SPITFIRE, MUSTANG

AND THE
'MEREDITH EFFECT'

SPITFIRE, MUSTANG

AND THE 'MEREDITH EFFECT'

HOW A SOVIET SPY HELPED CHANGE
THE COURSE OF WWII

PETER SPRING

AIR WORLD

AIR WORLD

SPITFIRE, MUSTANG AND THE 'MEREDITH EFFECT'
How a Soviet Spy Helped Change the Course of WWII

First published in Great Britain in 2024 by
Air World
An imprint of
Pen & Sword Books Ltd
Yorkshire – Philadelphia

ISBN 978 1 52677 350 0

Typeset by SJmagic DESIGN SERVICES, India.

Printed and bound in the UK by CPI Group (UK) Ltd.

Pen & Sword Books Limited incorporates the imprints of After the Battle, Atlas, Archaeology, Aviation, Discovery, Family History, Fiction, History, Maritime, Military, Military Classics, Politics, Select, Transport, True Crime, Air World, Frontline Publishing, Leo Cooper, Remember When, Seaforth Publishing, The Praetorian Press, Wharncliffe Local History, Wharncliffe Transport, Wharncliffe True Crime and White Owl.

For a complete list of Pen & Sword titles please contact

PEN & SWORD BOOKS LIMITED
George House, Units 12 & 13, Beevor Street, Off Pontefract Road,
Barnsley, South Yorkshire, S71 1HN, England
E-mail: enquiries@pen-and-sword.co.uk
Website: www.pen-and-sword.co.uk

or
PEN AND SWORD BOOKS
1950 Lawrence Rd, Havertown, PA 19083, USA
E-mail: uspen-and-sword@casematepublishers.com
Website: www.penandswordbooks.com

Contents

Table of Figures

The Figures have been largely taken from pre-war Royal Aircraft Establishment (RAE) and National Advisory Committee for Aeronautics (NACA) papers or material found online and modified and simplified. Excellent sources for illustrations of the Supermarine Spitfire are Morgan and Shackladay, *Spitfire: The History*, Guild Publishing, 1986 and for the North American Aviation P-51 Mustang, Marshall and Ford, *P-51B North American's Bastard Stepchild that saved the Eighth Air Force*, Osprey, 2020.

Acknowledgements

When I started to research this book on the 'Meredith effect' I had no idea how many unexpected directions it would take me or for how long. I have sought to read largely, and in the process have discovered more, primary material (some previously unpublished) and am very grateful to many libraries and librarians for making this available.

The research papers of the Royal Aircraft Establishment (RAE), where F.W. Meredith worked in the inter-war period, are largely in The National Archive (TNA) in Kew. Some very interesting, and seemingly unremarked, RAE papers are not in the TNA but in the Farnborough Air Sciences Trust (FAST) Library and I very grateful to Alan Brown for retrieving these from microfilm. These include Wind Tunnel Note No 267 titled, *Note on the problem of conducting a fluid into a duct with the minimum of losses*, May 1935, where Meredith dealt with the problem of getting air to flow into ducts without the turbulence created by the boundary layer. Also, there are two very interesting papers, *Model tests of the Hawker Interceptor radiator cowl*, May 1936, and *Addendum to Model tests of the Hawker Interceptor radiator cowl*, August 1936, by A.S. Hartshorn which cast new light on the evolution of Hurricane's ventral cooling duct and its boundary layer bypass 'lip'. Brian Riddle and Tony Pilmer of the National Aerospace Library have facilitated onsite research and sent relevant papers and offered new leads. The Imperial War Museum collections provided the otherwise uncited *Papers of J.L. Atwood*, Document 21441 which included otherwise unpublished material by Jay Leland (Lee) Atwood who was vice-president of North American Aviation in 1940 when the P-51 Mustang was designed. The library of the Royal Aircraft Museum, Hendon, provided the notes for the 30th R.J. Mitchell Memorial Lecture by E.J. Davis, *The Basic Design of the Prototype Spitfire* delivered in 1986. (Remarkably, Davis had been present in 1935 when Meredith inspected, rather critically, the aircraft's pioneering cooling duct.)

NASA sent *Tests of the XP-46 airplane in the NACA full-scale wind tunnel* (Nickle and Wilson, January 1940) which throws into question North American Aviation's claims that the P-51 Mustang design owed nothing to the Curtiss XP-46. Then NAA Aerodynamicist Ed Horkey said, 'we ran a quick study and said that this is just a rehashed P-40 … and we'd do better starting from scratch'. Examination of the report, however, shows it to be a very thorough analysis in its own right and changes to the NAA aircraft's cooling duct design, subsequent to its receipt by NAA, reveals surprising similarities to the XP-46 layout.

Stephen Marsh has very generously allowed me to read and quote from his illuminating PhD *The Air Ministry and the Bomb Dropping Problem: Bombsights, Scientists and Techno-Military Invention, 1918-45*, King's College London, 1 June 2019. This has a chapter about Meredith and demonstrates his critical contributions to the development of British pre-war and wartime bombsights. (Marsh's material is complimented by Smith, *Skua: The Royal Navy's Dive Bomber*, Pen & Sword Aviation, 2006, which outlines Meredith's frustrated efforts to develop a naval dive bombsight.)

As said, I have tried to write this book using primary material, but two books are of particular importance for their provision of information about the early development respectively of the Spitfire and the Mustang: Morgan and Shackladay, *Spitfire: The History*, Guild Publishing, 1986; and Marshall and Ford, *P-51B North American's Bastard Stepchild that saved the Eighth Air Force*, Osprey, 2020. A series of articles in *NAAR* (*North American Aviation Retirees Bulletin*) by Ford are exceptionally valuable as sources for the history of the antecedents of the Mustang. A special mention might also be given to Meekoms, *The British Air Commission and Lend-Lease,* Air-Britain (Historians) Ltd, 2000, which is a unique source of information about pre-1940 British purchasing activity in the US.

Writing this book has proved a crash course in aerodynamics and tested my physics and mathematics to the limit. I apologise for any errors which are entirely my responsibility.

I am very grateful to John Grehan and Martin Mace of Pen & Sword for publishing this book and to Kenneth Patterson for editing the text and Amy Jordan for handling production.

Introduction

On 7 March 1936 Supermarine's test pilot Jeffrey Quill recorded information on the Spitfire's pioneering ducted radiator cooling system on its second and his first flight:

> This had been designed as a result of basic research work done at the Royal Aircraft Establishment (RAE) by Dr [sic] Meredith and had been a major factor in reducing the cooling drag which would otherwise have constituted a serious 'barrier' to the performance of both the Spitfire and the Hurricane. Meredith's work at Farnborough was an excellent example of how basic research at the RAE [Royal Aircraft Establishment] could make a vital contribution to ad hoc design work carried out by industry. This was exactly how the system was meant to work.[1]

Lee Atwood, who in 1940 was vice-president of North American Aviation (NAA), wrote a letter, published in *Air & Space* in 1996, stating that he had produced papers with two objectives:

> The first is to explain and quantify the 'Meredith effect' of drag reduction. The simple fact is that it was the basis of the Mustang design, and its most efficient application required a buried radiator. My second objective is to give proper credit to the Royal Aircraft Establishment at Farnborough, which sponsored the research that [F.W.] Meredith and R.S. Capon published in 1935 and 1936.[2]

Thus, F.W. Meredith was linked to both the Supermarine Spitfire and the NAA Mustang which were fighters essential to winning the war in Western Europe. The first, in 1940, provided the winning edge in the Battle of Britain, thus securing Britain as the base from which Western Europe could be recovered from the Nazis. The second, in 1944, destroyed the Luftwaffe over Germany as a fighting force resulting in total control of the air at D Day when that recovery commenced. These two had in common radiator cooling exploiting the 'Meredith effect' where the radiator, by heating the cooling air in a duct, produced jet propulsion: the first pioneering and inefficient; and the second highly effectively, contributing to making the latter much faster than the former on the same power. This book initially arose out of curiosity to find out more about the 'Meredith effect'. Both quotes gave credit to the RAE, so its work merited further research.

The investigation of the 'Meredith effect' and the Spitfire and Mustang shifted, however, into a number of unexpected directions as further questions arose which were not anticipated when work on this book began. Firstly, it became clear that Meredith's areas of research extended hugely beyond the 'Meredith effect'. So what else had he worked on and how original and important were his contributions in these areas? Secondly, in the US the role of the 'Meredith effect' in the development of the Mustang was found to be subject to totally irreconcilable narratives which had become embedded in numerous accounts. So what was the truth of the 'Meredith effect' in the development of the Mustang? Thirdly, why, if Meredith was such an important scientist, had he apparently largely been written out of history?

While researching the 'Meredith effect' it became clear Meredith's work extended much further than the eponymous effect and his work was highly original, indispensable and versatile. A flummoxed official wrote in 1951: 'There is literally nobody in the country who can replace him. I am told that on account of his intimate knowledge of aerodynamics and instruments, he is unique.'[3] The word 'first' appeared constantly in descriptions of his ideas covering both aerodynamics and avionics (then called instruments) over a period of nearly thirty years and an unusually wide range of disciplines related to flight.

Aerodynamics:

> In England the RAE began research on simple automatic controls, and in 1923 conducted the *first* automatic landing experiments since the pre-war activity of Lawrence Sperry. The RAE activity arose from the desire of F.W. Meredith to test a theory he had proposed using a quarter of phugoid oscillation.[4]

> F.W. Meredith *first* theorized on paper and showed mathematically that it should be possible to not only offset most of the drag of a radiator installation, but possibly produce some thrust by shaping the duct properly and utilizing the added energy of the cooling air exit stream through an adjustable nozzle.[5]

> Supermarine is often regarded as being one of the *first* companies to make use of breakthroughs made by Meredith at RAE Farnborough in the design of ducts for cooling systems. In fact, the Spitfire's radiator ducts were designed using these guidelines.[6]

> [J.E.] Ellor of Rolls-Royce had previously patented [GB 447,283, 15 November 1934] the use of exhaust gas to induce additional flow through the radiator, but Meredith was the *first* to suggest converting the energy (either heat or kinetic) of the exhaust into thrust.[7]

Rolls Royce, for the first time, developed jet exhaust stacks, of which the *first* suggestion in Britain had been made by Meredith in the same paper in which he had pointed out the possibility of recovering the energy in radiator heat.[8]

The efficiency gains of active LFC [laminar flow control] were *first* discussed by Griffith and Meredith of the UK Royal Aircraft Establishment in a 1936 paper.[9]

Since the convection due to suction and the diffusion due to the solid wall are acting in the opposite direction, the [boundary layer] profile will reach steady solution at large distance … The [mathematical] solution was *first* obtained by [A.A.] Griffith and F.W. Meredith.[10]

Instruments:

The author [Meredith who designed the autopilot] discloses that shortly after production at the Royal Aircraft Establishment of the world's *first* pilotless aircraft in 1925, this country was the also the *first* to produce the flying bomb, given the code name Larynx.[11]

The *first* British automatic pilot was mechanised in this way [with a tilted directional gyroscope in 1937 in an article by Meredith and P.A. Cooke].[12]

Perhaps the *first* autopilot to adopt this solution [single gyro three axis] successfully was the British Mk. VIII which was based on my [Meredith] patents and extensively used in the Second World War.[13]

These [SEP1 and Mk 9] were to be Britain's *first* all-electric autopilots. Smith adopted the so-called 'rate/rate' concept for their systems. This was to be developed under F.W. Meredith.[14]

The *first* attempt at making a small instrument employing a vibrating mass [tuning fork gyroscope] to measure rate of turn was probably made by Meredith in 1942.[15]

Meredith's pioneering developments were of huge importance in the Second World War when nearly all liquid-cooled engined fighters incorporated, with varying degrees of efficiency, 'Meredith effect' ducted radiators. Also, many fighters used Meredith's ideas for resolving boundary layer duct entry problems. Further, British bombers used Meredith autopilots and, in the later war, bombsights containing Meredith-designed mechanisms. Modern jet fighters and bombers include various aspects of Meredith's solutions to the problem of duct entry. Meredith is widely regarded as having filed the first patents for solid state gyroscopes without which the modern world would grind, lost, to a halt or topple over – being built into smart phones and gaming devices, multimotor drones, robots controls, photographic stabilisers, and transportation devices like segways. Therefore, given its range and importance over time, Meredith's broader work deserves to be researched and told. This book is the first effort to cover the extraordinary range of his research – much of which found practical application.

Meredith's name largely lives on in the term the 'Meredith effect' which is a central feature in the veritable publishing industry producing books about the North American Mustang. This fighter was the best embodiment of Meredith's combined ideas on ducted radiators, duct entry and exhaust gas momentum, resulting in a much higher speed than the Spitfire on the same engine power. Aircraft histories, however, covering the development of the Mustang and the role of the 'Meredith effect' were found to contain irreconcilable information, leading to this author's conclusion that aspects of these accounts, which are found in most histories of the Mustang's development, were either misleading or simply wrong.

The role of the 'Meredith effect' in the Mustang's design became the subject of a fascinating and increasingly bitter debate in the 1990s, in which NAA's vice-president in 1940, Lee Atwood, played a controversial role, half a century after the aircraft's creation, which this book analyses – so adding, hopefully constructively, to the Mustang publishing industry. Astonishingly it became clear that Atwood's account of the fighter's conception, based on his claim he discovered Meredith's otherwise largely unknown work, which is deeply embedded in many Mustang histories, proved quite simply incompatible with surviving documentation.

Given Meredith's remarkable scientific contribution the question arose why is he apparently so little known? The answer is that he was not only well known to contemporary aeronautical scientists, but also, he was equally very well known to the British Security Services, both in the pre and post Second World War period, who maintained voluminous files on his activities and to whom he presented a hideous dilemma. The Security Service records contain the following quotes: 'This [Meredith's] case presents the problem of "Communism in industry" in as acute a form as I have seen it';[16] and 'It is a great pity that this brilliant man should have this failing. He is unique and if he has to be removed from our scene I do not know how we would replace him'.[17]

What then does a political system do when the individual within it is so uniquely qualified to do certain work that he is by common accord irreplaceable, yet he, by his own admission, cannot be regarded as anything but very politically unreliable?

Meredith made no secret of his admiration of the Soviet system and his dislike of the USA. It was only in the post-war period, however, that belated reading of captured Gestapo files, recording the interrogation of spy handlers working for the Soviets, that it was revealed how far Meredith had gone pre-war as a spy. This exacerbated the authorities' Meredith problem, as although the public generally knew little to nothing of his work, in scientific and governmental circles related to aviation he was regarded as unique. How the authorities attempted to resolve the dilemma is in itself a fascinating story and casts an intriguing – and not unpositive – light on British politics and society.

The book is structured in two parts. The first has as its core, although much else is discussed, Meredith's role in the development of the Spitfire and his life and work in Britain for the RAE and Smiths Instruments – including his often fraught relationship with the authorities; and the second focuses on the question of the part played by Meredith's ideas in the US, with particular focus on the debated role of the 'Meredith effect' in the conception of the Mustang.

In order to try to avoid overloading the text with material, much of which many readers will be familiar, some of the basic issues involved in cooling drag is covered in Appendix 1. Also, the story of Meredith's work on cooling systems, which started in 1935, built on earlier developments which are covered in Appendix 2. In order to tell the story it is impossible to exclude an equation $(0.177 \ (V/100)^2 - 1.725 \ (V_0/100)^2)$ which defines the 'Meredith effect'. Its derivation, which is key to understanding the originality of Meredith's work, is placed in Appendix 3. Also, Meredith spurred a systematic programme of wind-tunnel and other research into all aspects of the cooling process at the Royal Aircraft Establishment. Only that part of this programme between 1935 and 1936 is placed in the main text which otherwise might be overburdened, and the rest is in Appendix 4. US texts that possibly originated the term, the 'Meredith effect', are set out in Appendix 5.

Part 1

MEREDITH AND THE SPITFIRE

1935 – *annus mirabilis* sees two critical developments

The marriage of the Supermarine Type 300 airframe, with its beautiful elliptical wing, and Rolls-Royce's potent PV12 engine, the antecedent of the Merlin, would prove a major factor in winning the Second World War. There remained in late 1934, however, one seemingly insuperable obstacle to making the combination successful as the iconic Spitfire. The PV12 was designed to use evaporative cooling, that is heat dissipation through airframe surfaces, which could not be made to function effectively on a fighter which could not be expected to fly straight and level. Thus, the challenge remained how to reduce radiator cooling drag – at the then exceptionally high speeds of over 300mph that the Type 300 was designed to reach. The dilemma was elegantly explained by Frederick William Meredith of the RAE in May 1935:

> Cooling of aero engines involves the exposure of a large heated surface to a stream of air, a process which involves the expenditure of power owing to the viscosity of air. Until recently, it appeared that this fact imposed an intractable limit to the speed of aircraft since, whereas the heat transfer only varies directly as the speed of the air over the surface, the power expenditure varies as the cube. Thus, even though the exposed surface be adjusted until only the required heat transfer is effected, the power expenditure increases as the square of the speed. This fact and the recent increase in the speed of aeroplanes has brought the question of cooling drag into prominence.[1]

1935 would prove the *annus mirabilis* in the development of viable ducted cooling systems and the solution to the problem, defined by Meredith, following two developments at the RAE. Firstly, the RAE placed its highest priority on internally placed radiator systems. The Aerodynamics Sub-committee of Britain's Aeronautical Research Committee, when formulating its Programme of Aeronautical Research at the RAE in 1935, stated, 'Internally placed radiator systems [are rated] Priority A'.[2] Secondly, the RAE's brilliant scientist, F.W. Meredith moved from running its Instruments to its Aerodynamics unit. These two developments would transform the approach to ducted cooling systems and the associated major challenge of duct entry.

Meredith's enormous scientific contribution, particularly important during the Second World War, was facilitated by some coincidences, unfortunate depending on the point of view, making possible the 1935 *annus mirabilis*. Between 1919 and 1938 he worked at the Royal Aircraft Establishment (RAE), Britain's leading aircraft research organisation. In 1934 and 1935 the RAE lost in quick succession the heads of two of its most important departments, in freak accidents involving local trees, with consequences critical for the course of the coming war. Firstly, the head of the RAE's Aerodynamics unit, Hermann Glauert, was killed when struck by a wood fragment from a blown up tree on Aldershot Common. Secondly, the head of Instruments, Leonard Bygrave, was knocked off his horse by a branch incurring fatal injuries at a rally of the Guildford troop of Legion of Frontiersmen. (The Legion was a paramilitary organisation intended to support the regular army whose members wore scout-type uniforms.)

Meredith moved from Instruments to become head of Aerodynamics at the beginning of 1935 and then returned to head Instruments in the fourth quarter of the same year to work on autopilots and bombsights. At both departments Meredith led very different developments that were incorporated in literally tens of thousands of fighters and bombers, both British and American, that fought in and won the 1939-1945 war.

Chapter 1

Supermarine, Rolls-Royce and RAE – and the cooling challenge

In 1935 the design to be named the Spitfire faced a particularly exacting cooling challenge. How did this arise? The background is reviewed here in some depth to demonstrate the extent of the challenge and the originality of the work of Rolls-Royce and the RAE and particularly the latter's head of the Aerodynamics unit, Meredith.

The story of the evolution of the Spitfire is that the development of a dialectic between Supermarine airframes and Rolls-Royce engines. The initial marriage of the companies' airframes and motors in single-engined aeroplanes was in the S series of racing seaplanes, whose design was led by R.J. Mitchell in the late 1920s. In 1931 one Supermarine S 6 seaplane won the Schneider Trophy outright, while another raised the world air speed record to 407mph. The Schneider Trophy racers, in the final victorious S 6 form, combined all metal, low wing airframes with the then huge Rolls-Royce R engines of 36.7 litres capacity. These used evaporative cooling which made them supremely efficient for fast, low level, straight flight. (The R engines, first flight in April 1929, were developed from the Buzzard and would be developed into the Griffon which powered later marks of the Spitfire.)

Success with the Schneider racers left Supermarine overconfident that they could produce a speedy modern fighter. The company's Supermarine 224 was designed to meet the Air Ministry F7/30 specification issued in 1931 for a fighter to replace the Bristol Bulldog biplane. The Type 224 had replaced the floats of the S 6 seaplane with a fixed spatted undercarriage on a cranked thick wing. The Goshawk engine (21.25 litres), capable of 660hp, was based on the highly successful Kestrel having been adapted to use evaporative cooling. The Type 224, first flight February 1934, was a failure. The thick cranked wing and fixed undercarriage produced inordinate drag and the evaporative cooling could not operate reliably in positions other than level – pointless for a fighter.

July 1934 saw the initial redesign of the Type 224 to produce the Type 300. This persisted with the evaporative cooled Goshawk engine – as no other solution seemed available – but married it to an airframe with a thinner tapered wing, retractable undercarriage and a fully enclosed cockpit. Two changes – one from Supermarine and the other from Rolls-Royce – in late 1934 created the iconic Spitfire.

3

Firstly, the tapered wing was replaced by a beautiful thin elliptical structure, designed by the Canadian Beverley Shenstone who had graduated from the University of Toronto with a master's research degree into flying boat stability. In 1929 he went to Junkers in Germany. In the following year Shenstone worked in Walter Lippisch's design office where he learned of Ludwig Prandtl's work on fluid dynamics. In 1931 Shenstone returned to England and joined Supermarine after walking out of an interview with Hawker's irascible Sidney Camm, who was then still wedded to biplane fighters. Apart from his knowledge of up-to-date developments in Germany he could also read technical reports in German.

Secondly, the Rolls-Royce Goshawk engine was replaced by the PV12 (27 litres) late in November 1934. In that month, Rolls-Royce personnel, including supercharger expert J.E. Ellor – who that same month applied for a patent for a ducted radiator – visited Supermarine. The PV12 was a scaled-up Kestrel which Rolls-Royce had been working on since 1932 and was first run in October 1933. The engine would be named after another bird of prey making it the legendary Merlin. By the turn of 1934 and 1935 the Type 300 design, with its elliptical wing and PV12 engine, was recognisable as the Spitfire. The Type 300 design, however, still soldiered on with evaporative cooling for want of an alternative.

The size of the PV12 was significant and propitious. In the later 1920s most inlines, like the Kestrel, were just over 20 litres but these were largely replaced in the 1930s by engines approximately 15 litres larger.

V12 inline engine capacities				
Manufacturer	Name	Displacement (cu in)	Displacement (litre)	First run
Rolls-Royce	Kestrel	1,296	21.2	1926
Allison	1710	1,710	28.0	1930
Rolls-Royce	Merlin	1,650	27.0	1933
Rolls-Royce	Buzzard	2,240	36.75	1928
Mikulin	AM-34	2,864	46.9	1931
Daimler Benz	600 series	2,070	33.9	1932
Hispano Suiza	12Y	2,200	36.0	1932
Klimov	M-105	2,142	35.1	1938
Rolls-Royce	Griffon	2,240	36.75	1939

The Merlin at 27 litres was an unusual intermediate size. Only Allison and Rolls-Royce chose this capacity for supercharged V12s. Rolls-Royce's decision to select the same size as the Allison would prove extremely fortunate, facilitating the latter's replacement with the Merlin in 1942, as the P-51 Mustang's powerplant. (On 28 June 1942 Rolls-Royce works director E.W. Hives would write to Air Chief Marshal Sir W.R. Freeman: 'We are sold completely on the Mustang. The Merlin 61 goes into it with no alteration to the engine cowling or to the radiator cowling.'[1])

The British became astonishingly skilled at squeezing the most remarkable amount of power from comparatively small engines. The German Daimler-Benz family, which most notably powered the Messerschmitt Bf 109, was much larger, 36 litres against 27 litres, and when British engineers examined captured DB 601s, during the Battle of France, they were surprised at how little power the Germans were getting out of engines with one third greater capacity than the Merlin. (The German engines although larger were lighter.) The British, however, were helped after 1940 by the availability, at the time of the Battle of Britain, of American 100 octane petrol, while the Germans still used 87 octane. The higher octane was not, however, anticipated in the early 1930s when the Rolls-Royce PV12 was conceived, making the PV12 something of a gamble on more efficient supercharging and cooling systems.

The development of the Spitfire's pioneering cooling system was a story of remarkable cooperation between Supermarine, Rolls-Royce and the RAE. Rolls-Royce was the first engine manufacturer to set up its own flight-test department. In late 1934 Rolls-Royce established its own testing unit at Hucknall, in part having determined the previous year that low-drag radiators required actual flight testing. Problems with evaporative cooling made it imperative to reduce the drag of conventional radiator cooling systems. (See Appendix 1 for more background on the development of engine cooling.) Two areas were investigated: placing the radiator in a duct; and replacing water with glycol. Rolls-Royce first applied for a patent for a ducted radiator in November 1934. Also: 'Tests with the [Kestrel-powered] Hart were to examine the possibility of glycol as a cooling medium as an alternative to composite cooling [evaporative cooling with a small auxiliary radiator]. The results of its researches were communicated to Supermarine … on 3 December 1934.'[2]

In June 1935 R.S. Capon wrote an RAE paper which developed a methodology for comparing the relative efficiencies of unducted and ducted radiators that specifically cited Rolls-Royce. This said: 'Control of the flow at the rear exit has been suggested in connection with the NACA cowl and has been the subject of experiments proposed by Messrs. Rolls-Royce in connection with water and ethylene glycol radiators.'[3]

By 14 January 1935 a small auxiliary ventral radiator had been added to the design, necessary to provide cooling when stationary and taxiing, indicating that evaporative cooling was still intended.[4] In early 1935, however, the PV12 was adapted to use a conventional liquid-cooling system as the problems using evaporative cooling on a fighter were recognised to be insuperable. The Merlin B became the first of the series to use glycol cooling which raised the boiling point of the liquid increasing its efficiency. This passed Type [bench] Testing in February 1935, generating 950 hp. On 19 March 1935 Rolls-Royce personnel went to Supermarine to discuss cooling.[5] The replacement of evaporative cooling required a much larger radiator. This in turn raised questions as to where to place it and how then to reduce the drag which would otherwise make the 300mph plus speeds intended almost impossible. A glycol-cooled Merlin engine was flight tested by

Rolls-Royce in a Hawker Hart in April 1935 and Rolls-Royce sent Supermarine a copy of the test report. Supermarine now faced the challenge of designing an efficient cooling system for a compact aircraft requiring a large radiator. It looked to the RAE, which in June 1935 produced two seminal internal papers respectively by F.W. Meredith and R.S. Capon. (These were not published externally until the following year.)

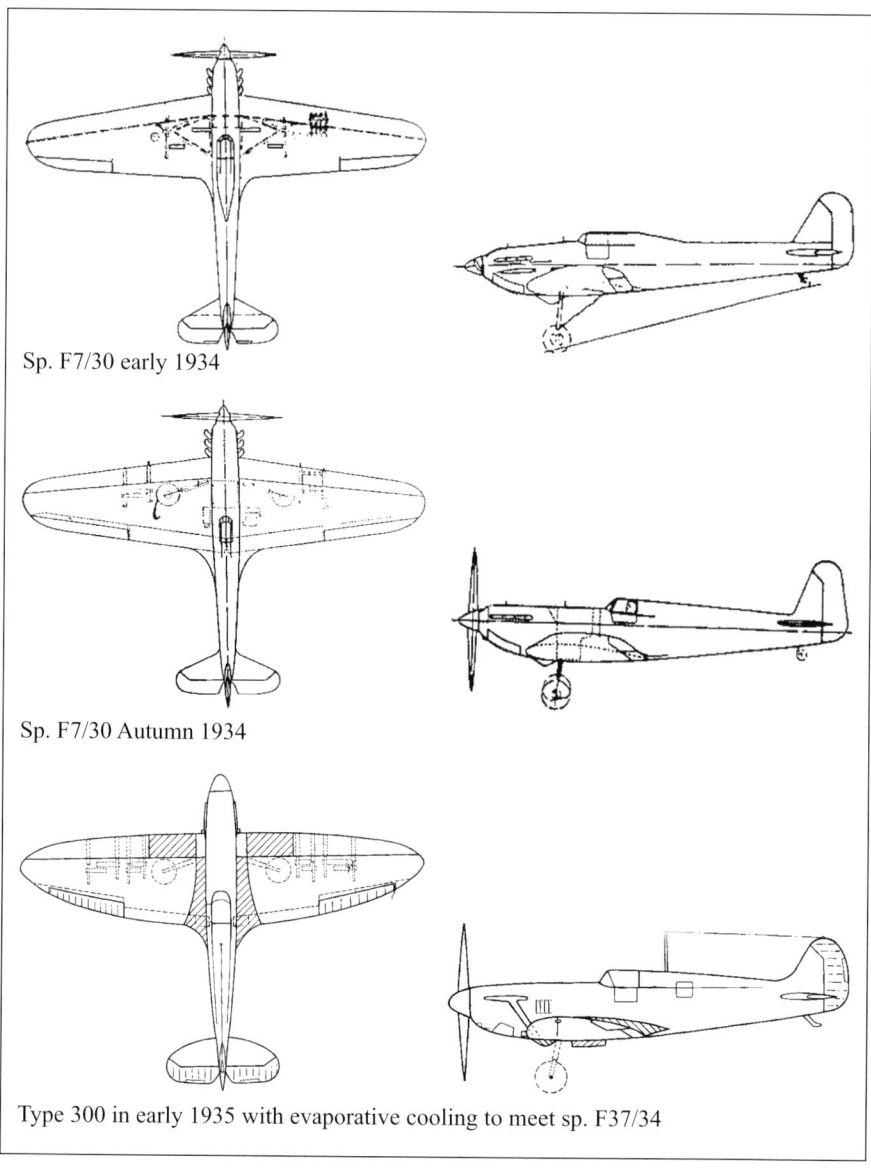

Sp. F7/30 early 1934

Sp. F7/30 Autumn 1934

Type 300 in early 1935 with evaporative cooling to meet sp. F37/34

Figure 1.1 – Development of antecedents of the Spitfire prior to adopting ducted radiators.[6]

Chapter 2

Royal Aircraft Establishment and Frederick William Meredith – Bolshevism rampant

J. Leland Atwood was vice-president of North American Aviation, or NAA, when in early 1940 the British ordered the airplane that was to become the Mustang. In 1996, when deep in controversy over who should take credit for its design, he wrote:

> I have recently written some papers with two objectives. The first is to explain and quantify the 'Meredith effect' of cooling drag reduction. … My second objective is to give proper credit to the Royal Aircraft Establishment at Farnborough, which sponsored the research that Meredith and R.S. Capon published in 1935 and 1936.[1]

The Kentucky-born Atwood, when commending the RAE whose scientists provided an essential resource to the British aeronautical industry, might have been surprised at its contemporary reputation in the 1930s as: 'The local police are inclined … to think that the majority of employees in the RAE are out-and-out Bolsheviks.'[2] What therefore was the RAE which combined both brilliant science and extreme left-wing politics?

Royal Aircraft Establishment

The Royal Aircraft Establishment or RAE – as the Royal Aircraft Factory had been renamed to avoid confusion with the now retitled Royal Air Force – located in Farnborough, Hampshire, was formed on 1 April 1918, when the organisation had stopped manufacturing airplanes to focus on research. It proved an exceptionally important institution, responsible for aeronautical research and development. Much of its activities were secret and important research papers were not released for fifty years making it difficult for contemporaries to measure its relevance. It was a civilian organisation, run by civil servants, beyond the authority of the Air Ministry and the RAF – and, so it proved, the Security Services who increasingly shared the opinion of the local constabulary as to its subversive tendencies.

In Britain a broad infrastructure was developed to coordinate civilian and military, and private and government research. In 1924 the Directorate of Scientific Research (DSIR) was established by the Air Ministry to facilitate adapting the latest scientific advances into aircraft development. The already existing Aeronautical Research Committee (ARC) refocused itself back to its original advisory role on scientific research. By 1925 the ARC had thirteen sub-committees, each with a number of panels, presided over by a member of the main committee and including representatives of the governmental bodies interested in aeronautical research. The Aerodynamics Sub-committee monitored aeronautical work at the RAE, often done on the recommendation of the committee itself.

The relevance of the ARC here was twofold. Firstly, it prioritised the investigation of radiators in ducts at the beginning of 1935. Secondly, it put key RAE research on ducted radiators into the public domain. (Most RAE research was marked secret for fifty years.) In August 1935 the ARC approved for publication Meredith's internal RAE June research paper on ducted cooling systems, *Cooling of Aircraft Engines With special reference to Ethylene Glycol Radiators enclosed in Ducts*. The date given at the bottom of the front page under the title 'printed and published', is 1936. In March 1936 it published, much revised in the light of Meredith's work, R.S. Capon's May 1935 internal RAE paper titled, *The cowling of cooling systems*. Thus, the RAE's work on cooling in ducts was internationally available. (German research soon built on and cited Meredith's and Capon's ARC papers on ducted radiators.)

In the US the Army Air Corps had no real counterpart for inputting civilian scientific developments into military aircraft development. In 1942 the US aerodynamicist, Edward Warner, when investigating in England the low drag of the Mustang, would express, 'the greatest admiration for the general quality of the British research effort, I find the variety and the quality of the work being done at the RAE and elsewhere most impressive'.[3]

In 1939 Squadron Leader 'Tubby' Vielle, a brilliant pilot and navigator, of distinctly non-leftist views, joined the RAE to work in the Navigation Section, run by Senior Scientific Officer Harold Pritchard, under the overall charge of the Instruments department then led by Jack Richards. Vielle had been disappointed in his hopes of university due to the Depression and joined the RAF where he demonstrated a genuine, and he perceived, frustrated scientific bent, reflected in his autobiography, *Not quite a boffin*. Vielle wrote of the RAE:

> The staff comprised as strange an assortment of boffins of all ages as one can imagine. Some of these scientists were so specialised in their particular field that they knew little about the outside world; others had wider knowledge – some had brilliant brains, others were just plodding along, waiting for their pensions. All, almost without exception, were interesting.[4]

Ironically Vielle's own often eccentric and violently expressed views might be seen as justifying what otherwise might be regarded as the paranoia of the Soviets and their western fellow travellers. Post-war he, 'wrote a paper (which I was later told had been considered by the Cabinet) suggesting that, for the benefit of future world peace, and before Russia developed their own atomic bomb, the US and Britain should threaten Moscow immediately with an atomic bomb attack unless Moscow disarmed completely and opened up their country to us'.[5]

Frederick William Meredith

At the beginning of 1935 the RAE faced some particularly pressing problems as the political situation deteriorated. One was how to resolve the problem of cooling drag. Another was how to handle the brilliant maverick 'Bolshevik', Frederick William Meredith, who was essential to numerous projects, but whose extreme left views were reported regularly to the national Security Services. In 1948, these recorded, 'we were fortunate [in 1926] in securing the services of an informant in RAE, who thereafter for some years provided us with a very useful inside picture of the extreme left-wing people at RAE'.[6] There proved to be a lot of them.

The Security Services held several fraught conferences with the Air Ministry and the RAE who said bluntly that Meredith was indispensable, regardless of his political views. Meredith made no effort to conceal his communist opinions and presented, over his exceptionally productive working life, a huge problem to his employees and the government. A flummoxed official would write in the later 1940s, 'this [Meredith's] case presents the problem of "Communism in industry" in as acute a form as I have seen it'.[7] Yet despite repeated alarming informant reports over the years it was considered that little could be done about the Meredith problem. 'As far as Meredith's open communist sympathies were concerned, the Air Ministry did not consider – in view of the lack of a definite policy at the time [pre-Second World War] – that any action could be taken.'[8]

Meredith worked in the RAE's Instruments section throughout much of the 1920s and 1930s and led the development of the British autopilot necessitating expertise dealing with gyroscopes in the disciplines of both instruments and aerodynamics. This combination of experience working in, and then having leadership, of both the RAE's Aerodynamics and Instruments units gave Meredith unique insights. When asked about Meredith's qualities a Security Services briefing on 6 April 1951, discussing possible cooperation with the US on guided missiles, recorded:

> There is literally nobody in the country who can replace him. I am told that on account of his intimate knowledge of aerodynamics and instruments, he is unique, and that through this background of experience he has already put forward lines of attack which have not been conceived of by anybody else, and which are considered to be of outstanding merit.[9]

Meredith himself remains an enigma. He got no gongs and has no biographer. He gave his name to the once ubiquitous system of ducted radiator cooling for liquid-cooled engines, the 'Meredith effect'. He led many developments in the British avionics industry, being the main driver behind the development of the British autopilot and aircraft remote control, and played an important role in the development of the British bomb aiming system.[10] So why is Meredith not acclaimed as one of the great British applied scientists of the twentieth century who made a huge contribution to winning the Second World War and generally to the British avionics industry? He was, after all, not alone in holding extreme left-wing views. The answer did not become fully clear until 2006 when The National Archives released papers about spy investigations and interrogations in the late 1940s and early 1950s.

A biography of Meredith is perhaps overdue but would be difficult to write because the most that is known about him, apart from scientific papers which cover an extraordinary range of aeronautical subjects, comes through the prism of Security Service documents in The National Archive. Meredith's life and works raises intriguing issues about scientific and political intelligence, and about the nature of reputation. There is justification in quickly reviewing it until the mid-1930s because of his critical contribution to the development of inline aero-engine cooling and his active involvement in these aspects of the design of the Spitfire as well as his contributions to avionics.

Meredith was born on 10 July 1895 at Killiney, County Dublin in Ireland to an old Protestant family. He was educated at Aravan Bray, in County Wicklow, from 1903 to 1909, which prepared middle-class Protestant boys from Ireland for English public schools. Then he went to Bromsgrove, Worcestershire, where he held the Mathematical Scholarship. His education continued at Trinity College, Dublin, where he obtained a Foundation Scholarship in Mathematics in 1914. There was no early sign of rebelliousness. He served in the Officer Training Corp (OTC) Bromsgrove School Contingent for three years until he resigned on leaving.[11] Meredith volunteered before conscription was introduced the following year in Britain. (Ireland never had conscription in the war.) He was certified as recommended by the Military Education Committee as a suitable candidate for appointment to a commission in the Regular Army for the period of the war by the University of Dublin.[12] His standard application, used by ex-OTC cadets, filed in 10 September 1915 and dated 24 September recorded he was 'desirous of serving Royal Garrison Artillery, failing this the RFA' and recorded, when asked whether able to ride, 'a little but would need to try'.

On 29 September 1915 he was commissioned as a second lieutenant in the Royal Garrison Artillery (RGA). The RGA had been formed in 1899 as a distinct arm of the Royal Regiment of Artillery alongside the Royal Field Artillery and the Royal Horse Artillery. It was the Royal Artillery's 'technical' branch, largely responsible for the professionalisation of gunnery during the First World War.

Meredith served in France in the Anti-Aircraft 2nd Army from January 1916 with 57 AA Section which became H Battery on reorganisation. He left his unit on 6 February 1917 with bronchitis and was invalided back to England on 17 March. He was discharged from hospital on 2 April having received three weeks sick leave and two months home service. On 28 April he was recorded as attached to Abbey

Wood AA depot. Whereupon, as related by the army, he disappeared. On 12 June 'a trace' was sought on his movements since 1 April, and on 30 June it was recorded 'no reply was received when attached to the Abbey Wood depot'. (This was after sick leave and home service had expired.) Notwithstanding his disappearance, records show he became a full lieutenant on 1 July 1917. Meredith appears to have returned home to Clonesleigh, Shankill, Dublin. On 16 September he sent a certificate from his doctor from Clonasleigh stating Meredith was, 'suffering from a rigor with temperature. He has Diarrhoea and his kidneys have been affected. In my opinion it would be unwise for him to travel and present as he is run down from the recent septic throat he had'. On 21 September Eastern Command, presumably not in receipt of the certificate, still noted 'efforts to trace the whereabouts of this officer have proved unsuccessful'. The next day, however, he was at Dublin Hospital and then went to London District and was recorded as in an officer's convalescent hospital on 17 October 1917.

On 3 December he was ordered to rejoin the AA Abbey Wood depot as soon as possible. On 2 January he was serving with his unit two days later at Parkhurst on the Isle of Wight and on 20 February he was with 34th Anti-Aircraft Company RGA at Staines under the Administration of London District. The London Air Defence Area of the RGA, established on 31 July 1917, manned the first integrated air defence system using tethered balloons, sound locators, searchlights, gun sites and aircraft patrols. By November 1918 this comprised 286 guns, 387 searchlights and eight Home Defence squadrons, with about 200 fighters. The new technology of wireless communication assisted in directing fighters. Ten German airships and twenty aircraft were brought down. Clearly the London Air Defence Area was not some obscure backwater. In fact it was one of the most technically advanced military bodies then extant anywhere in the world and possibly an ideally fertile ground for developing Meredith's scientific interest in aviation.

Meredith was demobilised on New Years Eve 1918. It might be noted that he had served on the Western Front for the entire period of the Battle of the Somme. Also, Meredith's war service initiated a pattern remarkable throughout his life. He had effectively gone AWOL, if through ill-health, yet there had been no known repercussions. As will be seen the authorities would show extraordinary tolerance towards Meredith throughout his life that in others, less gifted and useful, might have earned a far more hostile treatment.

Between 1918 and 1919 Meredith completed his BA at Trinity. The Irish War of Independence started in the latter year and Meredith was regarded later as a passionate Fenian. His school and war record, however, show no sign of earlier militancy.

Meredith's RAE scientific activity

Opinions provided over the course of many investigations by the Security Services revealed Meredith's exceptional scientific mind. The Air Ministry in January 1949 made clear both his versatility and indispensability. 'Mr Meredith is of such outstanding ability in the field of aerodynamics and auto-control that from technical considerations alone there is no one in the country whom the Department would be more anxious to employ.'[13] A March 1949 British Security Services report said curtly, 'Mr Meredith is in a high place in the category of indispensable people.'[14] In the 1950s the Security Services, investigating Meredith, sought advice from George Gardner, who became a senior technical officer, at the RAE. He provided a fascinating and sympathetic insight into how Meredith achieved his scientific results, having worked under his supervision starting in 1925:

> I was immediately struck by his very great scientific ability and soon came to learn how his enquiring mind worked. He had a preference for thrashing out the problems with which he was confronted by discussion and argument with those around him rather than by thinking in isolation. In tackling a new problem he would argue just as passionately for and against some hypothesis until he had resolved the issue. During the course of these arguments he was remarkably unemotional, and I have no recollection of him ever allowing emotion or personal feelings in any way to bias his scientific judgement.[15]

Another reference [January 1949] made clear Meredith's ability to achieve elegant solutions to design problems. 'It would not be true to say that if Mr Meredith were not employed, our particular problems would not find a solution. It was, however, stressed that from past experience of the quality of this man's work the solution would probably be far tidier from the design point of view than that of any other designer.'[16]

Perhaps Meredith's experiences with First World War anti-aircraft defence triggered his fascination with the technical side of aviation, for he joined the RAE in 1919, working in the Aerodynamics Department as a Technical Assistant. This Department specialised in aerodynamics, control, wind tunnel and mathematical analysis. Automatic aircraft control development became Meredith's responsibility.[17] Meredith's ability to reach across different disciplines is reflected in his early contributions to automated landing, autopilot and remote control.

Automatic landing

Meredith first came to notice in what sounds a madcap approach to automated landing. The RAE began research on simple automatic controls after the First World War and in 1923 conducted the first automatic landing experiments since the pre-war US activity of Lawrence Sperry. Meredith wanted to test his theory that a quarter of a phugoid, an up and down pitching oscillation, could produce simultaneously horizontal motion, stalling speed, and contact with the ground, if, in a gliding approach, the manoeuvre were initiated at a precalculated height and a prescribed airspeed.[18] Despite understandable RAF pilot misgivings – one of their number would first have to fly the aircraft and then sit back while it attempted to land itself – Meredith's challenge could not be honourably ducked.

A Vickers Vimy bomber was held at an appropriate steady glide speed and attitude for approach and then trimmed tail heavy. Following this a ground indicator, consisting of a weight on a line, was lowered to a fixed distance below the aircraft. When the weight was seen to touch the ground the observer signalled to the pilot to release the control column so that the tail heavy trim condition would then prevail, and the phugoid motion was seen to take effect and the Vimy would land itself. Meredith put himself at risk as he sat in the front gunner's cockpit. This idea proved practicable if unnerving. A trailing wire was used later for assisting the landing of flying boats on glassy misty surfaces when it was difficult to estimate altitude, the indicator being the retractable radio aerial cable.[19] It was also employed to land the Queen Bee, the first unmanned radio-controlled aircraft, for which Meredith claimed responsibility.[20]

Stabilisation and autopilots
While working in Aerodynamics Meredith made himself an expert on the stabilisation of aircraft. This involved issues of controlled movement to change direction and altitude. In 1924 he established his credentials with a report on the *Automatic control of aeroplanes*.[21] The origin of the RAE's development of the autopilot lay in its work on stabilising pilotless aircraft where the RAE was working on the pioneering flying bomb, codename Larynx. The secrecy of the RAE and Meredith's work has meant that its importance and originality has become obscured. 'The methods of dynamic stability analysis had been applied in the design of the RAE flight control equipment from 1924 on, but very few results were ever published in the open literature.'[22] (Dynamic stabilisation is the proactive movement of control surfaces to return an aircraft to its intended flight path.)

In 1925 Meredith moved to the Instruments Department to focus on aircraft stability.[23] He then worked with two breaks in the Instrument Department which specialised in advanced automatic controls until his resignation in 1938. (In 1932, he was Chief Technical Officer at Martlesham Heath, the base of the Aircraft and Armaments Experimental Establishment which tested new RAF aircraft. In 1935 he moved for nine months to Aerodynamics.[24])

Meredith's work was increasingly central to the development in Britain of the autopilot – the system used to control the trajectory of an aircraft without constant 'hands-on' control. Perhaps surprisingly, the origin of the RAE's development of the autopilot lay in its work on stabilising the Larynx in 1925. It was designed to carry a 250lb bomb at 200mph over 200 miles. Given that it was pilotless it needed by definition a system of automatic stabilisation along a pre-set course. The controls were designed by Meredith. The first clever insight was that to be functional (and economical) all that was needed was control of the rudder and elevator to stabilise altitude and direction. The second was that if the gyroscope were tilted then only one gyro was required to control two axes. (Its controls were, as Meredith pointed out post-war, almost identical to those used in the 1940s in the German V-1.)

Thus, in the mid-1920s the RAE developed an extremely clever economical single gyro, two axis aircraft stabilisation system. In 1925 Meredith filed three patents for a single gyro control system controlling only rudders and elevators. While the system was initially designed for the pilotless Larynx it could obviously be used to stabilise a piloted aircraft to reduce the burden on the pilot on long flights and to maintain course in poor visibility.

It was found that Meredith's single gyro two-axis RAE Automatic Pilot worked well when the air conditions were steady, however, it was inadequate to stabilise the aircraft for bombing and photographic work (vital to mapping the Empire) when the air was turbulent. The result was that the RAE developed the two gyro, three axis Mk I Automatic Control system which comprised basically two packages, each incorporating air-driven gyros, pneumatic valves and servos. The first had a tilted gyro which controlled the rudder and elevator. The second had a separate gyro for roll, through aileron control.

The late 1920s marked the start of the RAE's relationship with Smiths Industries when the latter was granted the manufacturing rights for the RAE's Mk 1 autopilot. The importance of Smiths to the Meredith story was that he moved there from the RAE in 1938. The RAE Mk 1 Automatic Control was developed, which was sold commercially as the Smith Automatic Control for civilian aircraft use. Its production started in 1931 and continued to 1946. The Security Services noted that on 9 May 1938 an Air Ministry official told Charles Gray, editor of *The Aeroplane*, that Meredith was the inventor of the Automatic Pilot built by Smiths.[25]

Blind flying and landing

Meredith's work extended beyond stabilising aircraft to the whole range of problems involving blind flying and landing. In 1930 Meredith read a paper to the Royal Aeronautical Society, titled *Air Transport in Fog*, which stated, 'air transport in fog is immediately practicable: but it involves an element of risk,' in which he outlined progress already made and the lines of future development. The following year he published a paper, with the same name, in the *Journal of the Royal Aeronautical Society*.[26]

An account of the results of the early efforts in developing an autopilot was presented by the pioneers Meredith and Cooke of the RAE in England in 1937. This 'describes the use of the automatic pilot in map-making and suggests its superiority over the Sperry three axis design for applications requiring manoeuvres'.[27] The development shows how Meredith and Cooke were aware of and drew on the expertise of fellow RAE workers. The account 'shows the considerable acquaintance of the authors with the theory, methods, and conclusions of their colleagues at the Royal Aircraft Establishment who had been engaged in the study of the dynamic stability of airplanes. The action of the automatic pilot was clearly explained in those terms'.[28]

In 1930 Meredith and C.H. Smith took out a patent for *Improvements in or relating to electrical indicating systems* (GB 357,968) for an invention 'applied to wireless direction-finding apparatus for giving a continuous and instantaneous indication of the bearing of a transmitting station, for example for use on aircraft'.[29] In 1935 Marconi announced it had acquired the rights for Meredith's Radio Azimuth patent.

This now familiar 'homing' device itself will be developed to provide a visual indication … for example in regard to fog landing operations. In practice, the pilot of an aircraft fitted with such an apparatus has only to watch a needle on a dial to know whether he is on his set course. If he deviates the movement of the needle shows immediately the direction of the deviation and also gives an approximate indication of its extent.[30]

Bombsights

In the mid-1920s it became clear that bombsights would have to be stabilised for effective operation and stabilisation was Meredith's particular area of expertise. In November 1926 Meredith wrote a report on the *Problem of Lateral Stabilisation of a Bombsight*.[31] This revealed his propensity for elegant solutions as he pointed out that if the aircraft itself were stabilised then the bombsight need not be. Meredith would go on to have a major role (outlined below) in the development of British RAF and RNAF bombsights.

Remote aircraft control and guidance – Larynx and Queen Bee

As seen, Meredith designed the controls of the pilotless Larynx which flew along a pre-set course. The next challenge was to design a system for in-flight guidance of pilotless aircraft. The RAE developed a pilotless radio-controlled aeroplane for use as a gunnery target requiring automatic control from take-off to landing, or destruction. The Queen Bee was de Havilland's response to the 1933 Air Ministry Specification F 18/33 for a wireless-controlled pilotless target aircraft to provide gunnery practice for Royal Navy ships and Royal Artillery anti-aircraft schools. There appears to have been earlier work, as in 1932 Meredith's Security Services file recorded, 'Meredith was employed on very secret work and invented two of the most secret W/T [wireless telegraphy] inventions'.[32] Another 1927 reference said, 'Meredith was responsible on the Aerodynamics side for serial target (W/T controlled aeroplanes)'.[33]

The Queen Bee incorporated Meredith's ideas on automated landing and autopilot. It was fitted with auto-controls based on the Smiths Mk 1a automatic pilot. A single gyroscope controlled the rudder and elevator. Meredith claimed the Queen Bee was his invention in somewhat compromised circumstances. In 1939 an alert customs officer reported on Meredith and his wife to the Security Services as they went to Eire from Holyhead, after he noted on Meredith's passport the three visits to the Soviet Union in 1932, 1935 and 1937.

Mr Meredith … volunteered the information that the visits were 'of purely a tourist nature, unconnected with his business capacity'. [This was completely untrue.] I gained the impression that both were admirers of the communist system of society. He informed me that he was the inventor of the 'Queen Bee' type of control for aircraft and did confidential work for the Government.[34]

The Queen Bee was first flown in 1935 and had a long operational life to 1947. It was a brilliantly simple adaptation of the de Havilland Tiger Moth biplane with floats. One gyroscope controlled two compressed air valves, which fed high-pressure air to pistons controlling the rudder and elevator. There was auto control for ignition and throttle but not the ailerons. The Queen Bee took off and landed automatically, performing the latter using the trailing wire system, here the radio antenna, pioneered by Meredith on the Vimy in 1923; it was controlled through nine commands sent by radio using a dash tone followed by dots (–• navigation lights on, –•• navigation lights off, –••• right turn, –•••• straight ahead, –••••• left turn, –•••••• climb, –••••••• level flight, –•••••••• glide, –••••••••• dive).

Queen Bee flights were not without, in retrospect, a certain humour. As targets they made plain the inadequacy of naval anti-aircraft gunnery and, having been comprehensively missed during show exercises, they might have to be put deliberately into a dive (radio command –••••••••••) unhit, in order to spare the blushes of the top brass. Unscathed Queen Bees were sometimes found floating on the sea having run out of fuel and adeptly landed themselves assisted by the trailing aerial. (As seen, Meredith had pioneered automatic landing assisted by a trailing wire in 1923.)

Meredith and the *Farnborough Group of Dictatorial Intellectuals*

'Tubby' Vielle, while seconded to the RAE, became convinced that Jack Richards, Ben Lockspeiser, a chemist, and Meredith had deliberately sabotaged the development of effective bomber navigation and bomb aiming systems. Following a stay at Richards' house Vielle believed he had tried to convert him to communism. He reported this to his department head Harry Pritchard who expressed little surprise: 'Didn't you know, Tubby, that Richards, together with Ben Lockspeiser and Meredith, was one of the ringleaders in the Communist uprising here back in 1926.'[35] (1926 was the year of the failed nine days General Strike which was called by the Trades Union Congress to force the British government to prevent wage reductions for 1.2 million locked-out coal miners.) The Security Services recorded:

> Meredith and Lockspeiser were both exceedingly active during the General Strike of 1926, when they addressed a meeting urging the workpeople in the Royal Aircraft Establishment to cease work. After the General Strike had been settled, a number of the ringleaders at the Establishment were dismissed. These two were brought before the Chief Superintendent, but apparently no action was taken against them.[36]

Meredith's conduct had been considered in 1926 by the Air Ministry but it was decided not to sack him even though he had said that if called upon for duties – other than those for which he was appointed – he would consider committing sabotage.

Meredith's fellow ringleaders in the 1926 RAE communist uprising went on to do important work. Richards become head of the Telecommunications Research Establishment, the main UK research and development organisation for radio navigation and radar for the RAF during the Second World War. Lockspeiser joined the Ministry of Aircraft Production (MAP) and supplied the spotlight altimeter method used to determine the correct very low flight altitude required during the Dambusters raid. He, as Sir Benny Lockspeiser, later became the first president of CERN.

In 1932 Meredith made the first of three visits to the Soviet Union. The Security Services investigated the matter. 'Henry Wimperis' (1876-1960) view was that Meredith and his associates were abnormal, but loyal, and that they would not disclose secret information to the Russians.'[37] (Wimperis designed the Course Setting Bomb Sight (CSBS) in 1917. In 1934 he set up the Committee for the Scientific Study of Air Defence which played a key part in developing radar.) Also, 'a reason given why Meredith was not prevented from travelling to the Soviet Union [in 1932] was although he was employed on very secret work, he was so conceited that it was thought unlikely that he would give away important work [which was his intellectual property] to the USSR'. [38]

Meredith left with eight other people from the RAE for Russia on 21 May 1932 and returned on 12 June. A colleague, Edward Calvert, changed his views of the USSR but clearly the visit had no similar impact on Meredith.

> Calvert described how he became completely disillusioned about Russia when he made a trip [with Meredith]. He went there with an open spirit of enquiry. He did have some contact with a Russian family [which] had returned from England to the USSR, and although the son of the family was convinced that everything in the USSR was lovely, the mother, with whom he had some confidential conversations, had told him some home truths about Russia.[39]

Calvert, 'described [Meredith] as a dangerous man who looked like an intellectual giraffe. He obviously disliked Meredith strongly; one thing which he had against him was that Meredith had acquired and cultivated a very cultured accent'. [40]

By 1934 the Security Services recognised the RAE risk to be considerable. A March report noted the address that 'a person under suspicion' visited 'where will be found two senior officers of the RAE, Messrs McKinnon Wood and F.W. Meredith. Both of these officers are highly skilled men and scientists of a very high degree. As leading scientists on the Experimental Staff, they are brought into daily touch with the latest inventions and experiments which are being carried out at this establishment'.[41]

On 15 March 1934, however, when considering suspending communists:

> It was suggested that it was preferable to have the benefit of Meredith's brains at the RAE and run the risk of a possible leakage. It was pointed out that if Meredith were dismissed, he might quite

possibly go to Russia where the Air Ministry would be completely deprived of his services and brain, which they value very highly.[42]

In 1934 Meredith was openly advocating Communism. His comments on 30 August 1934 at a meeting of the Cove Labour Party Discussion Circle were carefully recorded by the Security Services:

> We must work for the complete, immediate and simultaneous Nationalisation of all the Industries and Services, etc. The Socialisation of All Services Bill to be rushed through at the first opportunity, to nationalise all Services, etc., in one sweep. Although, in my personal opinion, the most pressing need at present is to wear down the word Patriotism before it is allowed to push Socialism and other 'isms' into the background as it did during the last war; I have just returned from a trip through France, Italy and Switzerland where vast preparations for war were evident on every hand. We, therefore, must make our first issue a determined and organised drive to create an uprising before any more war. Or if not successful before the next war, which is fast approaching, we must do all we can to bring it about during the war.[43]

On another occasion:

> Meredith and half a dozen others at the RAE, attended a private showing of the Soviet film – 'The General Line' a Soviet propaganda film. During the interval, a record of the 'The Internationale' was put on the gramophone, and Meredith is reported to have sung it and urged others to do likewise.[44]

The Security Services were becoming increasingly alarmed about sedition at the RAE. 'There seems no doubt that, until these subversive activities are dealt with very firmly, the RAE will continue to be a serious potential source of danger in the event of a national emergency'.[45] Particularly, Meredith was present at a private discussion regarding the 'urgent necessity for spreading Class Consciousness and Anti-War, etc, propaganda among the forces and affiliated Establishments'. At this it was decided to form a small Propaganda Committee 'to devise schemes to spread illegal propaganda among the Troops and local workers'.[46] In the Security Services file note for 8 November 1934 for Lockspeiser a name was given for this group. 'A talk on *The Transition to a Socialist State* was arranged by Vernon and others of the *Farnborough Group of Dictatorial Intellectuals* – Lockspeiser, Vernon, Meredith, Calvert, Spencer, Fisher and others. The above mentioned group of intellectuals run a private study circle, and meet various types of individuals, including foreigners.'[47]

The name reveals a lot about how Meredith and his fellow 'intellectuals' saw themselves. The term 'Dictatorial' must be derived from the Marxist term 'the dictatorship of the proletariat' when the Communist Party, having seized the means of production, required strong organisation to impose its authority, to prevent counterrevolution and to facilitate the transition to a communist society. Who would lead the proletariat? The 1848 *Manifesto of the Communist Party* of Karl Marx and Friedrich Engels, provided the answer: 'A portion of the bourgeoisie goes over to the proletariat, and in particular, a portion of the bourgeois ideologists, who have raised themselves to the level of comprehending theoretically the historical movement as a whole.' Meredith and his fellow bourgeois intellectuals naturally identified themselves as those who comprehended the historical movement. These Farnborough intellectuals knew they were cleverer than everyone else – a point frankly conceded by those who monitored their activities with increasing alarm—– and would naturally provide the leadership for the dictatorship of the proletariat.

That year the informant recorded:

> Meredith is an out and out Communist. There are about a dozen of the senior type mixed up with it – and God knows how many of the smaller fry. Meredith is a cunning swine with it and to create a good impression with the topnotchers he bullies and raves at underlings inside the establishment – but outside the Establishment he will shake them by the hand and slip them five bob or so for a drink, etc.[48]

Fellow communist Wilfred Vernon confirmed Meredith's duplicity in 1934. 'Meredith is very good and clever with it too. He has just been promoted to the charge of the new Air [wind] Tunnel [head of Aerodynamics following the death of Glauert]. He talks to the "Heads" in their own language, adopts their tactics and gets away with it.'[49]

The Security Services recorded: 'In December 1934, arrangements were made by the Air Ministry for all employees at Farnborough to be warned that they must not engage in political activities of any kind. Unfortunately, this only produced merely a temporary effect.'[50] As Vernon was noted as commenting, wryly, in 1935, 'we will have to go easy for a while, but the active old hands like Lockspeiser, Meredith, Sandford, Alexander, Calvert, Gurrey and co are too popular to lose any ground on account of a lecture'.[51]

In 1935 it was recorded that, 'an active and dangerous communist cell, of which the principals are the four individuals mentioned below [Meredith, Vernon, Lockspeiser, Hollingdale], exists at the Royal Aircraft Establishment South Hampshire'.[52] That year Commander Renwick RN reported on a meeting of RAE employees to the Security Services. A woman 'described her experiences in the USSR in a very biased manner'.[53] Another report continued the story. 'Those gathered expressed the opinion that when the eventual revolution came, it would be accomplished bloodlessly if possible, but that if the bankers etc did not do what they were told, they would have to be shot.'[54] (Ironically, Meredith had made himself so unpopular in some quarters of the RAE that it was mooted that he too would suffer this fate at the hands of his communist colleagues. An informant later reported: 'The trouble with Meredith is that he has had a very unhappy private life and bears a grudge against the world. He could best be described as an embittered Irish rebel, and in the old days at Farnborough [name redacted] had often told him if ever his revolutionary friends came to power, Meredith would be the first person they would shoot.'[55]) Again in 1936, 'Special Branch forwarded information obtained from a reliable source, which described Meredith as one of the four principal members of "an active and dangerous Communist Cell" at the RAE'.[56]

In August 1935 Meredith made a second visit to the Soviet Union. A Flight Lieutenant V. Harris wrote to Moscow Air Attaché A.C. Collier that Meredith 'was of the opinion that the establishment of a Soviet regime in England was not possible except through revolution'.[57] Clearly concerned, the Attaché made inquiries which elicited a response in a Security Services memo to him that recorded:

> For your private information, the three individuals in question [including Meredith] are all very capable, indeed brilliant, scientific workers, but have somewhat advanced views of a political nature. This may serve to guide you in your treatment of them, and I would suggest that beyond the normal courtesy given to any visiting Britisher you should not be connected with them in any way.[58]

Another memo from the Attaché in Moscow to the Director of Operations and Intelligence Air Ministry stated that, 'The Ambassador has asked me to record his opinion that it seems strange an officer such as Mr Meredith ['whose conduct was anything but correct'] should be allowed to take his leave in the USSR'.[59]

Despite the threat the Security Services file records curiously parochial events over the years. In 1935, 'Meredith and other members of the RAE were at a violin recital organised by the Bramley branch of the Friends of the Soviet Union'.[60] Also, 'Meredith was reliably reported to have gone "Spain mad" [due to the Civil War] and to have applied for the use of Farnborough Town Hall for a public meeting. This application was refused as likely to cause a breach of the peace'.[61] Then, Meredith suggested an outdoor meeting near the Town Hall as a protest and to refuse to close the meeting if requested to do so by the police. Mrs McKinnon Wood [born Gwendoline Spicer to Sir Albert Spicer, 1st Baronet] agreed to be arrested in order to draw attention to the matter. After further discussion it was decided 'for weather reasons' and 'so as not to prejudice the case with the [co-organiser] Council for Civil Liberties', to hold the meeting indoors.[62]

In 1936: 'Meredith and a number of others at the RAE were present at a meeting which was held to discuss the Spanish situation and kept the discussion on Left lines. One of the RAE employees present [Hollingdale] suggested the immediate formation of a *Popular Front in Farnborough and Cove* in order to spread suitable propaganda, etc..'[63] In the following year, '"Hops" [the informant] report states that Lockspeiser, Janeway and Meredith were among those who attended a 'Rally Conference and Camp' which was held at Broomsquires Camping Ground, Elstead, on 19 and 20 June'.[64]

Notwithstanding their alarm the Security Services were unable to get any kind of official action against Meredith and his fellow communists. They were considered as exceptional (which they were) in their abilities and had to be given special treatment. As seen, in 1934 Wimperis was of the view that, 'Meredith and his associates were abnormal, but loyal, and that they would not disclose secret information to the Russian'.[65] Even in this company Meredith was recognised as remarkable. Also that year, '[Meredith] is spoken of as one of the leading lights who should easily reach to the top of aeronautical experiments.'[66] Again:

> An Officer of the Security Services was informed by a reliable and well placed, separate source that Meredith was one of the most dangerous men employed at the RAE. Further, that the tendency on the part of Senior Officers at the RAE was rather to condone such activities, with the excuse that scientific men were prone to hold different views from their fellows.[67]

There was a further problem, captured later in 1937, when 'a staff officer entered with a wad of correspondence and remarked, "We can now proceed with the case against that Farnborough civilian"'. The basic response was, 'If they suspend all those on the List of Communists – it will include Meredith'.[68] The RAE (and Britain) could not afford to lose Meredith: so he and the other communists perforce survived. On 13 September it was recorded: 'If they suspend all of those on the list of communists it will include Meredith, Lockspeiser, Carter, Constance, Squire, Calvert, Hollingdale and Lord knows who. If they suspend all Socialists they will have to close the Factory [RAE].'[69]

At the beginning of 1935 Meredith moved back to the Aerodynamics Unit at the RAE following the untimely death of its head Hermann Glauert in August 1934, killed by a splinter from an exploded tree on Aldershot Common. Glauert had joined the Aerodynamic Unit of the Royal Aircraft Factory in 1916. (This became the RAE in 1918 to avoid confusion with the newly renamed RAF). He went to Göttingen where Prandtl did pioneering work on the boundary layer and wing theory post-First World War and on return became the head of RAE Aerodynamics. He wrote the *Elements of Aerofoil and Airscrew Theory* (Cambridge University Press, 1926) which became the standard introduction to fundamental principles of aerodynamics.[70] Thus, Meredith was seen to have the merit to follow highly distinguished footsteps.

At this time Supermarine and Rolls-Royce faced apparently insuperable problems with evaporative cooling. Meredith's recent work so far had been with aircraft stability and autopilot control. Immediately, however, he appears to have developed new approaches to engine cooling and the associated problem of duct entry, outlined in the next chapter.

Chapter 3

Meredith – papers on jet propulsion and duct entry

The return of Meredith to the RAE's Aerodynamics Unit led in 1935 to an extraordinarily fruitful line of development for ducted radiators where ideas were put forward and modified in the light of other, perhaps conflicting, ideas leading to solutions. In the 1950s the British Security Services, investigating Meredith, sought advice from George Gardner, who became a senior technical officer, at the RAE. As seen, he had provided a fascinating and sympathetic insight into how Meredith achieved his scientific results. 'In tackling a new problem he would argue just as passionately for and against some hypothesis until he had resolved the issue.'[1] The development of ducted cooling systems progressed through some very fruitful dialectics which cast light on how to make the system more effective. (In a dialectical cycle a hypothesis is proposed, then a counter-thesis, resolved possibly in a synthesis.) Meredith, as Gardner described, could combine the whole process in his own mind. The approach from different directions was seen in the output of research papers, many unpublished, which played a critical role in developing ducted cooling systems. In the following chapters several lines of dialectical development will be reviewed.

In Great Britain, in 1934 and 1935 Rolls-Royce (J.E. Ellor) and the RAE (C.J. Stewart and F.W. Meredith) applied for patents for ducted cooling systems whose development clearly interacted. Also, in Great Britain, two leading scientists at the RAE (R.S. Capon and F.W. Meredith) both produced internal papers in mid-1935 on ducted cooling systems. Capon significantly modified his mathematical analysis in the light of Meredith's work. Also, Meredith's and Capon's work stimulated critical analysis in Germany which developed a much more thorough mathematical basis for ducted radiators. Several German research papers were translated by the National Advisory Committee for Aeronautics (NACA) and used by North American Aviation to configure the Mustang's radiator.

In the first half of 1935 Meredith wrote three very original and related research papers, two of which have been entirely overlooked and the third much referred to but largely unread. The first indicates that his ideas for revolutionary approaches to the cooling challenge developed from an identification of ducted cooling systems with heat engines (systems that convert heat into mechanical energy) in the form of subsonic ramjets; the second provided solutions to the problem of the boundary

22

layer and duct entry; and the third gave a mathematical demonstration that it was theoretically possible for the power lost in the cooling duct to be exceeded by the power gained from the radiator heating the air passing through it. The first two ideas are dealt with in this chapter.

Jet propulsion

It is a paradox that the transfer of heat provided a remarkable new approach to the cooling challenge, but it would require a lateral thinker to promote and develop the idea. On 28 February 1935 Meredith submitted an application to the Air Ministry titled, *Invention relating to jet propulsion of aircraft* (marked 'Secret Closed until 1986'). This said: 'It has been proposed to propel aircraft or the screws of aircraft by the principle of the internal combustion reaction motor.'[2] (In 1926 the RAE's A.A. Griffith had described a two stage turbine, the first to drive a compressor, and the second a propeller. More recently the 1934 Frenchman René Leduc had patented a manned ramjet powered aircraft.) Meredith continued: 'For this purpose an internal duct is provided in which the air is compressed, by passing through an expanding passage, after which heat is added before the air expands in a contracting passage from the end of which the jet of augmented momentum issues.' (This also describes a ducted radiator.) The following image by Meredith formed part of the application. Meredith does not appear to be claiming this is original, but he is certainly early in describing jet propulsion in the form of a subsonic ramjet – an air breathing engine that uses its forward motion, not a mechanical compressor, to compress the air before heat is added – as in Figure 3.1.

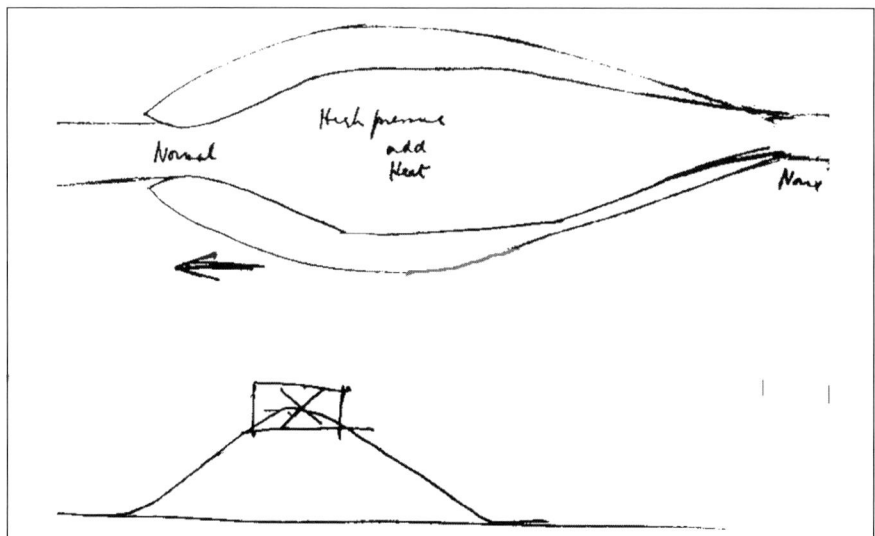

Figure 3.1 – Meredith's drawing of the 'internal combustion reaction motor', signed, 'F.W. Meredith 28/2/35'

Meredith then added: 'According to the present invention the same cycle is performed on the external stream past the body. The cycle is shown which may be of the form of a three dimensional streamline body or preferably in the form of a wing.'

Meredith stated that, 'the following advantage was achieved: (1) The total surface is less than with the internal duct'. [That is without an internal duct's additional interior skin area.] Meredith then suggested adding heat before the wing. 'According to the invention the heat may be added to the air by burning the fuel in the region of high pressure on the front of the body.' Given that he described earlier an 'internal combustion reaction motor' this new concept might be called an 'external combustion reaction motor'. (The addition of heat indicates that Meredith had anticipated the concept of the external burning ramjet which would be investigated in the post-war years.)

The importance of this document was threefold. First, Meredith's paper anticipates the 'Meredith effect' ducted cooling system as, in his first Figure 3.1, all that is necessary is to put the radiator in the place where is written 'high pressure add heat'. Second, the drawing of the internal duct shows the entrance is carefully

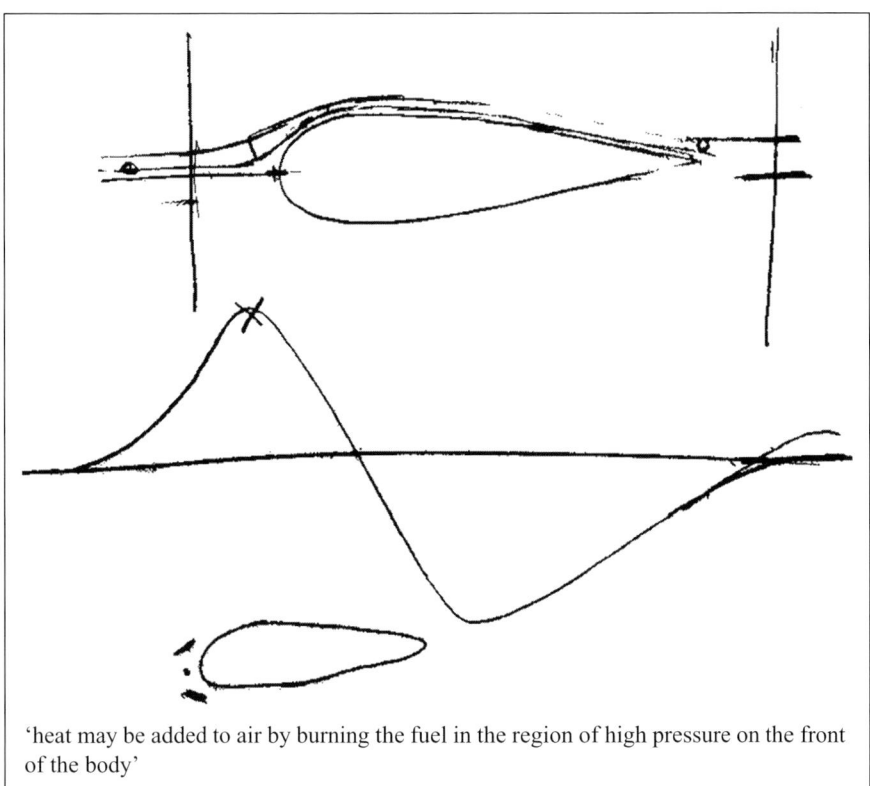

'heat may be added to air by burning the fuel in the region of high pressure on the front of the body'

Figure 3.2 – Meredith's drawing of the same cycle as in Figure 3.1 performed on the 'external stream'

profiled in an aerofoil form to facilitate entry. Third, he considered, as in the second figure, the process of compression could take place before the wing rather than within it in a diverging duct for his ducted cooling system. (This was of relevance when he could not patent the use of a diverging duct because Rolls-Royce had a prior patent claim.)

Meredith's application received a rather dusty response from the Air Ministry which marked the report as received 18 March:

> There is here the germ of an idea which might conceivably develop, probably in a very different form from anything now envisaged, into something practical; but I really think one can hardly say at this stage that the invention is likely to be of use to the Air Service. I agree there should be no application for patent at the public purse. D.R. Pye, D.D.S.R., 23.5.35[3]

(As seen in 1925, the Directorate of Scientific Research (DSR) had been set up at the Air Ministry. David Randall Pye had been invited to become Deputy Director.) In 1937, Pye would become Director of Scientific Research with responsibility for introducing into the RAF new methods and new equipment in preparation for the expected coming war, thereby reflecting the remarkable integration of British civil scientists and arms manufacturers. (In June 1939 a visit by Pye to Frank Whittle's Powerjets led to the Air Ministry finally properly funding the development of the jet engine.) In one way Pye's comment proved remarkably prescient: the idea with respect to internal ducts did develop into something 'very different', the Spitfire's radiator duct, which was intended from the outset to recycle heat. In another way it was not so prescient – for this idea would prove of profound use to the Air Service.

The interest in, and importance of, Meredith's paper lies not just in its description of a ramjet but in the manner it anticipates the Meredith's ducted radiator cooling system. The development is shown in the following Figure 3.3.

The questions might be posed: did Meredith's work on jet propulsion give rise to his realisation that the ducted cooling system was a (yet-to-be-named) ramjet which could generate thrust. As seen in his paper he said, 'it has been proposed to propel aircraft, or the screws of aircraft, by the principle of the internal combustion reaction motor'.[4] This would imply that he was aware of the ramjet concept or the 'internal combustion reaction motor'. Thus, when tackling the RAE's Aerodynamic unit's priority problem for 1935, ducted radiator cooling drag, Meredith had a solution. The ducted radiator, rather than being a problem, was an opportunity, because the cooling air heated by the radiator created a heat engine producing thrust. The challenge now was that the amount of thermal energy converted into kinetic energy is tiny – about 0.345%. Meredith, as will be seen, would now demonstrate that, if the aircraft was moving fast enough, then this would indeed be sufficient to counteract significant drag. The fact is, however, that Meredith was familiar with the ramjet concept and, as will be seen, saw ducted radiators as heat engines where, depending on the speed, the thrust created could exceed cooling drag.

The RAE did examine the ramjet concept in 1940 in a *Note on the development of additional power for aircraft by jet reaction*.[5] Joint author H. Constant

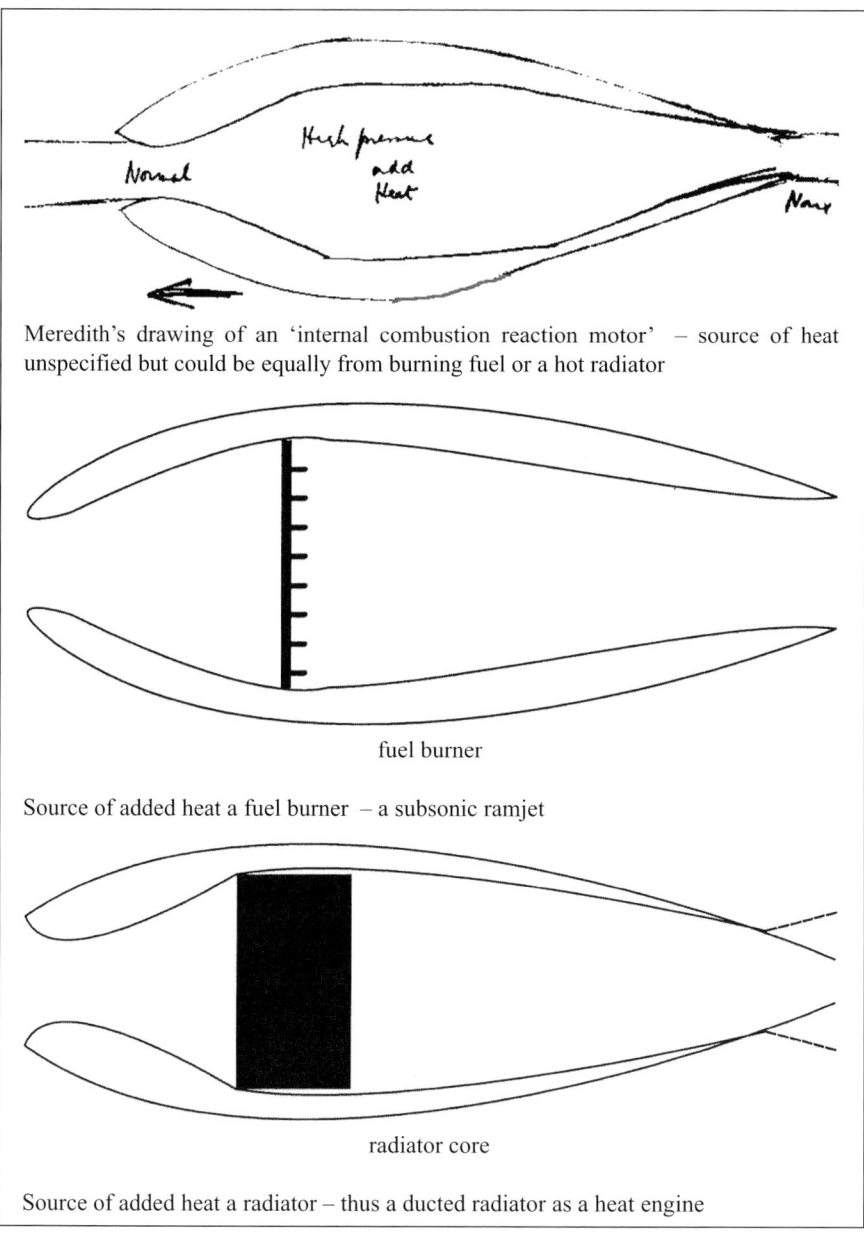

Meredith's drawing of an 'internal combustion reaction motor' – source of heat unspecified but could be equally from burning fuel or a hot radiator

fuel burner

Source of added heat a fuel burner – a subsonic ramjet

radiator core

Source of added heat a radiator – thus a ducted radiator as a heat engine

Figure 3.3 – Development of propulsion from recycling of heat in an internal duct.

(1904-1968) joined the RAE in 1928 and Imperial College in 1934. In 1936 the scientist Henry Tizard, who *inter alia* played an important role in the development of radar, persuaded him to return to the RAE from Imperial College to help with the development of A.A. Griffith's axial flow turbine engine designs. (The 1940 RAE report includes a diagram of a remarkably advanced axial flow jet engine made by Metropolitan-Vickers, which developed Constant's design and ran his Metrovick F2 for the first time later that year.)

In 1940 more speed was sought for existing British fighters. The report stated:

> It was desired to examine the possibility of augmenting the power of the main engine of an aeroplane by the use of units which provide thrust by jet reaction. Two schemes were considered:
> (a) Burning of fuel in a forward-facing duct.
> (b) The continuous flow internal combustion turbine.

(a) was a ramjet and (b) an axial flow jet engine. The report includes a detailed description of the former:

> The development of power for aircraft propulsion by jet reaction becomes possible by relatively simple means, involving no moving parts, when the forward speed of the aircraft is fairly high, a forward facing duct provided with a controlled exit is fitted to house a combustion unit consisting of burners and suitable baffles. Air enters the duct and is compressed almost adiabatically, so that its pressure and temperature rise above their values, and air is heated by the

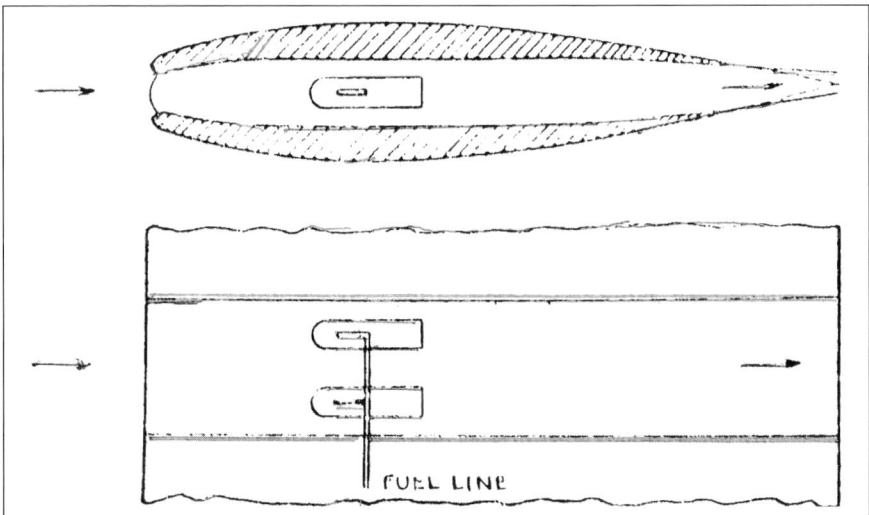

Figure 3.4 – Arrangement of burners in wing duct – *Note on the development of additional power for aircraft by jet reaction* (Hall and Constant, 1940).

combustion of fuel at the burners; finally, the heated air expands through the rear exit back to the atmospheric static pressure. Owing to the heating of the air, the velocity of efflux is greater than that of entry, and a forward thrust is therefore produced by jet reaction.

The process was explicitly recognised to be that of a heat engine.

The heat cycle involved makes use of adiabatic compression, heating by combustion, followed by adiabatic expansion. The system relies on the compression which takes place in the entry to the duct to elevate the pressure before combustion, to obtain a positive thermodynamic efficiency.

The drawing of (a) is remarkably similar to Meredith's drawing above. Also, it uses the in-wing position favoured, as will be seen, by Meredith for a ducted radiator.

Duct entry

In May 1935 Meredith completed a very interesting RAE paper, Wind Tunnel Note No 267. This was a *Note on the problem of conducting a fluid into a duct with the minimum of losses*. This dealt with the problem of how to get air to enter a duct efficiently in the first place. This was absolutely critical to the effectiveness of ducted radiators. (And it would prove so also for jet engine inlets.) Most drag was incurred at the duct entry when the boundary layer, the slower moving air adjacent to the airframe, had some distance over the airframe to build up and, inside the duct, where air tended to separate or break away from the duct sides.

The aerodynamic boundary layer was first defined by Prandtl in 1904. It simplified the equations of fluid flow by dividing it into two areas: one inside the boundary layer, dominated by viscosity and creating the majority of drag experienced by the boundary body, here the airframe; and one outside the boundary layer, where viscosity can be ignored. The issue of duct entry would be central to the relative drag of the Spitfire and the Mustang cooling systems: the former being poor (as Meredith would point out before the aircraft flew) and the latter eventually excellent.

Meredith's paper stated: 'General considerations. All serious losses arise from separation from a boundary and this separation may take place either by the internal or the external stream.' Particularly prescient for the Mustang was Meredith's addressing of the issue with ventral radiators which were particularly likely to incur boundary layer problems.

Ventral entries. In the case of underslung radiators enclosed in a cowl or duct the entry generally takes a form similar to Fig. 1 [showing a flat plate, this being a convention in boundary flow analysis] except that the bottom floor [here the upper side of the flat plate] represents the bottom surface of the fuselage and is curved in the destabilising direction both in front of and behind the entry. Such a system is bound to lead to separation as the boundary layer is thick and the depression at the surface is accentuated by the curvature of the boundary, serious losses associated are therefore common.

Meredith not only identified the problem, but he also proposed two solutions: '(a) deflection of the main stream back to the surface by controlling vanes; (b) removal of the boundary layer in the neighbourhood where separation would otherwise occur.' Meredith, in order to implement (b) suggested incorporating a passage through which the boundary layer could flow without turbulence.

Meredith considered external stream separation but did not view it as such a serious problem as internal separation. 'Separation of external stream. The conditions for this phenomenon are closely analogous to those of upper surface separation for an aerofoil and little difficulty should arise in preventing this phenomenon.' This required 'a rounded leading edge for precisely the same reasons as in the case of an aerofoil'. This can be seen both in the figure above and in Meredith's earlier drawing of 'a proposal relating to jet propulsion of aircraft'. (The effectiveness of the rounded leading edge would be confirmed in future wind tunnel tests as seen in *A review of wind tunnel experiments on ducted radiators* (Hartshorn, July 1936)). This May 1935 paper revealed that Meredith had very

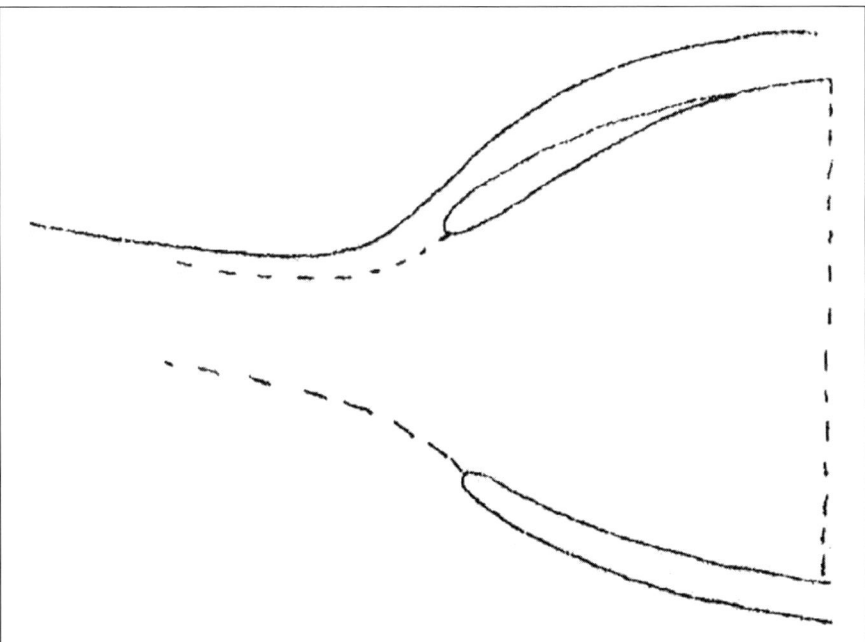

Figure 3.5 – Meredith's drawing of 'an auxiliary duct bypassing the cooling system for the purpose of removing the harmful boundary layer' applied 'to ducted underslung radiator'.

clearly anticipated the problems of the boundary layer and duct inlets. Also, he provided solutions which were utilised in practice and would be incorporated into the Second World War fighters with ducted radiators.

This paper was not Meredith's last word on duct entry. The internal June 1935 version of Meredith's *Note on the cooling of aircraft engines with special reference to ethylene glycol radiators enclosed in ducts* (Meredith's third important paper discussed below) included under 'Further developments': 'Wind tunnel experiments with ducted cooling systems for both liquid and air-cooled engines are being conducted. The avoidance of entry losses in the ducts is the main feature requiring exploration.'

It should be noted that in 1935, while Meredith was in charge of Aerodynamics, the RAE tested a 'ventral duct with both a bypass and vanes, solutions suggested by him resulting in a *Note on the installation of a ducted radiator in the ventral position,* (Hartshorn, November 1935). The report included the diagram below.

The report noted: 'The radiator was semi-recessed into the fuselage in front of the leading edge of the wing and the cowl was continued backward over the front of the wing. The cooling flow was controlled by a flap which altered the exit area of the duct.' It identified the particular problem of the boundary layer with the ventral location. The extent of entry loss was clearly serious, 'at top speed this entry loss is two to three times the loss through the radiator'. The boundary layer was identified as the cause of loss. 'This entry loss is probably linked up with the combination of a *well established boundary layer* on the undersurface of the fuselage.'

The methods tried to reduce this loss, which had been suggested in Meredith's paper on duct entry, were:

(a) Dividing the entry into separate compartments.
(b) Placing deflector vanes near the entry.
(c) By-passing the boundary layer near the duct entrance through a separate slot.

These methods proved on testing only partly successful. This paper is, however, of considerable interest for the insight it gives into the very real problems of ventral radiators, even those semi-recessed and with a boundary layer bypass. (This wind tunnel test is looked at in more detail in Appendix 4.)

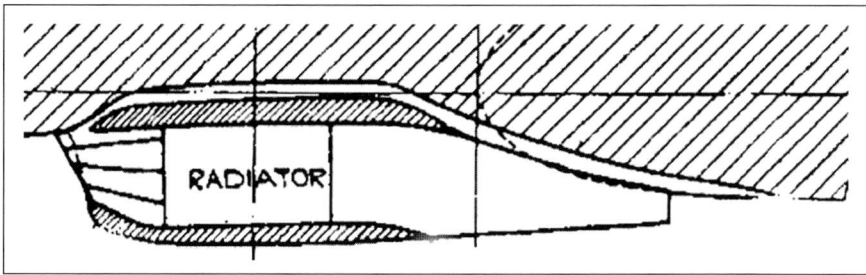

Figure 3.6 – 'Ventral radiator Model 2 with by-pass' – detail in *Note on the installation of a ducted radiator in the ventral position* (Hartshorn, November 1935).

As will be seen in September 1935 Meredith visited Supermarine to discuss the cooling system of the F37/34. His sketch showed that he recommended a boundary layer bypass called a 'vent passage' and 'guide vanes'. This was in line with his May *Note on the problem of conducting a fluid into a duct with the minimum of losses*.

At the Instruments unit Meredith had focused on autopilots. It reflects his unique abilities that Meredith could shift from Instruments to Aerodynamics and immediately write pioneering papers on both jet propulsion and duct entry that would be central to the conception and functioning of ducted radiators as a source of thrust that could greatly reduce and above certain speeds negate cooling drag.

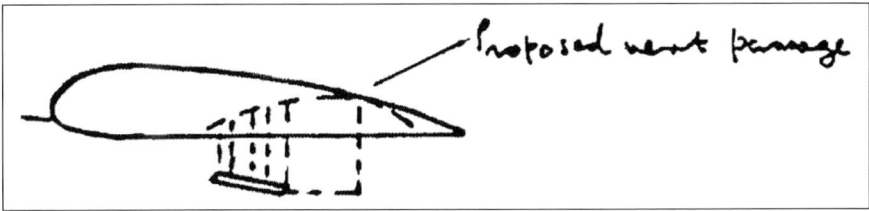

Figure 3.7 – Meredith's sketch (detail) made 11 September 1935 during visit to Supermarine here showing proposed addition of 'vent passage' and 'guide vanes' to the F37/34 cooling system.[6]

Chapter 4

Rolls-Royce and RAE – patents for ducted radiator systems

The British patent process provides a revealing insight into the development of ducted radiators. Patents were applied for by named individuals not their employer company or research institution, and so become identified with a particular person or persons. The process started at an initial 'Application Date' with a 'Provisional Specification'. This might be revised in the light of claims in other patent applications, then resulting in a second 'Application Date' and 'Provisional Specification'. There followed the 'Complete Specification Left', and finally the 'Complete Specification Accepted'. During this, possibly protracted, process patents might be substantially modified in order to differentiate themselves from other patents. There were, in 1935, three important applications for the development of ducted radiators, two by Rolls-Royce and one by the RAE. The revisions to these patents give revealing insights into the dialectical development of ducted radiator systems.

First Rolls-Royce patent (Ellor) – application stage

It was J.E. Ellor of Rolls-Royce who applied for the first British patent for a ducted radiator, GB 447,283, titled *Improvements in Cowling for Liquid Cooled Internal Combustion Engines for Aircraft*, on 15 November 1934. This application is particularly notable as it shows that Rolls-Royce pioneered the process of placing the radiator for cooling inline engines in ducts. Ellor had been the country's leading expert on superchargers at the RAE. In order to keep him in the country he was moved in 1927 to Rolls-Royce, who could pay more than a government position at the RAE and was made responsible for development work on superchargers. It was shortly after this that a single-sided centrifugal supercharger was fitted to the Rolls-Royce Kestrel. Ellor assisted in the development of a supercharger for the 'R' engine which powered the Supermarine S6, Schneider Trophy winner of 1929. His work on the 'R' engine led to the development of a single-stage supercharger for the Merlin. (During the war he would be Rolls-Royce's representative at Packard in the US when the latter built the Merlin.)

The Rolls-Royce patent application, GB 447,283 in its 'Provisional Specification' form, stated: 'This invention has for its object to provide a cowling in which the cooling of the radiator … shall take place.' There was a divergent entry duct. 'The radiator is housed … in a tube against the engine cowling with a divergent orifice.' Rolls-Royce proposed that the engine exhaust gases were piped through the duct behind the radiator 'and the exhaust gases are led [from the exhaust manifold] into the radiator tube … behind the radiator'. (The purpose is discussed in more detail below.) Finally, there was 'a converging exit for this air'. Thus, the patent described diverging and converging ducts respectively before and after the radiator. (This was not, however, a complete ducted cooling system as there was no provision for varying the air flow using rear flaps.)

RAE patent (Stewart and Meredith) – application stage

The RAE's first public reference to ongoing work on ducted radiators came in the patent application GB 454,266, by Major C.J. Stewart and F.W. Meredith, titled *Improvements in or relating to aircraft and other craft or vehicles*, on 28 March 1935. This built on Meredith's ideas for jet propulsion outlined in *Invention relating to the jet propulsion of aircraft*.

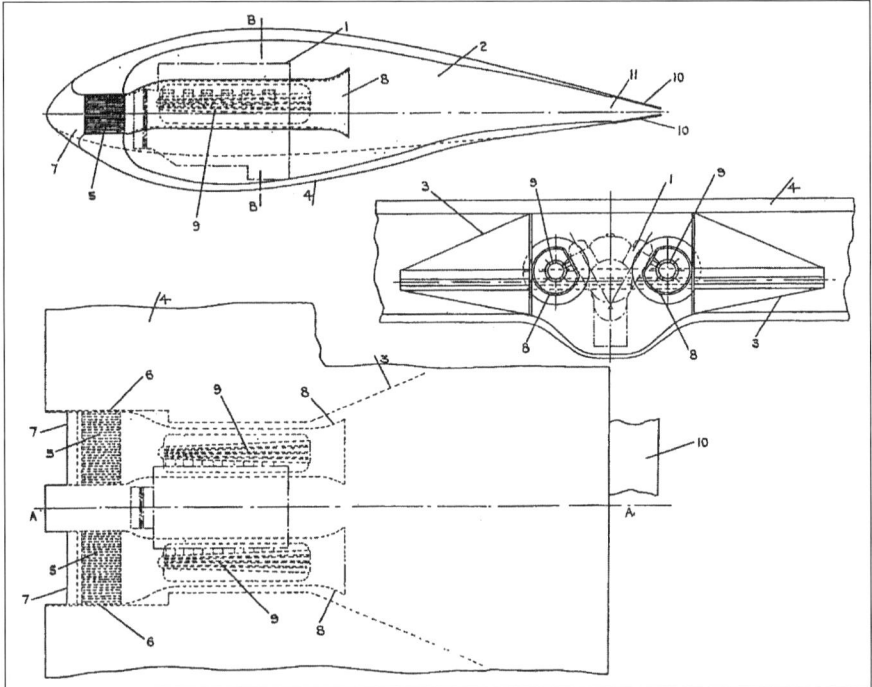

Figure 4.1 – Diagram from RAE patent *Improvements in or relating to aircraft and other craft or vehicles*, (Stewart and Meredith, GB 454,266, March 1935) showing in-wing design adding both radiator and exhaust heat.

The invention had a dual objective: 'To reduce the drag due to the cooling system. Also, the invention has for a further object to supplement the propulsive force obtained by engine driven airscrews … [as] waste heat is utilised to regenerate or augment the momentum of a stream of air utilised in the cooling system.' The patent application also discussed an issue where Meredith was also doing pioneering work, the drag created by the boundary layer. Here the objective was that, 'the resulting gain in kinetic energy is greater than the loss inevitably involved by the boundary conditions between the stream of air and the aero engine cooling system'. Figure 4.1 shows the radiator as positioned in the wing.

The patent application described the cooling system cycle as that of a heat engine in the form of a subsonic ramjet: 'Firstly the air is compressed by the recovery of part of the dynamic head of the main airstream past the aircraft, by expansion of the streamlines, in front of the aircraft.' It should be noted that compression does not take place in a divergent duct here, as in Ellor's Rolls-Royce patent. The reason why there is no diverging duct is possibly because this had already been claimed in Ellor's patent. (Figure 3.1, showing Meredith's *Invention related to jet propulsion of aircraft*, indicated he was quite aware of how to use the diverging duct to obtain compression and slow the air speed in accordance with the principle of low velocity cooling.)

Heat was added as, 'the cooling air passes over surfaces (such as a finned exhaust manifold) provided for disposing of the heat of the [engine] exhaust gases'. Alternatively, the possibility of adding the momentum of the exhaust gases was also considered, 'and/or the exhaust gases may be injected into the airstream with downward momentum'. There was a converging duct. 'The … cooling air … passes through a suitably shaped contracting [duct], in which the pressure is reduced substantially to the original value.' Finally, 'The … cooling air … is projected backwards'. The source of thrust was Newton's second law of motion. 'The thrust … is provided by the rate of change of momentum of the … cooling air in the direction of the main airstream.'

Importantly, there was the first patented provision for shutters (if a Junkers patent of 1918 is excluded – see Appendix 2), which had a dual purpose. Firstly, 'Shutters may be provided for the purposes of regulating or interrupting the cooling'; and secondly, by opening into external airflow, 'for causing drag or braking'.

First Rolls-Royce and RAE patents compared

Both Ellor of Rolls-Royce and Stewart and Meredith of the RAE submitted patent applications for systems where engine exhaust gases were injected into the duct, but these were for rather different purposes. (Drawings from the Ellor and Stewart and Meredith patents are shown in Figure 4.2 in single engine form.)

Ellor suggested the use of the exhaust gas, piped to the duct rear of the radiator, to induce additional air flow through the radiator. Basically, the Rolls-Royce system was optimised to ensure adequate cooling air in the most demanding low speed situations – as the priority, for an engine manufacturer pioneering new technology, was to make sure the engine kept going: that is, it did not overheat

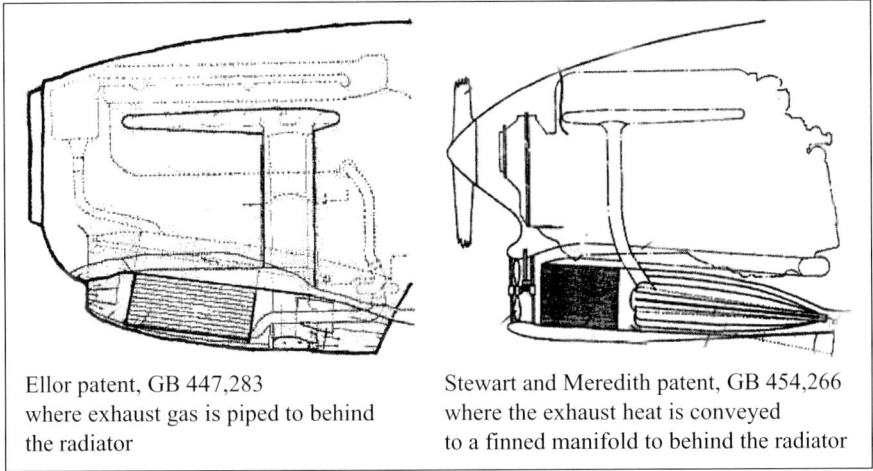

Ellor patent, GB 447,283 where exhaust gas is piped to behind the radiator	Stewart and Meredith patent, GB 454,266 where the exhaust heat is conveyed to a finned manifold to behind the radiator

Figure 4.2 – Comparison of Rolls-Royce and RAE patents showing different recycling of exhaust energy. (Drawings come from the respective final patent specifications)

when stationary, taxiing, or in a laden climb. Here, at zero or low speed, drag is less of a consideration.

Stewart and Meredith wanted to convert the radiator and exhaust heat into kinetic energy as their priority in adding exhaust heat was not, as with Rolls-Royce, to prevent overheating at the lower end of the speed range but higher speed operations when heat from the radiator, and possibly the exhaust system could produce thrust to overcome the serious drag problem at the upper end of the speed range. '[J.E.] Ellor of Rolls-Royce had previously patented [GB 447,283, 15 November 1934] the use of exhaust gas to induce additional flow through the radiator, but Meredith was the first to suggest converting the energy (either heat or kinetic) of the exhaust into thrust.'[1]

The Rolls-Royce Ellor patent looked back to the past, where overheating was the fear, while the RAE Stewart and Meredith patent looked forward by exploiting the cooling challenge in order to create thrust to make aeroplanes fly faster.

Second Rolls-Royce patent (Ellor) – application stage

In April 1935 Ellor of Rolls-Royce submitted a second very different patent application, GB 456,335, for *Aircraft engine accessories*. This was significant because it was the first such application to conform to the basic model of a ducted cooling system with diverging and converging ducts and an adjustable exit. Unlike Ellor's first Rolls-Royce patent, or that of Stewart and Meredith of the RAE, there was no provision for adding engine exhaust which meant that this patent was in line with what would become actual practice. The problem of varying cooling requirements in different flight conditions was outlined. This was an important development as it demonstrated that Rolls-Royce had adsorbed the lessons of

Beisel in the US about the use of cowl flaps to adjust for different flight conditions on radial engines. (See Appendix 1 and 2.)

> The tunnel [duct] which is designed to admit sufficient air for cooling purposes when the aircraft is normally flying level will not be large enough to cool the radiator sufficiently when the aircraft is climbing, while if the tunnel is constructed to admit sufficient air during the climb it will be unnecessarily large and have therefore an unnecessarily high drag coefficient during level flight.

The invention was intended to increase the flow when required for climbing. 'The object of this invention is to provide the means whereby the volume of air flowing through the cowling can be temporarily increased.' Thus: 'According to this invention means are provided for increasing at will the exit from the radiator tunnel.' The solution was a variable flap. (As seen in Appendix 1 this was pioneered in the US for radial engines.)

> Preferably part of the wall of the tunnel at the rear of the radiator is arranged as a single flap which can be opened outwards into the air stream thus increasing the area of the exit. The effect of so increasing the area of the exit is to cause eddies at the rear of the radiator and at the rear of the tunnel and these eddies will suck more air through the radiator.

Rolls-Royce's concern was still that at low speed, but during a powered fully laden climb, enough air would be available for cooling – so the flap was lowered into the airstream in order to induce flow through the radiator. It admitted that lowering the flap into the airstream would increase drag but considered this a price worth paying to ensure adequate cooling. 'The drag on the aircraft will be consequently slightly increased but as the increase of the exit is a temporary measure such increase of drag can be tolerated at such times as it is called for.' Rolls-Royce in its patents had now proposed all the features of a conventional ducted radiator 'cold' system. These were: diverging and converging ducts and an adjustable exit.

First Rolls-Royce (Ellor) patent – complete specification stage

On 15 November 1935 Ellor of Rolls-Royce submitted the complete specification of the first Rolls-Royce patent application, GB 447,283, for a ducted radiator, initially submitted in November 1934. This provided a much more detailed description of the system. The role of the entrance duct was clarified (possibly to ensure that the Stewart and Meredith RAE patent had no claim on the diverging duct). In order to diminish such drag, 'a cowling [is] shaped [diverging] so as to convert part of the kinetic energy of the admitted airstream into pressure before reaching the radiator face'. The patent implicitly included the use of a duct [necessarily convergent] to convert pressure into kinetic energy, 'to re-convert such pressure … into energy at the rear of this radiator cowling'. The key point about this first Rolls-Royce patent remains, however, that the engine exhaust gases were emitted into the duct behind the radiator, 'into this cowling behind the radiator the exhaust gases from the engine are discharged'.

The complete specification indicates that heat, perhaps drawing on Meredith's ideas available in patents, not just from the kinetic energy, from the exhaust gases, could be added to accelerate the airflow.

> The heat and kinetic energy of the exhaust gases may be utilised to speed up the airstream behind the radiator. By suitably proportioning the radiator cowling the airstream containing the exhaust gases may be caused to leave the same at the velocity of little less and possibly even greater than that of the airstream going past the outside of the cowling.

(Another possible reason why Rolls-Royce recognised that the radiator duct was a heat engine was that at this time an RAE employee, T.P. de Paravicini, who had worked with Meredith, moved to Rolls-Royce to work with Ellor and produced a series of patents for various types of ducted radiators. The first was *Oil coolers for aircraft* (Paravicini, GB 463,303, September 1935) which covered both radial and inline engines and showed for the latter a ducted oil cooler radiator.)

Thus, Rolls-Royce's revised patent appears to have acknowledged Meredith's concept of the radiator duct as a 'hot' system. (The difference was that the (marginal) effect of heat from the radiator was ignored – the impact of heat and kinetic energy from the engine exhaust gases only being considered.) In practice this Rolls-Royce patent was a dead end. It is notable, however, because it was the first patent, as it dated back to 1934, for a ducted inline engine cooling system. Also, it may have prevented Stewart and Meredith from using a diverging entry duct in their patent application.

These patent applications demonstrate that Great Britain had developed the concept of the ducted liquid cooling systems by the first half of 1935. Also, the pioneering role of Rolls-Royce has perhaps been overlooked, but it was the first to demonstrate in writing a cooling system for inline engines with diverging and converging ducts and an adjustable exit in a system uncomplicated by the addition of engine exhaust gases.

Patent completion

Looking forward, 1936 saw the final stages of the patent process for the two Rolls-Royce patents. The first was *Improvements in Cowling for Liquid Cooled Internal Combustion Engines for Aircraft,* GB 447,283. The second was *Improvements in Radiator Cowling for Aircraft* GB 456,335. Also, the RAE patent *Improvements in and relating to aircraft and other craft or vehicles,* GB 454,266 (Stewart and Meredith) for ducted radiators was accepted.

In January 1936 Stewart and Meredith submitted a short revised application for patent GB 454,266, followed in March by the complete application. In order to avoid issues of patent infringement, particularly after Ellor's Rolls-Royce patent was revised, the Stewart and Meredith patent was changed to incorporate a fan to increase compression before the radiator as there was no diverging duct. 'The pressure of the air in the stream flowing through a tunnel … is augmented by an engine driven blower or fan.' This explicitly recognised that Rolls-Royce had already claimed a diverging duct. This was a long text with substantial revisions to the first submission following Meredith's ARC approved report of August 1935.

The patent drew together the ideas in Meredith's three papers of 1935, discussed next, which treated a ducted cooling system as a heat engine and were particularly concerned with the problems of duct entry and the boundary layer. This document is nearly four densely written pages long and is a far more detailed exposition of the working of a ducted cooling system than Meredith's 1935 ARC paper discussed in the next chapter.

> It is known to enclose the cooling surfaces of an aircraft engine … in a duct … and it is also known to decrease the drag on the aircraft caused by frictional losses in the duct by shaping the duct so that the kinetic energy of the stream flowing through it is converted to pressure before the cooling surfaces are reached and is reconverted to kinetic energy before being discharged from the duct. These conversions are achieved by shaping the forward part of the duct so that the streamlines of the stream entering the same are expanded either in front of or inside the duct and by contracting the walls of the duct after the cooling surfaces have been passed.

The relevance of the patent is that it shows Stewart and Meredith explaining explicitly the functioning of the duct, but this was not used here, probably due to Ellor's prior claim. Later they wrote: 'Adjustment of the throat area of the nozzle is required to limit the stream through the duct to that required for cooling the engine.' Stewart and Meredith said that by recycling heat negative drag, in effect, positive thrust was possible:

> By means of this invention it is possible with an internal combustion engine of an aircraft given a substantial head of pressure at the front of the duct such as is available with an aircraft travelling at about 300 miles per hour, … to reduce the drag in a properly designed duct, to a figure which we believe has not hitherto been achieved and it may even be found possible to reduce such drag below nothing as the duct produces a thrust on the aircraft.

The Stewart and Meredith patent now explicitly recognised that this was a heat engine. 'The duct may be regarded as a heat engine from which a thrust is obtained by the reaction of a stream of air of which the kinetic energy has been raised by transferring to it waste heat from the engine.'

The authors were particularly concerned about the duct entry and stream separation – an issue that Meredith had considered separately in his paper on duct entry. 'Moreover, it is required that the entrance to the duct be designed to avoid the excessive entry loss associated with stream separation.' Ideally the duct entrance should be in the leading edge of the wing or fuselage front, or the boundary layer should be isolated.

> In general, this [stream separation] is difficult to achieve without special precautions to remove the boundary layer and the condition can most easily be met by avoiding surface in front of the entrance, or by arranging that the boundary layer over such surface, if it cannot be avoided, does not enter the duct.

Like the earlier Rolls-Royce patent, the in-wing engine design outlined in the Stewart/Meredith patent was a dead end before the end of the Second World War. The patent is important, however, because of the explicit discussion of the duct cooling process and the importance of dealing with the boundary layer. Also, the emphasis on leading edge duct entry would be followed by British aircraft design, particularly the Westland Whirlwind, the de Havilland Mosquito, and Griffon powered Fairey Firefly and the oil cooler of the radial cooled Hawker Sea Fury.

The response to the patent showed Meredith's ideas received attention and were taken seriously in aeronautical circles. Stewart and Meredith's completed patent was recognised externally as being for a heat engine – as this passage from *Flight*, April 1937, demonstrated:

> A contributory factor to the performances attained by some of our latest military machines fitted with Rolls-Royce Merlin engines is the 'ducted' radiator which produces a measure of thrust at high speeds. The principle on which these radiators function has been further developed by Messrs C.J. Stewart and F.W. Meredith, of the RAE, whose present scheme of supplementing airscrew thrust by that exerted by a mixture of air and exhaust gases pouring from slits in the trailing edge may prove highly beneficial to high-speed machines. Briefly, the scheme converts into thrust the drag presented by the cooling system, which may be regarded as a form of heat engine increasing the speed of an aircraft.[2]

In 1936 all three patents were accepted, fully completing the patent process. On 15 May Ellor's (Rolls-Royce) first patent, 447,283 then on 28 September Stewart's and Meredith's (RAE) 454,266. Then followed on 3 November Ellor's (Rolls-Royce) second patent (456,335). Rolls-Royce continued to patent many designs of ducted radiators but its two Ellor patents, and that of Stewart and Meredith were pioneering. The further Rolls-Royce patents were largely in the name of T.P. de Paravicini who until recently had worked with Meredith at the RAE underlining the close relationship between the RAE and Rolls-Royce.

Chapter 5

Meredith and Capon ARC research papers on inline engine cooling

In the US, books about the North American Mustang constitute almost a publishing genre in its own right. The 'Meredith effect' is generally mentioned but Meredith's actual analysis is not. This chapter looks at what Meredith (and R.S. Capon) actually wrote.

In August 1935 the Aeronautical Research Committee (ARC) approved for publication the *Cooling of Aircraft Engines With special reference to Ethylene Glycol Radiators enclosed in Ducts* by F.W. Meredith. (The date given with the printer's name, HMSO, is 1936.) In March 1936 the ARC published *The Cowling of Cooling Systems* by R.S. Capon. These papers, however, had an earlier genesis in 1935, seen in RAE papers that have not previously been considered. These show how ideas within the RAE mixed in a dialectical relationship with extraordinarily creative and valuable results.

In June 1935 Capon and Meredith had issued internal RAE papers on ducted cooling systems, respectively No B.A. 1208 and No. B.A. 1213. The papers can be seen as promoting mathematical analysis of the systems of patents for ducted cooling systems developed by Rolls-Royce and the RAE. Capon worked on the areas of interest to Rolls-Royce whose engines were used with shuttered unducted radiators, retractable radiators and ducted radiators, with and without adjustable exits (see above Ellor patents, GB 447,283 and GB 456,335). Meredith first compared unducted with ducted radiators. Then, at greater length, he compared the power lost overcoming drag with that gained by recycling heat (see Stewart and Meredith patent GB 454,266). The first two papers appear to have been initiated quite independently of each other but once Capon became aware of Meredith's work he revised his analysis.

Up until 1935 cooling was seen as a source of drag that could be reduced but not eliminated, let alone turned into thrust. The amount of thermal energy that can be turned into kinetic energy appears derisory at 0.345%. So no one considered that a cooling duct incorporating a radiator could be a practical heat engine in the form of a subsonic ramjet. That is until Meredith became head of the RAE's Aerodynamics unit after his predecessor's unfortunate encounter with an exploding tree late in 1934. Meredith demonstrated mathematically that because the relative faster speed of the airstream outside the duct and the slower speed through the radiator are both squared, that the seemingly negligible 0.345%, after various adjustments, could above certain

40

speeds produce enough thrust to exceed the drag. Only a truly original and lateral thinker might have had and pursued this insight and no one else apparently did before Meredith. It reflects the high respect in which Meredith's scientific views were regarded that such an apparently marginal conversion was subsequently taken seriously.

Meredith – June 1935 internal RAE paper

This chapter might seem to contain a fair amount of mathematics and physics which some readers might find tedious. When discussing Meredith's paper commentators often focus on the duct and its diffusing and converging elements and an adjustable exit to compensate for different flight conditions. This, however, is not what Meredith's paper is really about. At the core of his paper is a single equation based on two conclusions, one essentially aerodynamic and the other thermodynamic, and its derivation (this is further looked at in Appendix 3). Therefore, this equation is dealt with first.

The equation was composed of two parts: giving the net percentage of engine power lost or gained in the cooling process as equal to $0.177 (V/100)^2 - 1.725 (V_0/100)^2$, where: V is the aircraft speed; and V_0 is the speed of the cooling air through the radiator in a duct. V_0 is considerably lower than the aircraft speed (V) due to compression ahead of the radiator, in practice due to a diverging duct. The speed is also constant through the duct due to an adjustable duct exit regardless of changes in aircraft speed. The equation built on the first two of three conclusions outlined in Meredith's paper:

Percentage of engine horsepower lost and gained in the duct	=	Thrust $0.177 (V/100)^2$	-	Drag $1.725 (V_0/100)^2$
		Meredith's (thermodynamic) 'conclusion' 'The combined effect of compressibility [here changes in temperature and density with that of pressure] and heat transfer from the radiator may reduce the power consumption to nothing if the size of the radiator is adequate.'		Meredith's (aerodynamic) 'conclusion' 'The employment of low velocity cooling [placing the radiator behind a diffuser duct which slowed the cooling air] avoids the necessity of an increasing expenditure of power with increasing speed provided the exit conditions are adjusted to suit the speed [by a converging duct with a variable exit].'
For V=300mph, V_0=100mph		$0.177 (300/100)^2$	–	$1.725 (100/100)^2$
- 0.13%	=	0.177 (9)	–	1.725 (1)

That is to say 0.13% of engine power is lost in the cooling process. Thus, if the engine developed 1000 horsepower then 1.3 horsepower was the net loss. The originality of this equation lies in its demonstration that the apparently miniscule amount of kinetic energy created from the conversion of thermal energy can, at high speeds, outweigh the energy deficit lost due by cooling drag.

Looking at the derivation of the aerodynamic conclusion and second value of 1.725, on the basis of RAE research, Meredith said the power consumed by a ducted radiator when cold, where the air speed through the radiator was 100mph, was about 0.9% of engine power. This percentage was increased by several factors (largely related to the reduced efficiency due to the cooling air being heated by compression ahead of the radiator and radiator running in practice hot) to 1.725%.

So, looking at the thermodynamic conclusion and first value of 0.177, the conversion of thermal energy from the radiator into kinetic energy is extremely small at about 0.345%. As only about half of engine heat is dissipated through the radiator, about 0.16% of engine power, is thus converted. (The difference between 0.16 and 0.177 is the beneficial effect of lower temperature at an altitude assumed by Meredith of 14,000 feet.)

The clever part is that although the value of 0.177 in the first half of the equation for the power gain is only about one tenth of the power lost of 1.725, this can be reversed at higher speeds as the ratio of the airspeeds is squared. Thus, at 312mph the engine horsepower lost and gained in the duct is equal. The 'Summary' at the beginning of the paper said: 'It is shown that the power expended on cooling does not increase with speed for a properly designed ducted system but that, owing to recovery of waste heat, a thrust may be derived at speeds of the order of 300mph.'

Taking conclusions 1 and 2 taken together – Meredith stated:

> The purpose of this report [is] to show that, by correct design of low velocity cooling systems, in which the surface is exposed in an internal duct, the power expended on cooling does not increase with the speed of flight [conclusion 1], but … it should diminish to vanishing point at a practicable speed beyond which the cooling system contributes to the propulsion [conclusion 2].

The chart opposite gives – separately – lines for the two parts of Meredith's equation and the net combination.

- The bottom (aerodynamic) flat line $(1.725(V_0/100)^2)$ shows how 'low velocity cooling' avoids 'increasing expenditure of power with increasing speed provided the exit conditions are adjusted to suit the speed'.
- The upper (thermodynamic) curved line $= ((0.177(V/100)^2)$ shows how the 'combined effect of compressibility and heat transfer from the radiator may reduce the power consumption to nothing if the size of the radiator is adequate'.

- The middle curved line $(0.177(V/100)^2 - 1.725(V_0/100)^2)$ combines the values of the two above lines and shows that at 312mph the power gained equals the power absorbed in the cooling system.

Thus, Meredith's revolutionary insight was that the cooling system was a heat engine that could, above a certain speed, produce negative drag or thrust. This was the core idea of what became known as the 'Meredith effect'. E.J. Davis of Supermarine, who was present later in 1935 when Meredith inspected the Spitfire's cooling system based on his concepts, said, 'The cooling deserves recognition as a quantum leap forward'.[1]

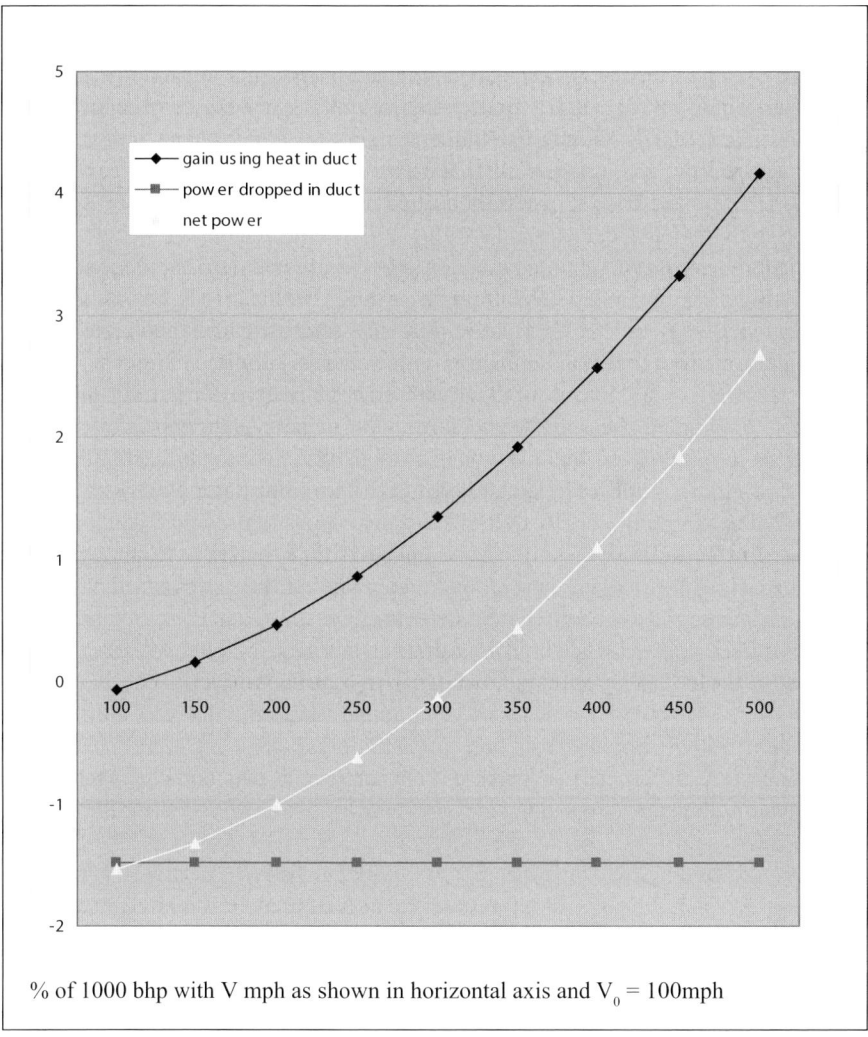

% of 1000 bhp with V mph as shown in horizontal axis and $V_0 = 100$mph

Figure 5.1 – Two parts of Meredith's equation shown as separate lines and net combined.

Constituent parts of Meredith's paper

1. Introductory – This stated that.

> It is purpose of this report to show that, by correct design of low velocity cooling systems … the power expended on cooling does not increase with the speed of flight, but that, on the contrary, it should diminish to vanishing point at a practicable speed beyond which the cooling system contributes to propulsion.

2. Classification of drag – Meredith divided cooling drag into three groups: skin friction; eddying due to separation; and expansion losses without separation. Eddying and expansion losses can be avoided by good design and burying the system, therefore, the main problem is the unavoidable drag of the internal stream within the duct. Here, there are three basic assumptions: the cooling air is slowed ('low velocity cooling'); there is a variable exit ('exit conditions are adjusted'); and the duct is buried so only internal drag is an issue.

3. The radiator considered as an actuator disc operating on a perfect fluid (derivation of aerodynamic conclusion) – Meredith considered first the 'cold' radiator which was looked at both unducted and then ducted, the latter having lower drag. Meredith developed formulas for the efficiency of induction for the freely exposed (unducted) and ducted radiator. The efficiency of induction was the ratio of the power utilised in the actuator disk (comparable to the energy derived by a wind turbine from the wind) to the power expended overcoming the drag of the wind turbine. (The closer to 1 the more effective the wind turbine is in converting the power in the wind into usable energy.)

   The point is made here, not simply for the sake of giving more equations, that Meredith gave one that was immediately used in the work of other RAE scientists. Meredith looked at first at an unducted radiator, which he called 'freely exposed radiator' where the induction efficiency (η) is given by the formula $\eta = 1 - a$ where a is the extent that the velocity of the airstream falls through the actuator disc. Meredith said that 'for conventional radiators the value of $1 - a$, when they are freely exposed, is about 0.6,' therefore, the value of a is about 0.4. Then he looked at the more efficient ducted radiator. Meredith provided a formula for the (greater) efficiency of induction (ηd) for a ducted system, $\eta d = (h/2H) \, 1/ \{1 - \sqrt{(1-h/H)}\}$, where: H is the dynamic head [pressure] of the stream; and h is the drop in pressure across the radiator associated with this flow. As dynamic pressure is given by the formula [½ (air density) multiplied by (velocity squared)] the greater the velocity and greater the efficiency of induction, that is the lower the drag. Meredith said that 'for the top speed conditions we have assumed, the duct efficiency (ηd) lies between 0.89 and 1.0'. Thus, the ducted radiator has a much higher efficiency of induction than the unducted radiator.

4. Effects of compressibility of the air' (derivation of thermodynamic conclusion) Meredith's work was original in that he examined 'compressibility', that

is the impact of changes in pressure and temperature now through the duct. Meredith gives four effects of the compressibility of the air. The first three increases the cost of cooling in terms of the power lost:

1. The effective temperature of the air is raised by the kinetic energy of the mainstream.
2. The drop in pressure across the radiator is increased for the same mass flow by the reduction of density resulting from heating the air.
3. At altitude, the power necessarily expended in the radiator varies inversely as the square of the density and inversely as the cube of the available temperature difference.

The fourth lowers the cost of cooling:

4. The available energy of the cooling system is increased by the expansion after the addition of heat.

5. Quantitative balance of the power in the duct – Meredith brought together the equations derived in the two previous sections producing his iconic equation $(0.177(V/100)^2 - 1.725(V_0/100)^2)$. He was aware that the gain from radiator heat was marginal and he produced an equation for the addition of both radiator heat and the much greater heat from the engine exhaust gas. (In his paper he put this equation first as he considered the addition of radiator heat necessary in practice to produce thrust from the cooling system at the speeds fighters flew in the mid-1930s.) This reflects his and Stewart's patent, GB 454,266. If heat from the radiator and the exhaust system is recycled, then the net percentage of engine power gained or lost is given by $0.88(V/100)^2 – 2.67(V_0/100)^2$. Here the ratio of values 0.88 and 2.67 is much smaller than in the previous equation, 0.177 and 1.725. Therefore, the point when power gained equals the power lost is much lower than for radiator heat alone (312mph), the result being $V = 174$mph.

6. Applicability of the foregoing theory to an actual installation – This considered the problems of an actual installation, particularly the factors reducing efficiency due to the problems of duct entry and the choice of the most suitable size of radiator to produce a sufficiently low velocity through the radiator without incurring too large a weight or drag penalty.

7. Effect of momentum of the exhaust gases on the drag of an engine installation (third 'conclusion' on exhaust gas momentum) – Meredith had an important further conclusion unrelated to the cooling duct regarding exhaust gas momentum.

Third conclusion: 'Finally, attention is drawn to the importance of the momentum of the exhaust gases for a high-speed aeroplane, although no attempt is made to deal with this point quantitatively.'

Under the heading, 'Effect of the momentum of the exhaust gases on the drag of an engine installation' Meredith continued, 'design to date has apparently been little affected by consideration of the momentum of the issuing gases'. He added:

> The thrust derivable from the rearward direction of the exhaust gases is given by the product of the mass flow and the velocity of the exit and the latter quantity depends upon the internal design of the exhaust system. The thrust power is, however, also proportional to the speed of flight. Thus, it becomes increasingly important to utilise this thrust as the speed of flight increases.

By correct design much of the energy of the exhaust gases can be retained and significantly add to thrust horsepower in high-speed flight. However, 'no attempt is here made to assess the power which may be available from this source. It is suggested, however, that if, an appreciable proportion of the original energy of the exhaust gases can be preserved, this will provide an appreciable increment to the thrust horsepower of a high-speed aeroplane'.[2] This idea had important consequences, first for the Spitfire and Hurricane whose exhaust stacks were, as will be seen, carefully redesigned by Rolls-Royce, and then for all high-speed piston-engined aircraft.

'Further developments'

In the June report there was a section 'Further developments' which was deleted in the published August version. These covered entry losses and heat energy recovery:

- Wind tunnel experiments with ducted cooling systems for both liquid and air-cooled engines are being conducted. The avoidance of entry losses in the ducts is the main feature requiring exploration.
- Experiments to verify the availability of the heat transferred to the air in the duct is desirable.
- A quantitative estimate of the thrust which may be derived from the momentum of the exhaust gases will be made.

The first two were done but not, as far as can be determined, the third. The point is that Meredith, while at Aerodynamics, initiated a programme of systematic research into ducted cooling systems. He considered the problem of duct entry particularly pressing. (His work here has been reviewed earlier.)

Meredith's June paper of the same name was approved for external publication by the Air Ministry in August 1935 as ARC R&M 1863. There was no difference between the August report and the June report except, as seen, the section 'Further developments' was deleted, and a third classification of drag was added to skin friction and eddying due to separation. That is 'drag due to expansion losses without actual stream separation'. The paper was not actually printed and published externally until the following year, which means that it has been dated to either 1935 and 1936 in references to it. Effectively, however, the analysis was completed by June 1935 and was not subsequently materially changed.

Immediate impact of Meredith's paper

Meredith's report had an immediate impact in several areas. 'Further developments' in May 1935 called for wind tunnel testing. In October 1935 his equation for the efficiency of induction for a ducted radiator was explicitly used in the first RAE wind tunnel test of a ducted cooling system in *A scheme for a radiator in a wing* (Shaw and Curtiss, October 1935).

In Capon's June 1935 RAE paper, he said revisions, discussed below, would be made due to points about 'compressibility' in Meredith's June paper. These revisions were published in Capon's August 1935 interim report also outlined below.

The recycling of heat was explicitly a design objective of the Spitfire's ducted radiator design which Meredith inspected in September 1935. In 1986, E.J. Davis, who worked on the Spitfire in 1935 said: 'About this time, Frederick Meredith evolved a novel ducted cooling system [where] the warmed air is speeded up and ejected at the rear making the system a rudimentary jet engine'.[3]

Meredith's aerodynamic concepts were possibly transferred to Rolls-Royce by T.P. de Paravicini who worked with Meredith at the RAE till late 1935. At Rolls-Royce he took out two patents which built on Meredith's work: *Oil coolers for aircraft* (Paravicini, GB 463,303, September 1935); and *Improvement in exhaust discharge arrangement for internal combustion engines* (Paravicini, GB 471,177, November 1935). These were followed by a series of Rolls-Royce patents for ducted radiators.

The November 1935 *The Aircraft Engineer* included a lengthy report by G.P. Douglas of the RAE which looked at the theory of duct design noting: 'The theory of duct cooling has been developed independently by Capon and by Meredith.'[4] Meredith's and Capon's work were not then published externally until 1936, so Douglas's report was the first to put Meredith's and Capon's work into the public domain. The article discussed in detail Meredith's formula for the efficiency of induction. 'This very important relationship, due to Meredith, enables us to compare the drag cost of any cooling system with that which is theoretically possible.'[5] The possibility of almost eliminating cooling drag, without the addition of heat, was recognised. 'If for a given installation we regard the cooling pressure loss as constant it appears that good efficiencies are possible over a wide range of flight speeds. At low values of h/H (pressure drop divided by dynamic pressure) corresponding to very high speeds, efficiencies approaching unity are possible.'[6] The importance of Douglas's report is that the informed public, including foreign aircraft manufacturers and scientists, could have known in 1935 that Meredith and Capon were working on the mathematics of ducted radiators.

Robert Stanley Capon

Robert Stanley Capon completed a paper on ducted cooling in June 1935. It seems that Capon initiated his research independently of Meredith, possibly at the behest of Rolls-Royce, which wanted to prove ducted radiators with adjustable exits were more efficient than the alternatives which included ducted retractable radiators. Prior to external publication by the ARC, Capon and Meredith learnt from each other's RAE work, leading to a productive dialectic between the ideas in the two papers and a substantial revision of Capon's work.

R.S. Capon (1886-1975) was born in Liverpool. After medical and musical training (the latter in Berlin) he entered St Johns College Oxford University, from 1909-14 and studied mathematical physics gaining a first. During the First World War he joined the RFC and having become a POW tried to escape. In 1919 Capon was posted to Martlesham Heath and the Armaments Experimental Establishment where he introduced many new developments in testing methods. In 1925 he accepted a post with the Aeroplane & Armaments Experimental Establishment as Civilian Technical Officer and later joined the RAE at Farnborough, becoming Principal Scientific Officer and then Superintendent of Scientific Research.

Capon wrote the first paper on Dimensional Analysis, *Note on dimensional relationships for air compressors* for aero-engine superchargers in 1928, where, 'dimensional relationships are derived by which the performance of a compressor may be deduced at one set of intake conditions from tests at another'. This facilitated understanding how a compressor might function in a different condition, for example at very high altitude, to that in a sea-level test centre. The ability to work out such functioning using only analytical means was extremely important. After Stanley Hooker joined Rolls-Royce in 1938 he used Capon's paper when he improved the Merlin supercharger.

Between 1937 and 1941 Capon was Deputy Director of Research and Development in Armament. In 1948 he and his family emigrated to Australia where he undertook further study of mathematics, including quantum mechanics. In 1951 he started lecturing at the Adelaide University mathematics department in fluid dynamics, classical mechanics and differential equations.

Capon – June 1935 RAE paper

In June 1935 Capon's first paper, *The cowling of cooling systems,* was issued internally at the RAE. This was started independently of Meredith's paper but before it was completed Capon became aware of Meredith's work and he wrote that his June document would have to be revised (as will be seen in August) in the light of some of Meredith's findings. Capon made explicit the direct connection to Rolls-Royce:

> Control of the air flow through a cowled cooling system by adjusting the exit orifice in accordance with the speed of flight and the heat to

be dissipated has been proposed in the USA for air-cooled engines, and Messrs. Rolls-Royce have applied the system of control to liquid-cooled engines.

Capon's work provided a mathematical analysis of Rolls-Royce's application of US radial practice to inlines. Capon said cooling flow adequate for climbing would result in wasted power at the upper end of the speed range and he explicitly discussed the varying cooling requirements for different flight conditions which inspired the introduction of rear cowl shutters in the US.

Capon compared a radiator with a variable cowl, a fixed cowl and a retractable radiator, showing the use of adjustable rear flaps to be the most efficient system. He concluded:

> The proportion of power expended in cooling by the three systems, placed here in order of efficiency, is:
>
> | | | |
> |---|---|---|
> | Cowled radiator, adjustable exit. | - | nearly constant. |
> | Retractable radiator. | - | varies as (flight speed)^2 |
> | Radiator having fixed cowl. | - | varies as (flight speed)^3 |
>
> The adjustable exit appears to be indispensable for a low value of the cooling losses over a wide speed range: in a well designed adjustable system it will probably be possible to maintain the losses below 2% of engine power.

Capon's first result for the cowled radiator with the adjustable exit was the same as Meredith's first conclusion, that is: 'The employment of low velocity cooling avoids the necessity for an increasing expenditure of power with increasing speed provided the exit conditions are adjusted to suit the speed.'

Capon took note of Meredith's analysis. For example: 'The very different optimum tube length required in the cowled radiator from that usually adopted in radiator design is of great interest: attention was first directed in this matter by Meredith.' (Meredith had written: 'The limitation of frontal area may call for a somewhat greater ratio of tube length to diameter than is customary for freely exposed radiators.') Meredith's point was not demonstrated by him mathematically. It reflected the fact that in most locations an internal ducted radiator could only have limited depth, thereby requiring longer tubes. (The exception was the fuselage ventral aft position which Meredith regarded as susceptible to boundary layer build up problems severely disrupting flow entry. In the US, where the boundary layer challenge was perhaps not then fully grasped, aft ventral fuselage locations, not apparently considered in the UK due in part to the boundary layer problem, seemed the more attractive.)

Both Meredith's and Capon's papers came from very different directions. As seen, Meredith's paper was written to demonstrate mathematically the paradox that a cooling system was a heat engine where thrust could exceed drag; while Capon's paper was written to prove mathematically the superiority of Rolls-

Royce's application of US ideas for radial cooling to inline engines, including an adjustable exit to cooling ducts (as seen in patent GB 456,335, *Improvements in Radiator Cowling for Aircraft*) compared with no adjustable shutters and a retractable radiator.

Capon – August 1935 RAE paper

Capon, referring to Meredith's internal RAE June paper, wrote that in the light of it: 'Certain corrections required by the change in density of the air due to heating will be included in a more detailed examination.' This was issued internally in August when Capon had revised his June paper to take into consideration variation of air density in the light of Meredith's June research. In this revision Capon examined in detail the impact of heat on pressure, temperature, velocity, and skin friction. He concluded: 'The pressure drop across the radiator is greater when the radiator is hot than when it is cold.' That is to say the power expended on cooling is greater. 'But the cooling drag is reduced and may become negative at high flight speeds.' Capon added later: 'If an air stream is expanded in a duct, heated, and then contracted before ejection, a thrust is derived.' He recognised, following Meredith, that such thrust power is a new term in his analysis which can exceed the power required to overcome the increased drag resulting from heat so there 'may even give a net thrust on the system of high flight speeds'. Thus, Capon confirmed Meredith's analysis.

Capon – March 1936 ARC paper

Capon's report published by the ARC was issued in March 1936. This was again titled *The Cowling of Cooling Systems* and was Air Ministry 'Reports and Memoranda No. 1702, March 1936'. This report is the one cited in the literature about ducted cooling systems. The summary stated that control [of] air through cowled cooling systems by adjusting the exit orifice has been proposed for both air-cooled engines and the radiators of liquid-cooled engines. Capon said that analysis would first ignore variations in air density and then, in response to Meredith's work, although Meredith is not specifically mentioned here, the impact of variations in density (due to heat) was analysed.

Cowled systems with and without adjustable rear exits and retractable radiators were analysed. Capon now added uncowled radiators with shutters at the entrance. (This was possibly because the Junkers Ju 87 Stuka dive bomber had first flown in September 1935 with a Rolls-Royce Kestrel engine cooled by an under engine radiator with front shutters.) Front shutters had anyway been the method generally used before the development of retractable and ducted radiators. It was employed on many Rolls-Royce powered aircraft and it may have been deemed useful to compare such shuttered radiators with later systems to see how relatively efficient, or not, they were.

Capon drew a number of conclusions:

- As engine power needed to overcome radiator drag increases at the square of the velocity through the radiator, expanding the flow [that is increasing the ratio of the radiator frontal area to the duct entrance area] to reduce the speed [of air as it impacts the radiator] is advantageous up to a limit, dependent on the weight and installation/location of the radiator. (Meredith made this point when he said that ever reducing the speed of cooling air through the radiator would eventually result in a prohibitively large radiator.)
- The relative efficiency of ducted radiators with and without variation of the cowl exit, retractable radiators and shuttered radiators. In the Appendix their impact is given:

Cooling type	Ratios of the power absorbed in overcoming cooling drag, for the speed ratio of 2 : 1 at full throttle
Variation of cowl exit	0.9 (1^{-1} decreases)
Retractable radiator	4.0 (2^2 increases as square of flight speed)
Uncontrolled flow	8.0 (2^3 increases as cube of flight speed)
Shutters at cowl entrance	10.7 ($2^{>3}$ increases as greater than cube of flight speed)

(It should be noted that this is 'at full throttle'. Therefore, the difference in speed is accounted for by different flight conditions, that is climb and high-speed level flight, not by different throttle levels in level flight.)

- Overall, if variation in air density is included (as Meredith) then this reduces the proportion of engine power absorbed in cooling in a manner proportional to the square of the flight speed.
- Confirming Meredith's result he says: 'The cooling losses in a well designed system are small, and this term may be large enough, in high performance aircraft, to give a net thrust on the cooling system.'

In the Appendix Capon provided a methodology for categorising drag in wind tunnel experiments. He said the following measurements could be made:

(1) The drag of the whole system.
(2) The loss of total head [combined static and dynamic pressure] up to the rear exit.
(3) The pressure drop across the radiator.
(4) The mass flow through the cowl.

This made possible establishing:

(a) The drag coefficient of the whole system.
(b) The drag coefficient of the internal drag.
(c) The drag coefficient of the minimum (ideal) drag.

In and after 1935 the RAE would develop a systematic methodology for comparing wind tunnel results for different aircraft and different radiator locations on the same aircraft.

Meredith and Capon – dialectic relationship and summary

Both Meredith and Capon looked at ducted cooling systems but started from very different positions: Meredith from his work on jet propulsion; and Capon to provide a mathematical basis and justification for Rolls-Royce's work on ducted radiators. Notwithstanding, both became aware of each other's work and used it to modify their own in a constructive dialect. Capon drew attention to several points first made by Meredith which he subsequently incorporated in his analysis:

- There is an adiabatic – that is derived from compression, not heat, addition – temperature rise ahead of the radiator.
- There is an increased density drop through radiator when radiator heat is considered.
- Meredith had demonstrated mathematically that for a radiator the same size of exit opening could be used for the same speed at different working altitudes.
- After Meredith: 'It is well known that if an air stream is expanded in a duct, heated, and then contracted before ejection, a thrust is derived.' In practice Capon saw the impact as marginal but recognised that, 'at higher speeds there might even be a net thrust'.

Meredith and Capon provided mathematical 'proofs' for concepts embodied in earlier patents, respectively, Stewart and Meredith's (RAE) and Ellor's (Rolls-Royce). The RAE patent focused on recycling heat. The Rolls-Royce patents considered a ducted cooling system with an adjustable exit. Both Meredith's and Capon's papers proved mathematically their respective objectives inherent in the patent design: Meredith; that heat could produce negative drag or thrust; and Capon; that a ducted radiator with an adjustable exit was much more efficient than the alternatives, no adjustable exit, or retractable or shuttered radiators. Capon modified his mathematical analysis in a constructive dialectic by Meredith's work by recognising the impact of changes in heat over the thermodynamic cycle, although he considered the net effect so marginal as not to change significantly his results.

Overall, their papers complimented each other and provided a formidable mathematical basis for analysing and comparing of radiator cooling systems, summarised in the following table.

Both Meredith and Capon's work of mid-1935 proved the superiority of the radiator in a duct with an adjustable exit to the alternatives of non-adjustable exit, front shutters, or retractable radiators. This was incorporated in the Spitfire's

	Meredith 1935 June and August	Capon 1935 June and August	Capon 1936 March
Unducted radiator	yes		
Ducted radiator without adjustable exit		yes	yes
Ducted radiator with adjustable exit	yes	yes	yes
Retractable radiator		yes	yes
Front shuttered radiator			yes
Heat type added to duct			
radiator heat added	yes	yes (August)	yes
radiator and exhaust heat added	yes		

design when the evaporative cooling system was replaced as impracticable in a fighter. Meredith's report recognised a propeller-powered aircraft had in practice three sources of thrust. The first, the propeller is obvious. Meredith also observed two further sources: radiator heat regeneration, which was quantified; and exhaust gas momentum, which was not, but was recognised as too important not to exploit if the exhaust heat were not added to the cooling air behind the radiator (or used in a turbocharger). Both further sources would be incorporated into the design of the Spitfire.

Capon's June 1935 report established the superiority of the ducted radiator with an adjustable exit compared to other systems at the time the Spitfire's cooling system was being redesigned. His March 1936 report set out a wind tunnel methodology that was built on in the May 1936 Spitfire wind tunnel test report. (The tests were done the previous November.) After Meredith and Capon's reports no other form of liquid cooling system other than ducted radiators was used on any significant new aircraft. Also, exhaust stubs were designed to exploit exhaust gas momentum. Meredith's and Capon's work was also built on in Germany. The German papers were in turn translated into English by NACA in the US and used by North American Aviation aerodynamicists to design the Mustang's cooling duct.

Chapter 6

RAE – research into heat and wind tunnel issues

Radiator and heat related issues

The RAE's systematic program of research into cooling systems, initiated when Meredith was put in charge of Aerodynamics in 1935, also looked at critical issues of heat dissipation and waste heat recovery, which were central to the 'Meredith effect'. Three RAE papers resulted.

In *Heat dissipation of ethylene glycol radiators and comparison with water radiators* (Anderton Brown and Barlow, May 1935) the introduction stated:

> With the object of improving aircraft performance of liquid-cooled engines, liquids of higher boiling point than water may be used and ethylene glycol has been employed for this purpose. Experiments with engine have been made but the influence of coolants other than water on the radiator performance has not been sufficiently investigated. This report presents radiator design data for such coolants.

The report concluded:

> Ethylene glycol, at a maximum temperature of 125°C., permits a large reduction of radiator area (about half) on account of the higher working temperature and greater proportionate direct heat loss from the engine jacket, pipes and tankage. Thus, the report demonstrated the clear superiority of glycol to water as a coolant.

In *Note on the performance data for honeycomb radiators in a duct* (Hartshorn, November 1935) the RAE examined the radiators themselves to see how heat dissipation could be made as efficient as possible. In November 1935 the RAE prepared a paper analysing the honeycomb radiator in a duct, 'To calculate the performance of the radiator in a duct, it is necessary to know the heat dissipation.' Formulas were established which gave the relationship between cooling flow, rate of heat dissipation and the pressure drop through the radiator. It was recognised that the value [h for pressure drop] must be modified for a hot radiator [reference 3 was to Capon, who followed Meredith on this point] since for a constant mass flow of air the velocity increases as it passes through the tube due to warming up. The finding depends on Meredith who stated in 1935, 'With a hot radiator the tube velocity is gradually increasing as the air passes along the tube due to heating up of the air'.

Recovery of energy from a ducted cooling system (Smelt, Davies and Callen, September 1936) tested the extent of energy recovery. Meredith's paper envisaged cooling systems as heat engines. In the internal May 1935 version of his seminal report Meredith wrote: 'Experiments to verify the availability of the heat transferred to the air in the duct is desirable.' In September 1936 the concept was tested by the RAE. The perception of a ducted radiator system as a heat engine was the central insight of Meredith's work. Given, however, the marginal impact of the addition of radiator heat alone, it was important to see if actual testing could determine whether the addition of such heat did have in practice any material benefit. 'The method of low-velocity cooling employed in a ducted cooling system involves addition of heat to air at high pressure and subsequent pressure reduction. Under such circumstances, a conversion of a small quantity of the waste heat into mechanical energy takes place, giving a reduction in the drag of the system.' The paper explicitly recognises that the ducted radiator cooling cycle is the same as that of a heat engine. In reference 2 [to Meredith] 'the adiabatic compression of the cooling air, the addition of heat at almost constant pressure, and the final expansion, are viewed as stages in a heat engine cycle represented by the following diagram'.

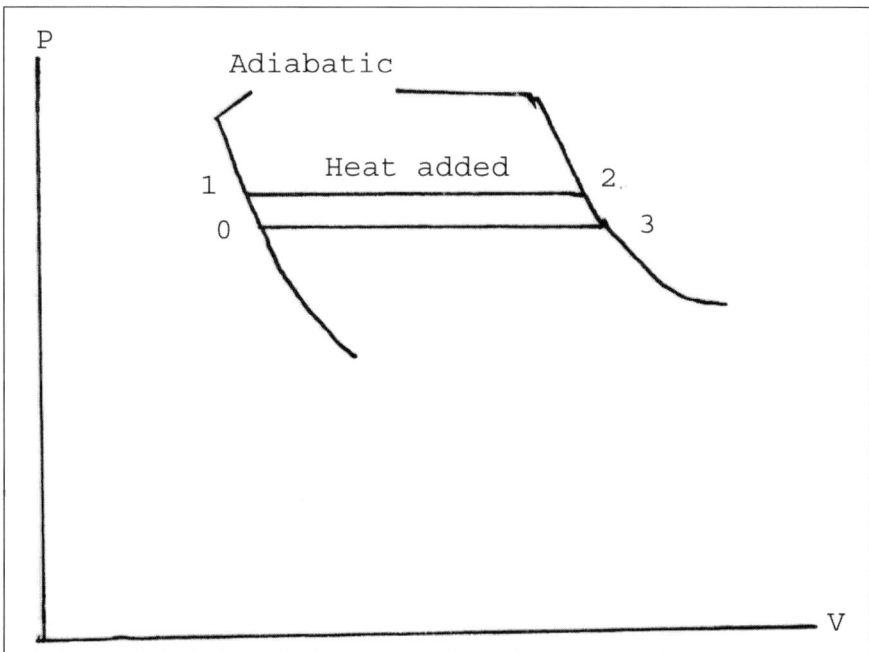

Figure 6.1 – 'Heat engine cycle' in *Recovery of energy from a ducted cooling system* (Smelt, Davies and Callen, September 1936).

Electrical heating elements were fitted in the low velocity regions of a duct in a model wing. The report concluded: 'That it is possible to recover energy from the radiator, the exact amount being given by the theory.' The drag decrease was quantified: 'In a glycol radiator for a 1,000 HP engine, in flight speeds between 300 and 500 m.p.h., the drag decrease, converted to a speed of 100ft/sec., stays almost constant at 1lb [that is 10 hp for 1000 hp engine].' The report specified: 'The internal drag becomes negative at speeds of over 290mph.' (This was somewhat better than Meredith's ARC report, published 1936, where with a speed through the radiator (V_0) of 100mph, there was negative drag, thrust was 312mph.) The paper recognised Meredith's recommendation that engine exhaust gas be directed to the cooling duct, although this was not done in practice:

> As much heat as possible must be put into the cooling air; so that a very great increase in the amount of heat recovered can be obtained by using the exhaust, expelling it into the duct just behind the radiator. If all the exhaust energy can be utilised, the drag reduction possible is of the order of four times that obtained from the cooling system alone.

Thus, by September 1936, the RAE had demonstrated the validity of Meredith's counter-intuitive insight that a cooling system in the form of a ducted radiator was a heat engine capable of creating thrust

Systematic methodology developed for comparing drag in wind tunnel tests

Before looking at wind tunnel tests for the Spitfire and Hurricane it might first be noted that the RAE developed a methodology for measuring drag in wind tunnel tests which enabled the RAE to determine the relative efficiency of different locations. This involved:

- expressing all measurements of drag in terms of lbs per 100 feet per second (fps). 1lb per 100 fps was equivalent to 10 horsepower (hp) at 300mph for a 1000 hp engine.
- dividing drag into categories finalised as four: minimum internal drag; residual internal drag; external skin friction drag; and residual external drag.

This made possible comparison of the drag of cooling systems in different positions and between different aircraft. The full RAE testing methodology was developed over three wind tunnel reports:

> Stage 1) Drag split into three types, two internal, one external – In *A scheme for a radiator in a wing* (Shaw and Curtiss, October 1935) an initial division of cooling drag was made. Internal drag was split into

two terms: minimum internal was derived using Meredith's equation for the efficiency of induction. Residual internal [due to inefficient design] was the remainder after minimal internal drag was deducted from total internal drag. External drag was not yet split as this drag was regarded as minimal due to burying.

Stage 2) External drag split and drag expressed in terms of lbs per 100 fps [feet per second] – In the second report *Note on the installation of a ducted radiator in the ventral position*, (Hartshorn, November 1935) there were two developments: a simple measure for drag was included; and external drag was also split into different types. Drag measurements were adjusted to represent the drag at 100 fps of an installation capable of cooling a 1,000hp glycol engine at a forward speed of 300mph. External drag was now divided into several types identified with specific features, these corresponding to minimal drag and avoidable losses [absence of filets, re-entrant flap, sharp entry].

Stage 3) Drag divided into four categories – The April 1936 report *Note on tests of a ducted radiator fitted to the nose of a ¼ scale Hart* (Patterson, April 1936) is significant because it was the first to provide a consistent methodology comparing the drag from different positions and on different aircraft. This involved dividing drag into four categories: minimum internal drag; residual internal drag; external skin friction drag; and residual external drag.

The report included a Glossary of terms that remained standard and was included verbatim in subsequent reports for several years. This is summarised without the algebra:

Cooling drag – is the difference between the drag of an aeroplane designed with no provision for cooling and that of the same aeroplane equipped with a radiator.
The cooling drag may be divided into two components, an internal drag calculated from the total head [pressure] of the cooling air at exit, and the difference between the total cooling drag and the internal drag, which is presumed to be an external drag.

Minimum internal drag – The loss of head [pressure] across the radiator for any given rate of cooling.

Residual internal drag – The difference between the internal drag, calculated as the measured loss of pressure, and the minimum internal drag, calculated from an estimated loss of head. (The main difference is due to bad entry conditions causing a loss in total head in the preliminary conversion [at duct entry] from kinetic to pressure energy.)

External skin friction – The duct may increase the total external surface of the aeroplane.

The skin friction drag due to the additional surface area is calculated from the theoretical value for a flat plate using a Reynolds number [ratio of inertial forces to viscous forces in fluid flow] based on the wind tunnel speed and the overall length of the model fuselage.

Residual external drag – The drag remaining after deducting the external skin friction drag and the internal drag from the measured cooling drag will be defined as the residual external drag.

All subsequent RAE reports used this methodology. It made possible comparison of the drag of cooling systems in different positions and between different aircraft. This gave it early powerful tools for comparing cooling drag across different airframe locations, and from different parts of the airframe. Meredith had said in his May 1935 paper on further developments, 'wind tunnel experiments with ducted cooling systems for both liquid and air-cooled engines are being concluded'. As will be seen in October 1935, Meredith recommended wind tunnel testing the Spitfire's cooling duct. Capon, in March 1936, had set out a methodology for calculating different types of drag. Now the RAE was implementing such a systematic programme.

Chapter 7

First aircraft with ducted radiators – Meredith critical of the Spitfire's

On 29 April 1935, the Air Ministry issued a specification, F10/35, for a new fighter aircraft with a minimum airspeed of 310mph (500 km/h) and six to eight machine guns. The Supermarine Type 300 was modified to take eight machine guns. Ten days later R.N. Dorey of Rolls-Royce was at Supermarine's Woolston plant to continue discussions on various properties of evaporative and glycol radiators. (Dorey joined the company in 1927 as an experimental engineer. In 1931 he inaugurated Rolls-Royce's flight development establishment at Hucknell which worked on ducted inline engines.)

Having decided to replace evaporative cooling with an ethylene glycol radiator the decision had to be made where to place what remained a sizeable and potentially draggy ethylene glycol radiator, at the then very high speeds envisaged. If a fuselage location were rejected for the radiator, then the only position on this aircraft left, given the very thin wing, was aft of the main spar partially buried in the wing. This choice was to have critical results for the Spitfire as the location was very challenging. The duct could never be really long enough or sufficiently buried due to the positioning of the main spar, the undercarriage wells and the flaps, and the thin wing. (That said, the Messerschmitt Bf 109E and particularly the Bf 109F, where the radiators had a similar aft wing location as the Spitfire, tried to deal with these challenges.)

In mid-1935 Supermarine's aeroplane was given the name with which it has been immortalised, Spitfire. (In Elizabethan times this described a fiery, ferocious, generally female, person.) It was suggested by Vicker's director, Sir Robert MacLean, after his daughter's nickname. Or so the story goes. In fact, the failed Type 224 was to have had the same name. Mitchell disliked it and wanted 'the Shrew' or 'the Scarab'.

Germany

Ironically, although the Spitfire was designed with a radiator deliberately intended to exploit the 'Meredith effect', neither it nor the Hawker Hurricane were, however, the first aircraft to fly with Rolls-Royce engines and ducted radiators

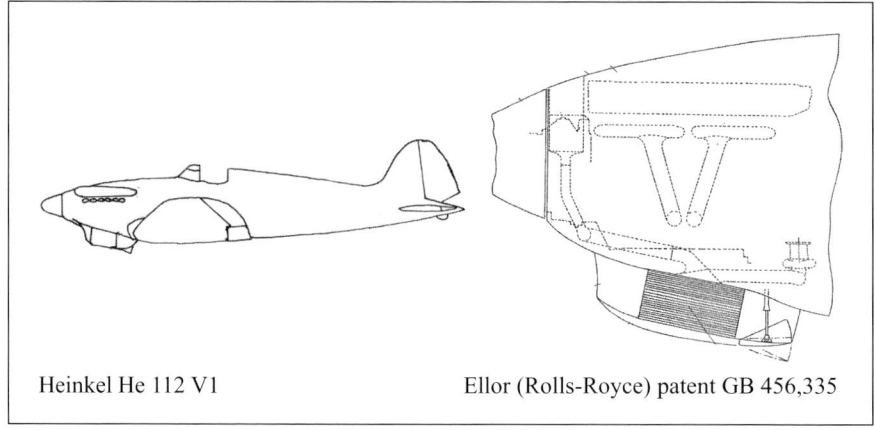

| Heinkel He 112 V1 | Ellor (Rolls-Royce) patent GB 456,335 |

Figure 7.1 – Heinkel He 112 VI with Rolls-Royce Kestrel engine, first flight September 1935.

with adjustable exits. Remarkably, the first flight of the Battle of Britain duo was preceded by the Rolls-Royce Kestrel powered German aircraft, the Messerschmitt Bf 109, the Heinkel He 112 and soon followed by the Junkers Ju 87.

A comment on an online forum from a late relative of T.P. de Paravicini records, 'he stated to our family many years ago that Rolls-Royce exchanged many patents with the Germans before 1939. Hence the 109 copying it'.[1] The Messerschmitt Bf 109 first flew with a ducted Kestrel engine in May 1935 as the Junkers Jumo 210 power plant was not ready. This, however, had a system of segmented flaps on a semi-circular cowl, not unlike that of the lower half of a radial cowl or an annular cowling as used on the Junkers Ju 88, first flown on 21 December 1936, powered by a Junkers Jumo. A Rolls-Royce package was incorporated in the Heinkel He 112 V1 prototype, whose first flight was in September 1935.

The Ju 87 dive bomber first flew in September 1935, again with a Kestrel engine. This did not have a ducted radiator but rather one with front shutters. It was important to ensure the engine did not overcool during the dive while ensuring the near vertical speed was not excessive. Thus, the high drag of the shuttered system was not perceived as a disadvantage.

France

France was early in the development of monoplane fighters and designed inline cooling systems that did not make use of the US insights provided by cowled radial systems with adjustable flaps. The all-metal, open-cockpit, fixed-undercarriage monoplane Dewoitine D.500, first flight June 1932, had a radiator with front shutters under the engine. The Morane Saulnier MS 405, first flight August 1935, was a pioneering French fighter with an enclosed cockpit and retractable undercarriage. The successor, MS 406, had an unducted retractable radiator, located underneath the fuselage. It became the only front-line monoplane fighter produced in significant numbers to use such a radiator. (Analysis by Capon of the RAE in 1935 had shown this to be a very inefficient system.) On 3 February 1938, the first pre-production aircraft made its first flight. The Loire-Nieuport 161 was in many ways more advanced and promising than the MS 405. It was pioneering in that its radiators were positioned in the aft wing position, like the Spitfire and Messerschmitt Bf 109E. There was a very shallow underwing entrance as the radiator was buried in the wing. The cooling air exited above the wing. Prototype crashes were blamed on the cooling system and the MS 405 was preferred. The Dewoitine D 513, first flight January 1936, tried a short nose radiator, but failed to get above 450 km/hr. It was rebuilt with a long duct from the chin entrance to exit near the wing trailing edge but failed to attract interest.

Spitfire development – Meredith leads delegation to Supermarine

In September 1935 Meredith – only recently returned from the Soviet Union where, as seen, 'his conduct was anything but correct' according to the British ambassador – led a delegation from the RAE to Supermarine, in order to inspect the mock-up and discuss the design of the ethylene glycol radiator, in the course of which he also pointed out various design flaws of the F37/34 (as the Spitfire antecedent was still called). There is a detailed record that shows it was Meredith who was doing the talking and his views were treated as authoritative not just on the radiator design but also on other features of the aeroplane.[2] Accompanying him from the RAE were Major C.J. Stewart, with whom he had made the patent application, GB 454,266, for the ducted radiator earlier in the year and Dr Harold Roxbee Cox who later chaired the wartime Gas Turbine Collaboration Committee which pooled ideas and experience about gas turbines and jet propulsion. Attending from Supermarine was E.J. Davis, head of the Technical Office, who would give an informative lecture, *The Basic Design of the Prototype Spitfire* in 1986 which made clear that Supermarine was fully cognisant of Meredith's work.

Meredith was not impressed by the aft wing positioning of the radiator. He 'expressed the opinion that the glycol radiator as proposed would cost us about 15% of engine HP, i.e. about 15mph in drag at top speed'.[3] But he added, 'he thought it might be improved considerably by tunnel testing a model. He explained why "the radiator position was not good". The chief point being that air should be taken from the nose of the wing or body where the pressure is normally atmospheric, instead of from a point further aft where it may well be less than atmospheric'. Meredith was particularly concerned about drag caused by too short a duct, resulting in breakaway and turbulence with the aft wing radiator location:

> The process of building up the necessary pressure to push air through the radiator requires careful fairing, and a length of cowling which depends upon the pressure difference [over internal length of the

diffusing duct], as there is a certain pressure gradient [i.e. change of pressure per unit length] which cannot be exceeded without causing a breakaway of flow and hence unwanted drag.[4]

A surviving drawing shows Meredith also recommended 'guide vanes' and a 'vent passage' for the Spitfire, both proposed in his 1935 paper, *Note on the Problem of conducting a fluid into a duct with a minimum of losses*. 'Mr Meredith was of the strong opinion we should get a standing eddy in our radiator cowling mouth unless we fitted vanes, and/or vented the opening.'[5] (The recommendation of the use of guide vanes was confirmed by Davis's lecture. 'The system was simple, although Meredith suggested a series of internal vanes to ensure non-turbulent flow.'[6])

Meredith was clearly a man whose views commanded attention and were to be considered carefully. As the result of the meeting, 'the Meredith radiator scheme was adopted for the F37/34'.[7] (Other changes included moving the engine louvres to reduce disturbance over the wing fillet and moving the oil cooler inlet rearward.[8]) Meredith had specifically recommended wind tunnel testing the duct. The Spitfire ducted radiator was the first designed for a particular aircraft to be tested in a wind tunnel. The tests were carried out in November 1935 although the final report was not dated until May 1936. Davis, who was present over fifty years earlier, recorded in 1986: 'The cooling system … was proved in a wind tunnel, as was the spinning test, and no other wind tunnel tests were made.'[9]

On 26 November, Air Commodore R.H. Verney (RAF Directorate of Technical Development (DTD)), visiting Supermarine noted: 'The glycol radiator is in the starboard wing, with controlled outlet cooling.'[10] This confirmed the presence of a variable flap to control the pressure drop across the radiator. In December 1935 Hartshorn, who wrote earlier that year the RAE report on the ventral radiator, went to Supermarine in effect to sign off the Spitfire radiator design. (He had written *Note on the installation of a ducted radiator in a ventral position* (Hartshorn, November 1935). He 'thought the radiator as then installed was close to the best possible. Dissipation was satisfactory and drag minimal'.[11]

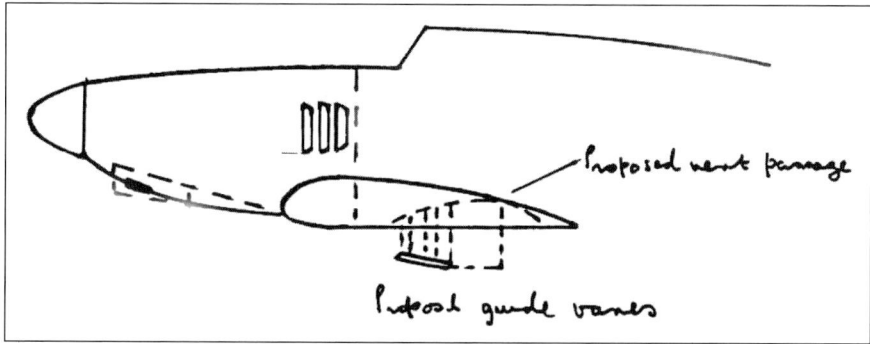

Figure 7.2 – Meredith's sketch, made 11 September 1935 during visit to Supermarine, here showing proposed changes – addition of 'vent passage' and 'guide vanes' – to the F37/34 cooling system.[12]

There was no doubt that the recycling of heat, in accordance with the 'Meredith effect', was designed into the radiator from the beginning. 'RAE tests on the ducted radiator proved it had low drag and Mr E.J. Davis recalls that he and his colleagues were of the opinion that the thrust of warm air from the radiator balanced the drag.' In other words the 'Meredith effect' had at least neutralised, if not rendered negative, the drag. 'It was, he said, in effect a rudimentary jet engine.'[13]

The ravishing looking Spitfire was the second of the eight gun fighters to fly in March 1936. The Hurricane, first flight November 1935, with its tubular fabric covered fuselage looked back. The all-metal monocoque Spitfire looked forward. Earlier on 6 November 1935, the first flight of the Hawker Interceptor, as the Hurricane was then called, took place. The original radiator is generally described as being a very simple affair adapted from earlier Hawker biplanes. As will be outlined below, RAE diagrams from wind tunnel tests show a more complex story.

The Air Ministry placed an order for 310 Supermarine Spitfires in June 1936. The same month saw the first public appearance of the Spitfire prototype at the Royal Air Force Pageant, Hendon. This hugely popular event in North London had been the location of hair-raising stunts by highly manoeuvrable biplanes. Now the people saw the monoplane fighter of the future.

The Hurricane's appearance was workmanlike: that of the Spitfire, with its beautiful elliptical wing, was fabulous. After the first flight in March 1936 by Vickers test pilot Mutt Summers the test programme was taken over by Supermarine's test pilot Jeffrey Quill. He noted after the Spitfire's second flight: 'I also recorded information on the ducted radiator system [which was] designed as a result of basic research work done at the Royal Aircraft Establishment (RAE) by Dr [sic] Meredith and had been a major factor in reducing the cooling drag.'[14]

Chapter 8

RAE – Spitfire and
Hurricane wind tunnel tests

In May 1936 the RAE completed two reports of wind tunnel testing of its cooling system of the fighter duo that fought the Battle of Britain. In September 1935, Meredith had recommended that the Spitfire's ducted radiator be wind tunnel tested and the actual testing ensued almost immediately in November. The following year the Hawker Hurricane's ventral radiator would also be wind tunnel tested with important consequences that reflected Meredith's proposals for diverting the boundary layer.

The Spitfire wind tunnel tests were carried out in November 1935 but the report was not given a date until May 1936. Thus, the Spitfire and Hurricane reports were finalised at the same time and both used the same RAE comparative methodology that broke down drag into the four components of: external skin friction drag; minimum internal drag; residual internal drag; and residual external drag. Also, drag in all situations is expressed in terms of lbs per 100 fps.

Supermarine Spitfire

Model tests of the Supermarine F.37/74 radiator cowl (Shaw and Kirkby, May 1936, tests in November 1935) was an analysis of the Spitfire's cooling drag using the four categories developed by the RAE:

	(lb. full-scale at 100 fps).
External skin friction drag	0.3lb
Minimum internal drag	1.3lbs
	1.6lbs
Residual internal drag	1.9lbs
Residual external drag	0.8lb
	2.7lbs
	4.3lbs

The wind tunnel tests showed that, as Meredith predicted, the Spitfire's ducted radiator was not particularly efficient. 'The cooling drag is thus 2.7lb higher than the theoretical minimum of 1.6lb.' As Meredith had anticipated: 'The larger part of this excess drag, 1.9lb., is due to loss of head [pressure] of the cooling air in the entry duct (hE), and to uneven flow distribution across the radiator, and is therefore directly related to the shape and proportions of the entry duct.' Various changes were tested:

Cowl A – initial Supermarine design. Partitioning the entry duct reduced uneven internal flow but increased external drag leaving overall drag little changed. Making the radiator entirely external to the wing showed a definite advantage in recessing part of the radiator.

Cowl B – having a longer more gradual duct. This shows that the entry loss can be reduced and the flow distribution improved 'by making a longer and more gradual entry. Owing, however to the large entry opening the shape of the cowl was poor and the external drag consequently very high'.

Cowl C – successive reductions in entrance area. 'The entry area was reduced [in three stages, C1, C2, C3] and though … the internal conditions suffered [due to stream separation], the improvement in cowl shape effected considerable reduction in external drag by comparison with cowl B. With cowl C3 the external drag was reduced and the cooling drag for top speed conditions fell to 3.7lb.'

	Original	C3	Change
External skin friction drag	0.3lb	0.35lb	+0.05lb
Minimum internal drag	1.3lbs	1.3lbs	no change
Residual internal drag	1.9lbs	1.5lbs	- 0.4lb
Residual external drag	0.8lb	0.55lb	- 0.25lb
	4.3lbs	3.7lbs	- 0.6lb

The report recorded: 'By lengthening the entry duct 0.9in full-scale the cowl drag has been reduced by 0.6lb. This is principally on account of improvement in the internal conditions.' The report recognised that the duct was still not very efficient. 'The measured drag is still more than twice the minimum and for this entry loss is largely responsible.' There was the possibility of further improvement. 'With this type of cowl the drag due to skin friction on the added external surface is only a small part of the total. It is therefore, conceivable that with a still longer entry duct, owing to the saving in internal losses, the drag would be still further reduced.'

Overall, variations of the Spitfire duct were extremely thoroughly tested by the RAE: Supermarine's original cowl, 6 forms; original with partitions, 2; original without recess, 3; longer cowl larger entry, 1; and longer cowl smaller entry, 7. The rectangular entrance shape was wide and shallow making it difficult to add an effective 'lip' as applied successfully to the Hurricane and later the Mustang. (As will be seen the testing of a 'lip' on the Spitfire Mk III in 1941 produced a disappointing result.) The undercarriage wells limited the space for a longer inlet duct.

The overall judgement of RAE's Hartshorn, in December 1935, of the Supermarine cowl, was that 'it should be satisfactory'. This was in fact somewhat

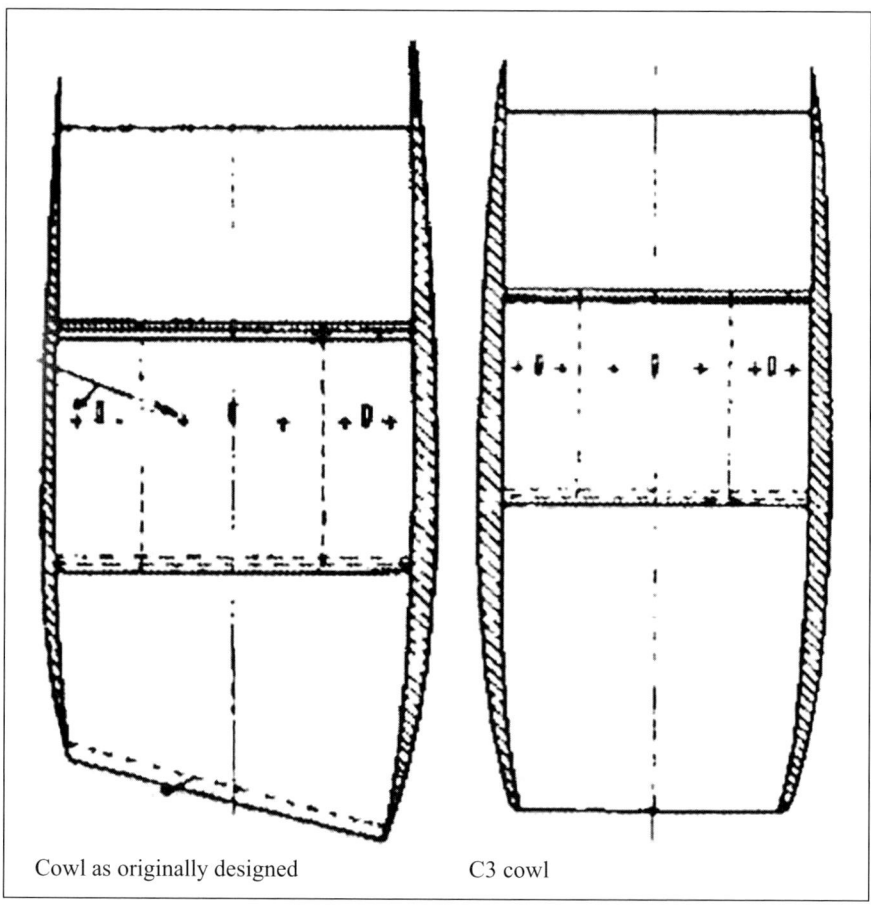

Cowl as originally designed   C3 cowl

Figure 8.1 – Cowls A and C3 from *Model tests of the Supermarine F.37/74 radiator cowl* (Shaw and Kirkby, May 1936, tests in November 1935).

damning with faint praise. It should, as Meredith had indicated in September 1935, have been much better. The fact is that the Spitfire laboured with an inefficient cooling system in terms of drag. The Spitfire was a beautiful but flawed design that failed properly to exploit the 'Meredith effect'. As Meredith said, 'the radiator position was not good'.[1] (As will be seen the Mustang, which exploited the 'Meredith effect' much more effectively, would be about 25mph faster that the Spitfire on the same power.)

Hawker Hurricane

The Hawker Interceptor first flew in November 1935. Wind tunnel testing was not, however, carried out until the following year on the cooling system. The ventral position followed that of the Hawker biplanes. The radiator was, however, positioned further to the rear than on the biplanes to make space for the wells for the retractable undercarriage wells.

In May 1936 the RAE completed a report, *Model tests of the Hawker Interceptor radiator cowl* (Hartshorn, May 1936). This report is not in The National Archive. Its existence was only known because of a reference to it in the RAE's, *A review of wind tunnel experiments on ducted radiators* (Hartshorn, July 1936). (It exists at Farnborough Air Services Trust (FAST) in microfilm form.) As seen, the RAE produced a report titled, *Note on the installation of a ducted radiator in a ventral position* (Hartshorn, November 1935). This report, however, highlighted the problem of ventrally placed radiators due to boundary layer build-up. 'This [high] entry loss is probably linked up with the [combination] of a [well established boundary layer] on the undersurface … The methods tried to reduce this loss were: dividing the entry; deflector vanes; and by-passing the boundary layer.' (The Wind Tunnel Note No. 267, *Note on the problem of conducting a fluid into a duct with the minimum of losses* (Meredith, May 1935) recommended the addition of vanes and a bypass duct.)

In May 1936 the RAE completed a report on the Hawker Interceptor's radiator cowl testing three versions. The first set of wind tunnel tests were done in March 1936. The report introduction recognised that the duct location lessened the opportunity to improve the design: 'An attempt has been made to reduce the drag of the existing cowl by small modifications within the limits imposed by this design.'

1. Original cowl on Hawker prototype – This was the original cowl used on the prototype which was first flown in October 1935. Given that drag was 8.5lbs at 100fps this was clearly very inefficient. In fact the duct was surprisingly pioneering as it had vanes and what was called a 'by-pass' gap' intended to separate the boundary layer. (Meredith had recommended vanes and such a gap for ventrally located radiators in his paper, *Note on the problem of conducting a fluid into a duct with the minimum of loss,* Wind Tunnel Note 267, on duct entry.) The gap is shown in the following diagram. Thus, although not generally recognised, the first aircraft to incorporate a boundary layer bypass was the Hawker Hurricane prototype.

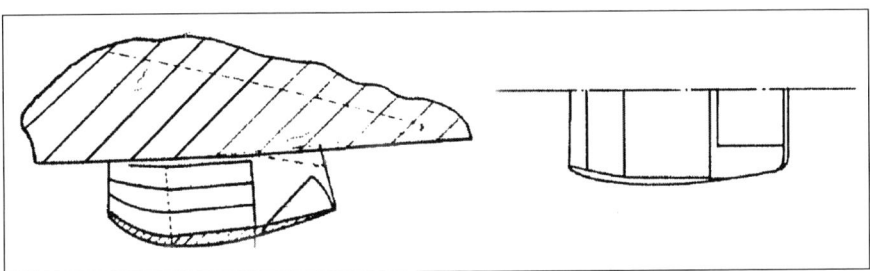

Figure 8.2 – 1. Original cowl on Hawker Interceptor prototype.

The by-pass gap's presence was confirmed in the text as wind tunnel tests were done with it removed. A test of the lengthened Hawker cowl, see next, was done blocking the gap to establish the difference which was about 0.45lbs. Internal drag due to excessive cooling and inefficient entry was 6lbs. Residual external drag was also high. This demonstrated that, in a duct that was overall inefficient, the bypass had had a positive effect.

2. Hawker's lengthened cowl – The modifications which might be done were restricted by the location: 'The cowl entry could not shift forward on account of the folding undercarriage but the cowl could be lengthened by moving the exit aft. This would involve a break in the landing flap. As indeed would prove the case. The radiator block could be moved back 4 inches but could not be recessed into the fuselage.' This confirms that the benefits of burying were known but not possible with the Hurricane.

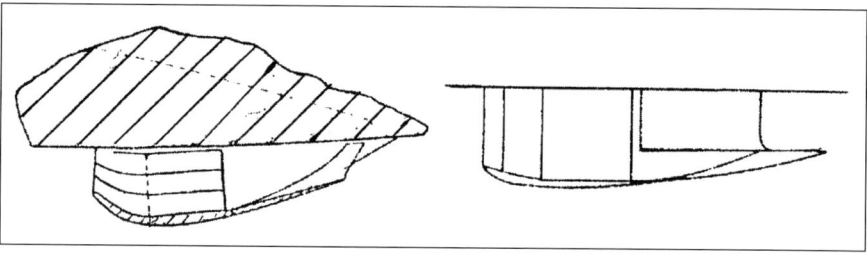

Figure 8.3 – 2. Hawker Interceptor's lengthened cowl.

The report initially tackled the minimum internal drag. 'The first step to reduce the drag is clearly to cut down the cooling flow to its proper value by reducing the exit area in the flap neutral condition.' This reduced minimum internal drag from 2.7lbs to 1.2lbs, this level remaining subsequently unchanged as further revisions were made. (Meredith's Wind Tunnel Note No. 267 on duct entry said of control of separation, 'two methods of avoiding or reducing the losses associated with separation immediately suggest themselves [one was] the deflection of the mainstream back to the surface by controlling vanes'.) Those steps reduced total drag from 8.5 to 6.3lbs at 100 fps. The report added: 'The cowl was first tested without deflectors (vanes) in the entry but the flow in the upper part of the radiator was found to be reversed. Inserting the single straight guide vane corrected this reversal.'

3. RAE's new cowl – The RAE's cowl tackled residual internal and external drag by lengthening the entry duct, moving the radiator rearwards, and reducing the number of vanes from two to one. Lengthening the diffuser duct reduced residual internal drag. Making the duct exterior frontage less abrupt lowered the external drag.

A further RAE report, *Addendum to Note on the installation of a ducted radiator in a ventral position* (Hartshorn, August 1936) revealed a development that had critically important future implications. Meredith's 'Wind tunnel Note

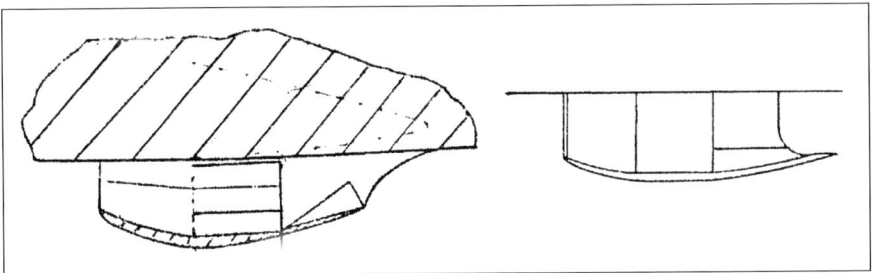

Figure 8.4 – 3. RAE's new cowl for Hawker Interceptor.

No. 267 on duct entry had considered the issue. 'Ventral entries. Such a system is bound to lead to separation as the boundary layer is thick and the depression at the surface is accentuated by the curvature of the boundary, serious losses ... are therefore common.' The second proposed method for the control of separation (the first being vanes) was 'removal of the boundary layer in the neighbourhood where separation would otherwise occur ... [by] an auxiliary duct by-passing the cooling system for the purpose of removing the harmful boundary layer'.

The RAE report, *A review of wind tunnel experiments on ducted radiators* (Hartshorn, July 1936), discussed below, included radiators in the chin position. The diagram showed a 'lipped' duct unlike the report in *Note on tests of a ducted radiator fixed to the nose of a ¼ scale Hart* (Patterson, April 1936). This was the first recorded use of a 'lip', but in the chin not ventral position.

The second recorded use of a 'lip' was in an August 1936 RAE report on the Hawker Interceptor, testing a fourth cowl which incorporated the 'lip' in the ventral position.

Cowl with 'lip added' – The introduction said: 'The advantage in this is that the lip so formed prevents the retarded boundary layer on the fuselage surface from entering the duct and, instead, deflects it around the cowl in the gully formed above the lip.' Meredith described a tunnel bypass but the 'lip' can be seen as an effective and simpler alternative.

Figure 8.5 – Hawker Hart Model in *A review of wind tunnel experiments on ducted radiators* (Hartshorn, July 1936).

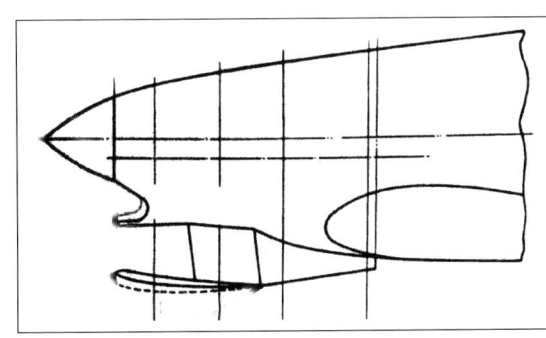

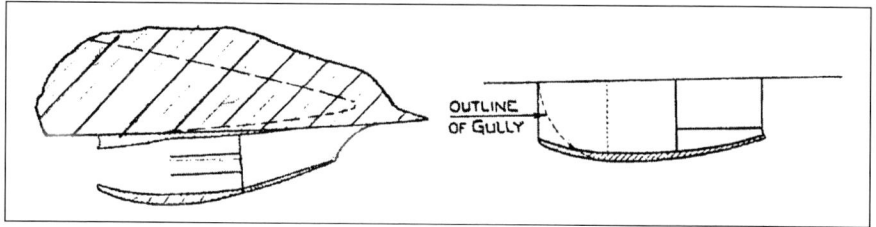

Figure 8.6 – Cowl with 'lip added' in *Addendum to Note on the installation of a ducted radiator in a ventral position* (Hartshorn, August 1936).

The drag of the four Hurricane cowls is set out in the following table:

Cooling drag at top speed (lbs full-scale at 100 fps)

	May report			**August report**
	1. Original cowl on Hawker prototype	2. Hawker's lengthened cowl	3. RAE's new cowl	4. Cowl with 'lip added'
External skin friction drag	0.3	0.4	0.4	0.5
Minimum internal drag	2.7	1.2	1.2	1.2
Residual internal drag	3.3	2.6	2.0	1.2
Residual external drag	2.2	2.1	1.7	1.3
	8.5	6.3	5.3	4.2

The RAE wind tunnel tests showed how the Hawker Interceptor's cowled radiator drag could be halved from 8.5lbs to 4.2lbs. Wind tunnel testing offered a huge reduction in the Hurricane's cooling drag as measured by wind tunnel testing. The impact on the Spitfire was more marginal as shown next:

	Spitfire original	**Spitfire final**	**Hawker interceptor original**	**Hawker interceptor final**
External skin friction drag	0.3	0.35	0.3	0.5
Minimum internal drag	1.3	1.3	2.7	1.2
Residual internal drag	1.9	1.5	3.3	1.2
Residual external drag	0.8	0.55	2.2	1.3
	4.3	3.7	8.5	4.2

The introduction of a 'lip' to the Hurricane's ventral radiator duct in 1936 would be paralleled again in 1941 with the Mustang. The Mustang had problems with ventral duct entry and, according to designer Ed Schmued, it was British input that solved the problem.

Chapter 9

Spitfire – a pioneering but flawed design

On 11 June 1937 Supermarine's leader of the Spitfire design team, R.J. Mitchell, tragically died of cancer, aged forty-two. The first production Spitfire (K9787) flew for first time on 14 June 1938. On 14 August 1938 the aircraft entered service with 19 Squadron based at Duxford. The first two Marks were very similar, the key difference here being in their radiators which were compared in tests in a 1941 RAE report (see Appendix 3).

E.J. Davis of Supermarine had been present in 1935 when Meredith had inspected and criticised the Spitfire's cooling system. In 1986 he said in the R.J. Mitchell memorial lecture:

> In this [radiator duct] a small quantity of high speed air is ducted into an expansion chamber. Thus the speed is reduced and the pressure raised before entering the radiator. Thereafter the warmed air is speeded up and ejected at the rear making the system a rudimentary jet engine. Thus drag is reduced to a negligible amount whilst the warmed air, in theory, gave some thrust. [1]

As seen he stated: 'The cooling deserves recognition as a quantum leap forward.'[2]

After Vicker's test pilot Mutt Summers made the first flight on 6 March 1936, the test programme was taken over by Supermarine's test pilot Jeffrey Quill. Testing the 'Meredith' radiator was a priority. After the Spitfire's second flight Quill reported:

> I also recorded information on the ducted radiator system. This had been designed as a result of basic research work done at the Royal Aircraft Establishment (RAE) by Dr [sic] Meredith and had been a major factor in reducing the cooling drag which would otherwise have constituted a serious 'barrier' to the performance of both the Spitfire and the Hurricane. The early recording of data on its functioning was therefore a matter of great importance.

Quill was fulsome in his praise of the RAE: 'Meredith's work at Farnborough was an excellent example of how basic research at the RAE could make a vital contribution to ad hoc design work carried out by industry. This was exactly how the system was meant to work.'[3]

Alfred Price, who wrote in *Spitfire: A Documentary History,* in 1977, when many of those involved in the evolution of the Spitfire were still alive, stated: 'The solution to the cooling problem came from the Royal Aircraft Establishment at Farnborough, where Mr F.W. Meredith had been experimenting with a new type of ducted radiator.' Also: 'Meredith pioneered the development of ducted radiator cooling which was to make it possible for Mitchell to dispense with the unpredictable evaporative cooling for his new fighter.'[4] Price explicitly recognised the Spitfire's cooling system to be a ramjet:

> The ducted radiator acted rather like the present-day ramjet: the ram air was compressed, heated, and then expelled from the rear with increased velocity to produce thrust. The amount of thrust produced from the ducted radiator was small and only under optimum conditions did it exceed the drag. But previous types of radiator had all been major drag-producing items, so Meredith's work represented a major step forwards.[5]

In 1995 David Lednicer wrote: 'Supermarine is often regarded as being one of the first companies to make use of breakthroughs made by Meredith at RAE Farnborough in the design of ducts for cooling systems. In fact, the Spitfire's radiator ducts were designed using these guidelines.'[6]

The Spitfire was a pioneering aircraft because its cooling system was designed to incorporate the 'Meredith effect'. This was, however, executed in a deficient manner as Meredith himself explained in September 1935 when, as seen, he declared the radiator position 'was not good'.[7]

Problems with the Spitfire's cooling system

1) Boundary layer build up – Lednicer, discussing Second World War fighter aerodynamics, continued: 'Experimentally, it was determined that the Spitfire cooling system drag, expressed as the ratio of equivalent cooling-drag power to total engine power, was considerably higher than that of the other aircraft tested by the RAE.'[8] Lednicer provided an analysis of the Spitfire's deficiencies. The Spitfire's 'considerably higher drag' was attributed to, 'the presence of a boundary layer ahead of the duct tends to precipitate separation and makes the ducting problem more difficult'.[9] The aft wing location resulted in substantial boundary layer build-up. Lednicer reported:

> The VSAERO [computer program to calculate non-linear aerodynamic characteristics] calculation indicates the boundary

layer on the lower surface of the wing is ingested by the cooling system inlet. Running adverse (increasing) pressure gradient ahead of the radiator, the boundary layer separates shortly after entering the duct, resulting in a large drag penalty.[10]

2) Area ratios – NAA's Lee Atwood, who claimed a central role in the development of the Mustang based on his claimed discovery of Meredith's otherwise ignored work, stated:

> The efficacy of the 'Meredith effect' depends on the area ratios employed in the ducts used. A greater area ratio for the entry duct produces a greater radiator drag reduction; similarly, a greater contraction ratio for the jet efflux increases the jet thrust. The drawings of the Spitfire's radiator duct … indicate area ratios around 2, these being limited by the duct's placement beneath the wing.[11]

This was contrasted to the Mustang: 'In the case of the P-51 Mustang, in contrast, the radiator's placement at the underbelly of the fuselage offered room for significantly greater area ratios, perhaps of the order of 4. Consequently, the Mustang benefitted rather more from the 'Meredith effect' than did the Spitfire.' [12]

3) Non-variable flap – The Spitfire exit flap had only two positions – top speed, the exit area is 35% of the radiator area; climb, the exit area is 65% of the radiator. The difference was the result of a 10° movement of the flap. In 1943 a Rolls-Royce experimental report reached the 'General conclusion':

> The airflow through a tropically suitable radiator is greater than is necessary at any lower air temperature. The airflow would be reduced to the required amount and a substantial increase in performance obtained, at these lower temperatures, by the use of a continuously variable radiator flap. Level Speed. 13mph at 21,000ft.[13]

An attempt was made to deal with the Spitfire's high cooling drag with the Spitfire Mk III where both bypass passages and lips were wind tunnel tested (see Appendix 4). Such were deemed the exigencies of war that these, and the Spitfire Mk III, were not continued and the Spitfire fought on with a high drag system – as was made very clear by the adoption into service of the Mustang by the RAF in 1942, which proved much faster on less power than the Spitfire Mk V, at all but high altitude given the limitations of the Allison supercharger.

Chapter 10

Rolls-Royce buys Heinkel He 70 for flight testing, including radiators and exhaust stubs

Although in 1939 Britain would be at war with Germany, throughout most of the 1930s the British airframe and aero engine industry maintained close relationships with German companies (much to Meredith's disgust). The Messerschmitt Bf 109, Heinkel He 112 and the Junkers Ju 87 prototypes first flew with Rolls-Royce Kestrel engines. In March 1936 a Heinkel He 70 was delivered to the Rolls-Royce's aerial test site at Hucknall. The four-passenger cabin allowed space for engineers to perform during flight testing. Rolls-Royce used the Heinkel to test two aspects of Meredith's ideas: ducted radiators; and engine exhaust gas momentum. The tests were realistic as this was an actual aircraft in flight with a running engine heating the radiator and not theoretical mathematical analysis or a wind tunnel test.

Ducted radiators

The first trials using the Heinkel He 70 were on the radiator position. These involved a 'hot' radiator system unlike most wind-tunnel tests. '[Flight] Tests confirmed in general the principles of radiator design which had been worked out by the RAE and by Wright Field.'[1] (Wright Field was the location since 1926 of the USAAF Matériél Division which combined research and development, procurement, supply and maintenance.) They demonstrated the very high drag of the fully exposed radiator in a position similar to that of the Hawker Interceptor. '30% of power developed was wasted in overcoming radiator drag when the latter was fully exposed to the airstream.'[2]

Rolls-Royce experimented with: 'Moving the radiator forward into the fuselage frontal area and greatly increasing the duct length produced a great improvement.'[3] Tests showed, 'a radiator entirely within the frontal area of the Heinkel, although not actually inside the airplane, … was the most desirable location'.[4] Thus, relocating the radiator in the chin as opposed to the ventral aft position was not necessarily sub-optimal if the frontal area were not increased. The ducted radiator

74

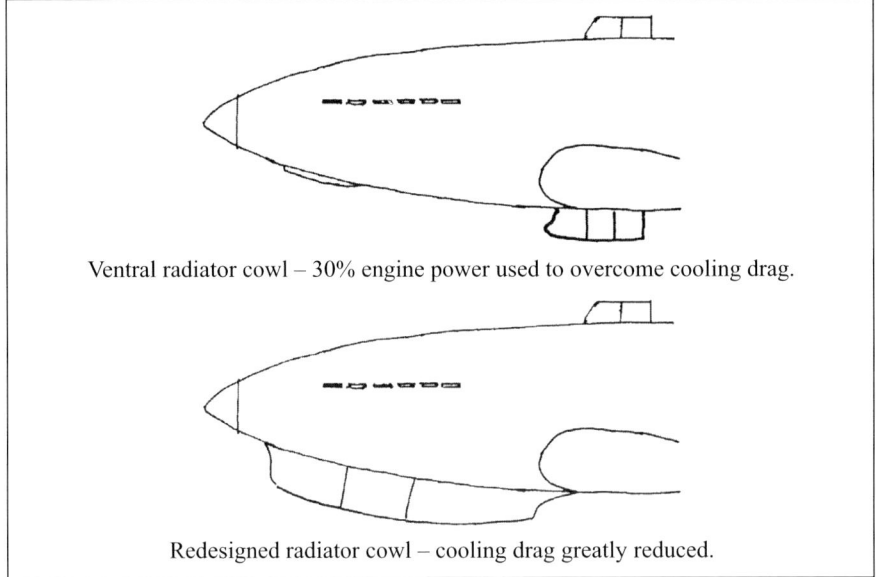

Ventral radiator cowl – 30% engine power used to overcome cooling drag.

Redesigned radiator cowl – cooling drag greatly reduced.

Figure 10.1 – Heinkel He 70 showing ventral and redesigned under engine radiator cowls.

was seen by Rolls-Royce as a jet propulsion system. Sir Stanley Hooker, who redesigned or designed the Rolls-Royce Merlin's superchargers and then headed its jet development, wrote in his autobiography, *Not much of an engineer*, that tests at Hucknall, 'included the radiators for cooling the water and oil, the air intakes and the exhaust system, which could be made to act like a small jet propulsion unit'.[5]

Exhaust gas momentum

The next series of trials were on the exhaust manifolds with five types under test. The tests on exhaust momentum built on Meredith's 1935 paper which put forward as an alternative to piping exhaust heat to the converging duct. 'Rolls-Royce, for the first time, developed jet exhaust stacks, of which the first suggestion in Britain had been made by Meredith in the same paper in which he had pointed out the possibility of recovering the energy in radiator heat.'[6] It was seen earlier that Meredith had written: 'It becomes increasingly important to utilise this [energy exhaust] thrust as the speed of flight increases.'[7]

Although the seminal Meredith paper of August 1935 had recommended using the momentum of exhaust gases, Rolls-Royce made the first patent for such use. On 30 November 1935 Rolls-Royce's T.P. de Paravicini, who had previously worked for the RAE, applied for a patent, *Improvement in exhaust discharge arrangement for internal combustion engines* (Paravicini (Rolls-Royce), GB 471,177, November 1935).[8] 'In an exhaust discharge system for an aircraft capable of a speed of 250 miles an hour the exhaust is discharged into a rearwardly projecting manifold or manifolds.'[9]

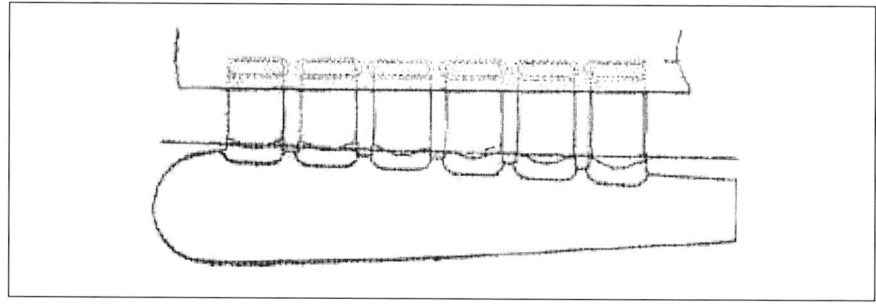

Figure 10.2 – Patent *Improvement in exhaust discharge arrangement for internal combustion engines* (Paravicini (Rolls-Royce), GB 471,177, November 1935).

The tests on the He 70 were for different types of groups of several 'stacks' or 'stubs' rather than one tapered pipe. The stubs tested included as follows:

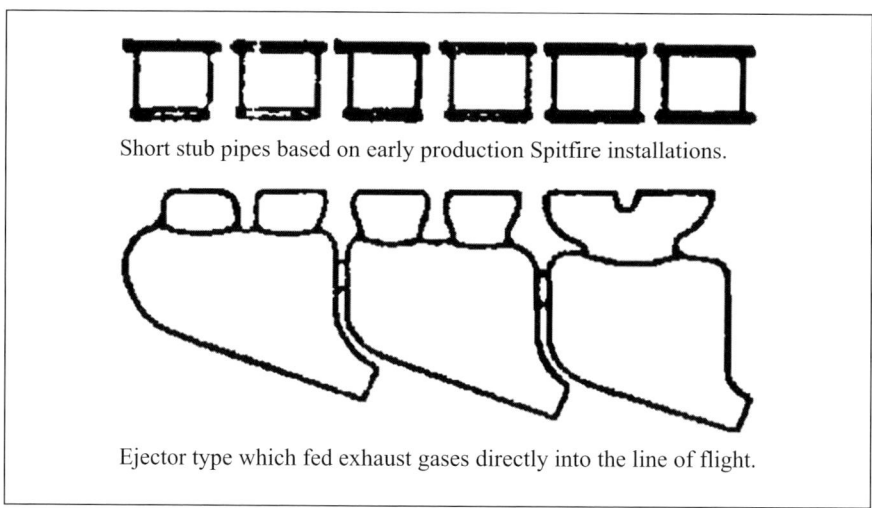

Short stub pipes based on early production Spitfire installations.

Ejector type which fed exhaust gases directly into the line of flight.

Figure 10.3 – Heinkel He 70 tested multiple exhaust manifolds, ejector type selected.

The tests led to modifications of the Spitfire's design:

> A distinct improvement emerged from work by Rolls-Royce which indicated that directing the engine's exhaust gases directly rearwards would augment thrust. This thrust augmentation could amount to 70lbs, equivalent to a 70hp increase at 300mph. … In September 1937 ejector exhausts producing this effect were fitted to K5054 and its maximum speed rose to around 360mph.[10]

Hooker put the figure rather higher. 'At Hucknall a great deal of work had been on taking the exhaust from the Merlin and ejecting it rearwards through very short exhaust pipes, it acted as a means of jet propulsion equivalent to about 150 extra horsepower'.[11]

The Battle of Britain fighter duo's exhausts were duly modified: 'Rolls-Royce believed that for the attainment of maximum speed in a fighter it was effective to make use of the energy in the exhaust by means of the jet exhaust stacks which it had been developed and which were used on all Spitfires and Hurricanes.'[12] Meredith's role would be explicitly recognised: 'It was on this airplane [Heinkel] that Rolls-Royce, for the first time, developed jet exhaust stacks, of which the first suggestion in Britain had been made by Meredith in the same paper in which he had pointed out the possibility of recovering the energy in radiator heat.'[13]

Chapter 11

RAE – wind tunnel analysis in 1935 and 1936

Meredith, as the head of Aerodynamics – to which position he was appointed at the beginning of 1935 after the untimely death of Glauert – was associated with the RAE wind tunnel; as seen in a quote from fellow revolutionary Vernon. 'He [Meredith] has just been promoted to the charge of the new Air [wind] Tunnel. He talks to the "Heads" in their own language, adopts their tactics and gets away with it.'[1]

In 1935, as seen, the RAE rapidly developed a methodology which facilitated comparison of wind-tunnel tests, building on ideas in both Meredith's and Capon's papers. The RAE now led the world with a systematic programme of research whose originality and breadth merits detailed analysis. Wind tunnel testing would be done on particular cooling designs, for example, the Supermarine Spitfire and the Hawker Hurricane. Also, testing was carried out comparing the relative efficiency of cooling systems in different locations; these being, leading edge and aft under wing, fuselage chin and ventral. Analysis was applied not just to locations but to all aspects of Meredith's ideas involving cooling. (Much work was also done on radial cooling drag.) As seen the heat dissipation of radiators was looked at in 1935 and the effectiveness of recycling heat in 1936. Duct entry was investigated as a specific issue in 1937. The main locations for ducted radiators were systematically tested.

Leading edge location

The RAE research paper, *A scheme for a radiator in a wing* (Shaw and Curtiss, October 1935), set out the results of wind tunnel tests conducted in February 1935. Here the engine was also buried in the wing. The RAE tests were at Rolls-Royce's request and reflected the close working relationship between the two organisations. 'Messrs Rolls-Royce asked that experiments should be made to determine whether an engine so installed [inside the wing] could be economically cooled by a radiator housed in a duct leading through the wing from the leading to the trailing edge.' It is of note that, 'a model wing was fitted with a duct having an adjustable exit nozzle'. This, in February 1935, is the first known physical use of a variable exit device with an inline cooled engine.

The report drew on Meredith's work. There was an implicit reference to Meredith's June and August 1935 papers on cooling in ducts with the use of the word 'compressibility' here meaning the impact of changes in temperature and pressure as the result of the ducted radiator being regarded as a heat engine. 'No account is taken of compressibility and in consequence this theory, although applicable to the wind tunnel measurements at low speed with a cold radiator, requires modification when applied to an actual aeroplane. These corrections are discussed in reference 1.' (This was Meredith's internal RAE June paper.) Also, Meredith's formula for the ideal efficiency of induction of a ducted radiator was explicitly used. The addition of engine exhaust gas was excluded in the actual tests but recognised as advanced by Rolls-Royce. 'It is proposed that the exhaust pipes should be contained in separate ducts and discharged into the main duct exit, but they are not represented in the model.' (Rolls-Royce's first patent *Improvements in Cowling for Liquid Cooled Internal Combustion Engines for Aircraft* (Ellor, GB 447,283, November 1934), for a ducted cooling system had also proposed piping engine exhaust gases to the duct behind the radiator.)

The paper was particularly concerned with the impact of different angles of incidence of duct entry. 'Entries to the duct in different positions around the leading edge were tried in turn and for each lift, drag and flow were measured over a range of incidence with a series of exit openings.' The tests showed the in-wing position to be extremely efficient as, 'the power expended in cooling at top speed is less than 1% of the B.H.P. of the engine'. The in-wing ducted radiator was theoretically attractive because the entrance was in the leading edge of the wing and therefore entirely avoided the duct entry problems caused by the build up of the boundary layer.

There followed a systematic series of wind tunnel tests designed to examine particular locations, sometimes for particular aircraft:

- Ventral location – *Note on the installation of a ducted radiator in the ventral position* (Hartshorn, November 1935) (See Appendix 4).
- Aft wing location – *Model tests of the Supermarine F.37/34 radiator cowl* (Shaw and Kirkby, May 1936 (tests in November 1935)).
- Chin location – *Note on tests of a ducted radiator fitted to the nose of a ¼ scale Hart* (Patterson, April 1936).

The key point is that the RAE had, by mid-1936, examined three obvious locations for ducted radiators.

Reviews of research

The RAE continued an active wind tunnel research programme after mid-1936. There were three papers reviewing earlier research on cooling systems issued in July and September.

- *A review of wind tunnel experiments on ducted radiators* (Hartshorn, July 1936).

- *A review of the RAE cooling research* (Perring, September 1936) (see Appendix 4).
- *Note on present position of cooling drag of aero engines* (Douglas, April 1937) (see Appendix 4).

These made use of the RAE's consistent wind tunnel methodology to make comparison of the different locations for ducted cooling systems.

A review of wind tunnel experiments on ducted radiators (Hartshorn, July 1936) outlined wind tunnel tests of ducted radiators that had already been conducted by the RAE. (In December 1935 Hartshorn had gone to Supermarine to sign off the Spitfire radiator design.) The report gathered data from a number of earlier RAE reports showing that the organisation had tested the key locations.

Position of duct entrance		Position of radiator		
		Underslung exposed	Underslung semi-recessed	Enclosed
Fuselage	Nose	1		
	Ventral	2		
	Aft	3		
Wing	Leading edge			5
	Aft lower surface		4	

1	*Note on tests of a ducted radiator fitted to the nose of a ¼ scale Hart*	(Patterson April 1936)
2	*Note on the installation of a ducted radiator in the ventral position*	(Hartshorn November 1935)
3	*Model tests on the Hawker Interceptor radiator cowl*	(Shaw and Cameron May 1936)
4	*Model tests of the Supermarine F37/34*	(Shaw and Kirkby May 1936)
5	*A scheme for a radiator in a wing*	(Shaw October 1935)

The locations are compared:

In-wing radiator – This is very efficient as there is little residual loss but is sensitive to change of incidence and offer structural difficulties.

Nose – There is very little residual internal drag but the position necessitates a relatively large increase in external surface giving an appreciable external drag which is in order of 2 ½ times the skin friction drag. The report is of note because it shows the Hart test with a 'lip'. This was not in the specific report for the Hart test, *Note on tests of a ducted radiator fitted to the nose of a ¼ scale Hart* (Patterson, April

1936). This is the first public drawing of a 'lip' on a duct entrance. (This was soon tested on the Hurricane, as seen above.)

Ventral and aft [wing] position – These have an appreciable residual internal drag due, in the main, to the effect of the aeroplane surface in front of the duct entrance. The external drag should be slightly less than for a nose radiator since the external surface is less. The paper drew attention to the importance of contouring the duct entrance.

Meredith's 1935 paper on duct entrance had said: 'If curvature is arranged to avoid a steep pressure gradient separation should not occur. These conditions, however, require a *rounded leading edge* for precisely the same reasons as in the case of an aerofoil.' The illustrated comparison of a sharp and rounded entry in the 1936 report reflects Meredith's comments in his paper on duct entry.

The paper compared overall results for each location but did not give a detailed breakdown of the drag numbers for different parts of each cooling system. Cooling drag was:

2lb. at 100ft/sec. for a radiator in a wing.	2% of the BHP
3lb. at 100ft/sec. for a nose radiator.	3% of the BHP
4 ½lb. at 100ft/sec. for the aft [wing] and ventral types.	4 ½% of the BHP

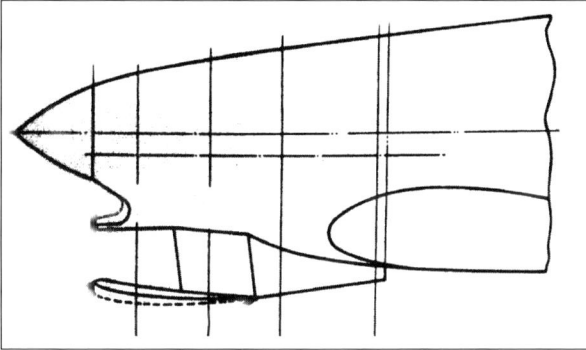

Figure 11.1 – Hawker Hart Model A with 'entrance lip' in *A review of wind tunnel experiments on ducted radiators* (Hartshorn, July 1936).

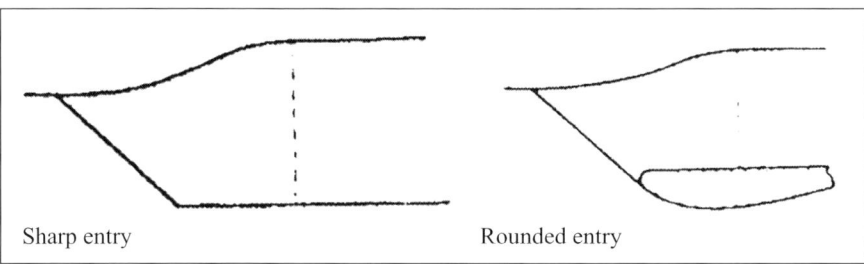

Sharp entry   Rounded entry

Figure 11.2 – Ventral duct sharp and rounded entry in *A review of wind tunnel experiments on ducted radiators* (Hartshorn, July 1936).

The paper included a retractable radiator (as did Capon's paper of 1935).

10lb. at 100ft/sec. for the retractable radiator.	10% of the BHP

The report confirmed British distrust of the ventral position and justified moving the cooling system forward to the nose as would be seen with the Curtiss XP-40 and the Hawker Tornado, particularly if the radiator could not be buried.

Duct entry

Meredith was particularly concerned about drag caused by too short a duct, resulting in breakaway and turbulence with the aft wing radiator location. He wrote in his *Note on the problem of conducting a fluid into a duct with a minimum of losses* (Meredith, May 1935):

> The process of building up the necessary pressure to push air through the radiator requires careful fairing, and a length of cowling which depends upon the pressure difference [over internal length of the diffusing duct], as there is a certain pressure gradient. [i.e., change of pressure per unit length] which cannot be exceeded without causing a breakaway of flow and hence unwanted drag.[2]

The unpublished June version of Meredith's August 1935 paper on ducted radiators included a section 'Further developments'. This reported: 'Wind tunnel experiments with ducted cooling systems are being conducted. The avoidance of entry losses in the ducts is the main feature requiring exploration.' The RAE specifically investigated this issue in 1937 and 1938 reflecting the importance given to it.

Some wind tunnel tests on internal expansion in duct entries (Patterson, May 1937), stated that ducted cooling, if the velocity of the cooling air at the radiator face was to be much lower than the flight velocity, required, 'efficient internal expansion'. To this end, 'various curvatures for the diverging walls and angles of expansion were tested'. The investigation established: 'Large internal expansions of the flow are possible without appreciable loss by using an expanding entry of suitable curvature and by arranging for the expansion to take place both externally and internally'.

Note on the scale effects on entry and duct losses in cooling systems (Davies, May 1938) investigated the reasons for the difference between model and full-scale measurements of entry and duct losses, to see whether wind tunnel tests, using reduced scale models, could give reliable results. 'The existence under certain circumstances of large-scale effects on entry and duct losses in cooling systems is well known, and some discrepancies which have recently occurred between model and full-scale measurements have made it desirable to reconsider the applicability of model tests in this connection.' Testing on the chin position had shown, 'Model and full-scale tests agreed in showing a negligible entry loss in the case of the "Hart" nose radiator'.

The RAE report shows the close cooperation and sharing research with Rolls-Royce. 'Full-scale tests on a ventral radiator fitted to the Heinkel He 70 confirmed the large entry loss obtained in model tests with a radiator in this [ventral] position.' The report confirmed that research in Britain presented the ventral position as problematical. 'Full-scale tests on a ventral radiator fitted to the Heinkel He 70 confirmed the large entry loss obtained in model tests with a radiator in this position.' The report concluded: 'The evidence given above shows that any analysis of internal drag measurements on models must be made with care, since the existence of large entry or duct losses on the model does not necessarily imply similar losses full-scale.'

To conclude, in 1935 – the year when Meredith was placed in charge of the RAE's Aerodynamics Department, which set research into cooling into the top priority – a systematic programme of wind tunnel testing was initiated. By 1938 the RAE had systematically tested different locations: wing leading edge, aft underslung wing, chin and ventral; specifically tested the two fighters that would win the Battle of Britain, the Spitfire and the Hurricane; and issues of specific concern to Meredith, duct entry and heat recycling. The RAE had devised a systematic methodology to compare wind tunnel results involving expressing all measurements of drag in terms of lbs per 100 feet per second (fps); dividing drag into four categories, minimum internal, residual internal, external skin friction, and residual external. It could be argued that this work would prove extremely important to the coming 1939-45 war effort and that it was stimulated by Meredith's comparatively brief period at Aerodynamics.

Chapter 12

Ducted radiators on aircraft generally

In the mid-1930s, Rolls-Royce and the RAE pioneered the use of ducted radiators for inline engines. This chapter will look at developments between 1936 and 1941 to see how Meredith's ideas impacted other countries.

Britain

Looking first, however, at Britain itself, other British mid-1930s Rolls-Royce Merlin powered monoplanes than the Hurricane and the Spitfire included the Fairey Battle (Specification P 27/32, 1933) and Fulmar (P 4/34, 1934) and the Boulton-Paul Defiant (F 9/35 1935). Both the Fairey airplanes, the Battle (first flight March 1936) and Fulmar (January 1937), had ducted cooling systems where a shallow [barely recessed] radiator was situated just behind the engine and the front duct extended ahead of the rear of the engine. There was a rear adjustable flap. Both had simple ducted systems, similar to those in Rolls-Royce patents, which were not developed in the airplanes' lifetimes. That said, RAE research saw front fuselage systems with shallow long radiators as relatively efficient. Both airplanes had top speeds below 300mph and therefore there was little to be gained from highly efficient ducts.

The turret gunned Boulton Paul Defiant had a simple ventral ducted radiator with a rear flap. Its top speed barely exceeded 300mph and therefore there was, even on a theoretical basis, little likelihood of positive thrust as the result of the 'Meredith effect'. The Defiant II had a Merlin XX engine requiring a larger radiator. The duct was deepened but otherwise unchanged.

The engine builder Napier had an aircraft designed to attempt the speed record using its 24-cylinder sleeve valve Sabre engine. The design of the cooling system is of considerable interest. The radiator was buried within the fuselage. The heated air was ducted to the either side of the tail surfaces. It also had a boundary layer bypass. The design appears to have been anticipated in a 1937 Rolls-Royce patent *Improvements in aircraft* (Ellor and Paravacini (Rolls-Royce), GB 472,555, April 1936). (The rear exits around the rudder anticipated the configuration of the French Arsenal VG 60, in drawing form only, and the rear engine of the Dornier Do 335, first flight October 1943, which had fuselage mounted tractor and pusher engines. See below for both.)

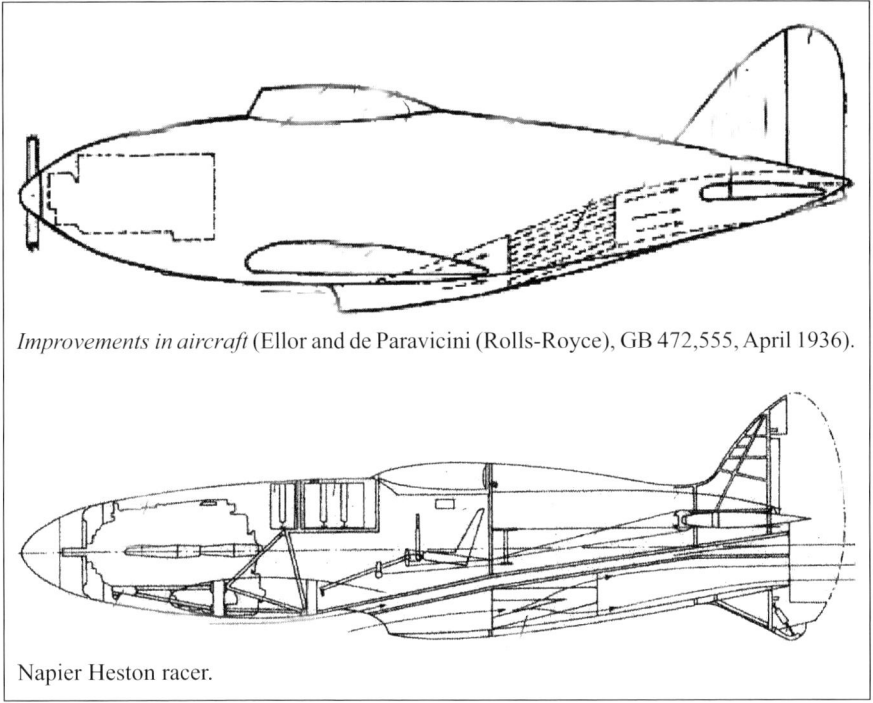

Improvements in aircraft (Ellor and de Paravicini (Rolls-Royce), GB 472,555, April 1936).

Napier Heston racer.

Figure 12.1 – Drawings from Rolls-Royce patent and of Napier Heston racer.

By the late 1930s the design of replacements and developments of the Hurricane, already obsolescent, and the Spitfire were underway. The Hawker Tornado was powered by a new engine, the 24-cylinder Rolls-Royce Vulture. The Spitfire Mk III, incorporated significant design changes by Supermarine. Wind tunnel testing of both was carried out in the late 1930s and early 1940s. (See Appendix 4 for wind tunnel tests.)

British twin engined airplanes included the Westland Whirlwind and the de Havilland Mosquito. (Tests are considered in more detail in Appendix 4.) Both had wing leading edge entry between the fuselage and the engine nacelle and radiators buried in the wing. The placement of the undercarriage system within the nacelle restricted the radiator duct to the inefficient chin position if this were placed in the nacelle. This was acceptable in larger bombers but undesirable in aircraft designed for speed. In the Whirlwind and the Mosquito, the location of the radiator and the duct were quite different.

In the first Westland Whirlwind design type the ducts passed through the wing spars. In the second, much simpler Mosquito design, the wing chord was extended ahead of the front spar and the whole duct placed before that spar with the exit below the wing. The Whirlwind's radiators were behind the main spar and the wing flap also varied the air flow through the cooling duct which exited at the rear. There was also a slat which opened to allow increased airflow when the flaps were down.

85

The Mosquito's radiators where ahead of the main spar where the wing chord was increased in order to contain the radiators and the ducts. The exit was ahead of the main spar and pointed downwards. Both airplanes' solutions were tested by the RAE. (See Appendix 4 for wind tunnel tests.) Meredith preferred the leading edge in-wing location and the Mosquito was notable for its low cooling drag and high speed.

Germany

Although, in 1939, Britain would be at war with Germany, throughout most of the 1930s the British airframe and aero-engine industry maintained close relationships with German companies. The first pioneer of ducted cooling systems was Junker who patented both ducted radiators, *Düsenkühler*, and adjustable exit flaps. Thus, Germany had its own traditions for such ducted systems. Notwithstanding, Rolls-Royce Kestrel engines were used in the Heinkel He 112, Messerschmitt Bf 109, and Junker Ju 87 prototypes. All had rather different cooling systems.

German research papers of 1937 and 1938, showed the work of Meredith and Capon was known in Germany where the impact of radiator heat was of particular interest. In 1938 and 1939 three German research papers on liquid cooling were translated by NACA. Two explicitly referred to Meredith's and Capon's work. (These are discussed in more detail in Part 2 which analyses Meredith's impact in the US.) In *Contribution to the theory of the heated duct radiator* (Winter, 1938, NACA, translated 1939), Winter, wrote: 'It was Meredith who first pointed out the possible gain in power required to tow [pull] the radiator systems under the operating condition as compared with the cold condition.' Göthert, in *The drag of airplane radiators with special references to air heating* (Göthert, 1938, NACA, translated 1939), cited Meredith's 1935 report under the heading, 'Effect of Heat on Radiator Drag'.

The Heinkel He 112 monoplane fighter was produced in very small numbers for export and was not used operationally by the Luftwaffe. The prototype, first flight September 1935, was powered by the Rolls-Royce Kestrel with a Rolls-Royce ducted radiator and exhaust manifold. Rather surprisingly, given its inefficiency, proven mathematically by Capon, later prototypes had retractable radiators, as did the He 112 B which was bought in limited numbers by the Hungarian (3) and Romanian air forces (30). The Heinkel He 100 fighter, which was largely a propaganda myth, first flight 22 January 1938, had evaporative cooling, Heinkel having experimented with it on the He 119 airframe. This fighter was never used operationally.

Willy Messerschmitt was very aware of the pioneering work by Junkers on the *Düsenkühler*. He explored the issues of high speed flight in this 1937 study *Probleme des Schnellflugs*.[1] Messerschmitt credited the invention of ducted radiators to Junkers. 'Due to the introduction of the *Düsenkühler* according to

Junkers, it was possible to considerably reduce the resistance of the cooling system.' (See Appendix 2.) He recognised, 'the adjustable *Düsenkühler* has the advantage that the cooling power is independent of the speed and the air speed in the radiator and thus the power consumption for the radiator can be kept constant'. (This reflected closely Meredith's first conclusion in his seminal 1935 paper.) And, 'The most beautiful installation of a *Düsenkühler* was in the wing'. (In this he again echoed Meredith who favoured the wing leading edge location.) As seen above, the Bf 109 prototype flew in May 1935 with a Kestrel engine. The initial production models of the A, B, C and D series were powered by the relatively low-powered, 660-690hp Junkers Jumo 210 series engines. All had under engine cooling ducts.

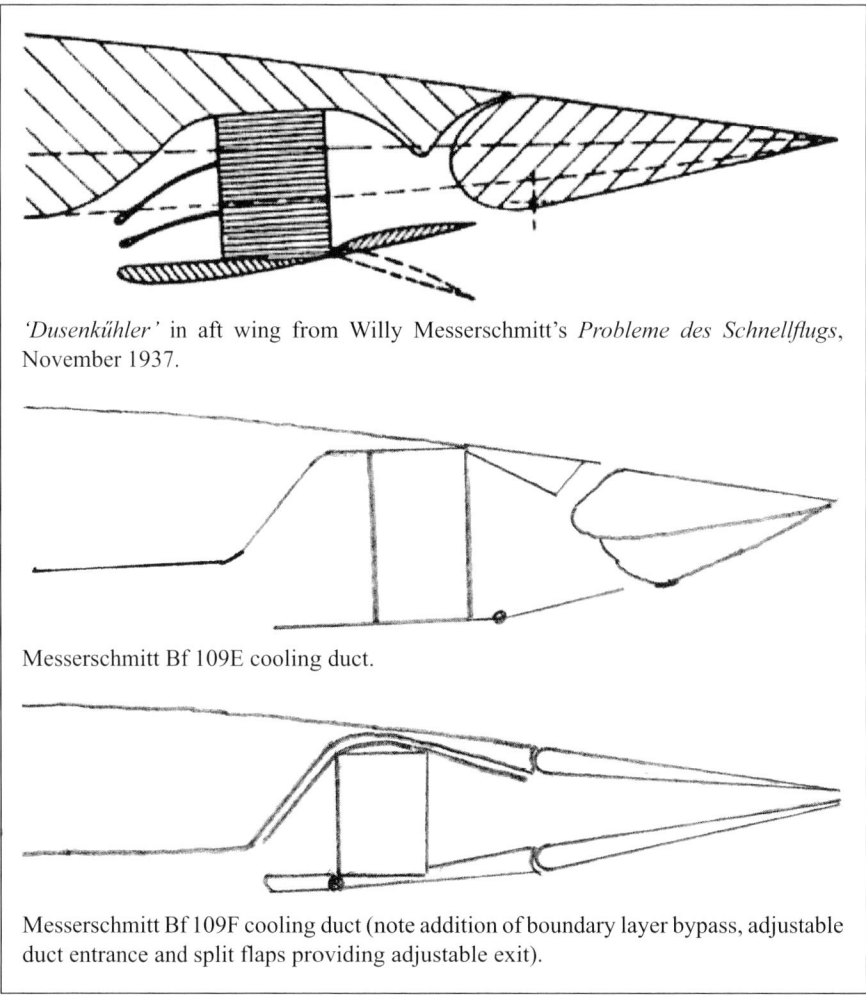

'Dusenkühler' in aft wing from Willy Messerschmitt's *Probleme des Schnellflugs*, November 1937.

Messerschmitt Bf 109E cooling duct.

Messerschmitt Bf 109F cooling duct (note addition of boundary layer bypass, adjustable duct entrance and split flaps providing adjustable exit).

Figure 12.2 – Messerschmitt Bf 109 radiator duct development.

The Bf 109E, first flight 1938, was powered by the more powerful DB 600 series engine. This required a much larger radiator and a total redesign of the cooling system. Like the Spitfire, this was placed in the wing aft position, but the design was much more sophisticated. It was anticipated in Willy Messerschmitt's *Probleme des Schnellflugs*, in 1937. The radiator was moved to the aft wing position to reduce drag to the aft wing position to both increase the radiator areas and to balance the greater weight of the engine.

The Bf 109E appears to follow the Spitfire's practice but became much more advanced with the Bf 109F, whose first flight was on 10 July 1940 and came into general use only in 1941. This was a complex system that attempted to resolve the challenges of the aft wing location – something that was never done with the Spitfire. There was a variable incidence intake linked with the trailing edge flaps in order to open at the same time as them. The variable incidence plate picked up the boundary layer on the underside of the wing, and discharged it on the trailing edge. There was also a boundary layer bypass over the radiator which significantly improved the pressure recovery at the radiator face. The exit section was split, serving the additional purpose of controlling the airflow through the wing radiators. Finally, the intakes and exits were continuously adjustable, automatically regulated to create thrust. [2] The boundary layer bypass had been suggested by Meredith. Also, the boundary layer bypass was tested on the Spitfire Mk III which was not put into production. (The Bf 109G removed the boundary layer bypass.)

Junkers had a tradition of ducted radiators going back to 1915 when Hugo Junkers patented a *Düsenkühler*. The Junkers Ju 87A to C had a chin radiator in a short duct placed below the engine. The D had a more powerful Jumo engine requiring a larger radiator. Also, the airframe was made more efficient aerodynamically. Like the Messerschmitt, the Stuka's engine's radiator cooling system, was moved to the aft wing position. Two radiators were placed under the inner cranked wing in short ducts with both adjustable entrances and exits.

Overall, Germany had its own traditions going back to Junkers's First World War *Düsenkühler*. Like Britain, and unlike France, Russia, Italy and Japan, companies developed very diverse practice. Messerschmitt may have followed Supermarine in the use of the aft wing location but greatly improved on it. Germany was very important in transmission of Meredith's research ideas to the US where NACA translated German papers into English and further developed the material in them.

France

France was initially resistant to foreign ideas about cooling drag before 1938:

> It should have been obvious that the British and Germans had solved the radiator problem. By using a flap at the rear to increase the flow of air at low speeds, radiators did not have to be so large. The flaps

were clearly visible on published photographs and aeronautical journalists were commenting on them and even describing how, by careful design, the new ducted radiators were using the heated air to generate some forward thrust. French designers, however, seemed to be completely unaware of these breakthroughs. [3]

In France, Louis Breguet and his chief engineer René Devillers published in 1938 a synthesis of the knowledge at that time in *La Technique des radiateurs d'aviation et de leur carénage*.[4] France began to catch up but it was late.

The MS 406 was Morane-Saulnier's response to a 1934 specification. The entry to service of the MS 406 in early 1939 represented the first modern fighter aircraft to be adopted by the French Air Force. It had an inefficient retractable radiator. (This was the only operational fighter design of the Second World War to be so cooled.)

The first two French aircraft to have ducted radiators, placed ventrally, were the Arsenal VG-30 and the Dewoitine D.520. The 1936 specification that led to the Arsenal VG series was for a fighter that could be built rapidly in large numbers. The prototype, Arsenal VG-30 first flew in October 1938 with a radiator in the forward ventral position. There does not appear to have been provision for an adjustable exit flap.

The D.520 first flew in October 1938. Like the Arsenal VG-30 it had a forward ventral radiator. It was the first French fighter to be brought into service in 1940

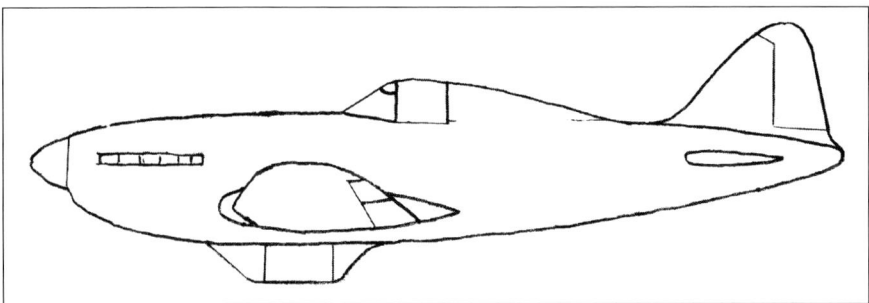

Figure 12.3 – Arsenal VG-30.

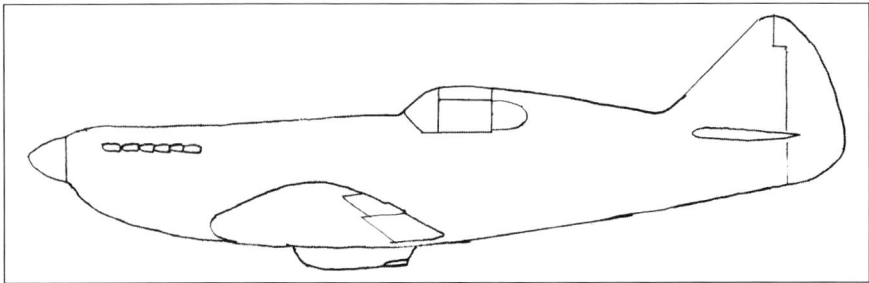

Figure 12.4 – Dewoitine D.520.

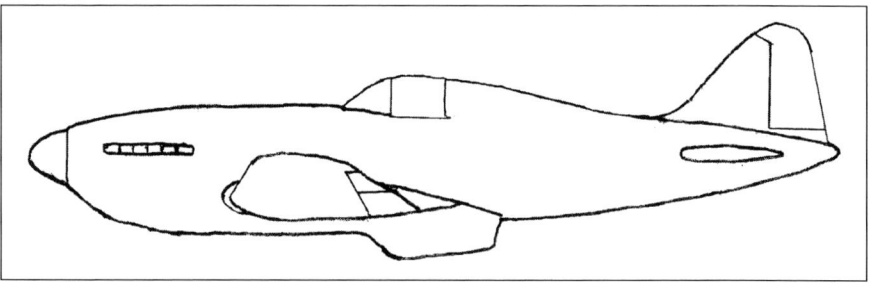

Figure 12.5 – Arsenal VG-33.

with a ducted radiator with an adjustable exit, thus France was well behind Britain and Germany, and to a lesser extent, the US in incorporating this system.

There followed an almost bewildering number of designs underway as French design caught up, but too late to save France at the time of the fall of France in June 1940. Few made it to production – but some continued to be developed in secretive conditions during the occupation.

The Arsenal series was particularly remarkable. The trend was towards increasing radiator duct burial with flush exits. The Arsenal VG-31 differed from the VG-30 by having the radiator bath moved aft to improve the centre of gravity. The VG-31 flew in 1939 and proved to have excellent performance. It had an adjustable exit. The VG-32 was expected to be powered by an Allison engine. The radiator was partially buried and the duct had an adjustable exit. The prototype VG-32 was completed in 1940 and awaiting its test flight when it was captured by the Germans. The VG-33 was a modified version of the VG-31, and first flew on 25 April 1939 and was capable of nearly 350mph. It was the first production model, but most of the airframes had not received engines when captured by the Germans.

The Dewoitine 550 had a ventral radiator, first flight June 1939, similar to the 520. It proved fast but the operational version 551 lacked engines before France's defeat. While the MS 406 was entering squadron service in 1939, an upgrade series was initiated with the aim of improving the design. This had a fixed radiator in a duct with an adjustable exit in place of the earlier retractable design. Production of

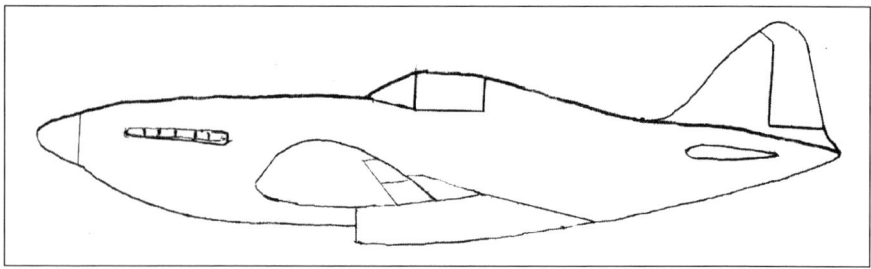

Figure 12.6 – Arsenal VG-36 (Hispano Suiza powered) and VG-50 (Allison powered) – externally similar.

the MS 410 had only just started when France fell in June 1940. There were two other fighters again with ventral radiator, the Potez 230 and the SNCAO 200 which flew before the war but played no part in it.

The Arsenal group then designed some rather advanced ducted radiators. The Arsenal VG-36 was a more developed and refined VG-35. The aircraft had a modified rear fuselage and used a shallower and more streamlined radiator duct. The VG-36 was first flown on 14 May 1940 but was later destroyed. There were plans to use foreign Rolls-Royce and Allison engines. The VG-40 was to have a Rolls-Royce engine. The VG-50 was an Allison version with an advanced nearly fully buried ventral duct. It is of interest as it shows that there was an advanced ventral design before the full development of the Mustang.

France had been complacent. When it did follow Britain and Germany it standardised on the ventral location. Defeat came before it could exploit some interesting and advanced designs.

Belgium

Belgium attempted to build its own fighter in the late 1930s the Reynard R-36 as a replacement for the Fairey Firefly. It was a modern all metal design, initially engined with a Hispano-Suiza engine. This had a very advanced fully buried aft ventral radiator. It first flew in November 1937. It was re-engined with a Merlin II and the cooling was moved forward to a more conventional ventral position.

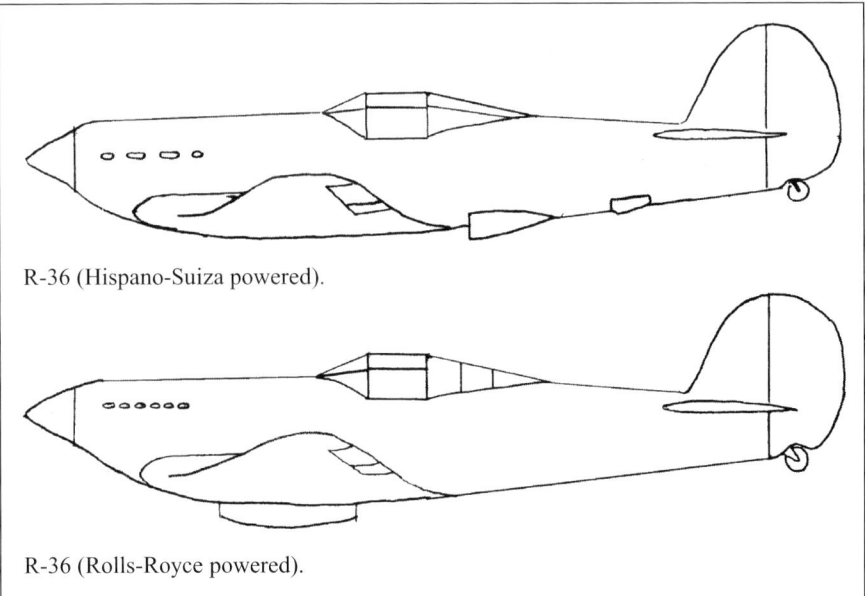

R-36 (Hispano-Suiza powered).

R-36 (Rolls-Royce powered).

Figure 12.7 – Reynard R-36.

Soviet Union

In the run-up to 1940 the USSR produced three groups of inline fighters: Mikoyan Gurevich or MiG, Yakovlev or Yak, and Lavochkin or LaGG. The design and production system was different to the west in that aircraft were designed by design bureaus and construction was passed out to production organisations. The Yak and the LaGG series were powered by the Klimov M-105/6 V12 engine and the MiGs 1 and 3 the huge Mikulin AM-34 engine.

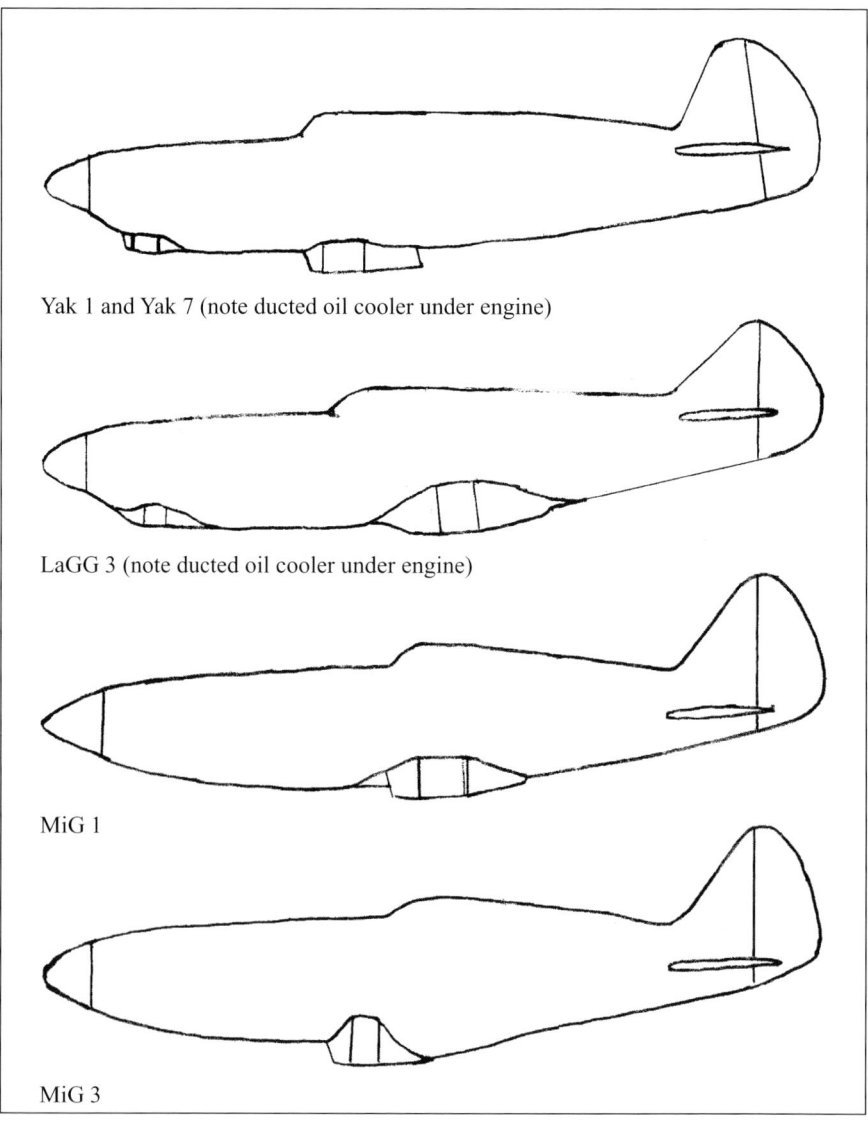

Yak 1 and Yak 7 (note ducted oil cooler under engine)

LaGG 3 (note ducted oil cooler under engine)

MiG 1

MiG 3

Figure 12.8 – Soviet ventral ducted radiator fighters.

The Yak-1 first flew in January 1940. The prototype suffered from oil overheating problems which were never completely resolved. The Yak-7 followed in July with a similar duct. The LaGG-1 was designed in 1938 as a light-weight aircraft designed around the Klimov M-105 engine and it first flew on 30 March 1940. Although forced into service too early the LaGG-3 had a cooling system of advanced appearance with a largely buried duct, an angled entrance and an adjustable exit. Like the Yak-1 it had an under engine ducted oil cooler with an adjustable exit. The Mikoyan-Gurevich MiG-1 designed to meet a requirement for a high-altitude fighter, issued in 1939, powered by the huge Mikulin 47 litre engine. (First flight April 1940.) The MiG-3 was a development of the MiG-1 to remedy problems in the MiG-1's development and operations. It started production on 20 December 1940. (First flight October 1940.)

Italy

Italy's fighters used radials until German Daimler-Benz inlines were bought or built under licence. Ducted radiators were introduced into front line Italian aircraft with the Macchi and Reggianne fighters during the war. Anticipating these are some earlier aircraft. The Macchi C.202 Folgore, first flight August 1940, had a design similar to the Yak and LaGG with the ventral engine coolant system and the oil coolant duct under the engine.

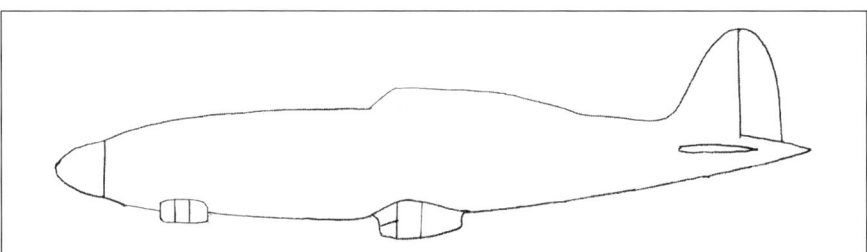

Figure 12.9 – Macchi C.202 Folgore (note vanes recommended by Meredith in 1935).

Japan

Japan used radial engines almost exclusively. The exception was the Kawasaki Ki-61 Hien, which had a comparatively short central ventral radiator. (First flight December 1941.) It used vanes to equalise the pressure distribution over the radiator. Meredith had suggested the use of vanes in 1935.

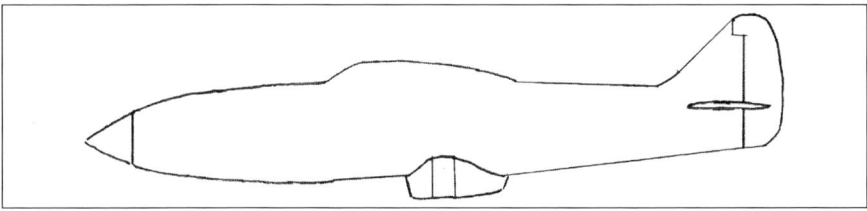

Figure 12.10 – Kawasaki Ki-61 Hien.

US

Apart from the Curtiss P-40, dealt with elsewhere, two other Allison powered fighters were under development in the later 1930s. Although very different in type both had fully or partially buried radiators behind the pilot. The Bell P-39 Airacobra first flew in April 1938 with a turbocharger. In August 1939 it was decided to remove the turbocharger, leaving only a one stage supercharger, as its weight and complexity, in such a small airframe, was perceived as demanding too much development time. The Airacobra had a genuinely fully buried ducted system of remarkable tidiness. The main engine glycol radiator was buried in the fuselage centre behind the main spar with two inlets in the wing roots and a single exit below the rear fuselage. There were two oil cooler radiators with inlets in the wing to the outside of the glycol radiator inlets and two exits on either side of the single glycol radiator outlet. All three exits had adjustable flaps which when closed were flush with the fuselage and inner wing.

The Lockheed P-38 Lightning twin had turbocharged twin engines. Unlike the Bell and Curtiss inlines it retained its turbochargers which could be buried in the twin booms and thus it had good high altitude performance. Therefore, the P-38's radiator position was effectively comparable to the aft location on a single-engined aircraft as the radiators were placed well behind the engine. It first flew in January 1939. The booms behind the twin engines allowed space for the turbochargers but also made possible the partial burying of the radiators, facilitating low drag installation. The prototype had duct entrances which were rather smaller than on the production versions and there was a single adjustable exit placed on the upper surface of the boom. The production version had exits which were placed on the side of the boom.

To conclude, in practice, the Second World War single inline engined fighters had engine coolant radiators in three positions, ventral, aft-wing and chin. Overall, there are some simple points. Britain's main fighters, the Hurricane and the Spitfire, used respectively the central ventral position continuing Hawker's biplane practice and Supermarine aft wing position for a possible combination of aerodynamic or possibly aesthetic (a chin or ventral radiator would have compromised the Spitfire's fine lines) reasons. European and Japanese design largely followed these models. Germany's Messerschmitt Bf 109, with the E versions onward followed the Spitfire, but with a much more sophisticated design, and all other countries dealt with here, France, Russia, Italy and Japan, followed the Hurricane, with ventral radiators. The US the Curtiss XP-40 followed an advanced ventral aft position that was to be moved into the inefficient chin location. The Bell P-39, which had its engine behind the pilot, buried the radiator with front wing inlets. The evolution of the Mustang is dealt with later, but it was unique in using the aft ventral position.

Chapter 13

Meredith – scientific contribution post-1935

Aerodynamics – Boundary layer suction

In March 1936 Meredith, who had returned from Aerodynamics to Instruments in later 1935, co-wrote a paper with fellow RAE senior scientist A.A. Griffith on boundary layer suction titled, *The Possible Improvement in Aircraft Performance due to the use of Boundary-layer Suction* (Griffith and Meredith, March 1936), an active form of laminar flow control where turbulent separation was avoided by sucking the boundary layer into the airframe. Avoiding breakaway of the boundary layer by actively inducing laminar flow was proposed not just across the wing but the whole airframe. Meredith and Griffith had been at the RAE since the early 1920s and had worked together in the Aerodynamics unit. This paper on boundary layer suction was the last known contribution by Meredith on the subject of drag reduction.

Griffith had joined the Royal Aircraft Factory, the predecessor of the RAE, in 1915. He did extremely important work on metal fatigue and supercharger turbines. In 1926 Griffith published a seminal paper, *An Aerodynamic Theory of Turbine Design,* where he demonstrated that the poor performance of existing turbines was because the blades were 'flying stalled' and proposed an airfoil blade shape that would dramatically improve their performance.[1] From 1931 to 1939 Griffith was in charge of the RAE's Engine Department. He is partly remembered for his negative assessment in 1929 of Frank Whittle's thesis on turbine engines which delayed their development. In 1938 he would start work on an axial-flow jet engine having recognised he was wrong about Whittle's ideas. (Whittle's engines used a centrifugal compressor.) It might be added that Griffith had been on the Security Services suspect list. On 24 May 1934 it was recorded, 'Dr Griffith is said to hold the same Communist views as Lockspeiser and that this is known to his superiors, which indicates that influences are brought to bear enabling him to retain his job'.[2]

Griffith and Meredith claim to have conceived the idea of boundary layer suction in the later 1920s, when speeds, and thus drag, were lower and the latter less of a pressing concern:

In 1927, B.M. Jones [Brian Melville Jones, a famous Cambridge University aerodynamicist] showed how great an improvement in the aeroplanes of the time was possible by proper streamlining. At about the same time it occurred to the present authors that still better results could be obtained by using perforated surfaces and sucking the boundary layer into the machine by an exhausting fan, the air being finally ejected with its total head [pressure] being restored by the fan. In this way the formation of a wake by skin friction could be avoided and power could be saved.[3]

In the late 1920s poor general streamlining made suction pointless, but in the mid-1930s the suction approach could be revisited as streamlining had improved so much. 'The process of streamlining has now proceeded so far, however, that the best modern aeroplanes are within reasonable distance of the ideal and in consequence the greater part of their drag when cruising arises from skin-friction.' Mathematical analysis shows the suction gains to be very great. 'The combined saving possible by boundary suction, may amount ideally to five-sixth of the power at present consumed by skin friction.'

Boundary layer suction is an active form of laminar flow control [LFC]. It was first suggested by L. Prandtl, who had identified the boundary layer in 1904 as one of the means of preventing or 'delaying' boundary layer separation. Griffith and Meredith concluded: 'Comparing an ideally streamlined aeroplane with a similar aircraft having boundary suction ideally applied, the latter has about a fourfold greater range at the same cruising speed and about 80% greater speed and range at the same cruising power.'

Griffith and Meredith developed the mathematics of boundary layer suction. Paul Blasius (1883-1970), a pupil of Prandtl, had produced equations for the profile of the boundary layer which would grow indefinitely if it moved along an infinitely long flat surface. Griffith and Meredith produced the first equations for the boundary layer, moving along a similar surface but with regularly placed suction holes, with the result that the boundary layer would have a constant thickness. For this achievement they are widely cited in relevant boundary layer literature.

On 25 May 1936, the RAE wrote to the Air Ministry asking whether a patent should be taken out to protect the Griffith and Meredith's boundary layer suction proposal. On 29 May the Director of Contracts wrote that it did not intend to file an application for a patent at the public expense. The following comments were appended which show early awareness in Britain of the advantages of laminar flow. 'There is no need for secrecy. The study of the boundary layer is now engaging general attention among workers in aerodynamic research, and the advantage that would come from the maintenance of laminar flow is already fairly well known.'[4]

A further minute reported the RAE was conducting experiments on laminar flow in 1936.[5] 'Experiments have already begun at RAE in an endeavour to prove the practicability of this idea, which as suggested [earlier] is more or less common property. The only need for secrecy might be introduced in connection with a design which successfully achieved boundary layer removal in a practical aeroplane.'

The US was, by the late 1930s, doing practical work on boundary layer suction. 'In 1939, [NACA] research engineers tested the effect on boundary-layer transition of suction through slots in the surface of wind-tunnel models and obtained laminar flow up to a length Reynolds number of 7 million, a phenomenally large value at that time.'[6] Attempts to produce similar results with an actual wing section with suction holes on a Douglas B-18 produced more marginal results and work was suspended, when the US entered the war, to focus on passive laminar flow systems.

The paper shows Meredith at the forefront of ideas to reduce drag and working productively with other great minds. Having produced ideas to reduce turbulence at duct entry, including the boundary layer bypass, he and Griffith now proposed ways to reduce turbulence on the surfaces ahead and inside the duct, suction. NAA's Lee Atwood made an insightful comment on laminar flow as: 'In general, attempts to extend laminar flow have been unsuccessful without boundary-layer control devices such as perforated wing surfaces.'[7]

Instruments

In early 1935 Meredith moved from the Instruments to the Aerodynamic unit of the RAE following the death in a freak accident of its head Glauert, when he was struck by a splinter from an exploded tree on Aldershot Common. Bizarrely, Meredith's stay at Aerodynamics ended after about nine months when the head of Instruments, Bygrave, was killed in a riding accident, involving a branch, during a Legion of Frontiersmen exercise. Thus, Meredith returned to Instruments having made remarkable contributions to ducted radiator and duct entry design. Probably no other man had the capability to head the RAE's main units, Aerodynamics and Instruments, let alone lead groundbreaking developments at both.

Autopilots
The standard Second World War British autopilot was the RAE Mark IV and was developed under Meredith in the mid-1930s. This had a pneumatic three-axis system with two gyroscopes. (It was similar to the Mark I in having twin gyroscopes controlling three axes, but in the Mark IV the gyros and servos were in separate packages, while in the Mark 1 the gyros were packaged with the servos.) By 1939 Meredith had designed an all-electric, fully manoeuvrable autopilot using free gyros, but this was not put into production as war effort focused on improving existing designs.

Bombsights
Recent research has greatly clarified the development of British Second World War bombsights and Meredith's role within it. Stephen Marsh has generously allowed access to his unpublished thesis, *The Air Ministry and the Bomb Dropping Problem: Bombsights, Scientists and Techno-Military Invention, 1918-45,* which has a chapter devoted to Meredith's work on bombsights. Peter C. Smith's book *Skua! The Royal Navy's Dive-Bomber* has a fascinating chapter, in which Meredith plays a prominent part, about the Navy's desperate effort to build an automated dive bombsight and the RAF's (largely successful) effort to thwart it due to its increasing obsession with higher level strategic bombing.

SPITFIRE, MUSTANG AND THE 'MEREDITH EFFECT'

In the 1920s the RAF used the Course Setting Bombsight (CSBS), designed by Wimperis, which was a simple vector sight developed in the First World War. This identified the bomb impact point on the ground. Before the bomb run the bombardier fed into the sight, the speed and direction of the aircraft, that of the wind, and the aircraft altitude. The bombardier then had to direct the pilot so that the impact point coincided with the target when the bombs were released. The vector sight was adequate for stationary targets, but the US navy was concerned about hitting moving ships. This resulted in the development of the tachometric bombsights of which the most famous was the US Norden. The tachometric sight synchronised the movement of the aircraft with that of the target, requiring both aircraft and target data to be fed into the sight before the bomb run. Then the bombsight was trained by the bombardier on the target and the aircraft movement synchronised by the sight with the target and the bombs automatically dropped.

Theoretically, the tachometric bombsight had the advantages of automating many processes and being able to deal with a moving target. In practice, the settings required time and could be easily disrupted by changes in direction by the aircraft or the target. Also, it only functioned effectively in daylight when the target movement was visible. The simple vector sight could be automated to adjust for manoeuvres by the aircraft during the bomb run and as night bombing involved largely stationary targets there was no need to synchronise aircraft and target movement.

Newly returned to the Instruments unit Meredith took over two bombsights: the archaic vector Course Setting Bombsight (CSBS) and the under development Automatic Bombsight (ABS). Also, Meredith replaced the late Bygrave on the Air Ministry Bombing Committee, which was responsible for bomb aiming and bombing tactics. At this time the imminent introduction of faster monoplane bombers rendered insufficient Meredith's earlier policy of stabilising the aircraft not the bombsight. Neither the CSBS or the ABS were stabilised and stabilisation using gyros was Meredith's particular area of expertise. Meredith was also doubtful that the tachometric ABS system would work effectively in wartime conditions where neither aircraft nor target could be expected, due to weather conditions and evasive action, to maintain a single course. A further complicating factor was that whereas biplanes could be induced to perform flat turns, faster monoplanes required banking turns and that meant that the bombardier and his sight, during the turn, faced away from the target. This was a particular problem for a tachometric system like ABS where the bombardier needed to keep the sight aligned on the target, but it also disrupted the antiquated CSBS.

In the mid-1930s not just the RAF was in search of a bombsight suitable for modern conditions. So too was the Royal Naval Air Service (RNAS) and Meredith became involved in this effort as well. The RNAS was desperate to develop a dive bombsight. The US and Japanese navies had recognised that dive-bombing would play a central role in forthcoming naval warfare and developed the necessary doctrines and hardware. So did the German land-based Luftwaffe. The RAF, however, was already obsessed by level and area bombing and not only refused to develop its own dive bombers but also did its best to stymie the Royal Navy's ability to produce its own effective dive bomber and bombsight. (The consequence was that despite the best efforts of the Navy, and indeed Meredith, the RNAS went to war with the obsolete Blackburn Skua without a modern dive bombsight.)

The Royal Navy did manage to lobby for a dedicated Dive-Bomb-Sight sub-Committee of the Bombing Committee which first met on 11 May 1936. This included Meredith who already sat on the main Bombing Committee. The Royal Navy insisted that the sight was capable of hitting a moving target. Meredith was a very active participant, always trying to come up with suggestions to get around the hostility of the Air Force to divebombing generally and some very naïve suggestions as to how to circumvent operational problems, particularly how to adjust for wind.[8]

He made two proposals: a simple sight comprising two concentric rings with radial spokes painted on the aircraft windscreen, and a gyroscope wired to the bomb release which would automatically release the bomb to help deal with the wind problem.[9] The second meeting of the Dive-Bomb-Sight sub-Committee on 2 December 1936 discussed a more developed 'simple' bombsight Dive-bomb Sight Experimental Type A which, as described by Meredith, incorporated a moveable foresight to adjust for wind, a ring and a bead sight; and a warning signal light which lit 500 feet above pre-set sight and went out at that pre-set height. The committee also discussed the RAE's more advanced multi-directional sight with gyro release. The RAF said this should be shelved until the simple sight results were analysed. Meredith reported that due to pressure of work the RAE had relegated multi-directional sight to category C. He proposed an Automatic Dive-Bomb Sight (ADBS) where 'a gyroscope' would 'communicate its movement by electric repeater motors to the sight' and the targets movements would be automatically incorporated in the data.[10] He suggested that this was made Category Priority B, but this was not taken up. In 1937 the Dive-bomb Sight Experimental Type A was tested and proved almost useless due to the RAF requirement that nonsensical dive angle and height settings were used. The results were only respectable because the pilots used their own judgement to overrule the sight.

At the second meeting of the Dive-Bomb-Sight sub-Committee on 18 December 1937 Meredith rejected trials of Dive-bomb Sight Experimental Type A as inadequate. He said the multi-directional sight would provide greater accuracy. Preliminary trials showed that relative wind movement and changes in target direction remained problematical. Meredith said all this would be resolved by his ADBS. This was resisted by the RAF due to its ever engrossing obsession with level flight area bombing of stationary targets and it was decided to proceed only with the multi-directional sight.

Reverting to the development of the high altitude bombsight, in April 1937 Meredith wrote a seminal paper, *Memorandum on High Altitude Bombsights*.[11] In it he asserted that in wartime a reflector stabilised vector sight would be in practice superior to a tachometric sight. (The use of a reflector greatly reduced the length of a sight.) The same Pye who saw no need to prioritise Meredith's proposals on jet propulsion made the development of a stabilised bombsight priority A. (In early 1935 finding a solution to inline cooling drag had been made priority A at the same time as Meredith moved from Instruments to Aerodynamics. Thus, in two years Meredith had been in charge of two of the RAE's most important projects in very different fields.)

The decision to focus on the antiquated CSBS was, notwithstanding, a February 1938 RAE Instruments report on *High Altitude Level Bombsights* which developed Meredith's analysis.[12] The paper argued for the development of a stabilised reflector vector bombsight which would be superior in practice to a tachometric sight as Meredith asserted in 1937. Work proceeded at the RAE, to develop a stabilised Reflector Vector Bombsight Type B. This was of little interest to the Committee for Scientific Study of Air Offence (CSSAO) which pursued CSBS and the Azimuth Bracket (a long unsightly contraption which facilitated resetting the bombsight after a banked turn).

Meredith's own position was now compromised by his involvement in the Vernon spy scandal (see below). Also, Henry Tizard, who chaired the Aeronautical Research Council (ARC), and the eminent aerodynamicist Brian Melville Jones intervened, concerned that the disruption caused by anti-aircraft fire and over complexity in operational conditions would mean advanced bombsights would be futile. Therefore, the focus was redirected to making an unstabilised vector bombsight, the CSBS, functional in a banked turn with the Azimuth Bracket.

The story of the ADBS and the high altitude bombsight became intertwined. In November 1938 the decision was made to develop Meredith's Automatic Dive Bombsight (ADBS) for the navy, which he proposed in 1936. R.S. Capon, who, like Meredith, wrote a seminal paper on ducted radiators in 1935, wanted to give the work to Smiths who, 'were at present in a particularly favourable position for undertaking this work' because Meredith now worked for Smiths who were allowed a fortnight over Christmas to analyse the issue. [13]

In that period, on 6 January 1939, Meredith submitted a patent application (*Improvements in or relating to apparatus for repeating the movements of a member such as the movable member of an instrument* (Meredith, GB 526,101A, January

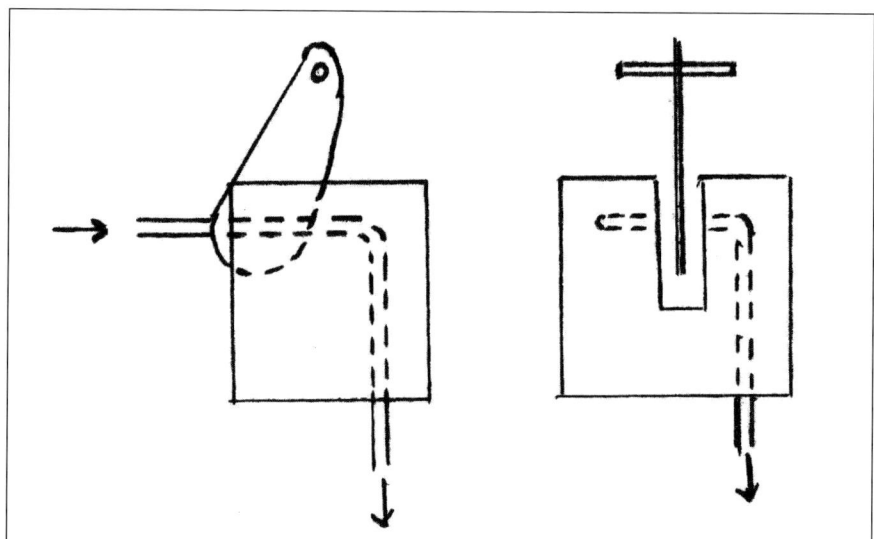

Figure 13.1 – Airblock and chopper servo-mechanism (much simplified).

1939)) for a pneumatic air-jet and chopper-block servomechanism. This was a form of powered relay which sensed low-power movement and converted it into higher-power movement with little impact on the low-power source. This functioned through the interruption of an air-jet – here by an input blade which the air pressure controlled – from an air-supply nozzle to an air-receiver nozzle. The output was amplified by a clever system through which a servomotor registered the changes in air pressure.

Ivor Bowen of the Ministry of Aircraft Production recorded that Smiths was the best firm to approach 'because the Chief Research Engineer of this firm, Mr Meredith, is probably more acquainted with the design problems than any other person in the country outside the department' as 'the only person the Air Ministry could trust with this difficult design task was Meredith'.[14] Bowen stated that the automatic dive bombsight 'is very far from simple and indeed is so difficult to achieve that a considerable body of opinion would probably call it impracticable'. Meredith was cited as, 'the main protagonist of the automatic dive bombsight and is already well aware of the extent of the problem and the mechanical and flight difficulties involved'.[15] Smiths was awarded a fixed price contract to undertake 'a definite and agreed plan of research'.[16]

Gunsights

Meredith's versatile mind meant that he was also interested in gunsights. His experience with aircraft stabilisation, autopilots and bombsights was reflected in his ideas here. As flight speeds increased the time to aim and fire decreased and the required deflection increased and the requirement for a deflection gunsight became pressing. In October 1937 Meredith wrote a short paper, *Note on the problem of aiming fixed guns in aeroplanes* (Meredith, October 1937).[17] This proposed simplifying the task of the pilot by designing the aeroplane and training the pilot to control it in two axes – thus obtaining the required angle of bank. Meredith and George Gardner, in October 1938, applied for a 'patent GB 576,359 (application 27 October 1938, publication 29 January 1940) relating to *Improvements in or relating to controlling aircraft,* which dealt with the problem of stabilisation (using gyroscopes) of a plane of sight during a banked turn.[18] This was accepted in January 1940. They 'proposed a stabilised gyroscopic sight for use in an aeroplane such that when a turn is required the sight is rotated, the aeroplane being turned at a rate depending upon the extent of the original movement of the sight'.[19]

Positions and awards

After Meredith left the RAE in 1938, where he was head of the Instruments Department, he remained deeply integrated into the aerodynamic scientific community. In 1937 the Royal Aeronautical Society honoured – with silver medals for outstanding achievers in global aerospace – Meredith and P.A. Cooke. In November 1938 the Security Services noted he gave a lecture to the Scientist's Group of the Left-wing Book Club, as the late Principal Scientific Officer in the Air Ministry.[20] He was recorded in the 1938 Airforce List as sitting on the Technical Equipment Committee.

Chapter 14

Meredith – from Spitfire to spy

In 1935 Meredith made critical contributions to the development of the Spitfire resolving the cooling problem. At the same time he took definitive steps towards becoming a Russian spy. Indeed, in the month of August, when Meredith's seminal paper was approved by the ARC, he spent time in the Soviet Union and the Russians perceived him as ripe for recruitment to the cause. On his return, as seen, he went to Supermarine in September to comment, rather critically, on the Spitfire's ducted radiator.

The earlier account of Meredith's political activities largely draws on The National Archive [TNA] file KV2/2199 which was closed in 1937, at which time the Security Services were unaware of Meredith's actual involvement in spying and his activities do not seem dangerous – indeed often they appear almost comical. The subsequent story is based on material in post-war KV2/2200, KV2/2201 and KV2/2202, after Meredith was denounced and much more of his activities in and after 1935 was known, and the story took a more compromised turn.

Political developments made Meredith increasingly susceptible to Soviet approaches. His post-war interrogator in the late 1940s reported:

> In 1935 he [Meredith] was quite satisfied that the British Government was pursuing the wrong foreign policy. It was showing a blind hatred of Russia and watched with equanimity the re-armament of Germany. At an early stage he, Meredith, realised that if Germany succeeded in beating Russia, it would turn on the West. He thought that his country was being dishonoured by its foreign policy, a view which was confirmed by the rape of Spain. [1]

Also: 'He felt that war between Hitler and Russia was inevitable, and that it was owed to the future of humanity that Russia should not lose this war. He realised that he had to pay a very high price at grave personal risk in taking some positive action, but that in the circumstances this risk was well warranted.'[2] Meredith believed his motives for recruitment as a Soviet spy were based on the most principled motives. 'He therefore had to communicate to the Russians anything that might be of military advantage to them in the war with Germany which he felt completely convinced was inevitable.'[3]

In 1934 Meredith had been involved with the Union of Democratic Control (UDC) a British pressure group formed in 1914 to press for a more responsive foreign policy. In the 1930s the UDC was led by Dorothy Woodman (1902-1970) who had joined in 1928 and reshaped it as an anti-fascist research and propaganda campaigning group. In the 1930s she worked for the Soviets recruiting spies. 'At this time Woodman was living with a Soviet citizen and was rabidly communist in outlook. It is known that she paid visits to the USSR.'[4] Meredith read the proofs of a pamphlet edited by Woodman called *Hitler Rearms* – an exposure of Germany's war plans which was very influential and even quoted by Winston Churchill, published in 1934. Woodman would suggest to Meredith that his knowledge would be *of great use* to 'the cause'.[5] This confirmed the 1934 Secret Service's view which was recorded as: 'It was considered, by those in a position to know, that Meredith had information in his possession which would be *of great use* to a foreign power.'[6]

Dorothy Woodman was a key figure in Meredith's recruitment. In her UDC role, she was closely watched by the Security Services, who (rightly) believed she was a Soviet agent. The Security Service wrote, 'one of her callers resulting from the publication of *Hitler Rearms* was a man who was either French or German'.[7] According to Woodman he, 'particularly asked to see an expert in Meredith's subject, namely the remote control of aircraft'.[8] As Meredith had designed the Queen Bee he was clearly their man.

In later 1935 the forty-year-old Frederick William Meredith married the eighteen-year-old Margaret Gwendoline Barnard (born 28 December 1918) in Aldershot Parish Church. This marriage was not popular with Meredith's brother-in-law whose views were reported to and recorded by the Security Services. Petty Officer Barnard told (unaware) an informant: 'Meredith is a Communist, is well supplied with money and has been in the habit of visiting Russia. Petty Officer Barnard and his wife are not very friendly with Meredith and his wife, who is Petty Officer Barnard's sister, because Barnard does not like Meredith or his Communistic views.'[9] The marriage, however, proved happy, according to the Security Service reports, and produced three children.

The English public school educated, car owning Meredith, for all his Bolshevik tendencies, could seem remarkably bourgeois. Before the war he married in a home county parish church and he played golf with the Aero Golfing Society. Post-war records show he was a member of the Wengen Curling Club and the Cheltenham Croquet Club – in the Championship of Ireland, 1967, he beat one Lady Fitzgerald. An RAE colleague, Calvert, had not liked Meredith in part as he, 'had acquired and cultivated a very cultured accent'.[10] Meredith did not join the Communist Party of Great Britain where he would probably have felt profoundly uncomfortable as a highly educated intellectual working in an advanced scientific institution at a time in the mid-1930s when the Party was aggressively working-class.

The following description by Meredith of his first meeting with a Soviet Intelligence Officer at the turn of 1935 and 1936 is so clichéd as to be laughable:

> Dorothy Woodman suggested that his knowledge would be of great use to the cause. She visited Russia and, upon her return, fixed it with Meredith to go to Dublin. He was to meet a man who would be carrying a certain newspaper and wearing something in his

buttonhole, at a pre-arranged time and date at the gates of Trinity College, Dublin. At this meeting Meredith's *bona fides* were discussed, and it was affably arranged that he should pass on such information as came his way.

The man he met was, 'definitely Russian, but spoke fair English'. He is described as born about 1895, 5'7" or 8", broad shoulders, heavy build, wore spectacles that may have been rimless'.[11] His Soviet contact appeared to know how to manage Meredith's sensitivities: 'He was not pressed to take any positive steps to make enquiries or the like, but merely to advise on scientific questions within his knowledge.'[12] Woodman disputed Meredith's recollection as to how he first met Soviet intelligence. She explained how:

> She insisted that she had made no arrangements at any time for a *rendezvous* in Dublin. She felt that Meredith had been talking wildly, for she felt sure that had there been such a *rendezvous* to which she was privy, the fact would clearly have stuck in her mind. She explained that she is more Irish than British and that anything connected with Dublin, or the Irish, would remain clearly in her mind.[13]

A security services report later summarised the situation. 'Ernest David Weiss, formerly German, but since 1946 a naturalised British subject, confessed that from 1932 until the outbreak of the war [1939] he was working in this country as a member of a Soviet espionage network.' Two such persons were, according to Weiss, Major [Wilfred] Vernon and a colleague of the latter at Farnborough, one Frederick William Meredith.

The first attempted meeting ended in failure. Weiss had apparently waited for Meredith and Vernon on the wrong side of Frimley Green. It was, appropriately, a dark night and raining at the time.[14] The actual first meeting with these men took place in May 1936 at Farnham:

> Weiss, under the name of Walter Lock, was introduced to them by his then spymaster, an individual known to him merely as Harry II. At this meeting, arrangements were made for the supply by Meredith and Major Vernon to Harry II of technical information from the RAE. The ultimate destination of any material so collected from Major Vernon and Meredith was in terms acknowledged to be the USSR.[15]

Meredith saw himself as an honourable spy. '[He] decided to exercise certain moral scruples and to pass on nothing which was not a child of his brain. He felt no wrong was done by sharing his own ideas, inventions and the like, with his Russian friends.'[16] It might be noted now that: 'He resolutely refused to become an active spy, confining his disclosures always to matters arising from his own inventive mind.'[17] The range of areas embraced by that 'inventive mind' were, however, vast indeed.

Meredith spy activity 1936 to 1939

In late 1936 RAE employees F.W. Meredith and Wilfred Vernon were under Security Service's suspicion but there was no inkling they were active Soviet spies. 'In November 1936 a summary of Vernon's activities was prepared and the Security Services decided that there was not sufficient information to put up a note to the Air Ministry to ask for the discharge of Meredith.'[18] The following year the pair continued to attract attention. In January 1937 the Security Service's informant at RAE reported that: 'Meredith and others were forming an extreme left book-club and discussion circle, and that Vernon was local recruiting agent for the International Column of the Madrid Forces. It was said that "he works through a man outside Golders Green station".'[19] That year Meredith met the Soviet spy ring handler, Harry II, in Paris, 'Through Weiss he made it known that he and Mrs Meredith were visiting Paris during 1937. An arrangement was made for Meredith to meet Harry II in the Florian Restaurant'. The handler's gallantry was noted, 'Meredith has a clear recollection that he last saw Harry II in 1937 when he turned up at Farnham out of the blue with a bottle of perfume for Mrs Meredith'.[20]

That year Vernon and Meredith were nearly found out and events set in motion that precipitated Meredith leaving the RAE. Members of the fascists, Blackshirts, one had worked at RAE, objected to a left-wing study group organised by Vernon. 'On 18 March 1937 Vernon's house was burgled and this caused some consternation amongst the ranks at RAE including Meredith.'[21]

> What he [Vernon] was worried about was that the thief had stolen some secret technical publications which he had, with his superior's permission, taken home to study. He was also worried because in his hut he had an enormous amount of left-wing literature. Vernon was subsequently prosecuted and defended by D.M. Pritt, to whom, according to Meredith, who was in Vernon's confidence, he told the full story of his dealings with Weiss' [Soviet] organisation.[22]

The Security Service report records: 'Vernon must have got from Meredith some of the documents which he had in his hut; he [Weiss] did not think this came out at the trial, but thought Meredith's subsequent departure from RAE might have been due to this.'[23] After Vernon's arrest Weiss was assigned a new controller in place of Harry II, or Henri Robinson, born in Belgium of Russian and Polish descent. (Robinson's arrest in 1942 by the Gestapo would have significant consequences for Meredith and Vernon.)

Vernon was convicted and fined £50 for 'retaining information' and 'not taking proper care of information' under the Official Secrets Act. Meredith reported in post-war interrogation that Vernon's £50 was paid by his defence counsel D.M. Pritt QC MP, who defended the Soviet show trials, and had been told by Vernon he was a spy. Pritt asserted an entirely innocent explanation for Vernon's possession of classified documents: thereby advancing a defence, false by his client's admission contrary to professional ethics.

At this time the Security Services recorded Meredith's third visit to the Soviet Union:

> On 24.4.37 Meredith and his wife left London for Leningrad on the Soviet vessel *'Felix Dzerzhinsky'* to attend the First of May celebrations in Moscow. Through the Air Ministry we were told the Superintendent of the RAE, who said that he knew Meredith, would be going to Russia, but saw no objection to his doing so. Meredith and his wife returned to the U.K. on the *'Sibier'* on 23.5.37.[24]

Meredith and his wife were given VIP treatment in the Soviet Union. 'Having made arrangements through Weiss they were picked up and entertained at the May Day Parade in Moscow. In addition, Meredith heard from the anonymous Russian who picked him up that his material was safely reaching the USSR through his contacts.'[25] Also: 'Meredith told Weiss on his return from Russia that he had been treated with great respect – taken out of the passport queue and so on. He was taken to Moscow and met a great many technical people.'[26] But 'in view of his wife's non-political attitude and her anxiety to treat the trip wholly as a holiday, they quickly went off to South Russia to the seaside, instead of spending the time as he would have preferred making scientific contacts in Moscow'. [27]

Meredith visited Moscow at the time of the show trials between 1936 and 1938 of former senior Communist Party leaders accused of conspiring with fascist and capitalist powers. Vernon's defence lawyer and Member of Parliament D.N. Pritt, mentioned above, commented: 'Once again the more faint-hearted socialists are beset with doubts and anxieties', but 'once again we can feel confident that when the smoke has rolled away from the battlefield of controversy it will be realized that the charge was true, the confessions correct and the prosecution fairly conducted.'[28]

In November 1937 the Security Services were told by an informant about RAE fears of a 'Domestic Enquiry' into leakage and slackness at the RAE. There were calls for Vernon to resign before he can be called to give evidence at any enquiry. The majority of those 'in the know' expressed concern about Meredith's actions and likely future.[29] It is not clear to what extent Meredith jumped or was pushed into leaving the RAE. He explained his actions in his resignation letter in terms of opposition to Government foreign policy:

> About a month ago I told you that I would take no further action about my resignation for a month, in order to avail myself of the fullest consideration. Since that date the developments in the international situation, following the resignation of Eden, have given much support to the view I took of the present [Government's] policy. Finally, the blatant support of the Fascist conquest of Spain, by the Prime Minister in tonight's debate, creates a situation in which I feel that I cannot conscientiously work for the Government.[30]

The Security Services duly noted:

> Meredith resigned from the RAE on 28 April 1938 and soon afterwards took a post with S. Smith & Son Ltd. Smiths were then closely associated with Henry Hughes & Son Ltd., who were carrying out confidential work for the Air Ministry, such as automatic pilots, automatic bombsights and certain accessories for pilotless (Queen Bee) aircraft. The automatic pilot [for the Queen Bee] was marketed by S. Smith & Sons and manufactured for them by Henry Hughes. Meredith was of course the co-inventor of this automatic pilot.[31]

The Security Services decided not to alert Smiths:

> We are inclined to agree that no warning about the Official Secrets Act should be given. Actually, he will have less opportunity now to acquire really secret information than he has had in the past: perhaps 'acquire' is not the correct word, for much of the secret information in his possession emanates from his own brain.

A letter to Colonel J. Harker (MI5) of 10 May 1938 showed Meredith was still much valued. 'I gather from our technical people that they still hope to take advantage of Meredith's knowledge, and it is probable that S. Smith & Son may become of increasing importance to the Department now that they have taken Meredith into their employ.'[32]

On 16 May 1938 another Security Service letter from Harker concluded:

> I think it is most fortunate that Meredith has left the RAE and [I] do not consider that any opportunity should be offered to him of re-entering Government service. In view of his valuable technical knowledge, I can quite understand that the position is a difficult one but hope that your technical branch will bear in mind in any future dealings with Meredith that he cannot be regarded as a loyal British subject.[33]

After Meredith joined Smiths his handler continued to see him. 'Weiss continued to meet Meredith spasmodically. The latter said there was little he could do, except occasionally give Weiss copies of a bombsight he was developing commercially for Smiths.'[34] (Earlier, Meredith appears to have given RAE material on bomb aiming. 'The only document that Meredith purloined from RAE was a lantern slide of the schematic of an automatic bombsight. This disclosure by Meredith caused him the greatest personal anxiety.'[35]) 'He did continue to provide information and answer such problems as were posed on his own subject, and these were always day-to-day improvements of a highly technical character.'[36] Weiss reported the 'last business meeting rendezvous' as somewhere in the summer of 1939.

After leaving the RAE Meredith continued to live in Farnham and ran the Left-Wing Book Club there.[37] Other fellow revolutionaries were deradicalized. In 1938 the informant 'Hops' reported Meredith said: 'Lockspeiser has his family to consider and is now lost to the movement.'[38] (Indeed many revolutionaries became pillars of the establishment. Those asked to consider the Meredith problem in 1948 included, 'Sir Ben Lockspeiser, Sir Alex Coryton, Air Vice-Marshal Cuckney and Mr Gardner, [who] are all aware that some suspicion attaches to Meredith'.[39])

Quality of information supplied

Looking at the information provided to the Soviets, Vernon's material was risible. 'On one occasion he [Weiss] received from Vernon a set of blueprints of an Avro-Anson.'[40] The Anson was a simple aircraft of no technical interest. While it seems unlikely that Vernon provided much of value to the Soviets himself, the situation was different in the case of Meredith. According to Dorothy Woodman, who played a crucial part in Meredith's recruitment, a Soviet agent, following Meredith's visit to the Soviet Union, had 'particularly asked to see an expert in Meredith's subject, namely the remote control of aircraft'.[41] Meredith had designed the Queen Bee unmanned remotely controlled seaplane. Meredith's handler Weiss recorded: 'Meredith always provided details of current developments to Weiss. This was his special subject. Details of the successful efforts to make the Queen Bee type of target aircraft with remote control was perhaps the most interesting information obtained by him.'[42] There are two references to bomb aiming equipment. Before joining Smiths Industries: 'The only document that Meredith purloined from RAE was a lantern slide of the schematic of an automatic bombsight.'[43] After joining Smiths Industries: 'Weiss continued to meet Meredith spasmodically. The latter said there was little he could do, except occasionally give Weiss copies of a bombsight he was developing commercially for Smiths.'[44] Meredith's visit to the Soviet Union in 1935 may have led to him being noted as both a possible and valuable recruit. As seen in 1937, Meredith, 'was taken to Moscow and met a great many technical people'.[45] 'Weiss thinks that Meredith's visit to Russia may have been of much more value to the Russians than any material he passed to André.'[46]

Chapter 15

Meredith – war years

Meredith's contribution to the British effort during the war has been largely overlooked. In terms of its ubiquity in the air war it was massive.

Autopilot

The RAE Mk IV autopilot was used in Wellingtons, Stirlings, Halifaxes, Sunderlands, and Lancasters. This was difficult and expensive to build as it incorporated two gyroscopes and production did not exceed 900 sets a month. Therefore, the simpler Mk VIII was developed with a single gyroscope using Meredith's patents. By 1943 production was 50% above the Mk IV and it became the basic installation in Lancasters and Lincolns. Meredith wrote:

> Perhaps the first autopilot to adopt this solution [single gyro three axis] successfully was the British Mk VIII which was based on my patents and extensively used in the Second World War. In this case, by selecting an inclined axis in the plane of symmetry or the insensitive axis, the ailerons, which controlled the steering as well as the banking, responded to either saw or roll.[1]

Bombsights

Britain, as seen, started the war without a modern divebomb sight as Meredith's ADBS had not been sufficiently developed. Much more seriously overall, the country did not have a modern level bombsight. In early 1939 the RAE staff designed and tested a stabiliser for the tachometric automatic bombsight ABS Mk II, so making the SABS Mk II. The tachometric un-stabilised automatic bombsights (ABS Mk I and II) were, however, operationally non-functional. (Eventually the tachometric SABS was successfully stabilised, but it was only used for special operations.)

At the beginning of the Second World War, the un-stabilised un-automatic vector bombsight, the CSBS Mk IX vector bombsight with the clumsy Azimuth Bracket was the RAF's operational bombsight. The bombsight problem was resolved from an unexpected direction involving Meredith's concepts and designs. As seen, in 1937, Meredith had written a paper, *Memorandum on High Altitude Bombsights*.[2] This pointed in the right direction, particularly as Bomber Command had learned very painfully that daylight operations were too dangerous and switched to night bombing. Also in 1939, Patrick Blackett (1897-1974) emerged as a key figure. Blackett was an experimental physicist who would win the Nobel prize for Physics in 1948 for his investigation of cosmic rays. During the Second World War he developed operations research which resulted in often counter-intuitive but effective analyses and solutions of military problems. Blackett designed a simple stabilised bombsight for anti-bomber bombs. Soon after the war began he joined the RAE to continue his bombsight work. By the end of 1939 Blackett and Sir Henry Tizard advocated developing Blackett's sight for low-level ship bombing. In August 1940 Blackett left RAE, but the RAE continued to develop his sight. It was tested in July 1941 as the Mk XIV and became Bomber Command's area bombsight.

In 1940 there was still no working automated dive bombsight. (Notwithstanding obsolete Blackburn Skuas managed on 10 April the 'major achievement' of sinking the *Königsberg*, 'the first major warship to be sunk by divebombing alone'.[3]) The ADBS had not passed the trial stage by mid-1941 and the results were deemed disappointing. Meredith rejected the critical RAE analysis. In the light of factual errors, Bowen reported, 'we have had a fairly protracted argument with Mr Meredith of Smiths and as a result we are all agreed (RAE included) that the mechanism deserves further trial in an aircraft which is more suitable to diving attack than are the Skua and Swordfish'.[4] Trials in mid-1943 in a Vultee Vengeance dive bomber proved unsatisfactory. (The Vengeance was used effectively by the British in Burma where sighting was still done late in the war by the 'Mark I eyeball'.) Marsh, in his unpublished PhD, *The Air Ministry and the Bomb Dropping Problem,* attributes the failure of the ADBS to Air Ministry 'vacillation' and the lack of effective involvement of Smiths.

> The flight testing was effected as a one-off affair, conducted without any involvement of the design experts at Smiths. The ensuing acrimonious debate reflected a situation in which the performance of the sight was clearly inadequate, but in which the designers had no opportunity interactively to effect the necessary iterative improvements essential to improve the sight's performance.[5]

Marsh concludes:

> Nevertheless, I claim that the ADBS was one of the most significant British bombsight developments of the Second World War, because it was causative in the invention and development of Meredith's air-jet and chopper-block pneumatic servomechanism, a mechanism which played an important role in the development of the SABS and the Mk XIV bombsight.[6]

Thus, Meredith's instruments were used in the Bomber Command offensive which flattened German cities in the second half of the war. Ironically, his pioneering work on the automatic divebomb sight was never used operationally.

Gunsight

In 1938 Meredith and Gardner patented a gyroscopic sight *Improvements in or relating to controlling aircraft* (Meredith and Gardner, GB 576,359, application October 1938, publication January 1940). They 'proposed a stabilised gyroscopic sight for use in an aeroplane such that when a turn is required the sight is rotated, the aeroplane being turned at a rate depending upon the extent of the original movement of the sight'.[7]

It might be noted that the RAE would play a critical role in the development of an extremely successful gunsight first used in late 1943. In 1936, Dr L.B. Cunningham, while working for the RAE, conceived of using the gyroscope's resistance to rotation to compensate for deflection. In 1938 M. Hancock at the Royal Air Force Fighting Development Unit independently proposed the use of gyroscopes. His idea was brought to the attention of the RAE, which developed the Gyroscopic Gunsight (GGS). [8] The resulting Ferranti gunsight and the US the K-14 gunsight, based on the RAE GGS, were installed respectively on the Spitfire Mk VIII and IX and the P-51D Mustang and markedly improved kill rates. The pilot dialled in the enemy wingspan, fed in the target range and got the wingtips of his target lined up on the ring projected on the gunsight.

Instruments

Autopilot

In 1942 Meredith applied for patent GB 576,248 for an electric motor (using the hysteresis effect where magnetization lags behind the magnetizing force) which recognised that while such motors had many advantages (smooth and silent operation) they were very inefficient.[9] (In 1949 Meredith gave a paper, *The Modern Autopilot,* to the Royal Aeronautical Society *The Modern Autopilot A Dissertation on the Fundamentals of Modern Autopilot Design*, reported in *Flight* 13 January 1949. He 'reviewed the development of the hysteresis servomotor, an achievement made in the face of established authoritative theories as to the impracticality of such work'.[10]) These would be used in all-electronic Smiths Electric Pilot 1 (SEP1) launched after the war in September 1945.

Tuning fork gyroscope

Also, in 1942 Meredith registered *Improvements in or relating to devices for detecting or measuring rate of turn* (Meredith GB 611,005, application July 1942, publication October 1948) which proposed a gyroscope device for measuring rate-of-turn, in the form of a vibrating tuning fork where the vibrating tines detect coriolis (inertial) forces.[11] Such vibrating structure gyroscopes, once developed, are simpler, being bearingless, than rotor gyroscopes and apart from avionics have many uses in modern technology. At the time the urgent need for autopilots meant Meredith continued to focus on rotor gyroscopes but the tuning fork concept was flight tested towards the end of the Second World War as the following documents revealed.

> Sir. Your report on the vibrating gyro reminds me that just after the war F.W. Meredith, then head of S. Smith & Sons research department developed a gonitachometer [instrument allowing an object to be rotated to a precise angular position] to such a stage that we did some flight trials with it at the Royal Aircraft Establishment in 1946. The urgent need, both military and civil, for a British automatic pilot, led Meredith to concentrate on the development of more orthodox rotor type rate gyros which was thought to have fewer problems at zero stability than the tuning fork system. Certainly the tuning fork system was dropped with great regret for both Meredith and the late James Sudworth.[12]

Also,

> It is of interest to note that some original research into such a possibility was conducted in the UK some twenty-five years ago under the direction of Mr F.W. Meredith. The device produced and actually flight tested in the closing years of the Second World War was a single-tine version of the so called 'tuning-fork gyroscope'.[13]

Spy activity

In August 1939 the Ribbentrop-Molotov pact was signed. Many earlier Soviet sympathisers were alienated. On the outbreak of war in September 1939 Meredith was evacuated with his firm to Cheltenham. In 1940 Meredith was recorded by the Security Services as regularly reading the *Daily Worker*.[14] Meredith again met his pre-war handler in 1941.

> After Weiss' release from internment, when he was serving in the Pioneer Corps, he found himself at Reading Station having missed his train connection. He says he decided on the spur of the moment to go to Cheltenham and look up Meredith [who earlier had sent him his address]. He telephoned to say he was coming, and Meredith met him at the station. They spent the evening together, but Weiss sensed a rather strained atmosphere.[15]

Meredith remarked that the behaviour of Russia in allying itself to Germany in 1939 'was beyond his comprehension' before Russia's entry into the war in 1941. Weiss said he had not seen Meredith since. In 1943, again the Security Services noted that he held left-wing views.[16] That year he was under consideration for employment by the Ministry of Supply for additional [Extra-Mural] research to his work at Smiths

Industries. A minute of 24 September 1943 recorded that while at the RAE he 'came under serious suspicion for betraying secret information'.[17] On 25 October 1943, a further minute from Michael Serpell of MI5 said Meredith 'is so highly qualified I do not think we can suggest that his employment should be in any way limited'.[18]

Arguably few men made a more ubiquitous contribution to air war over Western Europe in terms of what, and the sheer numbers of what, was incorporated in aircraft. Meredith's seminal 1935 ARC paper (published 1936) had two elements: the treatment of radiators in ducts as heat engines and the requirement to exploit exhaust gas momentum. The Spitfire was the first aircraft to have a cooling duct system specifically designed to produce the 'Meredith effect'. Meredith recommended that the design which he called 'not good' could be improved by wind tunnel testing, which it was. Indeed, while Meredith was at the RAE's Aerodynamics unit a systematic investigation of particular aspects of cooling ducts was instituted as well as those of specific aircraft. After Meredith's and Capon's papers virtually all inline engined powered fighters were designed with ducted radiators of very varying efficiency. All powerful inline engines had exhaust stubs designed to exploit exhaust gas momentum. The Hurricane incorporated a lip on the cooling duct to divert the boundary layer in 1936.

As will be seen the US Mustang fighter embodied all aspects of Meredith's aerodynamic drag reduction and thrust addition concepts: ducts as heat engines, boundary layer lips, and exhaust gas momentum. The Lockheed P-38 J incorporated a boundary layer bypass. The first US production jet fighter the Lockheed P-80 Shooting Star used a boundary layer bypass to resolve the problem of duct entry for a jet engine.

Remarkably, Meredith's contributions included not only aerodynamics but also instruments. All larger British aircraft incorporated his designs in the form of Mk IV and Mk VII autopilot. Meredith advocated the use of vector in preference to tachometric bombsights. He suggested the use of a reflector mechanism to reduce its length. Both of these features were part of the successful stabilised Mk XIV sight. Meredith's air jet and chopper servo mechanism was also an important feature of the design.

Any measure of importance of a particular individual as to the outcome of a war is fraught with complexities. Not least most inventions are of their time and if one individual had not made them then, given that they satisfied a pre-existing requirement, someone else would have done so. One point, however, that might be made about Meredith is that it is questionable whether any other scientist would have had the original insight that the tiny amount of energy converted from a heat to a kinetic form could be sufficient at high speeds to overcome cooling drag. A second point is the extraordinary ubiquity of the use of Meredith's ideas across both aerodynamics and avionics. The sheer range of the use of his inventions and the number of aircraft they were used in is remarkable. Literally tens of thousands of fighters used ducted radiators of which the Spitfire was the pioneer and the Mustang the apogee. All British bombers used his autopilots and after the mid-war bombsight design followed his recommended reflector vector concept and incorporated his air jet and chopper servo system. And a third point was that Meredith's wartime work on hysteresis motors and solid-state tuning fork gyroscopes would have a huge impact on the post-war world.

Chapter 16

Meredith – post-1945

Scientific work

During the Second World War Meredith continued actively to work on new ideas which could not be fully developed because the focus was on rendering functional existing technologies. Some, like hysteresis motors, were immediately incorporated post-war into new systems. Others, like solid-state gyroscopes, were simply too far ahead of their time and would not be developed for years or even decades.

Rate/rate autopilot incorporating hysteresis servo motors
In September 1945 Smiths launched the Smiths Electric Pilot 1 (SEP1), the first electric three axis automatic pilot which incorporated three gyroscopes. (Meredith's previous autopilots had incorporated one or two.) This was the Smiths Mk 9 in RAF use.

> To meet the British Air Staff requirements both for civil and military aircraft, the Research Organization of Smiths Aircraft Instruments, Ltd was entrusted with the development of an all-electric automatic pilot system. Under the leadership of Mr F.W. Meredith, who has been connected with British automatic pilot development since 1925, the Smiths' team decided to approach the problem from an entirely new angle, starting afresh to take the fullest advantage of the vast electrical field plus anything that could be gained by a comprehensive survey of the latest American and German types. The result is the SEP1.[1]

Three identical gyros measured the rate of turn about the vertical and two horizontal axes and separate servomotors controlled rudder, ailerons, and elevators. It was an advanced system for several reasons.

1) This was the first British all electric autopilot. 'Smiths contend that discarding the old hydraulic and pneumatic operation and substituting modern developments in electrical techniques has resulted in increased flexibility, increased reliability, and freedom from maintenance.'[2]
2) It was the first autopilot successfully to incorporate the rate/rate system. 'The rate/rate system provides for servomotors [which

114

electrically push or rotate an object with great precision] to actuate each control surface at a rate appropriate to the rate of rotation of the aircraft about the relevant axis of motion, rather than to an extent relative to the extent of displacement in yaw, pitch, or roll. This permits a very high degree of response and a reduction in time lag such as to allow the use of high-geared controls without incurring hunting.'[3]

3) The servomotors were pioneering, being electric hysteresis motors which developed torque due to the magnetic hysteresis, or lag, loss induced in its permanent magnet alloy rotor. Such motors allowed for especially smooth operation but had low efficiency. '[Three] identical, interchangeable servomotors are used for rudder, aileron, and rudder control. These motors feature high torque, low inertia, and almost immediate response.'[4] A practicable hysteresis motor was invented in 1916 by Henry Ellis Warren which was simple but inefficient. In 1942 Meredith applied for a patent GB 576,248 for a hysteresis motor which recognised that while it had many advantages it was very inefficient and sought to resolve the problem.[5] (In 1949 Meredith gave a paper, *The Modern Autopilot,* to the Royal Aeronautical Society. *The Modern Autopilot A Dissertation on the Fundamentals of Modern Autopilot Design*, reported in *Flight* 13 January 1949. He 'reviewed the development of the hysteresis servomotor, an achievement made in the face of established authoritative theories as to the impracticality of such work'.[6])

4) This autopilot was developed so it could be coupled to radio landing approaches and formed the basis of blind landing experiments. In 1949 Meredith gave a paper to the Royal Aeronautical Society on *The modern autopilot* where anticipated safe blind approaches using radio and SEP1 would be practicable.[7]

Tuning fork gyroscope

As seen, in 1942 Meredith registered a patent GB 611,005, which was not published until 1948, that proposed a gyroscope device for measuring rate-of-turn, in the form of a vibrating tuning fork.[8] Meredith was not able to continue work in this area but clearly it intrigued him. In 1949 he wrote an article in *Nature* pointing out *halteres*, small oscillating structures on some insects, enabled them to stabilise themselves in flight.[9] This was the inspiration behind the tuning fork gyroscope. On 7 May 1957 Meredith gave a very warmly received lecture titled *Invention and Nature* for the Annual Lecture of the Measurement and Control Section. He pointed out man can learn from the achievements of nature. He highlighted the *halteres* in flies, rod like vibrators behind the wings, which act like alternating gyroscope stabilisers. He gave 'a detailed account of the efforts of various inventors, including himself, to make use of this same principle (that of Foucault's pendulum) to stabilize aircraft. Man has here been less successful than nature'.[10]

Missiles

After the war the future was increasingly seen to lie with unmanned guided missiles and Meredith rapidly made Smiths central to development in this field. (Meredith had been the leading light in pre-war unmanned aircraft stabilisation and guidance systems with his work on the Larynx and Queen Bee.) In 1953 a report by Sir Stewart Mitchell, the Controller Guided Weapons and Electrics (CGWL) stated:

> It would be well to reiterate the immense value of Meredith from the technological aspect of our guided weapon work. He is quite unique in this country and his value to us is extremely high. I would not say he is indispensable – nobody is, but it is fair to say that he is the leading expert in this country on matters such as automatic pilots for aircraft and guided missiles, etc. [11]

The Guided Weapons Directorate (GWD) was created after the war to develop rocket-based armaments by the Ministry of Supply. In 1947 the Defence Research Policy Committee (DRPC) started four missile programmes intended to reach service in 1957: these were, Red Hawk, Blue Boar, Seaslug, and Red Heathen. Meredith was known to have become involved in the development of the first two, respectively an air-to-air missile and a television guided glide bomb, through Security Services records.

Red Hawk was a drone aircraft in the form of a small swept wing fighter, powered by solid fuel rocket motors to be carried in a recessed bay of the mother aircraft which did not attract RAF interest. The initial development contract was given to Gloster Aircraft in 1947. The Red Hawk air guided weapon project was granted to Folland Aircraft (in 1937 Henry Folland left Gloster Aircraft) which was expected to sub-contract to Smiths for work on an electrical guidance unit.[12] The Red Dean project was split off from the Red Hawk in mid-1951 to be developed by Folland, which gave it up in November 1951. Vickers took over development of this version from Folland. Neither the Red Hawk nor Dean were successful.

The Blue Boar, whose development contract was won by Vickers, was a guided glide bomb with a guidance system designed to hit moving targets from high altitude. The nose had an EMI television camera and the rear a stabilised antenna which sent television images to the mother aircraft and received commands from it. It was designed to fall at an angle of 40 degrees above the horizon. A gyroscopic system was used to produce a 'datum' point in the television signal that represented that desired angle. The autopilot was designed by Smiths. It was eventually dropped in 1954 as it was too large for naval strike aircraft.

Fighter aircraft stabilisation

There is a hint that Meredith was continuing to develop innovative ideas for manned aircraft. In 1952 he had suggested to the Ministry of Supply – a year earlier – a new scheme in connection with the stabilisation of fighter aircraft which had been well received and attracted British and American interest.[13]

Meredith uncovered

In 1942, Henri Robinson was arrested by the Gestapo in Paris with files that were analysed after the war, known as the 'Robinson papers'. The *Rote Kapella* spy ring was broken and Robinson executed in Germany the following year. In the July 1945 General Election Wilfrid Vernon was elected to Parliament as a Labour MP, although having been a member of the Communist Party of Great Britain he was to be counted as one of thirty CPGB Labour Party sleepers. Astonishingly, the Robinson Papers were lost, having been captured by the Gestapo during the war, and it was not until 1947 that they were properly studied. A Security Services report summarised the situation after an interrogation. 'Ernest David Weiss, formerly German, but since 1946 a naturalised British subject, confessed that from 1932 until the outbreak of the war [1939] he was working in this country as a member of a Soviet espionage network.' Two such persons were, according to Weiss, Major [Wilfred] Vernon and a colleague of the latter at Farnborough, one Frederick William Meredith.

In January 1948, Meredith was 'denounced by Weiss as one of the individuals from whom he was receiving secret material for transmission to Soviet spy masters'.[14] At the same time Meredith had attracted the attention of the managing director of Smiths, who passed to the Security Services Meredith's name as a crypto-communist or fellow traveller.[15] It was agreed, however, that 'Meredith was best left alone'.[16]

First interrogations – September 1948 to March 1949
In September 1948 the Security Services considered Meredith had to be investigated more thoroughly after he was heard, 'taking the usual Communist line of laying all the blame for the existing international unrest at the feet of "British-American imperialism" and was generally extremely outspoken in his comments'.[17] Also, the Guided Weapons Directorate (GWD) wished to place a secret contract with Bristol to sub-contract autopilot work to Smiths Instruments, meaning Meredith would be heavily involved. After efforts to stop the sub-contract going to Smiths the GWD said it was very doubtful whether any other suitable sub-contractor for the autopilot work could be found. The Security Services were told:

> Mr Meredith is of such outstanding ability in the field of aerodynamics and auto-control that from technical considerations alone there is no one in this country whom the Department would be more anxious to employ. It was stressed from past experience of the quality of this man's work the solution would probably be far tidier from the design point of view than that of any other designer.[18]

On 1 October, after investigations confirmed Meredith was a Soviet agent from 1936 until 1939, there were discussions as to whether to tell Smiths.[19] In December the decision was made – as Meredith's exceptional technical ability was required in connection with an important and secret sub-contract proposed to be given to Smiths and he was basically indispensable despite open communist views – to interrogate him to find out his current views.[20] The case was sufficiently important that the Prime Minister, Clement Atlee, was consulted. The interrogations were to be conducted by Jim Skardon of MI5, who would go on to successfully interrogate Klaus Fuchs, but fail with Kim Philby, Anthony Blunt and John Cairncross. He also interrogated two women and was partially successful with Edith Tudor-Hart (Edith Suschitzky), but also failed with Ursula Beurton (Agent Sonya, or Colonel Ursula Kuczynski).

Meredith was interrogated on 23 December. The process was conducted with quite extraordinary civility and lack of security.[21] (Skardon's report is so detailed that it is often possible to recreate dialogue.) He was summoned to Gloucester Constabulary Police Headquarters. Skardon told him he was a 'representative of the Security Services. He asked various questions confirming Meredith's identity and when challenged by Meredith as to whether he had the right was informed by Skardon that he had a 'perfect right' to do so. 'I told him that the one question to which I required an answer, and the whole purpose of the interview might be found in it, was "where did Meredith stand in relation to the State in an emergency".'

> I then said to him: 'Are you then a Communist?' Meredith answered evasively, saying that he supposed he might be, but went on: 'Are you seeking to control my opinions or those of people holding Communist views? Do you arrogate to yourselves the right to enquire into my political opinions?' I told him I had no right to enquire into his political beliefs but that I should certainly make enquiries on behalf of the Security Services into those of his actions which tended to involve the security of the State and made it clear to him that I was enquiring into his past conduct.

Skardon then made it clear he had 'positive knowledge of his past conduct'. By this point Meredith was rattled: 'It should be explained that at this time Meredith was clearly a very frightened person, in spite of the belligerent stand which he took.' Skardon confronted him with a photo of Weiss, who Meredith denied recognising despite being told that he had been in regular contact with him between 1936 and 1939. After various discussions of issues of legal advice which would be seen as an admission of guilt, Skardon reiterated the 'original question, that is to know where Meredith stood in relation to the State in the event of an emergency'. Following various hypothetical questions Skardon recounted: 'Meredith was clearly on the point of breaking but was obviously uncomfortable at the Police Headquarters and asked whether the interview had to take place there.'

There follows what might seem extraordinary considerateness, but it worked. Firstly, Meredith was uncomfortable at the police station and asked if they could go to his home, 'if that would be convenient'. Secondly, as 'Meredith thought this idea was desirable,' he asked Skardon, 'to allow him to go ahead to warn his wife and make arrangements'. Thirdly, Skardon had no means of transport to Meredith's house, and Meredith 'offered to take me but needed a few minutes to explain to his wife what was happening'. And fourthly, at 6pm they went in Meredith's car to his house in Cheltenham: 'where I met Mrs Meredith, a very pleasant young woman, his daughter and nephew. I allowed him a few minutes to make explanations to his wife and he took advantage of that opportunity to arrange that the family should go off to a cinema, leaving us alone … except for the youngest child who was already in bed.'

His family off to the cinema or tucked up in bed, Meredith then immediately agreed that he knew Weiss and explained his motivation, which was the realisation that Germany would attack Russia and having defeated Russia would turn on the West. He initially refused to name Dorothy Woodman as the person who had recruited him, but Skardon said he knew her involvement which Meredith then conceded. Meredith insisted he only provided the Russians with ideas he himself had generated. There followed outlining of Meredith's visits to Moscow and his meetings with his handlers.

Meredith now volunteered his answer to the question:

> As to where he would stand in the event of an emergency in the following way, he said that in any war with Russia – he would blame the United States for forcing it if GI Jo can be persuaded to fight and us for allowing this country to be their unsinkable aircraft carrier; he would just quietly wait for the end. He thinks that he would probably be a Conscientious Objector. He does not think he can make tools to fight a people whose efforts he admires.

Skardon recorded an acknowledgement of Meredith's 'big stake in this country and its prosperity' and his love of his work and family. He was loyal to both the country and his employer and was 'no security threat whatsoever at the present time'. Now it seems best of friends:

> Just after 8 pm Meredith and I went off together to have a meal in Cheltenham until about 9.15 pm. During this meal there was a general political discussion and throughout he was advancing the Communist line of thought. We made arrangements for future meetings at which I proposed to exploit him for full details of his association with the Russian Intelligence Service.

The civility and respect demonstrated in the whole process is astonishing. Meredith was fortunate in never having to confront the NKVD or KGB organisations of the country he so admired. Skardon failed dismally with Philby and Agent Sonia. Meredith was not a proactive Soviet agent with a Secret Service background and had no training in resistance to interrogation. He broke quickly and easily. But he probably sensed that with Skardon he was safe and, what might be termed as knowing he was caught red handed, was relieved to confess to someone as considerate as Skardon.

After further discussions Skardon reached the following conclusions:

1) For idealistic motives he [Meredith] undoubtedly lent assistance to the Russians over a period of four years between 1935 and 1939.

2) He has had no contact with them since that date.
3) I feel sure that he has no means of establishing contact.
4) I believe that he has loyalty:
    a) to his family,
    b) to his employers,
    c) to some extent to his country
5) He would certainly be very foolish following this interview to engage upon any espionage activity and I think it unlikely that he ever will.
6) In the event of hostilities breaking out between this country and the Soviet Union, I think that he might easily be a danger to security if left at liberty, but he would make an honest pronouncement of his feelings in that event.

Meredith basically proposed an accord. He 'made the point himself that if the Security Services were satisfied with him, his employer's interests might be best served for them, then their activities might be extended'.[22] This was to do secret work Meredith was aware was in the offing. In a further interrogation on 6 January Meredith was told that there was no intention to prosecute. Within two weeks the decision was made that the government could not afford *not* to employ Meredith, who had a wife and family to maintain and enjoyed his work. On 7 March it was concluded Meredith was not currently associated with the Communist party and unlikely to divulge classified information to Russians. 'Mr Meredith is in a high place in the category of indispensable people. This outweighs the security risk.'[23] At the end of the month the Security Service file was closed as the Ministry of Supply chose to accept the security risk of continuing to employ him.[24]

Second interrogations February 1951 – April 1952
From April 1949 to February 1951 the Security Services heard nothing of Meredith. In March the situation became sensitive again as he was reported as a close friend of a well-off Communist Party election candidate the Hon. Wogan Philipps. Also, Smiths was already working on missile project Blue Boar and on 12 March the Red Hawk air guided weapon project was given to Folland Aircraft, which was expected to sub-contract to Smiths for work on the electrical guidance unit.[25]

Meredith was again interrogated by Skardon on 15 March.[26] Meredith asked if something was worrying the Security Services and was told the Services were always worrying about him and the pressure of international events did not relieve anxieties.[27] Meredith said he had recently discussed the [Red Hawk] contract with Folland and the RAE and would see Vickers to discuss a new contract for Smiths which was only coming to Smiths because of Meredith's position with it.[28] On 20 March, Skardon reported Meredith had recently been to the US and was not seen as a security risk. He was under the impression that he was likely to be chosen to go to the US to discuss the latest Top Secret developments on Red Hawk, where Meredith had been consulted by Folland.

On 25 October 1951 the Conservatives won the general election. Edwin Duncan Sandys, the new Prime Minister Winston Churchill's son-in-law became Minister of Supply. (In 1957 he became notorious when appointed Minister of Defence, he produced the 1957 Defence White Paper which proposed replacing fighters with missiles. The policy, later rescinded, destroyed much of the Britain's aircraft industry.)

Meredith had been to the US recently.[29] The FBI was understood to have certain information about Meredith and it was considered unwise for him to go again to the US to discuss guided missiles. On 22 March 1952, the Security Services concluded that Meredith was still a Marxist but, 'he is not now a very serious one and may well maintain his views more from Irish perversity than from conviction. We are, however, really in the position that if we trust M, it is in our belief in bourgeois honesty and in the face of his past record and his proclaimed Marxist view'.[30] Meredith, however, should not be sent to the US, even if this does not avoid risk of embarrassment with America and kept on Guided Weapon work as he will undoubtedly gain knowledge of US secrets in this field. 'If the Americans were fully aware of his past, they would think that we had committed a grave breach of security and feel that co-operation with us in the field of Guided Missiles was no longer possible.'[31]

The Security Services were caught in a hard place as again it was reiterated that: 'If Meredith is sacked there is literally nobody in the country who can replace him [as] on account of his intimate knowledge of aerodynamics and instruments, he is unique.'[32] Thus, on 6 April, it was concluded that Meredith could continue on guided weapon work, subject to the condition of severe limitation on access to US material of which he was not to be informed.[33] The author lamented, 'It is a great pity that this brilliant man should have this failing. He is unique and if he has to be removed from our scene, I do not know how we would replace him.'[34] Despite the risk and his friendship with a known local communist it was decided to continue to employ him. When considering the risk of defection, on 12 April the extent of British civil protections were made clear: 'No power exists whereby a British subject can be prevented from leaving the country if he wishes to do so, unless evidence exists which will justify his detention under warrant.'[35] Again: 'The plain fact is that a British subject with a head full of knowledge and ideas can leave the country at his own sweet will, and I do not think that any department ought to be allowed to entertain the notion that there is anything which the Security Service can do about it.'[36]

On 26 April, it was decided that Meredith should continue to be used but not have access to US or joint US/UK information.[37] The next day a paper outlined the increasing impossibility of maintaining the agreed line that Meredith should continue secret guided missile work but not be allowed access to US research. This was because he met many people and could draw conclusions from actual US developed products. 'The Americans cannot be prevented from learning that Meredith, of whose security record they are informed, is employed in the Guided Weapons field and if and when they do they are likely to assume that he has access to US information.'[38]

Third Interrogations – September 1951 onwards

On 10 September a visitor to Smiths at Cheltenham reported to the Security Services that Meredith had lost no opportunity during the lunch break to air his views in the Manager's Dining Room. 'These views took the form of declaring that America was preparing for war and followed the Communist line. The presence of visitors did not deter him in any way.'[39] On 26 September 1951 a party of four Americans, two American Air Force Officers and two scientists engaged in a parallel project, were to arrive in the country. They had specifically asked to see Meredith to discuss guided missile developments.[40] The problem was that a meeting would challenge the arrangement whereby Meredith was debarred from US secret information.[41]

On 5 October, after another interrogation,

> Meredith said he was continuously heckled by his colleagues and admitted that in self-defence he had from time to time spoken rather wildly. He was quite prepared to give an undertaking that he would watch his tongue in future and declared that he was not a communist and that he was completely loyal to the Company and to the Country. A special dining room has now been arranged for the four senior men in the factory, which includes Meredith.[42]

On 29 May 1952, the Directorate of Guided Weapons said it was becoming difficult to keep American information from Meredith and sought advice. There existed 'the impression that Meredith in fact had knowledge of a considerable amount of the latest developments, both British and American, in this special field'. Reflecting ironically on the success of light touch surveillance, 'it was therefore possible that the Ministry of Supply Restrictions were so ineffective that Meredith was not aware of them'.[43]

Meredith approached Skardon seeking an interview on 13 December.[44] Two days later a meeting at the Ministry of Supply with the Security Services discussed whether a symposium should go ahead to discuss ideas proposed by Meredith.[45] The head of the Security Services [Roger] Hollis wrote the record. Sir Stewart Mitchell, Controller Guided Weapons and Electrics, did not want the symposium to take place as this would mean that Americans would investigate the security clearance of those taking part. Mitchell and Dr G. Gardner, Directorate of Guided Weapons (Research and Development, DGW (R&D)) had recently visited Smiths and Meredith made no secret of his dislike of the Americans. Mitchell thought Meredith's view had not changed but Gardner disagreed. Gardner had joined the RAE in 1926 and worked under Meredith and thought very highly of his scientific abilities.

At the end of this discussion Mitchell gave it as his opinion that the Ministry of Supply should make plans gradually to 'fade' Meredith out of defence work. Gardner on the other hand, thought that his value was so great that he should be retained on the present basis.

He [Gardner] said we were well ahead of all other countries in
Meredith's field and that this was solely due to Meredith. We might be
able to retain our leading position for a year or two without Meredith
while we were still exploiting his ideas, but if we did not have his
continuing services we should undoubtedly fall behind in the future.[46]

On 17 December Skardon reported on his meeting with Meredith.[47] At Claridges
Meredith said he had suggested to the Ministry of Supply a year earlier a new scheme
in connection with the stabilisation of fighter aircraft which had been well received.
He proposed to arrange a symposium to discuss ideas and this was later enlarged to
include US representatives. He had been told by Smiths in a guarded way that problems
had arisen and his presence would be highly undesirable. It was proposed that his
presentation be given by someone else, or his paper be forwarded anonymously, or
be read by a junior in his absence. But Meredith said it was impossible for another
to talk with authority. Meredith supposed that he did not have the necessary security
clearance. Skardon responded that it was a decision for the Ministry of Supply.
Meredith responded that he had been well received in the US and given unrestricted
access and entertained Americans at Cheltenham and received eulogistic letters. He
added an American paper he had obtained from RAE had been withdrawn and he
suggested there was a security ban on his access to American information and officials.
He offered personal assurance to Smiths and the Security Services.

On 31 December 1952 and 6 January 1953 there were yet more reports by
Mitchell and Gardner on Meredith. That by Mitchell stated:[48]

It would be well to reiterate the immense value of Meredith from the
technological aspect of our guided weapon work. He is quite unique
in this country and his value to us is extremely high. I would not
say he is indispensable – nobody is, but it is fair to say that he is the
leading expert in this country on matters such as automatic pilots for
aircraft and guided missiles, etc.

Notwithstanding, Mitchell thought Meredith had a split personality and could tip
over into helping Russia against the Americans. 'I think this is a genuine risk, and
it is the focus of my personal anxiety concerning the whole Meredith situation.'
But on balance it was right to continue the present policy of keeping him in current
work and accepting the security risk. Mitchell advised consulting Gardner whose
subsequent report started by saying he was struck when he joined the RAE in 1926
by Meredith's great scientific ability.[49] He was 'a first-class scientist and a man
extremely interested in political theory and liable to allow his emotions to distort
his judgement in this sphere'. Gardner believed he was not a risk now as 'he is very
pleased at the prospect of becoming a Director of Smiths' new research company'.

By 14 February 1953, however, the Ministry of Supply had decided Meredith
must be removed from secret work.[50] His ideological attachments made him
unsuitable for the secret government guided weapon work on which he was at

present engaged. On 28 February, Hollis wrote a memo saying the Ministry of Supply considered the possibility of getting Meredith a job outside Smith and suggested discussions with Imperial College.[51]

On 30 March, Smiths told the Ministry of Supply Meredith was going on holiday to France with family.[52] An informant reported concerns about Meredith on 28 April as in the past he was a professed communist. He invariably took all his leave at different addresses on the Continent, which has caused the informant to wonder whether he used these opportunities for contacting Communist sympathisers.[53]

An MI6 report said on 5 May:

> Meredith was a self-confessed Russian spy before the war, that he is a Marxist, but as far as we know has never been a member of the Communist Party. And that in spite of this his virtually unique technical skill was considered by the Ministry of Supply to outweigh the obvious security risk of employing him on Secret Government work. Recently the Ministry decided that they can no longer accept this risk and arrangements are being made to take Meredith off Government work.[54]

No specific reason was given and there is no record of any precipitating action by Meredith. The decision may have been taken at ministerial level that consequent on the defections, the risk could no longer be taken to Britain's shaky standing with the US, which had taken a dim view of the defections of Burgess and Maclean in 1951 and in 1954 and would be in the throes of the McCarthy show trials. Everything seems to have been done very discreetly.

The last entry in his third Security Services file KV2/2202 was on 8 June 1953 reporting a meeting that discussed whether Meredith should be included on a list for internment in the event of war or emergency. It was decided not, but the question would be addressed again in six months when a Home Office Committee had discussed how best to deal with, 'communists or communist sympathisers who have access at their place of employment to classified government work.[55] After that nothing is heard of Meredith's government related scientific activities.

Internet searches give random finds which reveal a quietly prosperous and respectable retirement. In 2009 a close relative of Meredith left an internet message saying they knew that he had lost his security clearance and passport but no more or why. Meredith continued to live in Cheltenham. Briefly in the mid-1960s his wife Gwendolyn owned the Montpellier Hotel. He was the star of that most intellectual and cruel game, croquet. In 1967 he reached the semi-finals of the Croquet Championship of Ireland, having beaten one Lady FitzGerald and in 1970 he won Cheltenham's Godfrey Turner Cup. In 1970 his first wife died and he remarried two years later. Meredith himself died in 1980 in Cheltenham. He had no obituaries. His name now largely lives on in a stream of books on the North American Aviation P-51 Mustang which continue to describe at length his eponymous effect while ignoring the man behind it. The next part of this book looks at the impact of Meredith's ideas in the US, largely through the prism of this remarkable aircraft.

Part 2

THE 'MEREDITH EFFECT' AND THE MUSTANG

1939 – North American Aviation's Lee Atwood discovers Meredith

Lee Atwood, who in 1940 was Vice-President of North American Aviation (NAA), wrote a letter published in *Air & Space*, October/November 1996, stating that he had produced papers with two objectives: 'The first is to explain and quantify the "Meredith effect" of drag reduction. The simple fact is that it was the basis of the Mustang design, and its most efficient application required a buried radiator.'[1] (Atwood also wanted the RAE, whose work has featured so prominently in this book so far, to be given its due recognition. 'My second objective is to give proper credit to the Royal Aircraft Establishment at Farnborough, which sponsored the research that Meredith and R.S. Capon published in 1935 and 1936.'[2])

In 1985, Ed Schmued, who had been in charge of NAA's Preliminary Design unit at the time the Mustang was developed, died leaving biographical tapes and a manuscript which started, 'Many stories about the design of the P-51 Mustang have been told, most of them out-and-out fabrications, or not really reflecting the actual history'. In Schmued's own account the 'Meredith effect' played no role in the design and its presence was discovered fortuitously later. (At which point Schmued recognised the 'Meredith effect', without using the name, provided ramjet levels of thrust.) But can either Atwood's or Schmued's accounts be considered reliable? Schmued commented frankly on the milieu in which the Mustang was designed: 'Companies would steal ideas from the best organizations. It was a dog-eat-dog affair. We lied like hell, made promises. But the government asked for competitive people. We were not always honest, to say the least. Yet there was patriotism from the word go.'[3]

Atwood's first objective is the main subject of much of the second part of the book. It is a dramatic claim that Meredith's eponymous 'effect' was the basis of the North American Aviation P-51 Mustang design. This was arguably the best all-round land-based fighter of the Second World War, when NAA's airframe was combined with the Rolls-Royce Merlin engine resulting in a fighter from the P-51B variants onwards, of exceptional speed, high altitude performance and long range. Thus, the claim's validity merits investigation. Reichsmarschall Hermann Goering stated: 'When I saw Mustangs over Berlin, I knew the jig was up', as it was clear that allied fighters could now accompany bombers to Berlin and back. The primary objective of the Mustangs was not to escort the bombers but to lure up and then attack the German fighters. The Mustang's remarkable qualities enabled it to destroy the Luftwaffe as a day fighting force in Western Europe in the first half of 1944, clearing the way for the D-Day landings.

This part of the book is, however, largely about the P-51A which was designed for the British in 1940 and sold to the RAF as the Mustang I, entering service in 1942. The P-51A was powered by the Allison engine which had a single speed supercharger. Although it had excellent low altitude performance this was poor at high altitude and restricted the potential of the remarkable airframe. Without the P-51A, however, there would not have been the war winning P-51B, C, or D.

The book now examines Meredith's ideas developed in the US in a manner both fascinating and controversial. Meredith the man is entirely ignored in the US story. While it was not known in Britain before the post-war period that he was an actual Soviet spy, his fellow workers and the security services were well aware of his Soviet and communist sympathies in the 1930s, not least because he made no effort to hide them. In the US, however, there might have been at the very least raised eyebrows if there had been awareness that Meredith, whose 'effect' has become central to the Mustang story, was a 'Bolshevik'.

To recapitulate, what was the relevant research that Meredith did at the RAE? In his aerodynamic *annus mirabilis* of 1935 he wrote four very important documents while in charge of the RAE's Aerodynamics unit. It might help to recap that these were:

1935		
February	*Invention relating to jet propulsion of aircraft*	Application for financing to a patent while with RAE
March	*Improvements in or relating to aircraft and other craft or vehicles*	Patent GB 454,266 (with Stewart)
May	*Note on the problem of conducting a fluid into a duct*	RAE Wind tunnel note 267
June	*Cooling of Aircraft Engines With special reference to Ethylene Glycol Radiators enclosed in Ducts*	RAE research paper – approved in August for publication by the ARC

The book now looks at how the idea in these papers were disseminated in the US, how they affected the development of the Mustang and the controversy surrounding the claim that the 'Meredith effect' was indeed the basis of the Mustang's design. It is thus rather different in character to the first part of the book, but without that first part there could be no second.

Particularly the book will test Atwood's overarching claim was that, 'the "Meredith effect" of drag reduction was the basis of the Mustang design.'[4] Implicit in this claim were two others.

- The first was that Atwood determined that 'a considerably better design could be developed' than the Curtiss P-40 fighter which the British Purchasing Commission (BPC) wanted NAA to build under license, but which had an inefficient chin radiator.
- The second was that to improve the poor P-40 design: 'I [Atwood] evolved a design concept which involved placing the coolant radiators back of the wing and designed a ducting system to recover some of the cooling energy in an efficient manner. This principle [identified as the "Meredith effect"] involved discharging the heated air under as much pressure as possible in a rear facing jet as in the yet-to-be-developed ramjet engine.'[5]

The book will also examine a number of Atwood's subsidiary claims that: he had read Meredith's 1935 ARC paper in 1939; Meredith's work was not well understood at the time – except implicitly by Atwood; in late 1939 early 1940 he told Ed Schmued, NAA's head of preliminary design, about placing the radiator in the aft ventral position; he used freehand drawings only in informal presentations to the BPC – that is why there were no formal drawings; the BPC ordered 320 aircraft called NA-73X on 11 April 1940; and that the aircraft was to be named the Mustang in April 1940.

Companies and organisations in the Mustang story

At this stage it might be helpful to set out the key organisations and characters in the development of the Mustang and the debate over the 'Meredith effect'. The original Mustang airframe and engine were built respectively by companies, North American Aviation (NAA) and Allison, which were controlled by General Motors. In 1934, James H. 'Dutch' Kindleberger and Lee Atwood left Douglas to develop NAA as respectively president and chief engineer. NAA's main experience was designing radial-engined trainers, observation aircraft, and medium bombers, again successfully with the B-25. Allison designed the inline V12 V-1710 during the early 1930s.

Atwood (1904-1999) is a major figure in this second part of the book which focuses on his claim that the 'Meredith effect' was the basis of the Mustang's design. In 1939 he was promoted from Chief Engineer to First Vice-President. His duties included Engineering, Operations and, with Kindleberger, Sales.[6]

Post-war Atwood became president of NAA in 1948, which produced the F-86 Sabre, F-100 Super Sabre, X-15 rocket plane, XB-70 Valkyrie bomber, and the B-1 Lancer bomber. NAA developed in new fields like the Apollo programme. In 1962 Kindleberger died and Atwood succeeded as president and chairman. In 1967 NAA merged with Rockwell to become North American Rockwell. In 1967 Atwood retired but remained on the board until 1978. In later retirement he wrote many articles and papers emphasising his role in the conception of the Mustang design based on his use of the 'Meredith effect'.

Edgar Schmued was born in Germany in 1899. He emigrated to Brazil in 1925. In 1931 he went to the US to work for Fokker Aircraft, which developed into NAA. In 1936 he became a preliminary design engineer and then head of Preliminary Design. He, not Atwood, is generally identified as the designer of the P-51 Mustang. Later he developed the twin Mustang fuselage F-82. He left NAA in 1952, unable to work with Atwood, and joined Northrop for five years, developing the cost-efficient F-5 light fighter and the T-38 trainer.

In 1938 aerodynamicist Ed Horkey had joined NAA from CALTEC where 'through the leadership of Dr Clark B. Millikan and Theodore von Karman, the GALCIT [Guggenheim Aeronautical Laboratory California Institute of Technology] became the premier wind tunnel testing facility for several years'.[7] NAA got access to the most up-to-date aerodynamics developments at CALTEC as well as to wind-tunnel facilities. In 1939 Horkey recruited Irving Ashkenas from CALTEC.

There needed to be some agency within NAA to draw together the features of the design of the Mustang. In early 1936 Edgar Schmued worked as a preliminary design engineer, subsequently becoming, as seen, Chief of Preliminary Design. Kit Carson, in 1978, gave a description in his insightful history of the Mustang, as both fighter ace and engineer, *Pursue and Destroy,* gives in some detail of Design's function. 'It fell to the lot of the Preliminary Design Group to keep abreast of the technology advances. Edgar Schmued was an exponent of the preliminary design concept and as a consequence he got the job of heading it up.'[8] And: 'It was their job to block out the preliminary design of fighters, bombers, or trainers as the demand for estimates and quotations came in from the boss [Kindleberger]. Thus, there are many preliminary designs in the technical files of an aircraft that have never seen the light of day as an airplane or a mock up.'[9]

A couple of US organisations played important parts in the development of the Mustang. The National Advisory Committee for Aeronautics (NACA) was formed in 1915 by Congress, alarmed that, despite the US being the nation to make the first powered flight in 1903, it had fallen behind European nations in aeronautical research. NACA was in part initially modelled on Britain's Advisory Committee for Aeronautics (ACA), established in 1909, which was renamed in 1919 the Aeronautical Research Committee, later becoming the Aeronautical Research Council (ARC) which put Meredith's and Capon's key paper into the public domain.

NACA, although this was not originally planned, developed its own research capabilities. In 1920 its first research and testing facility, the Langley Aeronautical

Laboratory, was created. It recruited engineers and scientists to develop a powerful research and testing capability with particular strength in evaluating aircraft designed by US companies. In 1940 the Ames Aeronautical Laboratory was opened in California in what is now Silicon Valley. This specialised in wind-tunnel research on the aerodynamics of propeller-driven aircraft. Of relevance to the cooling story here is the development of the NACA radial-engine cowling which improved upon the British Townend Ring (see Appendix 2). Also, NACA produced a systematic series of aerofoils which included, in the late 1930s, laminar flow profiles. This would play an important part in the design of the Mustang.

USAAF Matériel Division had been set up in 1926 at Dayton Ohio, bringing together research and development, procurement, supply and maintenance. The following year its centre was established at nearby Wright Field. Unlike the RAE it was a military organisation. As will be seen, the Matériel Division did early and important US work on the dimensions of ducted radiators.

In 1938 the British Air Ministry sent a purchasing mission to the USA and Canada, headed by Sir Henry Self, both to manage purchases of aircraft in the USA and to explore the manufacture of British types under licence. On 7 November 1939 the British Purchasing Commission (BPC) was established at 15 Broad Street, New York. Self had good relations with NAA due to the success of its Harvard trainer in British service. In January 1940 the BPC became the Anglo-French Purchasing Board (AFPB). When it became apparent that the fall of France was imminent, the AFPB became again the BPC in May 1940 and French contracts were assigned over to Britain. (For simplicity the AFPB will generally be referred to as the BPC.) In June 1940 increased demand for US products saw the formation of the British Air Commission (BAC) under Self.

The next chapters look at the areas where the ideas in Meredith's four 1935 papers may have impacted the US looking through the prism of the Mustang. These are first the 'Meredith effect' itself; the second is duct entry; and the third is exhaust gas momentum. Later the role of 'Meredith effect' in the development of the US ramjet is analysed.

Chapter 17

(1) Mustang and Meredith – the 'Meredith effect'

Lee Atwood, as seen, claimed the 'Meredith effect' of drag reduction was the basis of the Mustang design.[1] F.W. Meredith thus has the term named after him, this so-called 'Meredith effect'. He never used it and had no known part in its coining and quite probably never knew it existed. So, what was the source of this term and when did it come into existence?

The 'Meredith effect' term origins

Meredith's own description of what constitutes the 'Meredith effect' is found in the first two conclusions in his seminal paper *Cooling of Aircraft Engines With special reference to Ethylene Glycol Radiators enclosed in Ducts* (Meredith, August 1935).[2] The aerodynamic conclusion stated: 'The employment of low velocity cooling avoids the necessity for an increasing expenditure of power with increasing speed provided the exit conditions are adjusted to suit the speed.' The thermodynamic conclusion said: 'The combined effect of compressibility and heat transfer from the radiator may reduce the power consumption to nothing if the size of the radiator is adequate.' In Britain, however, the term the 'Meredith effect' was never used so where did it come from?

In 1941, NACA carried out experiments involving a heated element within a duct. John Becker, describing this work in 1981, wrote:

> In 1936, F.W. Meredith pointed out that the waste heat of a piston engine, which is transferred to the cooling-air flow in a radiator, is not all lost; it produces a small thrust provided the pressure at the exhaust of the radiator tubes is higher than the free static pressure of flight. This phenomenon became known as the 'Meredith effect'.[3]

The actual term the 'Meredith effect' has first been found in 1943, following these 1941 experiments in the written record in an *Analysis of Heat and Compressibility Effects in Internal Flow Systems and High-Speed Tests of a Ramjet System*, (Becker and Baals, NACA, 1943), based on the research in 1941 into electrically heating air passing through a shaped duct.[4] This stated: 'The power recoverable from the heat added to the cooling air ('Meredith effect') was found to be about 3 per cent of the brake horsepower for an existing air-cooled engine at a flight Mach number of 0.60 at sea level.' Thus, the term the 'Meredith effect' had appeared by 1943, but there is no evidence of it being used in 1939 when Atwood claimed to have discovered it on the basis of some, as will be seen uncertain, reading of Meredith's work.

Mustang concept pre-1940

'Dutch' Kindleberger, NAA's president, was quoted in the early 1960s as saying: 'You can't pull a rabbit out of a hat unless you put a rabbit into the hat beforehand.'[5] According to the legend the rabbit was put in in early 1940 and taken out in October and was developed in 100 days. Analysis of the background of the Mustang might establish whether, in fact, Kindleberger's rabbit went in the hat rather earlier than 1940. Therefore, this chapter considers the broader context in which the Mustang was developed.

The Mustang had certain clearly visible defining features: an inline liquid-cooled engine; an 'oversquare' radiator which was buried in the aft fuselage (with a prominent 'lipped' ventral entry); and a straight edged wing and tail area surfaces which greatly facilitated production. (Not obviously visible, there was also a laminar flow wing.) If these features were, however, largely in place in NAA's pre-existing fighter designs, both flown and on the drawing board, before 1940, then Atwood's claims, particularly with regard to his use of the 'Meredith effect', can be reappraised.

This chapter focuses on the extent that the form of the Mustang was the result of NAA designers answering a series of basic questions: what is the lowest drag engine – radial or inline; what shape of radiator provides the best compromise between cooling efficiency and drag – 'oversquare', or 'undersquare'; where can that oversquare radiator (excluding in-wing as impractical on a single engined fighter) be located to create the least drag? Looking at the wing and control surfaces where did the best balance lie between cost and efficiency with round or squared edges? If these questions were posed and at least some answers found before 1940 then the conception of the Mustang might be seen as lying before that year. Then Atwood's assertion that the 'Meredith effect' as presented (in his freehand drawings) to the BPC in 1940 – and particularly its thermodynamic elements – was the basis of the Mustang's design can be challenged.

Factors within NAA determining the Mustang's design

1) Inline-powered fighters

Both the US and Japan, where the role of aircraft was largely seen as naval, favoured the simplicity and lightness of the radial, seeing these qualities as more important than the lower drag of the more complex liquid-cooled inline. Why then was the inline adopted by NAA and used for the Mustang? In Europe, with the exception of the British navy, aircraft were largely seen as land or coast-based and inlines were increasingly favoured for land-based interceptors, due to their lower drag. By the mid-1930s Rolls-Royce and the RAE, where work was led in 1935 by Meredith, were developing ducted radiators with adjustable exits which greatly reduced inline cooling drag.

While commercially there was an incentive to combine NAA airframes with Allison inlines in the mid-1950s the *zeitgeist,* at least in the US, seemed against it. In the mid-1930s cowled radials with adjustable flaps were proving remarkably efficient while, before the adoption of ducted radiators, inlines, despite their smaller head-on dimensions, had no particular advantage. Thus, there were several radial powered-fighters – notably the Curtiss P-36 Hawk, first flight 6 May 1935, and the Seversky P-35, 15 August 1935.

Lee Atwood, when NAA chief engineer, believed that liquid-cooled inline engines could be superior to air-cooled radials even when these used low drag NACA cowlings.[6] In 1935 he selected the Allison to power the NAA entry in the Air Corps [twin seat] pursuit [airplane] competition of 1935.[7] This fighter concept was not continued but NAA had established a precedent for designing an Allison powered fighter.

Europe's development of fast inline fighters put pressure on the US Army Air Force (USAAF) to address the inline cooling challenge.[8] In 1937 and 1938 the USAAF Materiél Division issued specifications for Allison powered fighters. In January 1937, Materiél Division sent Circular Proposal-608, or CP-608 and in March CP-609, respectively, for twin and single-engined fighters using the turbocharged Allison engine, to nine manufacturers, excluding NAA.

In April 1937 the radial-powered Curtiss P-36 was re-engined with a turbocharged Allison engine and redesignated the XP-37. The Air Corps issued in March 1939 a new specification for an advanced design long range fighter, superior to the Bell P-39 and the Curtiss P-40, using either the inline Allison or the 24-cylinder Pratt & Whitney X-1800.[9] These were intended to use turbochargers for high altitude performance. The twin-Allison engined Lockheed XP-38 had sufficient space for a turbocharger in its tail booms. The single-engined XP-37 and XP-39, which had turbochargers, were discontinued. The former was replaced by the single stage only supercharger XP-40 and the latter continued as the XP-39 with the turbocharger removed. With simple superchargers both had poor high altitude performance. (The turbocharged radial-powered Republic P-47 Thunderbolt was developed from the AP-10, Republic's Allison-powered response to Specification CP 39-770.)

2) Preference for an 'oversquare' radiator

The inline engine's requirement for a radiator meant that a decision had to be made as to its length and dimensions. If a radiator were to be buried a critical consideration is how wide it is relative to its length, or how 'undersquare', or 'oversquare'. An 'oversquare' radiator cannot be buried in the wing or chin position. The most successful US and British inline-powered fighters had very different radiators in this respect. The Mustang's was 'over' and, relatively, the Spitfire's 'under' square. In Britain, Capon's work could be interpreted as favouring an 'undersquare' radiator. In August 1935, he had written, 'it is advantageous to use a radiator of small frontal area having long tubes: the optimum conditions indicate a tube length which will cause the rise of temperature of the air to be about 85% of the radiator-air temperature difference'.[10] This presupposed two factors: the radiator was substantially unburied so the frontal area needed to be relatively small to avoid inordinate drag; and the absolute optimum was required – when in practice a satisfactory result could be achieved at a significantly lower percentage.

In April 1936, NACA's D.H. Wood addressed the radiator challenge: 'The whole radiator question requires a complete overhaul. There is little doubt that the drag of radiators can be greatly reduced by proper cowling.'[11] Wood said most existing tests were useless as they applied to exposed not ducted radiators. Therefore: 'The radiator problem should be approached without preconceived notions. It will not be surprising if the radiator drag can be reduced to less than half of its present value. The liquid-cooled engine will then become a most serious competitor of the air-cooled engine.'[12] The challenge of doing such research was taken up by the Matériel Division, which examined the particular issue of radiator dimensions, coming to a different conclusion to Rolls-Royce, by favouring an 'oversquare' radiator. This emerged in an important debate that followed a Rolls-Royce presentation in the US in 1936.

By mid-1936 the US had clearly been directly exposed to British work on ducted radiators. This, however, was through Rolls-Royce, which had developed ducted radiators in 1934, not the RAE, based on Meredith's and Capon's work. On 4 June 1936 H. Wood of Rolls-Royce presented a paper on *Liquid-Cooled Aero Engines* to the Society of Aeronautical Engineers (SAE) at its semi-annual meeting at White Sulphur Springs, West Virginia.[13] The paper gave a brief résumé of the development of the Rolls-Royce Kestrel engine and then analysed the requirements of the high-performance engine of the future, developing at least 1500 bhp. There was much very interesting material about Rolls-Royce research on cooling drag.

Wood of Rolls-Royce said: 'Modern development has indicated that the cooling flow is better controlled by means of varying the exit from the duct rather than by using shutters at the front or inside the duct.'[14] (This point had been proved mathematically by the RAE's Capon at the instigation of Rolls-Royce.) Also, Wood confirmed the value of ducts with adjustable exits. 'It has been demonstrated, both by model and full-scale flight tests that a considerable reduction in drag can be effected by cowling the radiator and by regulating the flow of the cooling air by means of adjustable flap at the rear exit.'[15] Wood reported that in practice: 'The lowest figures yet obtained for the cooling cost of an ethylene-glycol-cooled installation are of the order of 3 ½ per cent for engine bhp at 300mph.'[16]

The presentation revealed the open relationship between American and British aero engineers. It stimulated an animated debate on the dimensions of radiators, with British delegates arguing for 'undersquare' radiators with smaller frontal areas and longer tubes, while their American counterparts favoured strongly 'oversquare' radiators with large frontal areas and shorter tubes. Wood of Rolls-Royce had favoured relatively longer radiator tubes.[17] This was challenged by American engineers who said that shorter tubes and a larger frontal area were preferable in all circumstances. In July 1936, W. Worth of Materiél Division added to the debate on radiator proportions:

> Studies at the Materiél Division indicate that, when external drag can be neglected [as when buried], the same surface arranged with a large frontal area and shallow depth will dissipate more heat for a given available pressure. If this condition is true, then it seems practical considerations and available space should be determining factors in all cases where the radiator is located within the structure.[18]

Thus, the large frontal area, as with an 'oversquare radiator' was preferable – with the key condition that the radiator could be buried. This was because adequate efficiency could be obtained with a ratio of coolant temperature increase of less than 60%, meaning shorter tubes were acceptable. The gain, however, in drag reduction from slowing the cooling air – by having a large ratio of diffuser duct entry and radiator areas – was much more important. NACA Special Report No 112, *Radiator design and installation* (Brevoort and Leifer, NACA, 1939) would conclude: 'The analysis of the length of passage on the liquid side of the radiator shows it to be a secondary consideration.'[19]

3) Ventral aft cooling duct location
In the US the advantages of the 'oversquare' radiator, provided it could be buried, were identified early by the Materiél Division. This raised questions as to where such a radiator could be located in a single-engined fighter? Certain locations – in the wing as too thin, or the forward and mid-fuselage, as occupied by engine or pilot – were in practice eliminated. (Analysis of this issue is greatly facilitated by research available in the twenty-first century in articles in *North American Aviation Retirees* (NAAR) journal by Lowell F. Ford and a very informative book '*P-51B Mustang North American's Bastard Stepchild that saved the Eighth Air Force*, by J.R. Marshall and L.F. Ford.)

The answer was soon made clear to the question of the location of a buried radiator. In February 1938 General Hap Arnold, Assistant Chief of Air Corps, responsible for procurement and supply at the Materiél Division, asked NAA for studies comparing American and foreign aircraft and describing the best next generation fighter.[20] Kindleberger hired Dr Clark Millikan (1903-1966) professor of Aerodynamics at California Institute of Technology (CALTEC) to analyse the issue. Millikan's report, submitted by Kindleberger to Arnold, dated 29 March 1938, was titled *The Performance Estimate For Idealized 1938 Pursuit Airplane*. The report said cooling drag, 'could be reduced perhaps by 50% if the radiators were placed entirely inside the wing or fuselage and a carefully designed ducting system used to lead the air to and away from them'.[21] Millikan's report was passed onto then NAA Chief Engineer Lee Atwood who was thus aware by early 1938 – that is before he said that he had read Meredith's work in 1939 – that drag could be reduced by a buried radiator in practice in the fuselage as the wing was too narrow in a fighter if the radiator was to be placed entirely within it.[22]

(1) MUSTANG AND MEREDITH – THE 'MEREDITH EFFECT'

Explicit recognition that the radiator could only be placed in the rear fuselage came on 6 May when Materiél Division issued a request, titled *Engineering Section Memorandum Report [ESMR] Serial Number P-51-643*, asking for comments about an aircraft design similar to Kindleberger's specification and Millikan's report which had included the cooling system housed within the fuselage. Thus, by the first half of 1938, two concepts behind the Mustang's ducted cooling system were potentially in place: that the radiator should be 'oversquare'; and that it should be buried in the rear fuselage based on aerodynamic reasons without any recourse to Meredith's work. Schmued who headed NAA's Preliminary Design unit analysed the report. This unit then began a secret study for an Allison-powered fighter.[23]

On 11 March 1939 the Air Corp issued a specification, CP39-770, for an advanced fighter which could be powered by inlines as well as radials. NAA was not asked to submit a design but was invited to comment.[24] NAA, however, now confirmed that the only location could be the aft ventral position. Schmued commented: 'Due to the small size of the engine compartment, the oil radiator, coolant tank and cooling radiator will have to be placed in the fuselage to the rear of the pilot.'[25] (So before Atwood claimed to have advised Schmued in late 1939 and early 1940 to use the ventral aft position, based on the basis of his reading of Meredith's work, Schmued had already reached his conclusion about the same position.)

To summarise, aerodynamic reasons – based on the requirement to bury an 'oversquare' radiator – can be produced to explain the selection of the aft ventral position and not, as Atwood claimed, to exploit the thermodynamic 'Meredith effect'. Given that the Allison was a liquid-cooled engine it had to have a radiator, thereby raising the question where it was located in Schmued's secret project. The answer might seem obvious, given that Schmued had read reports which located the radiator in the aft ventral position and had himself advised this location. Therefore, NAA personnel would likely have determined that the location of the radiator should be located in the rear fuselage in 1939, quite independently of any reading by Atwood of Meredith's work in that year. It appears the case, however, that NAA, through its relationship with Caltec and Millikan, and the comments by NAA's Schmued, could have played an important part in developing the US predilection for a ventral aft radiator.

4) Squared off wings and tail surfaces

In the later 1930s NAA designed a number of radial and inline powered aircraft with squared features that anticipated the Mustang. A defining quality of NAA aircraft was their relatively low cost, as they were carefully designed for mass production. This was no accident, as both NAA and Allison were part of the General Motor's stable of companies where efficient mass production techniques were applied to car production. (Allison's engines had far fewer parts than Rolls-Royce's.) NAA was keen to enter the rapidly growing international fighter market, particularly as it was excluded from the US market. The company designed, built and sold two radial-powered fighters derived from its trainers which impressed many nations by their functionality and low cost.[26]

Seven 840hp Wright Cyclone powered NA-50 fighters, developed using parts from NAA trainers, were sold in 1938 to Peru. The 875hp Cyclone NA-50 A also named NA-53, and then the NA-68 and P-64 was a more advanced development with a new wing and more streamlined engine cowling, first flying in 1940. The six built were retained by the US. NAA aerodynamicist Horkey wrote of the NA-50 and NA-50 A: 'The numbers were not large and the performance moderate, but the experience was very valuable.'[27]

NAA also designed some inline powered aircraft. In 1939 an earlier project, the NA-35 primary trainer, was reinstated under Ed Schmued. An all-metal prototype was designed and built in thirty-nine days and first flown on 9 December 1939, powered by a 150hp Menasco engine. 'This two-place low-wing monoplane was clearly planned with mass production in mind. Except for the open cockpits and fixed landing gear, its clean-cut lines foreshadowed the Mustang.'[28] In July 1940 NAA sold the NA-35 to Vega. 'The Vega 35 remains noteworthy because the diminutive craft, with a mere 150 horsepower, was an essential precursor to the Mustang.'[29]

Figure 20.1 shows the similarities of the P-509/NA-50 B to earlier air-cooled NAA radial and inline designs. In turn the X-73, which had the same dimensions as the Mustang, was a development of the P-509/P-50 B. (The relationship of the P-509/P-50 B with earlier designs was explicitly recognised by the BPC, which in April 1940 ordered 400 P-50 Bs, this design being seen as following in series the P-50 A.)

Summarising, so far, an argument can be created that the predecessor of the Mustang, the P-509/NA-50 B, could have developed as the result of several assumptions that have nothing directly due to the thermodynamic element of the 'Meredith effect'. These were generally that: an inline engine had lower drag than a radial engine; if liquid-cooled it required a radiator; and an 'oversquare' radiator was more efficient than an 'undersquare' radiator if buried; such an 'oversquare' radiator could only be buried in the aft ventral position in a single engined fighter. Specific to NAA, squared off wing and tail surfaces simplified production and kept costs down. Thus, it is possible to outline the development of the predecessor of the P-509/NA-50 B, the aircraft actually ordered by the BPC, until mid-February 1940, without recourse to Meredith's ideas as claimed by Atwood.

The existence by mid-1939 of the project that developed into the P-509 is supported by evidence of its presentation to British officials.[30] In July 1939, H.C.B. Thomas and Charles Luttman met with NAA to discuss potential fighter designs. This is the first documented meeting between BPC's technical representatives and the NAA engineering group.[31] Thomas had been Head of Mechanical Engineering Department at the RAE. In 1938 he became an AID/RTO (Aeronautical Inspection Directorate/Resident Technical Officer) in the US. He was appointed by the Directorate of Technical Development (RTO) for the NAA Harvard trainer (and the Lockheed Hudson).[32] Luttman had previously worked from 1936 to 1938 for the Aeronautical Inspection Directorate (AID) of the British Air Ministry in England. In March 1938 he was the Directorate's inspector at NAA in Inglewood, California.

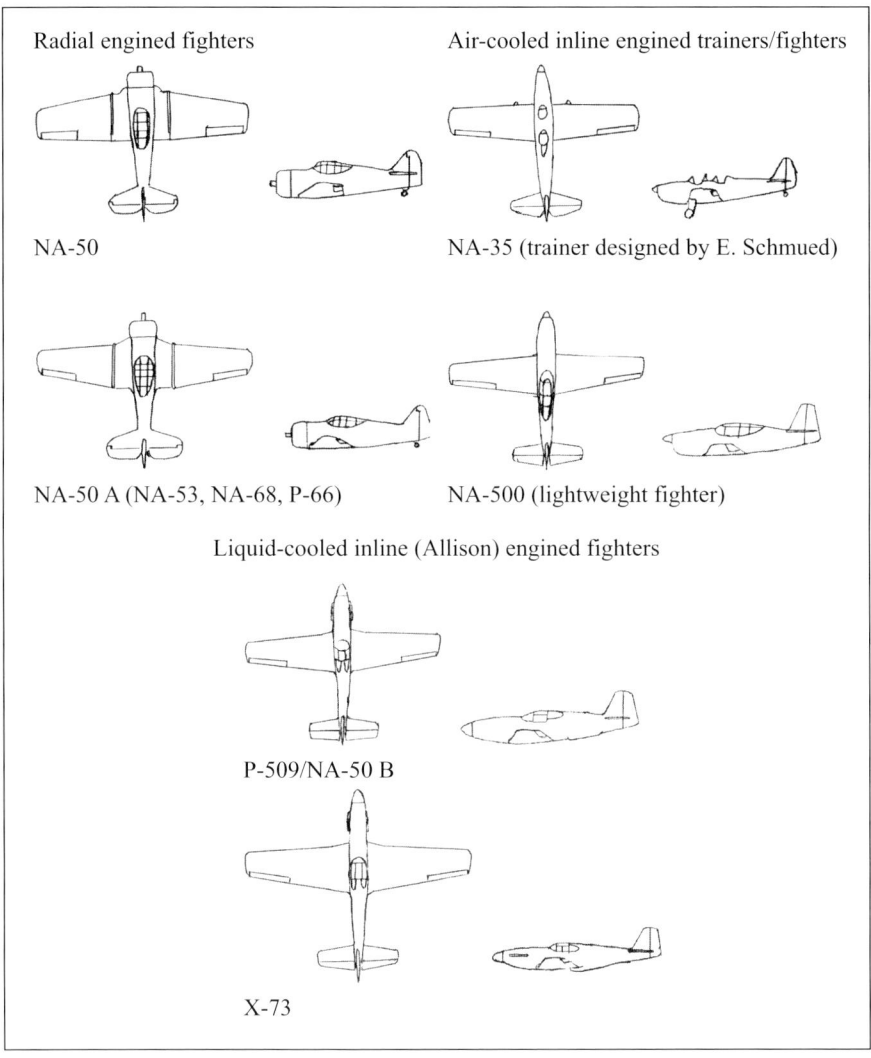

Figure 18.1 – NAA monoplanes showing squared off flying surfaces.

There is also evidence that Atwood was aware of the P-509 project at a time he would claim no design existed. From 1938 to 1940 Luttman was the liaison official with direct responsibility for working with NAA on the production of the Harvard trainer and he also became very familiar with NAA personnel. He had impressed on NAA the requirement to conform to AID standards of 'interchangeability', whereby Data Sheets showing tolerances meant inaccuracies in part mating were promptly determined and corrected.[33] 'The Inspector-in-charge AID [Luttman] recalls being asked by Lee Atwood early in 1940 to advise Ed Schmued, the Preliminary Design Group Supervisor at North American, on British aircraft interchangeability and other design requirements as a background to the new fighter design.'[34] This indicates that by early 1940 Atwood knew there was a fighter design, not just freehand sketches, and that Schmued was, at the very least, involved in its design. Thus, writes K.J. Meekcoms, in *The British Air Commission and Lend-Lease*, 'they [Luttmann and Thomas], and other members of the BPC were acquainted to varying degrees with the New Fighter proposal, when it finally became "official"'.[35]

This chapter looked at the question: Could the Mustang design have evolved without NAA designers having read Meredith's work? As seen, Atwood claimed that 'Meredith effect' drag reduction was the basis of the Mustang's design and this required a buried radiator which could only be located in the ventral aft position. Also, he asserted there was no formal design until effectively the second quarter of 1940. It has been argued here that Schmued could have chosen the same ventral aft location, without reading Meredith's work, for aerodynamic reasons. For example, as seen, he commented in March 1939: 'Due to the small size of the engine compartment, the oil radiator, coolant tank and cooling radiator will have to be placed in the fuselage to the rear of the pilot.'[36] Thus, Schmued did not need Atwood's input to have placed the P-509/P-50 B radiator (the design ordered by the BPC) in the ventral aft position.

Chapter 18

Meredith's work – availability and impact in the US pre-1940

Atwood claimed that Meredith's work was little known or understood at the time he read it in 1939. Therefore, his application of it to the design of the Mustang reflected his unique comprehension of the significance of Meredith's ideas. Before analysing the stages of the design of the Mustang, the availability and impact of Meredith's work in the US might be considered in this chapter; also, the possible impact of his ideas on other aircraft, both US and non-US in the next chapter. This would establish the milieu in which NAA's own designers operated. It would also test Atwood's assertion that the 'Meredith effect' was little known or understood at the time.

NACA published research building on Meredith's ideas

In 1938 and 1939 three German research papers on liquid cooling were translated by NACA which all recognised the thermodynamic element of the ducted radiator. The second and third explicitly referred to Meredith's and Capon's work. (Atwood stated that as NAA's chief engineer to end-1939 he had read NACA reports.)

The conversion of energy in a radiator (Weise 1937, NACA, translated 1938) started: 'The aerodynamic refinements on the airplane itself have made the share of the radiator on the power loss stand out.' [1] The report examined the impact of radiator heat. As aircraft fly at greater altitude:

> The result is that the radiator air is heated very considerably in relation to its absolute inlet temperature. This has far-reaching results for the behaviour of the radiator. This report [aims] to give a comprehensive discussion of all the fundamental principles and physical phenomena that offer a key to the understanding and the solution of modern cooling problems.

The report presented the effect of 'the air forces on a duct radiator, particularly on the radiator cowling, explaining the change of state of the air in the radiator with the aid of a velocity-pressure diagram'.

A Contribution to the theory of the heated duct radiator (Winter 1938, NACA, translated 1939) explicitly discusses heat, citing Meredith's 1935 paper.[2] The Introduction records:

> It was Meredith who first pointed out the possible gain in power required to tow [pull forward] the radiator systems under the operating condition as compared with the cold condition and showed how the momentum or power gain resulting from the heating of the air by the coolant may be approximately computed with the aid of simple momentum and energy considerations.

The comment on Meredith's work was interesting and insightful. 'Since the computation, however, involves rather extensive simplifications, the results may be used tentatively as a first approximation only.' Thus, 'In the present paper simple formulas are derived with the aid of which the lowering in the drag of a radiator due to heating may be computed with an accuracy sufficient for practical requirements'. Like Meredith, the case is considered first of the cold radiator and then the effect of the heating of the radiator on the rate of air flow and on drag. The analysis confirmed that a point can be calculated where, at a given velocity and altitude with the addition of heat, there is no internal cooling drag.

The drag of airplane radiators with special references to air heating (Göthert, 1938, NACA, translated 1939) again cites Meredith's 1935 report under the heading, 'Effect of Heat on Radiator Drag'.[3] The report contained a survey of past radiator research, including practical tests, with the object of ascertaining the most important loss sources. It noted that, 'losses due to the diffuser are to be looked into closely as they can be of preeminent magnitude. Generally, applicable equations and charts are developed for the rapid determination of the heating effect of radiators as regards flow and drag, and then checked by routine tests on hot radiators'. The report deals extensively with the issue of 'The hot radiator in a duct', stating in the summary; 'The effect of heating on the drag and flow of the radiator is elaborated in formulas and diagrams', and problems with ventral radiator, which is translated as the 'belly' radiator, discussed. The summary stated that if 'resistances' can be avoided, 'the entire radiator resistance would be practically eliminated and, in special cases, even a lift [negative drag] produced'. Later, this analysis is elaborated:

> Heating increases the pressure drop in the [radiator] core. This increase in pressure drop, which on a ducted radiator results in increased drag with rising heat, is confronted [counteracted] by the favourable effect of heating on the pressure exerted by the radiator duct. As a result of the greater pressure volume due to heating, the air leaves the core at greater velocity than from the core. According to the law of momentum, there must therefore be an additional force.

Thus, by 1939, NACA had produced three translations of German papers on the thermodynamic aspect of ducted radiators, two of which specifically cited

Meredith's work. The German analysis was of much more practical application than that of Meredith, who sought only to prove that it was mathematically possible for cooling drag to be neutralised when heat was factored into equations.

The German papers produced more complex equations and analysis of designs that could be and were used by NAA aerodynamicists. NAA aerodynamicist Ed Horkey said the report, *The drag of airplane radiators with special references to air heating* (Göthert, 1938, NACA translated 1939), was used to develop the Mustang cooling system.[4] The report contained intake, radiator and exit designs with the resulting drag from each of these.[5] Irving Ashkenas, who worked with Horkey at NAA, referred to the paper,[6] *Contribution to the theory of the heated duct radiator* (Winter, 1938, NACA, translated 1939).[7]

Ed Horkey wrote in 1996: 'We applied calculus in place of algebra for most of the analysis work. The mathematical work of a British professor [Meredith] was never used by us at any time.'[8] This is somewhat disingenuous as Göthert's and Winter's work, used by Horkey and Ashkenas, cited Meredith and built on his insight that a ducted radiator was a heat engine. As seen, the paper, *Contribution to the theory of the heated duct radiator* (Winter, 1938, NACA, translated 1939) recognised that Meredith's 'computations' involved rather extensive 'simplifications' and produced still 'simple' formulas. Thus, 'In the present paper simple formulas are derived with the aid of which the lowering in the drag of a radiator due to heating may be computed with an accuracy sufficient for practical requirements'. At the basis of the German work, however, was Meredith's insight. Therefore, although Horkey claimed that Meredith's mathematical concepts were never used by NAA, German work building on Meredith's work certainly was.

By 1939 NACA's own research reports showed the organisation had analysed Meredith's work independently of any German reports through their own investigations on the effects of heat in internal flow systems. Although Meredith is cited by NACA researchers no record has been found that NACA directly published his actual 1935 paper. It is clear, however, that NACA researchers were very familiar with his report.

In *Experiments on the Recovery of Waste Heat in Cooling Ducts* (Silverstein, NACA, 1939) ducts were tested with electric heaters in place of radiators to ascertain the extent of waste heat recovery. The first reference in Silverstein's report is to Meredith, who is cited after the statement: 'The possibility of recovering a small part of the heat energy wasted in the cooling air of aircraft engines has been indicated by theoretical considerations.'[9] Electrical heaters were placed in the duct. (This followed the RAE investigation of 1936, *Recovery of energy from a ducted cooling system* (Smelt, Davies and Callen, September 1936) and anticipated *Analysis of Heat and Compressibility Effects in Internal Flow Systems and High-Speed Tests of a Ramjet System* (Becker and Baals, NACA, 1943) which included the first mention found of the term the 'Meredith effect'.[10])

First, Silverstein considered the addition of radiator heat. He wrote: 'From the standpoint of performance calculations the effect of heat may usually be neglected; that is, the duct efficiencies obtained with cold radiators may be applied with sufficient accuracy to represent the operating condition.' Indeed, even at very high speeds for 1939, the heat effect appeared quite marginal.

> Assuming a high speed of 400 miles per hour and a conversion of 0.8 of the dynamic pressure into static pressure in the duct, a theoretical efficiency of 4% is indicated. Further assuming the average value of 0.4 for the ratio of the heat in the cooling air to the brake horsepower, the maximum power return possible is 1.6% of the brake horsepower. Since the actual accuracy may be only one-half of the theoretical, the actual maximum power regain may be less than 1 per cent of the brake horsepower. From this value must be subtracted the loss due to heating of the radiator and several other minor losses [Reference 1, is to Meredith who pointed out the adiabatic temperature rise due to compression ahead of the radiator]. The actual regain in power even for the higher speed airplanes may, therefore, be less than 1 per cent of the engine power, which is smaller than the possible accuracy of the calculations.[11]

The experimental results regarding the practical achievement of thrust did not appear particularly encouraging. Some thrust, however, was obtained. Silverstein also considered the addition of engine exhaust gas heat. (This was the real objective of Meredith who indeed recognised that the impact of radiator heat alone was marginal except at high speeds.) If exhaust gases are discharged into the cooling duct then a substantial recovery is possible but this would be no greater than discharging the exhaust gases rearward. (Meredith had also pointed out the importance of exploiting exhaust gas momentum.)

Radiator design and installation (Breevort and Leifer, NACA, 1939) broadly examined radiators and their installation and gave much practical advice on balancing theoretical optimums for cooling efficiency and practical considerations of space and location. [12] The summary says: 'The recovery of mechanical energy from the heat energy dissipated by the radiator in the duct is shown to be possible.' Thus, after Silverstein's somewhat dismissive report, radiator heat recovery was not seen by NACA as a lost cause.

In Silverstein's paper only Meredith was cited. Both he and Capon are referenced by Breevort and Leifer: 'The effect of heating an airstream after expansion in a duct and then contracting the duct before expulsion of the air is to convert some of the added heat energy into thrust. Meredith and Capon have made estimates of the thrust so derived.' The report's detail shows that in 1939 NACA had adsorbed Meredith's and Capon's work. For example, the report recognised: 'As pointed out by Meredith, the adiabatic compression of the air entering the duct causes a rise in air temperature.' (This reduced the available temperature difference in the radiator between the coolant liquid and the cooling air.) The report confirmed Capon's finding about the superiority of a ducted radiator with an adjustable exit: 'An efficient radiator installation within a duct or nacelle where the quantity of flow is controllable is superior to any installation where the radiator is exposed to the airstream, whether the radiator is retractable or shuttered.'

In *Drag Analysis of Single-Engine Military Airplanes Tested in the NACA Full-Scale Wind Tunnel* (Dearborn and Silverstein, NACA, 1940) consolidated the results of wind tunnel tests on single-engined airplanes over the previous two years. It included the Allison engined, XP-39, XP-40 and XP-46. It made clear that radiator heat recycling was of practical and not just theoretical consequence as: 'Some progress has recently been made in recovering a part of the waste energy in the form of jet propulsion.'[13] First, the use of waste heat was outlined. This demonstrates awareness of Meredith's work and its focus on heat:

> The efficiency of recovery of waste heat from the cooling may be calculated by the method of Meredith. The theory has been verified in some degree by experiment. The gains are not large but may be sufficient with a well-designed cooling system on a high-speed airplane to compensate for the cooling losses.[14]

Thus, by 1939, NACA researchers were well aware of both Meredith's and Capon's work and had both absorbed its detail and tested it experimentally. Particularly they focused on the second, thermodynamic conclusion in Meredith's research. While initially somewhat sceptical, as in Silverstein's work, they became more alive to the possibilities first in reports by Breevort and Leifer and then by Dearborn and Silverstein. Thus, through a combination of translated German and indigenous US research there was a substantial body of work building on Meredith's (and Capon's) work with a particular focus on Meredith's insight that a ducted radiator was a form of heat engine. Given that Atwood almost certainly did not read Meredith's 1935 paper in 1939 he may have derived his ideas on the ramjet quality of ducted radiator cooling by reading one of these NACA papers. Overall, however, it is hard to reconcile the sheer volume of NACA's research with Atwood's statement that: 'This subject "Meredith effect" has been misunderstood or poorly described in the literature available to me, and even Meredith's report No. 1683 in 1935 does not seem to have been clearly understood by a considerable number of airplane designers in the 1930s and 1940s.'[15]

Chapter 19

'Meredith effect' and US and non-US aircraft

The exploitation of the 'Meredith effect' is, outside Britain, generally associated with the US Mustang. Meredith's ideas were, however, broadly disseminated in Britain, Germany, and eventually France. Thus, this chapter looks at some other aircraft where the design of cooling ducts might have reflected Meredith's ideas.

US aircraft

Curtiss may have designed aircraft with the ventral duct capable of exploiting the 'Meredith effect' rather earlier than NAA. This raises the question, what was the source of Curtiss's design? The Allison-engined XP-40 first flew on 14 October 1938. This is the first US airplane where the engine cooling system was in the ventral position aft of the pilot. This might have followed the dissemination of Materiél Division work to US aircraft manufacturers. As seen, Millikan's report, submitted by Kindleberger to Arnold, dated 29 March 1938, was titled *The Performance Estimate For Idealized 1938 Pursuit Airplane*. The report said cooling drag 'could be reduced perhaps by 50% if the radiators were placed entirely inside the wing or fuselage and a carefully designed ducting system used to lead the air to and away from them'. Also, as seen on 6 May 1938, Materiél Division issued a request for comments, titled ESMR P-51-643, which included the cooling system housed within the fuselage.

Photographs and most drawings of the Curtiss XP-40, first flight October 1940, show it with a comparatively short duct that was replaced by a chin radiator. The restricted length could hardly have generated the full 'Meredith effect'.

Blueprint drawings, however, found online show an advanced design, with a longer duct whose front is ahead of the wing leading edge. Also, it shows the radiator to be half buried and its diameter greater than its length. The design with the long duct might have been intended to produce the 'Meredith effect' and could in practice have done so.

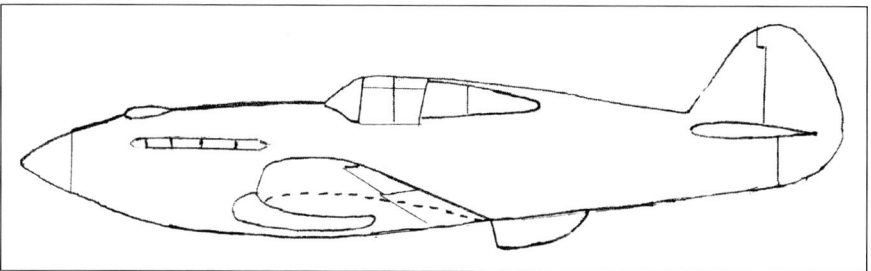

Figure 20.1 – XP-40 with short ventral duct as flown.

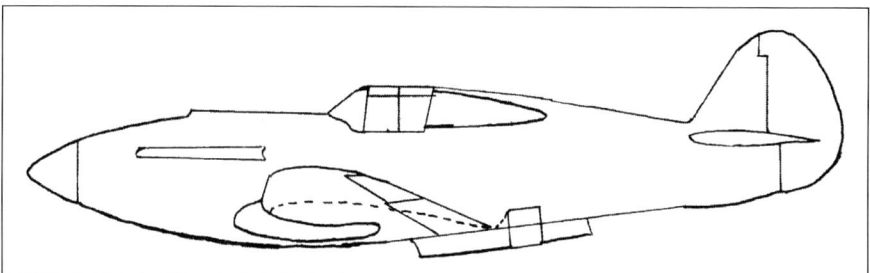

Figure 20.2 – XP-40 drawn with longer ventral duct and partially buried radiator.[1]

The XP-40, with the radiator moved to the chin position, won the 1939 fighter competition at Wright Field. Given the later success of the Mustang with the aft radiator this seems a retrograde step. Various explanations have been given for the radiator move to the chin position forward from that ventral aft. Gruenhagen wrote in 1969: 'Engineering problems prompted the designers to revert to a nose mounted radiator in order to meet production schedules.'[2] (Production was certainly facilitated when glycol and oil cooling were a unit below the engine.) Ethell, in 1981, reported that P-40 designer Donovan R. Berlin said: 'The Curtiss-Wright management thought it looked better that way.'[3] Research in Britain by the RAE and Rolls-Royce showed there were actually sound reasons for moving the radiator from the ventral to the chin position. The RAE's wind tunnel work confirmed the ventral aft location could produce high drag due to the long build-up of the boundary layer. The November 1935 report into the ventral position stated: 'Further tests are to be made with radiator moved forward so that the duct entry is in the plane of the nose of the fuselage. It is hoped that the entry loss will be reduced considerably.'[4] Rolls-Royce experimented on the Heinkel He 70 with, 'moving the radiator forward [from a ventral position] into the fuselage frontal area [which] produced a great improvement'.[5] In 1939 the ventral radiator of the Hawker Tornado was moved to the chin position after incurring compressibility problems.

The Curtiss XP-46 was intended to replace the P-40. This was wind-tunnel tested at end-1939 and early 1940.

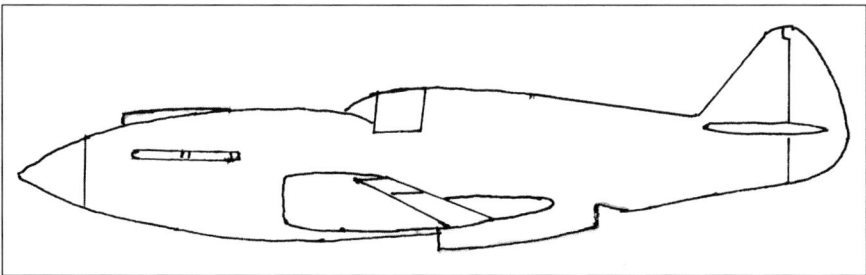

Figure 20.3 – XP-46 based on report *Tests of the XP-46 airplane in the NACA full-scale wind tunnel* (Nickle and Wilson, NACA, January 1940).

The XP-46 also had a ventral aft duct demonstrating that Curtiss still favoured the position. Its cooling systems may have been consciously designed to achieve the 'Meredith effect' given its long and carefully contoured duct. Marshall and Ford wrote: 'The company [Curtiss] placed great expectations on achieving significantly lower drag via an embedded radiator and duct system to achieve a "Meredith effect".'[6] The BPC technical team noted to NAA that Curtiss and the USAAC had represented that the P-46 was also designed to achieve 'Meredith effect' radiator cooling benefits.[7] Thus, Curtiss had an advanced design in 1939 indicating that in the US there were then designs that could achieve the 'Meredith effect'.

The overall point about the US is that there was sufficient information available from Materiél Command and NACA and probably other sources for Curtiss to have designed an advanced 'Meredith effect' system in the period before NAA was marketing an advanced fighter design to the BPC in March and April 1940. The Curtiss aircraft are particularly interesting as the XP-40, as in the internet drawing, and the XP-46, had ducts that could have developed the 'Meredith effect' and were believed, in the case of the latter, by the BPC to have done so.

Non-US aircraft

The Americans were not the only nation to consider buried cooling systems below and behind the pilot position. In Europe there were, before 1940, examples of aft-located fully buried ducted cooling systems and of Allison-powered aircraft with

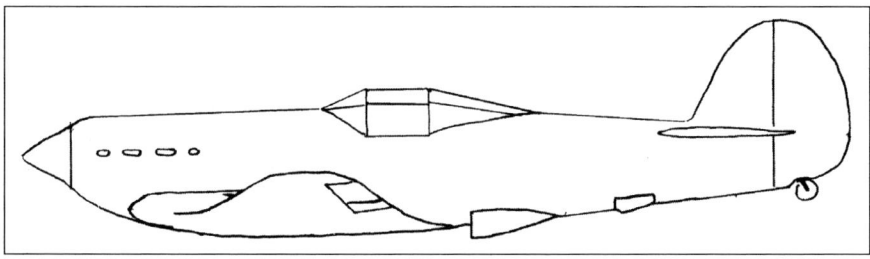

Figure 20.4 – Reynaud R-36.

partially buried systems. The Belgian Reynard R-36, first flight November 1937, had a fully buried aft ducted radiator.

The French VG-30 series had ventral radiators. The VG-32, which had a semi-buried duct similar to the VG-33 production version powered by a Hispano-Suiza engine was intended to be Allison-powered but did not fly as the engine was not delivered.

The VG-50, which had an almost fully buried radiator, was also intended to be Allison-powered and did not fly for the same reason. The Hispano-Suiza-engined VG-36 on which the VG-50 was based, did fly in May 1940.

To conclude, there is evidence that Curtiss aircraft, certainly, could have been designed to exploit Meredith's ideas. Also, European aircraft, possibly Reynard and Arsenal, had cooling ducts capable of exploiting the 'Meredith effect'. Thus, there were aircraft precedents for NAA's selection of an aft ventral position and some of this may have been designed to exploit fully the 'Meredith effect'.

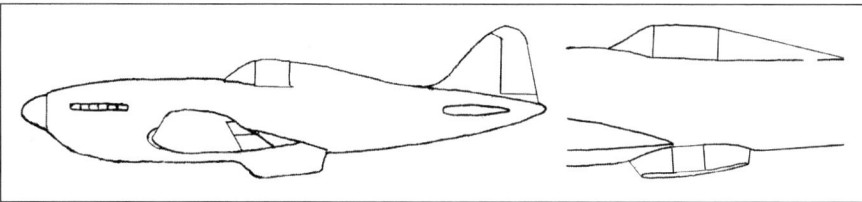

Figure 20.5 – Arsenal VG-32 (Allison engine).

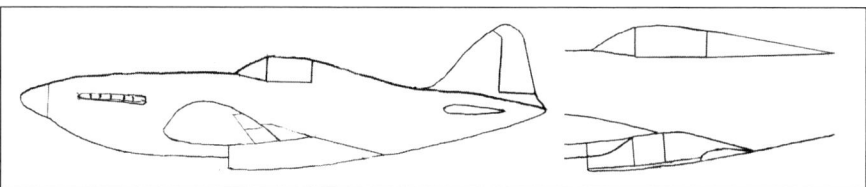

Figure 20.6 – Arsenal VG-50 (Allison engine).

Chapter 20

Stages in the evolution of the Mustang

Previous chapters looked at the question of whether the designs that developed into the Mustang had a ventral aft radiator designed with the intention to generate the thermodynamic 'Meredith effect', or whether aerodynamic factors based on the need to bury an 'oversquare' radiator could alone explain the ventral aft location of the radiator duct. Now the question of the possible role of the 'Meredith effect'

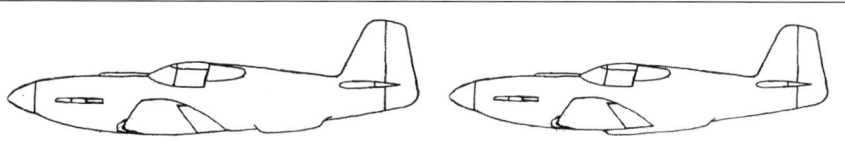

Stage 1 and Stage 2 – February 1940 – NA-50 B/P-509 first known configuration and March 1940 – change in configuration of cooling duct.

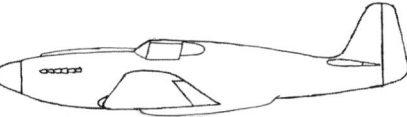

Stage 3 – May 1940 – Increase in X-73 overall dimensions, lengthening ducts, change in tail horizontal surfaces location.

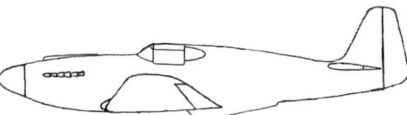

Stage 4 – June 1940 – Changes to X-73 internal duct configuration and cockpit glazing.

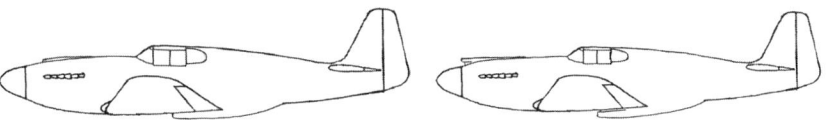

Stage 5 and Stage 6 – October 1940 (first flight) – Further changes to X-73 duct configuration, carburettor and cockpit glazing – February 1941 – Addition of 'lips' to the Mustang radiator duct entrance and extended carburettor duct entrance.

Figure 21.1 – Stages in the development of the design of the Mustang.

on the development of the aircraft that become known as the Mustang is analysed. This development is already the subject of many books. Therefore, to simplify the issue, the evolution of the design has been broken down into six stages. Each of these stages will be considered in order to analyse the impact of Meredith's ideas.

Stage 1) and 2) – revision of the cooling duct – February/March 1940

Drawings of the P-509, the predecessor of the Mustang, in February and in March show a major change in the location and length of the cooling duct. The first drawing reveals the duct in the fully aft location. It is not known when the design first had this layout, but it seems likely by end-1939 or early 1940. It will be recalled that Schmued commented in March 1939: 'Due to the small size of the engine compartment, the oil radiator, coolant tank and cooling radiator will have to be placed in the fuselage to the rear of the pilot.'[1] In the second drawing, dated 10 March, the duct is longer as it had been moved forward and its entrance is ahead of the wing trailing edge.

The event precipitating this change might have been a meeting of NAA engineers in later February, who gathered in an attempt to break the impasse between the BPC and NAA, the former requesting the latter to produce P-40s under licence, while the latter wanted to produce a new design for the former. The P-509 project, which had been rejected by the BPC in January, needed to be more advanced in order to convince the BPC. NAA's Aerodynamicist, Ed Horkey recorded: 'We had a meeting in the War Room on the second floor of the Admin Building. Here we reviewed the pursuit design and formulated a plan to move the proposal ahead without delay.'[2] The P-509 design was then revised by Schmued who relocated the radiator duct entrance forward.[3] (It might be noted that Atwood had insisted that there were, before April 1940, no formal drawings, only his freehand sketches.)

The revision had several impacts which would have made the ducted radiator more effective in exploiting the 'Meredith effect'. It placed the duct entry in a high pressure position under the wing. 'The Meredith duct should be embedded in the fuselage or in the wing to avoid excessive external drag. The optimized intake is positioned in the lower part of the aircraft at about two-thirds of the wing chord, where the pressure reaches its maximum.'[4] It made possible an increase in the length of the duct, allowing for much longer diffusing and converging ducts. Also, it decreased the length in which the boundary layer could build up (a key concern of Meredith), it reduced the length of piping from the engine to the radiator, it

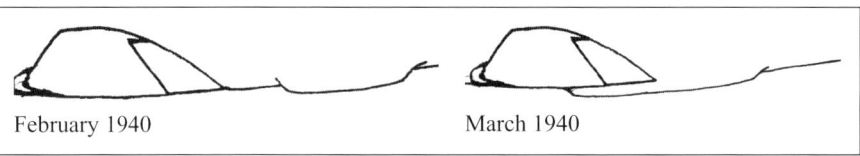

| February 1940 | March 1940 |

Figure 21.2 – Change in NA-50 B / P-509 configuration of cooling duct.

placed the heavy radiator nearer to the centre of gravity, and the location of the duct entry avoided interference drag of the wing trailing edge.

This change is particularly significant as Schmued might have placed the cooling duct in the ventral aft location for purely aerodynamic reasons. As seen in March 1939 he had stated: 'Due to the small size of the engine compartment, the oil radiator, coolant tank and cooling radiator will have to be placed in the fuselage to the rear of the pilot.'[5] This position might have reduced cooling drag but it would not have produced much of a 'Meredith effect' thrust. The redesign by NAA engineers, with its long duct, would have been much better. It might be argued that these engineers would have been aware of the 'Meredith effect' – even if it were not as yet named such – on the basis of reading multiple NACA reports. Also, Atwood played no part in this meeting and the resulting repositioning.

P-509/NA-50 B design presented to the BPC

In mid-March NAA presented the P-509 design to the BPC. Atwood claimed that before April only freehand drawings existed demonstrating how the 'Meredith effect' could be derived in the aft ventral location. Thus, the question needs to be asked what was presented to the BPC. Schmued recorded that earlier Kindleberger had instructed him to prepare such documents:

> In March, Dutch Kindleberger said, 'Ed, do we want to build P-40s here?' From the tone of his voice, I knew what kind of answer he expected. I said, 'Well, Dutch, don't let us build an obsolete airplane, let's build a new one. We can design a better one and build a better one.' And that's exactly what he wanted to hear. So he said, 'Ed, I'm going to England [New York] in about two weeks and I need an inboard profile, three-view drawing, performance estimate, weight estimate, specifications, and some detail drawings on the gun installation to take along. Then I would like to sell that new model airplane that you develop.'[6]

The 'new model airplane' identified by Schmued was the P-509.

On 6 March NAA sent the BPC a proposal to 'build a plane of its own design that would be better than the P-40'.[7] Five days later NAA sent a proposal for the P-509 that included three-view drawings and Specification 1592 giving preliminary design data. This stated NAA could deliver a better fighter due to proven systems, evidenced by the BT9/Harvard, faster if NAA reconfigured the Curtiss's P-40 for its own production.[8]

In 1981 Jeffrey Ethell published *Mustang a documentary history* and the documents included a BPC letter of intent, dated 11 April, text shown boxed below, to purchase NA-50B fighters from NAA in accordance with North American Spec 1592. (The BPC knew the P-509 as the NA-50 B following the radial engined NA 50 A which NAA had previously unsuccessfully marketed to the BPC.) Paul A.

Ludwig in *Development of the P-51 Long-Range Escort Fighter Mustang* (2003) wrote that he contacted Atwood in 1981, who told him in that, 'Specification 1592 is no longer available'.[9] This indicates Atwood knew that Spec 1592, which included three view drawings and hence more than freehand drawings, had existed.[10]

Sometime in mid-March Kindleberger and Atwood presented the P-509 to the BPC.[11] As seen, Atwood insisted there were 'only some freehand sketches' – a point that will be returned to later.[12] Other accounts, however, state that Atwood presented rather more than freehand drawings. In 1969 Gruenhagen wrote: 'The three view drawings and preliminary weight estimates which were used to secure the confidence of the British were presented by Kindleberger's right hand man and Vice President of NAA, John Leland Atwood.'[13]

On 18 March, Spec 1593, *The High Speed of the Allison Powered Pursuit* was sent by NAA to the BPC.[14] This contains work by NAA Aerodynamics and Thermodynamics experts on the cooling system and a new low drag/high speed airfoil. NAA's aerodynamicists Horkey and Ashkenas, and thermodynamicists, George Beerer and G.R. Mellinger outlined new developments in the P-509.[15] These included two ideas which had been central to Meredith's 1935 paper, the duct configuration and the use of exhaust gas momentum. By 15 March NAA was sufficiently confident in progress with the BPC to issue *Research and Development Order Shop Charge [SC] 1050* and to start a mock-up.[16]

10/11 April – BPC letter of intent/Atwood's 'birthday' of Mustang

In Atwood's account he was invited to see Sir Henry Self of the BPC after presenting only freehand drawings, setting out how best to exploit the 'Meredith effect' in the aft ventral position:

> Finally, early in that month [possibly 10 April], I was invited into Sir Henry's office and was advised approximately as follows: that they had decided to accept our proposal; that I should *prepare a letter contract* for his signature; that it should provide for the purchase of 320 aircraft of our design; and finally, that a definitive contract would be negotiated on the basis of this *letter contract*.[17]

There are again diverging accounts of events. Atwood's describes a contract for 320 NA-73 X aircraft. Surviving documentary evidence in The [British] National Archive shows a copy of a *Letter of Intent* to purchase 400 NA-50 Bs. (A *Letter of Intent* outlines an understanding between two parties which is intended to be formalised later in a legally binding agreement or contract.) In 1989 Bill Yenne, based on material provided by Atwood, wrote that on 11 April Atwood presented Self, 'with a draft of a letter contract which called for "the production of 320 NA-73 X aircraft equipped with an Allison engine and an airframe to be designed and built by North American Aviation"'.[18] The National Archive document, however,

N.A.A.

I am directed by His Majesty's Government to inform you that it is their intention to purchase from you 400 single-seat fighter aeroplanes, plus spare parts therefor in the amount of 20% of the value of the aeroplanes.

Material Ordered

(a) 400 North American model N.A.-50B single-seat fighter aeroplanes fitted with Allison GV-1710 engines and three bladed metal propellers all in accordance with North American specification No.1592 as finally altered and amended and agreed upon.

Letter of Intent, dated 11 April 1940, in The National Archive.

shows that on 11 April the BPC's Self stated: 'I am directed by His Majesty's Government to inform you that it is their intention to purchase from you 400 single-seat fighter aeroplanes.' The 'Material ordered' was '400 North American model NA-50 B, all in accordance with North American specification No 1592 as finally altered and amended and agreed upon'.[19] (This aircraft was called the NA-50 B thus identifying it as following the radial engined NA-50 A.)

Stages 2) and 3) – Changes in dimensions – March/May 1940

Drawings of 10 March and 15 May show that the aircraft, identified at the latter date as the X-73, was significantly longer than the P-509/NA-50B. The wingspan and area were also increased. At this stage the future Mustang's dimensions were effectively determined.

Other detail changes were; the horizontal tail surfaces were moved forward relative to the vertical surfaces; and the carburettor duct entrance moved forwards. The first reduced interference drag between these horizontal and vertical surfaces.

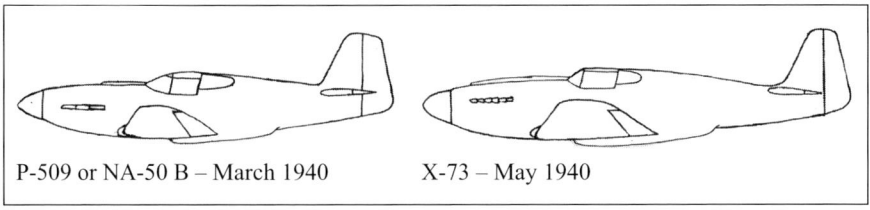

P-509 or NA-50 B – March 1940   X-73 – May 1940

Figure 21.3 – Increase in overall dimensions, lengthening ducts, change in tail configuration.

The second decreased the length for the boundary layer build up to the duct entrance. Also, the number of exhaust stacks was doubled from three to six.

The laying out of the larger design by Schmued incorporated in developed form the use of second-degree curves or conic sections in the design of the fuselage. He wrote:

> This is the kind of shape the air likes to touch. The drag is at a minimum and it was the first time that a complete airplane, with the exception of the lifting surfaces, was designed with second-degree curves. I laid out the lines myself and it was a first.[20]

The completed NA-1620 Detail Specification was delivered to both to the BPC and USAAC on 24 April.[21] This showed a significant increase in dimensions. (No specific explanation has been found for this change, but the requirement for equipment to meet British requirements like self-sealing tanks may have needed greater wing area in order not to raise wing loading.)

	P-509 (March)	NA-1620 (April)
Span	34 feet	37 feet
Length	26 feet	31 feet
Wing area	180 square feet	236 square feet

NAA Vice President Lee Atwood had sent a letter to the BPC on 1 May 1940, which is in The National Archive, promising initial deliveries of the 320 NA-73 airplanes to begin in January 1941: 'We are proceeding with the design of a single seat fighter airplane, our Model NA-73, incorporating an Allison engine and fitted with provisions for equipment and armament as detailed more completely hereunder.'[22]

Other changes included: the carburettor duct was greatly lengthened but remained exposed. The P-509 drawings and mock-up started after mid-March shows three doubled up exhaust stacks per cylinder bank. This was probably as part of the effort to increase exhaust thrust, the potential of which was recognised by Meredith as his third conclusion in his seminal 1935 paper. NAA's Spec 1593, *The High Speed of the Allison Powered Pursuit*, had highlighted the importance of exploiting exhaust gas momentum. (This is further discussed below.)

Stage 3) and 4) – Changes to internal duct design, and cockpit glazing – May to October – debate re role of Curtiss material

Between May and October there were further changes, particularly to the duct design where there is debate as to the extent that, following receipt of material from the Curtiss, this was incorporated into the design of the Mustang. NAA vehemently denied taking anything from the XP-46, but a careful analysis of the XP-46 and changes in the NAA design might cast doubt on these denials.

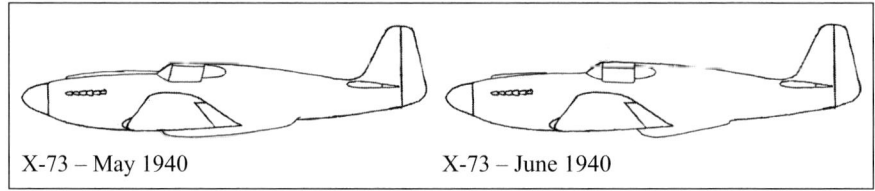

X-73 – May 1940   X-73 – June 1940

Figure 21.4 – Changes to internal duct configuration and cockpit glazing.

On 10 April the BPC's Self had advised Atwood to obtain P-40 data from Curtiss. The XP-46's cooling systems was consciously designed to achieve the Meredith effect according to Marshall and Ford. 'The company placed great expectations on achieving significantly lower drag via an embedded radiator and duct system to achieve a "Meredith Effect".'[23] The BPC may have known more about Curtiss and its deliberate use of the 'Meredith effect' than it overtly disclosed to NAA but wanted NAA to get information direct from Curtiss so as

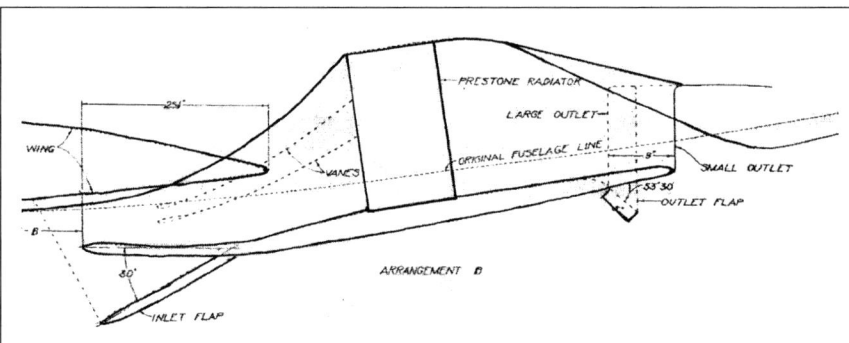

Tests of the XP-46 airplane in the NACA full-scale wind tunnel (Nickle and Wilson, NACA, January 1940). (This drawing shows the adjustable duct entrance – a feature of the June iteration of the X-73.)

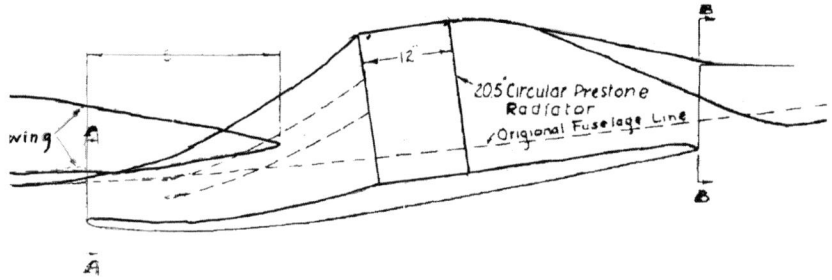

Drag Analysis of Single-Engine Military Airplanes Tested in the NACA Full-scale Wind-tunnel (Dearborn and Silverstein, NACA, October 1940). (This drawing shows a 'circular Prestone [glycol] radiator' – a feature of the June version of the X-73.)

Figure 21.5 – XP-46 duct design drawings in NACA reports.

to avoid charge of passing on Curtiss proprietary information. Marshall and Ford in 2020 wrote:

> The BPC technical team noted to NAA that Curtiss and the USAAC had represented that the P-46 was also designed to achieve 'Meredith Effect' radiator cooling benefits. Verbal approval for the X-73 was granted under the proviso that NAA obtained data on the XP-46 design from Curtiss that may have been beneficial to the company in the new project.[24]

Atwood returned to New York from Curtiss on 11 April and reported the purchase of data for the XP-37, XP-40 and the XP-46 to Self. On 16 April, Curtiss put together a list of documents considered to be of interest to NAA. On 1 May, Atwood informed Self that Curtiss, 'are furnishing to us data covering a comprehensive series of wind tunnel, cooling and performance tests of a similar aircraft, which data will assist us in the design and manufacture of these airplanes'.[25] On 21 May, Atwood paid Curtiss, who sent the data.[26] A drawing in the XP-46 wind tunnel test of January 1940, *Tests of the XP-46 airplane in the NACA full-scale wind tunnel* (Nickle and Wilson, NACA, 1940), is very revealing as it shows distinct similarities to the revised NA-73 duct.[27] The drawings of the XP-46 duct design are shown opposite (below). The first is in a report specifically covering the NACA tests on the XP-46. The second is in the report for all single-engine aircraft tested by NACA, including the XP-46.

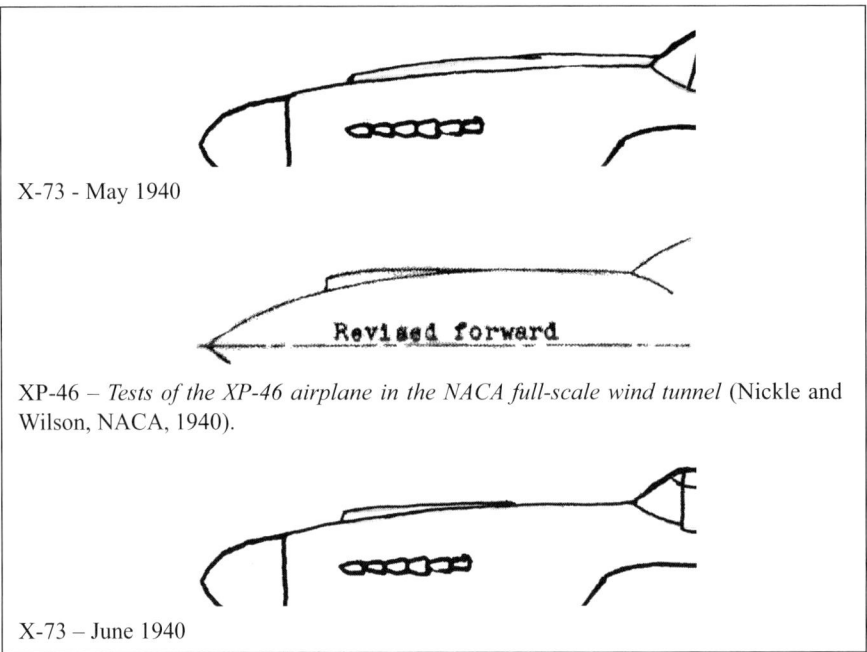

X-73 - May 1940

Revised forward

XP-46 – *Tests of the XP-46 airplane in the NACA full-scale wind tunnel* (Nickle and Wilson, NACA, 1940).

X-73 – June 1940

Figure 21.6 – Changes in the carburettor inlet design.

Accounts of the Mustang's origins generally state that by this time the design of the NA-73 was set and the Curtiss data had no impact. Careful examination of various drawings dating to mid-1940 reveal a rather more complex story.

The May drawing of the exterior of the X-73 shows the longer fuselage, but the external configuration of the duct is similar to the 10 March drawing and quite different to the drawing of late June. Therefore, it is assumed that the duct configuration remained unchanged between March and May. Also, between 13 May and 27 June there appear to have been significant changes not only to the cooling duct but also to the carburettor duct and to cockpit glazing. This raises questions as the whether NAA drew on material that it received from Curtiss after 21 May 1940 and before 27 June? For example, as seen opposite, the carburettor duct appears to have been buried in the area close to the cockpit in a manner similar to drawings in the XP-46 wind tunnel test.

Another area of change, bringing the design closer to the XP-46, was the cockpit canopy frames were made vertical and the quarter light changed so that the bottom edge was lowered and it was shortened.

Debate over extent NAA used Curtiss material

The question of the extent that NAA used Curtiss's duct design is now examined in more detail. The XP-37 and XP-40 data set by Curtiss was of no interest to NAA. The debate lies in the use made of the XP-46 wind tunnel test which included drawings of the internal duct. In the future, NAA would deny that it had used the data. Atwood wrote: 'Dutch Kindleberger quipped that we didn't even open the package, although I am sure that some of our technical staff did examine the reports.'[28] Schmued claimed, 'nothing was owed to the XP-46 design'.[29] Horkey, in an interview in 1986, 'does remember seeing a wind-tunnel report on a P-46 model'. (This does confirm NAA saw the drawing in Figure 21.5.) 'We ran a quick study and said that this is just a rehashed P-40, and we don't see where it's all that great, and we'd do better starting from scratch.'[30] Might it be possible that NAA personnel protested too much? As seen, Schmued commented frankly on borrowing ideas: 'Companies would steal ideas from the best organizations. It was a dog-eat-dog affair. We lied like hell, made promises.'[31]

Also, NAA had a vested interest in denying the use of the XP-46 data. Apart from company pride it could laid itself open to lawsuits by Curtiss. The company would have been right if it did anticipate Curtiss sensitivities over use of its wind tunnel tests and therefore deny taking account of Curtiss data. 'Curtiss-Wright Corporation felt that NAA had infringed upon its XP-46 design features and sued NAA while its NA-73X and NA-73 programmes were ongoing.'[32] In 1981 Jeffery Ethell published *Mustang A Documentary History*. This quoted Curtiss chief engineer Fredric Flader which told Curtiss-Wright employees on 28 October 1943:

> A comparison of the outlines and construction of the XP-46 with those of the highly successful Mustang will show that Curtiss

Engineers have contributed substantially to this aspect of winning the war. Incidentally, the performance of the XP-46 and the original Mustang were strikingly similar, even to certain difficulties with cooling; and recent great improvements are due primarily to greatly superior engine performance.[33] [This last referred to re-engineering the Mustang with the Rolls-Royce engine.]

NAA personnel and many commentators have dismissed Curtiss's claims. Might they, however, have any justification? The issue is whether detail changes were made following access to the XP-46 design. On 21 April Schmued began detailed

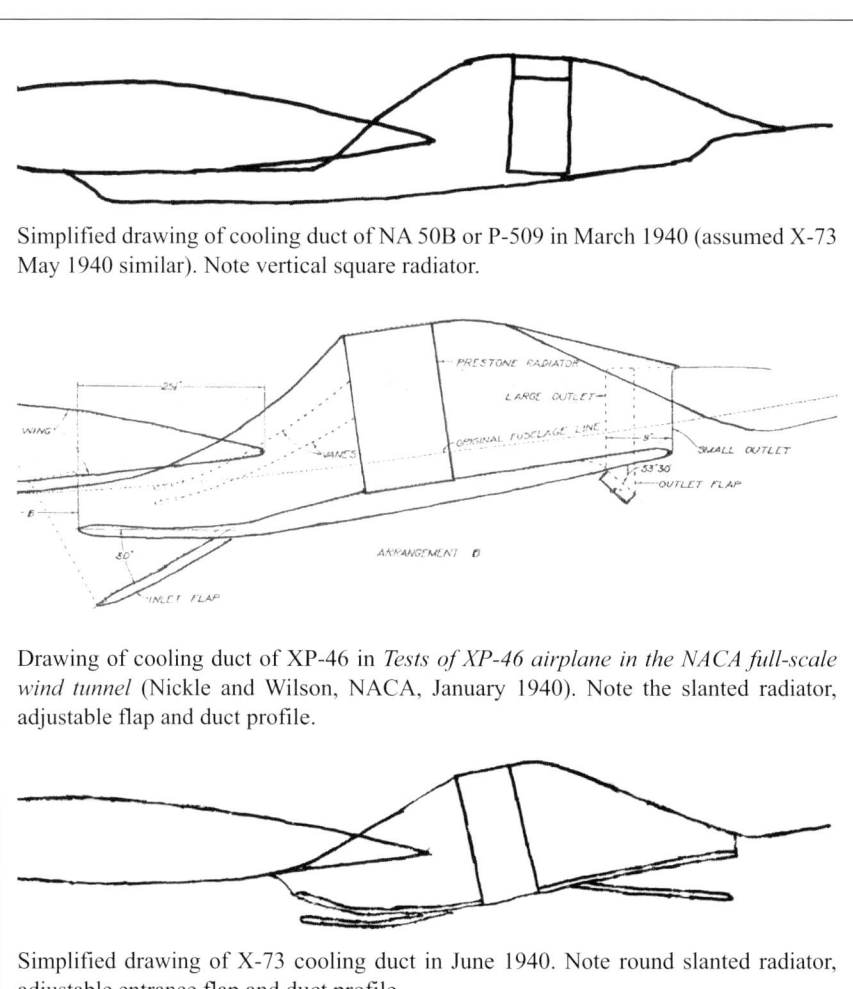

Simplified drawing of cooling duct of NA 50B or P-509 in March 1940 (assumed X-73 May 1940 similar). Note vertical square radiator.

Drawing of cooling duct of XP-46 in *Tests of XP-46 airplane in the NACA full-scale wind tunnel* (Nickle and Wilson, NACA, January 1940). Note the slanted radiator, adjustable flap and duct profile.

Simplified drawing of X-73 cooling duct in June 1940. Note round slanted radiator, adjustable entrance flap and duct profile.

Figure 21.7 – Simplified drawings of X-73 cooling duct in pre-June and June 1940 and XP-46 duct.

design of a larger aircraft than the P-509/NA-50 B. This was delivered to the BPC on 24 April as the NA-1620 Detail Specification. (It is not clear if the larger version had the same duct configuration, but it is likely.)

As seen in Figure 21.5 there are two NACA drawings of XP-46 ducts. The first was in a NACA summary of the wind tunnel tests on many US single-engine aircraft dated October 1940, delivered by Curtiss to NAA after 21 May 1940. The second was in the NACA wind tunnel test of the XP-46 in late 1939 and early 1940 which was seen by NAA in May 1940. Both reveal interesting aspects of the design. The first reveals there was an adjustable entrance. The second explicitly describes the radiator as circular. 'The rear radiator installation used a single 20-1/2-inch diameter radiator located in the fuselage behind the wing.'[34]

The NACA wind tunnel tests of the XP-46 can be compared with a drawing of the interior layout of the NA-73 in June 1940. The June 1940 iteration of the NAA design shows major changes to the May design. These changes make the NAA duct similar to the XP-46 duct. To summarise:

- Both the XP-46 and the X-73 (June iteration) had adjustable entrances.
- The May X-73 iteration had a square vertical radiator. The June X-73 iteration was similar to the Curtiss XP-46 in having a round radiator at an angle to the vertical so it faced the airflow more directly. The slanting of the radiator results in a continuation of the upper line of the diffuser duct to avoid an abrupt change in airflow on both the XP-46 and the June iteration.
- The May iteration of the X-73 had a long passage before the duct diverged. In the June iteration this passage was eliminated and the duct diverged from the entrance.

The one area of clear difference is that the variable exit flap is much larger on the June iteration than the XP-46. Overall, however, the profile of the XP-46 and the X-73, June iteration, ducts are similar and very different to the X-73 May iteration.

The Curtiss XP-46 had a sophisticated cooling duct that the BPC considered was designed to incorporate the 'Meredith effect'. The BPC was keen that NAA looked at the XP-46 design. The similarity between the redesigned NA-73 duct and the Curtiss XP-76 duct seems striking. Therefore, it might be arguable that, as a result of reviewing Curtiss's work, the NAA Mustang was redesigned to enhance the derivation of the 'Meredith effect'. Thus, as the design of the aircraft progressed the 'Meredith effect' again became increasingly basic to it.

Stages 4) and 5) – June to October

There were further changes between June and October to the cooling duct.

The airframe was completed in early September. Therefore, these changes took place mostly in July and August. The lower duct profile bottom was flattened and the exit was given a steeper angle. This had the effect of facilitating parallel entry and exit to the external airflow. Apart from the later introduction of the 'lip' in 1941

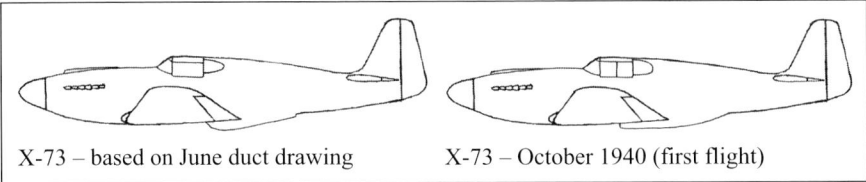

| X-73 – based on June duct drawing | X-73 – October 1940 (first flight) |

Figure 21.8 – Further changes to duct configuration, carburettor and cockpit glazing.

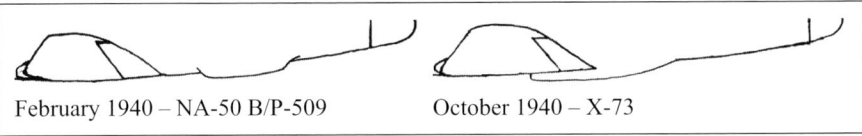

| February 1940 – NA-50 B/P-509 | October 1940 – X-73 |

Figure 21.9 – Change to duct configuration between February and October 1940.

(discussed below) the duct was approaching its final form. Other changes included, in late June the cockpit structure was revised with vertical supports and a shorter but deeper quarterlight.

This chapter has looked at the development of the Mustang in terms of a series of stages. The point, developed later, is that in the course of these stages the area that saw the greatest development was the cooling duct.

In February the ventral duct would hardly have generated the 'Meredith effect', but by October it would have developed this effect much more effectively. These changes were largely made in two stages: the first after the 'war room' meeting of NAA engineers, including aerodynamicist Horkey; and the second, arguably, after Curtiss XP-46 material had been reviewed.

Chapter 21

Atwood's subsidiary
Meredith claims re-examined

Lee Atwood, as seen, made an overarching claim that the 'Meredith effect' of drag reduction was the basis of the Mustang's design. He also made a number of subsidiary claims which are considered in this chapter and then the overarching claim is returned to in the following chapter. These subsidiary claims are relevant as they obscure analysis of the central claim and need to be cleared away first. They are also repeated in many accounts of the development of the Mustang, resulting possibly in inaccurate and often internally conflicting histories.

1) Atwood read Meredith's work in 1939

In 1993 Atwood wrote:

> As chief engineer, I had regularly reviewed the NACA reports and in 1939 one (NACA report) came to my attention that was a review of some British experimental radiator work at Farnborough. An investigator named Meredith had experimented with energy recovery from aircraft radiators.[1]

There is no evidence that Atwood read Meredith's 1935 paper (published 1936) *Cooling of Aircraft Engines With special reference to Ethylene Glycol Radiators enclosed in Ducts* in 1939 (or indeed before late 1993 or early 1994).

The 1993 quote above is the first known description by Atwood of Meredith as a man as opposed to reference to the 'Meredith effect'. Meredith undoubtedly existed as a man, but otherwise the broader description is inaccurate and indicates that Atwood had not read Meredith's actual paper. Meredith was not an investigator, nor did he conduct actual experiments with energy recovery from radiators. Meredith was the head of the Aerodynamics division of the RAE in 1935 and wrote the mathematical paper *Cooling of Aircraft Engines With special reference to Ethylene Glycol Radiators enclosed in Ducts*, demonstrating, with equations, not experiments, that recycling radiator heat could theoretically result in thrust greater than drag above a certain speed.

Atwood probably first read Meredith's actual paper in late 1993 or 1994 when David Birch of Rolls-Royce sent him many documents. In 1997 Atwood wrote:

> David Birch of the Rolls-Royce Heritage Trust and author of *Rolls-Royce and the Mustang* has most generously supplied me with copies of some very pertinent documents involving Royal Aircraft Establishment reports, patents, and wartime research and typed reports from the Rolls Experimental Department then at Hucknall. Among these papers are RAE Report No 1702 by R.S. Capon, dated 1936, in which he extends and amplifies Meredith's thesis.[2]

Atwood does not mention receiving and reading Meredith's report (as opposed to Capon's) for the first time, but this is the first recorded occasion he gives its name and quoted from the actual report, giving its correct reference number.

Schmued stated: 'Atwood didn't even know what the 'Meredith effect' was, until Dr Shenstone told him.'[3] (At a time that was almost certainly after the ventral location of the Mustang's radiator had been determined. Shenstone, as will be seen, went to NAA in 1941 to help resolve duct entry issues.) Atwood, however, probably knew the Meredith concept on the basis that: 'Charles Luttmann recalls conversations with Lee Atwood on the ramjet quality of radiator ducting.'[4] From 1938 to 1940 Luttmann was the British liaison official in the US with direct responsibility for NAA.

Overall, Atwood claimed that in 1939 he read a NACA report that reviewed British RAE experimental work on cooling by a researcher called Meredith. No such report has been found and Atwood almost certainly did not read Meredith's 1935 paper, published by the ARC in 1936, until 2003/4. He was, however, aware of Meredith's insight about the 'ramjet quality of radiator ducting' from reading NACA reports that built on and cited Meredith.

As seen, Atwood probably first read Meredith's actual paper in late 1993 or 1994 when David Birch of Rolls-Royce sent him many documents. Atwood's *Meredith Mystery*, 1994, stated:

> The subject of the cooling drag of radiators had been under study by the Royal Aircraft Establishment in Farnborough in 1935 or earlier. The F.W. Meredith report, No. 1683 of August 1935, and the R.S. Capon report, No. 1702 of March 1936, rather well defined the radiator drag problem in a mathematical way.

This is Atwood's first known reference to Meredith's actual 1935 report and subsequently (but not before) he referred frequently, specifically, to it. Here in 1994, rightly, Atwood said the problem was defined in a mathematical way. (In 1993, wrongly, he said Meredith had experimented with energy recovery from airplane radiators.[5]) Atwood now actually quoted Meredith's work for the first time (possibly because he has just actually read the original text) as confirming his interpretation. 'The employment of the principle of low velocity cooling avoids the necessity for an increasing expenditure of power with increasing speed provided the exit conditions are adjusted to suit the speed.' Ironically, what Meredith was saying does not support Atwood. Meredith and Atwood were discussing different points. Meredith was referring to different speeds in level flight, regardless of specific flight conditions, while Atwood was comparing climb with faster level flight conditions.

Subsequently, Atwood referred specifically to Meredith's 1935 paper. In 1995-8: 'The most significant contribution to the problem [adjusting airflow] came from Report No. 1683 by F.W. Meredith in 1935. This was followed by Report No. 1702 by R.S. Capon, also of the RAE, in 1936, who elaborated on Meredith's rather taut analysis.'[6] And:

> Regarding the Mustang, I have always referred to the work of F.W. Meredith of the RAE, whose report (RAE No. 1683) of August 1935, greatly influenced me as chief engineer for North American Aviation to offer the British Purchasing Commission the ducted radiator design configuration in 1940.[7]

In a 1997 document, *Mustang Design Retrospective,* Atwood appeared to confirm that in 1939 he had not read Meredith's 1935/6 report. He wrote: 'I had read a modified version of this report [Meredith 1935], published about 1939.'[8]

The question might be asked what had Atwood read in 1939 and 1940? NACA put a lot of work into the public domain between 1939 and 1943 which drew on Meredith's work. As seen, NACA did indeed publish several papers in 1939, both translations of German work by Winter and Göthert and research by NACA by Silverstein, Breevort, Leifer and Dearborn, that examined and experimented with what was the 'Meredith effect' without using that term but did cite Meredith. Atwood said that as Chief Engineer he read NACA research.

2) Atwood maintained that Meredith's work was not well understood

In 1995 Atwood wrote of the 'Meredith effect':

> This subject has been misunderstood or poorly described in the literature available to me, and even Meredith's report No. 1683 in 1935 does not seem to have been clearly understood by a considerable number of airplane designers in the 1930s and 1940s.[9]

Two years earlier he had said: 'It is rather interesting to note also that there is no record of any recognition at that time of the 'Meredith effect' by anyone in England or [in the US] by Dr Edward Warner, formerly professor at MIT.' He said in the *Lo-Technology Analysis of the 'Meredith effect* in 1996: 'This subject has been misunderstood or poorly described in the literature available to me, and even Meredith's report No. 1683 in 1935 does not seem to have been clearly understood by a considerable number of airplane designers in the 1930s and 1940s.'[10]

An assessment of the design of other aircraft before and contemporary with the Mustang indicates that Meredith's work was well understood and incorporated into them. Meredith's report had an immediate impact in several areas. In R.S. Capon's June 1935 RAE paper he said revisions, discussed below, would be made due to points made about 'compressibility' in Meredith's June paper. These changes were included in Capon's August 1935 interim report. The November 1935 *The Aircraft Engineer* included a lengthy report by G.P. Douglas of the RAE which looked at the theory of duct design noting: 'The theory of duct cooling has been developed independently by Capon and by Meredith.'[11]

Flight, April 1937, wrote:

> A contributory factor to the performances attained by some of our latest military machines fitted with Rolls-Royce Merlin engines is the 'ducted' radiator which produces a measure of thrust at high speeds. The principle on which these radiators function has been further developed by Messrs C.J. Stewart and F.W. Meredith, of the RAE, [patent GB 456,335] whose present scheme of supplementing airscrew thrust by that exerted by a mixture of air and exhaust gases pouring from slits in the trailing edge may prove highly beneficial to high-speed machines. Briefly, the scheme converts into thrust the drag presented by the cooling system, which may be regarded as a form of heat engine increasing the speed of an aircraft.[12]

As seen, German researchers Winter, Wiese and Göthert published research on the thermodynamic aspect of ducted radiators in 1937 and 1938, translated by NACA in 1939 and 1940. Also, NACA's Silverstein, Breevort and Leifer did further research in this area in 1939 and 1940. In France, Louis Breguet and his chief engineer René Devillers published in 1938 a synthesis of the knowledge at that time,[13] *La technique des radiateurs d'aviation et de leur carénage,* which described the new ducted radiators were using the heated air to generate some forward thrust.[14]

Other aircraft which would have been known to the Mustang designers incorporated the 'Meredith effect'. The recycling of heat was explicitly a design objective of the Spitfire's ducted radiator design which Meredith inspected in September 1935. In 1986, E.J. Davis, who worked on the Spitfire in 1935 said: 'About this time, Frederick Meredith evolved a novel ducted cooling system [where] the warmed air is speeded up and ejected at the rear making the system a rudimentary jet engine.'[15] The BPC believed that Curtiss had incorporated a 'Meredith effect' radiator duct in the XP-46.

Also, German and US NACA researchers built on Meredith's and Capon's work in the later 1930s. Thus, Atwood's implicit claim that he discovered and appropriately interpreted Meredith's otherwise overlooked and misunderstood work does not hold up and was indeed contradicted by Atwood himself. In 1997 he wrote:

> Horkey denies any use of the Meredith analysis for his work, and so I must conclude that he was one of the few technical personnel

who was unaware of that publication and that he never saw it until I gave him a copy two or three years ago. The NACA published an adaption of the Meredith analysis in the late 1930s as a regular technical report.[16]

In the same year, Atwood wrote: 'It is apparent that the principle of cooling drag reduction by restoration of the momentum of the air after it passed through the radiator was well known before the war and had been applied in aircraft configurations of the Spitfire, Bf 109 and others.'[17]

3) Atwood used freehand drawings only in informal presentations to the BPC, that is, there were no formal drawings

In 1989 Yenne wrote in *Rockwell The Heritage of North American,* based on interviews with Atwood:

> North American had not at that time [10-11 April] presented the British Purchasing Commission with drawings or specifications of any kind, except for the freehand sketches Atwood had used to demonstrate the concept during the informal conversations and the letter contract was the sole document available. [18]

Yenne also wrote: 'Atwood began by making it clear to the British that NAA had no design.' (In 1989 Yenne may have checked whether there were no drawings, showing he was uncertain about the claim. 'However, as far as Atwood remembered no drawings of this new concept were made at that time.' [19]) And in 1993, in his *Origin and evolution of the Mustang,* Atwood insisted there were 'only some freehand sketches'.[20] As seen, there is, however, incontrovertible evidence that NAA presented to the British the Allison-powered P-509/NA-50 B in 1939, which developed into the Mustang.

Gruenhagen's account in 1969 makes clear Atwood presented rather more than freehand drawings. 'The three view drawings and preliminary weight estimates which were used to secure the confidence of the British were presented by Kindleberger's right-hand man and Vice President of NAA, John Leland Atwood.'[21]

In 1996, Ed Horkey wrote criticising Atwood's claims about using only freehand sketches: 'No purchasing commission buys something from a "sketch on the back of an envelope".'[22] Atwood responded in 1997:

> Horkey outlines the routine peacetime method in general use in the United States in developing a contract for airplanes involving design drawings, weight, performance estimates, etc., and extensive negotiations before a contract award is made. He does not consider it credible that a purchasing authority could or would bypass these procedures and award a 320-airplane order. He was not there, however, and that is exactly what was done, and the letter contract with a not-to

both in the United States (at the National Advisory Committee for Aeronautics, NACA) and in England, as the "Meredith effect".' Atwood describes his concept as being a form of a ramjet. 'It involved discharging the heated air under as much pressure as was possible in a rear facing jet, as in the yet-to-be-developed ramjet engine. Thus, the cooling drag could be reduced to very little or even nothing at all in theory.'[33] Thus, it would appear that Atwood initially identified the 'Meredith effect' with the 'ramjet' quality of radiator ducting.

In 1993, Atwood appeared to modify the interpretation of the 'Meredith effect' in his paper *The origin and evolution of the Mustang*. As seen above, he wrote: 'An investigator named Meredith had experimented with energy recovery from airplane radiators. Meredith experimented with fully ducted radiators and showed that substantial recovery was possible.' And later: 'Meredith experimented with ducting it [airflow] out to the airstream. By making the outlet variable he could restrict the air passing through the radiator to just that amount needed for cooling.' Thus, Atwood interpreted Meredith's work in terms of both the cooling system as a heat engine and the adjustable exit for different flight conditions. The latter was the insight behind Beisel's adjustable cowl flaps for radial engines, subsequently applied by Rolls-Royce to the ducts of inline engines, which restricted the pressure drop to that necessary for different flight conditions.

In subsequent papers Atwood began to give greater emphasis to controlling the pressure drop than the creation of thrust. In the *Mustang Margin Aviation History: A Clarification*, in the Air Power History Journal of Air Force Historical Foundation, 1996, Atwood reiterated: 'The basic reason for its [Mustang's] speed margin, in my opinion, has never been adequately described.'[34] Atwood here focused on the different cooling requirements of different flight conditions. 'Since an airplane may use full power in a climb the radiator must have enough air forced through it to cool the engine at best climbing speed, which, in the fighter planes, was about half the maximum speed in level flight.' Atwood now discounted Meredith's original contribution, which was the examination of 'compressibility' in the thermal sense. 'Contrary to some rather capricious reports he [Meredith] never suggested that cooling could be effected with a net increase in propulsive power.' Actually, Meredith demonstrated that mathematically it was possible for the power generated by the cooling system to exceed the power absorbed by it.

In a speech to the Yorkshire Air Museum Elvington, England, 1998, titled *Yorkshire Air Museum, June 13, 1998*, Atwood said that the thermodynamic element of Meredith's work could be ignored completely.

> I would like to interpolate what is, to me, a most fascinating element in Meredith's 1935 report. As you may have noted, I have made no reference to the thermal element in the momentum recovery of the radiator cooling air and at the temperatures involved, the air expansion was relatively small and could be neglected. Real jet propulsion, however, involves fuel burning, and the velocity of the gases and heated air is greatly augmented by this high temperature.[35]

This reflects a complete misinterpretation of Meredith, who said the air expansion of cooling air, due to radiator heat, could above certain speeds produce thrust that exceeded cooling drag.

Thus, it appears that the more Atwood became familiar with Meredith's actual work the less accurately he described it. Indeed, when he was simply describing the 'ramjet quality of radiator ducting,' without mentioning Meredith's name, he was more accurate than he specifically described Meredith's work later in terms of controlling the pressure drop.

Summary

Overall, it is regarded here as very hard to reconcile many aspects of Atwood's account of events with other available information. That said, is it possible to reconcile at least some aspects of Atwood's account with other evidence?

Firstly, Atwood's use of freehand drawings to win over the BPC in April 1940 is not incompatible with more formal drawings being presented in mid-March as well as Spec 1592 and 1593. (The problem is that Atwood denied the existence of such drawings.) Secondly, there are possibly parallel lines of development – one based on Atwood's use of the Meredith effect as a thermodynamic concept, and the other, Schmued's desire to reduce aerodynamic drag – which are not mutually exclusive that resulted in the adoption of the aft ventral position. In 1939, with respect to positioning the Mustang's cooling duct, Atwood's reading of NACA documents built on Meredith's 1935 paper and may have alerted him to the possibilities of heat regeneration in a ducted radiation. This, to be properly exploited in a single engined airframe, required positioning in the aft ventral position and Schmued could have selected the same position as it was the only place an 'oversquare' radiator could be buried. The two routes led to the same result.

It remains, however, difficult to avoid the conclusion that many aspects of Atwood's account are unreliable or simply wrong. If these, however, are cleared away, Atwood's central claim about the role of the 'Meredith effect' as the Mustang's basis might be analysed more clearly next.

Chapter 22

Atwood's overarching
'Meredith effect' claim re-examined

What then about Atwood's overarching claim that 'the "Meredith effect" of drag reduction was the basis of the Mustang design', given that so many of his subsidiary claims are regarded as questionable?[1] It has been argued that the P-509, the design ordered by the BPC in April 1940, with its ventral aft radiator, could have been laid out by Schmued without drawing on Meredith's work due to the requirement to bury an 'oversquare' radiator which could only be done in the ventral aft location in a single engined fighter. Therefore, Atwood's main claim might seem weak.

Might it, however, be argued that while the 'Meredith effect' was not initially the basis of the Mustang design, it increasingly became so as that design progressed. There are a number of times when Meredith's ideas might have had an impact, as the design progressed.

> Stages 1) and 2) – February-March 1940 – The radiator duct was refined in later February or early March by lengthening it and placing the entrance under the wing. This improved both its aerodynamic and thermodynamic qualities. This followed a meeting involving a group of engineers including Horkey's aerodynamic group.

> Stages 3) and 4) – May and June – Following receipt of the design of the XP-46 from Curtiss there appears to have been another redesign of the duct. As seen, Curtiss placed great expectations on achieving significantly lower drag via an embedded radiator and duct system to achieve a 'Meredith effect'. [2]

Competing narratives

The role of the 'Meredith effect' in the evolution of the Mustang is complex. Elucidating it has not been helped by the information, or misinformation, provided by Atwood, Schmued and Horkey, all of whom had different and conflicting motivations.

Atwood

So far, the focus has been on Atwood's role in positioning the Mustang's radiator which he insisted followed his reading of Meredith's work. Basically, his motivation appears to have been to project himself as the fundamental designer of the Mustang in place of Schmued and his vehicle for this projection was his discovery of the 'Meredith effect'. If 'the "Meredith effect" of drag reduction was the basis of the Mustang design' and Atwood read Meredith's work in 1939 and sold a design using his freehand drawings incorporating it to the BPC in 1940, then he was *de facto* the Mustang's designer and Schmued and others had only secondary roles.

There is evidence that Atwood had long nursed the belief that he was the true designer of the Mustang. In 1962 *Air Power Historian* carried a tribute to the late Dutch Kindleberger by Ed Rees of NAA. The same article, with subtle changes, was republished two years later, described Rees as a 'former Assistant Corporate Director of Public Relations at North American Aviation'.[3] Atwood, who ceased to be chief engineer by the beginning of 1940, is identified as the designer of the Mustang. 'Even before the British had approached him, he [Kindleberger] had Atwood design a basic fighter.'[4] A paragraph of *Flying Magazine* article of 1944 and the Rees' article of 1962 might be compared.

Mighty Midget *Flying Magazine* Ed Churchill 1944 [5]	A Tribute To Dutch Kindleberger: The Mustang – A Great War Horse *Air Power Historian* Ed Rees 1962[6]
Use of a liquid-cooled engine	This [from previous sentence 'liquid-cooled inline Allison engine']
presented the problem of a large, drag producing radiator scoop, conveniently placed at the nose of the plane.	presented the problem of a large drag-producing radiator scoop conventionally placed at the nose of the ship.
Efforts to relocate it had failed.	
Merle Beaupré and his fuselage group aided the power plant group	Atwood
in placing the radiator just aft of the pilot.	placed it [radiator] under the fuselage and aft of the pilot.

This is the first mention found of Atwood's role in placing the radiator aft. After Rees left NAA the text of two years earlier was revised in another otherwise similar article to give Schmued some design credit. This might indicate that Rees in 1964 was unhappy with Schmued's earlier total exclusion in 1962, when he was a public relations official for NAA.

A Tribute To Dutch Kindleberger: The Mustang – A Great War Horse *Air Power Historian* Ed Rees 1962	How the North American P-51 Mustang emerged from the shadows and helped assure Allied air superiority over Europe *Airforce Magazine* Ed Rees 1964[7]
The plane was designed	The plane was designed
	by a team headed by Raymond Rice and Edgar Schmued,
to be made in many parts; large units were broken down into smaller components for ease of assembly and installation.	to be made in many parts; large units were broken down into smaller components for ease of assembly and installation.

Atwood wrote an unpublished memo titled *Origin of the Mustang Fighter Plane*, dated 8 August 1973, which was drawn on in three later books which incorporated language that show use of this memo, particularly the word 'concept', in relation to the design of the cooling system.

1) *Pursue and Destroy: 8th Air Force's Fighter Group in WWII*, 1978 – 'Kit' Carson relates that Atwood 'had produced a *concept* which put the radiators aft of the wing in a well contoured inlet that would recover some of the energy lost in the cooling process ("Meredith effect")'.[8] Carson wrote at some length that the Mustang's wing did not achieve laminar flow. The radiator, however, was important. 'The advantageous position of the coolant air scoop has already been touched on in other portions of this narrative.'[9]

2) *Lee Atwood, Dean of Aerospace*, 1980 – Lee Atwood retired as President and CEO of North American Rockwell in 1970 but remained on the board until 1978. This tribute book to his remarkable record was issued in 1980. This states: 'Having criticised the P-40s for its bulbous front located radiator and its large pressure drop Atwood said, 'My *concept* was to take advantage of the [hot] cooling air to add momentum to it, which in those days was known as the "Meredith effect". It wasn't anything new aerodynamically'.[10]

3) *Rockwell The Heritage of North American*, 1989 – Bill Yenne reports Atwood in words similar to the memo cited earlier: 'It seemed apparent to me that a considerably better design could be developed [than the P-40], and I evolved a design *concept* which involved placing the coolant radiators back of the wing and designed a ducting system to recover some of the cooling energy in an efficient manner.'

This account emphasises:

Although some technical work was by then being done in California, North American had not at that time presented the BPC with drawings or specifications of any kind, except for some freehand sketches Atwood had used to demonstrate the concept during the informal conversations, and the letter contract was the sole document available.[11]

In Yenne's book Atwood is frequently mentioned, Horkey once (in the context of the Mustang's laminar flow wing), and (incredibly) Schmued never. The team was described as what 'would be responsible for what well may be the greatest piston-engined fighter of all time included J. Stanley Johnson and Raymond Rice'.[12] There is no mention of Schmued in the entire book – an oversight that is hard to see as accidental but is remarkable.

The debate over the Mustang's origins might seem to have started in 1993 when Atwood published the *Origin and Evolution of the Mustang*. As seen, however, this debate over the Mustang's origin started much earlier. Something, then in 1993, made Atwood determined to reassert his role in the conception and selling of the Mustang design in 1993. That something, although Atwood did not make this explicit, was possibly Ray Wagner's *Mustang Designer, Edgar Schmued and the P-51,* published in 1990 after Schmued's death in 1985, which focused on Schmued's design role and did not attribute any design contribution to Atwood.[13] Atwood's 1993 *Origins* paper was probably his riposte to the Wagner's book and expanded on his unpublished 1970s paper.

Schmued

Edgar Schmued is generally regarded as the principal designer of the Mustang. For example, an article in 1975 on *The restoration of the XP-51* by restorer Jack Cox attributed the actual layout of the aircraft to Schmued. 'In 1940 North American's small engineering department, headed by Raymond H. Rice was resourceful and had some brilliant designers – particularly Edgar Schmued, the person who actually laid out the P-51 as we know it today.'[14] An analysis of his role in its layout and particularly the ventral aft location of the radiator shows this was due to aerodynamic reasons with no part played by Meredith's work or the intention to generate the 'Meredith effect' which was a fortuitous accident. As seen in response to 11 March 1939 Air Corps Specification, CP39-770, for an advanced fighter.[15] Schmued commented: 'Due to the small size of the engine compartment, the oil radiator, coolant tank and cooling radiator will have to be placed in the fuselage to the rear of the pilot.'[16]

In 1971 a symposium on the *Conception and Development of the P-51 Mustang* gave Schmued the opportunity to present his side. He does not mention Meredith or say anything about the location of the cooling system. Nor does he mention Atwood. A transcript was not published until 2015 in NAAR. In the first paragraph he recounts that Kindleberger came into his office in [early March] and said, 'Ed do we want to build P-40s?' I was horrified at the thought of building an obsolete airplane at North American. I said, 'No I hope not!' He said, 'Well, then get going and get me a proposal out. I am going to England in the next ten days, and I need an inhouse profile, a three-view drawing, specifications, performance and a weight statement.[17] Clearly this went beyond Atwood's freehand sketches.

In 1985 Schmued died. He left biographical tapes and a manuscript which started: 'Many stories about the design of the P-51 Mustang have been told, most of them out-and-out fabrications, or not really reflecting the actual history.' Ray Wagner says his book *Mustang designer Edgar Schmued and the P-51*, 1990, was suggested by Schmued's widow Cristel who tracked down leads and won their cooperation. In 1986 Horkey gave an interview to Wagner, material from which is also included in his book. Atwood was not included in Wagner's acknowledgements. Schmued's account in Wagner's book expands on that given to the 1971 symposium. In March 1940, Kindleberger asked Schmued if NAA should build P-40s. Schmued said they could build a better one and Kindleberger requested 'an inboard profile, three-view drawing, performance estimate, weight estimate, specifications and gun drawings'.

In a 1985 interview in Wagner's book Schmued had described the problems of the entry duct in 1985. Schmued claimed he placed the radiator aft to reduce interference drag:

> It is very important to locate the radiator in a position where it cannot interfere with either wing or main fuselage drag, because any spillage is turbulent air, producing drag. To keep that to a minimum, I moved the radiator as far aft as I could, and as far below the wing as I could. With the radiator located in this position, we really got an optimum. We had a world beater![18]

Schmued describes the thermodynamic element of the 'Meredith effect' as discovered later, accidentally revealing that it was unplanned:

> We also found out, later on [in wind tunnel tests], that the heat from the engine actually produced thrust in the radiator by increasing the velocity of the air flowing through. That horsepower gained by the radiator was only discovered by wind-tunnel investigation. We were contractually required to wind-tunnel test the P-51, and long after the first airplane flew, we got around to test a model which had an electric motor to drive a three-bladed propeller. We found from wind-tunnel data that the P-51 should not be as fast as it was actually clocked. Our chief thermodynamicist, Joe Beerer, studied the problem and noticed the favourable effect of the radiator.[19]

Thus, it was the thermodynamicist Beerer who later discovered the favourable but unplanned 'Meredith effect'.

Schmued's account is hard to reconcile Atwood's assertion that the thermodynamic element was deliberately incorporated in the design from the beginning on the basis of his reading of Meredith's work. Also, Schmued asserted that Atwood was unaware of Meredith's work: 'Atwood didn't even know what the "Meredith effect" was, until Dr Shenstone told him.'[20] (That, as will be seen, would most likely be January 1941 when Shenstone advised on duct entry problems.)

What motive might Schmued, or colleagues, have had for possibly denying Atwood or the 'Meredith effect' any role in the development of the Mustang? Schmued had a poor relationship with Atwood and Ray Rice, Atwood's successor as Chief Engineer in 1940. In 1952 he resigned, stating Atwood and Rice's 'adverse attitude towards me made it mandatory to find employment elsewhere'.[21] At fifty-two he was below the retirement age of fifty-five and received no pension after twenty-two years with NAA. It is, however, quite possible, indeed likely, that Schmued laid out the basic design of the aircraft that would become the Mustang without any knowledge of Meredith's work and particularly its thermodynamic aspect.

Horkey

NAA aerodynamicist Ed Horkey supported Schmued when opposing Atwood's claims, but had his own agenda. Horkey played a leading role in the Mustang's pioneering use of a laminar flow wing. The decision to use such a wing was made in California when Atwood was in New York marketing to the BPC. He was not involved in the decision and resented it. He insisted, probably rightly, that the Mustang's wing did not produce actual laminar flow and hence much lower drag. Thus, Atwood stated the reason for the Mustang's high speed lay with its efficient 'Meredith effect' radiator, again probably rightly. Horkey was an ally of Schmued, who saw Atwood as attempting to write Schmued out of the story of the Mustang's design, but he also wanted to ensure that the role of the laminar flow wing was given due attention.

In AAHS Journal [1996] titled *The P-51: The Real Story*, Horkey spread responsibility for the Mustang among many NAA employees with the exception of Atwood and Rice, who were not mentioned.[22] His two key points relevant here are set out next:

> THE BRITISH WERE IMPRESSED BY SOME FREEHAND SKETCHES AND PROCUREMENT OF SOME CURTISS-WRIGHT P-46 WIND TUNNEL DATA AND *PROCEEDED TO ORDER THE FIRST P-51 (NA-73X) AIRCRAFT* [Capitals follow the original text] False: The standard procedure in those days was to have Ed Schmued and his group make an inboard profile and three-view drawing and the start of a specification. No purchasing commission buys something from a 'sketch on the back of an envelope'.

Atwood had said only freehand drawings were presented before 10 April. Inboard profile and three view drawings were presented in mid and later March of the P-509 (Spec 1592 and Spec 1593) which was identified by the BPC as the NA-50 B.

> THE COOLING RADIATOR AND DUCT WERE DERIVED BY THE AERODYNAMICS GROUP IN CLOSE COOPERATION WITH ED SCHMUED AND HIS DESIGNERS True: Irv Ashkenas, George Mellinger and I were well-educated in aerothermodynamics.

> We applied calculus in place of algebra for most of the analysis work. The mathematical work of a British professor [Meredith] was never used by us at any time.

This might be seen as disingenuous. The mathematics actually used by Horkey and Ashkenas was in German papers by Winter and Göthert, translated by NACA in 1939. Both dealt with the recycling of heat and cited Meredith. Meredith's maths was quite simply intended to demonstrate that above a certain speed the power generated by heating the cooling air could exceed the drag of the duct. Horkey's fellow aerodynamicist Ashkenas used Winter's paper which said: 'It was Meredith who first pointed out the possible gain in power required to tow [pull forward] the radiator systems under the operating condition as compared with the cold condition.'[23] (As seen, Winter wrote, since the computation involves extensive simplifications, the results may be used as a first approximation only. Thus, simple formulas for lowering radiator drag with an 'accuracy sufficient for practical requirements'. Also, as seen, Horkey drew on Göthert's paper which again referenced Meredith. Thus, both Horkey and Ashkenas read German work, translated by NACA, which explicitly cited and built on the thermodynamic element of Meredith's work. Also, Horkey, moreover, was clearly aware of Meredith's work, for in 1986 he said:

> Meredith had brought forth the theory or proposal to take in air at a high velocity and slow it down, which, of course, builds up pressure. As it goes through the radiator core, the pressure helps some, but primarily you have more dwell time. Then with the increased pressure and temperature, you squeeze the air down again as it goes out the back and you actually get some thrust from this, or what can be called negative radiator drag.[24]

As seen, Horkey made clear the aft ventral location was a pragmatic choice and not based, as Atwood claimed, on the position best to implement Meredith's ideas:

> Locating the radiator aft was an overall fuselage/aerodynamic choice, heavily influenced by the fact that the radiator size, computed by us [Aerodynamics group] and *powerplant people* in preliminary design, was too big to fit forward under the engine.[25]

The reference to the powerplant group in Horkey's quote is supported by the 1944 *Flying Magazine* article which said: 'Use of a liquid-cooled engine presented the problem of a large, drag producing radiator scoop, conveniently placed at the nose of the plane. Efforts to relocate it had failed. Merle Beaupré and his fuselage group aided the power plant group in placing the radiator just aft of the pilot.'[26] The powerplant group worked with Horkey's Aerodynamics group.

In 1996 Horkey was killed in a car crash, leaving the field to Atwood who, by now a very old man, wrote a number of increasingly inconsistent papers and articles – until his death in 1999 – on the development of the Mustang. Horkey's account was intended to downplay the role of the 'Meredith effect' in the development of the Mustang. Horkey and Atwood disagreed over the reason for the high speed of the Mustang. Horkey saw it as due to the laminar flow wing which he played a leading and pioneering role in applying to the Mustang design. Atwood explained the high speed by the 'Meredith radiator' whose potential he, uniquely at the time, recognised. On the reason for the high speed of the Mustang Atwood was probably right in that it had more to do with the low net drag radiator than the laminar flow wing, although this had other benefits, particularly delaying compressibility facilitating a high diving speed.

Atwood's motivation

Why was Atwood so determined to promote his own role and suppress that of Schmued? On 2 April 1979, Jeffery Ethell's letter to Jack Reeder showed Atwood had not planned to use a laminar flow wing. 'I do know that Lee Atwood has stated that it was not his initial intention to use the NACA laminar flow wing, but this was thrown in after work had started on the final design.'[27] Schmued explained: 'We had planned to use a NACA-23 series airfoil. But when we heard that the NACA had developed a laminar-flow, low-drag airfoil, we decided to use it on the P-51 Mustang.'[28] Atwood was particularly concerned in the article, *Atwood – an engineer's perspective on the Mustang* (*Flight Journal*, June 1999) to emphasise that laminar flow was not his intention and was less important to the Mustang's speed than the 'Meredith effect'. [29] The main advantage of the laminar flow profile was 'not in drag reduction but in high-speed dives', in dealing with 'compressibility', giving it a high critical Mach number.

Atwood appears to have resented the adulation, as he perceived it, given to Schmued in England in 1943 when he was investigating why the Spitfire was so much lighter than the Mustang? On 23 March, Rolls-Royce's Bill Lappin wrote to NAA's P.H. Legarra. 'It has been a most valuable thing to have Schmued visit us, and after meeting him a few times, one has no difficulty in realising why the Mustang is a good aeroplane.'[30] In 1996 Atwood wrote to Larson:

> I knew Ed quite well and thought I had a reasonable relationship with him. After Ray Rice sent him to England during the war for liaison work for a short time, he was never quite the same. The British and our attaché, Tom Hitchcock, lionized him and he ate it up. He was an under-age conscript in the Kaiser's Army and in poor health when mustered out. He never finished school and started a bicycle shop in Germany. He was always enterprising and got a job with General Motors Holden in Brazil and somehow got a transfer to the United States. Since General Motors had picked up an interest in U.S. Fokker, an antecedent to North American, he got a job there on a drawing board. He was one of about twenty in the Engineering

Department, and I first met him in 1934 when I came to Baltimore from Douglas and Chief Engineer with Dutch Kindleberger. Schmued was a good draughtsman with a good mechanical sense and also a bit of artistic flair. However, he knew nothing of aviation technology and was never near Messerschmitt in Germany. [31]

(The last refers to the British misunderstanding in 1943 that Schmued worked for Messerschmitt prior to his leaving Germany, partially as he retained a strong German accent.) It is, however, difficult to understand quite why Atwood felt it necessary to behave as he did in suppressing Schmued's role as his own role in the marketing of the aircraft that was to become Mustang was crucial. He did have the insight that a buried ducted radiator acting as a heat engine could only be located in the ventral aft location in a single engined fighter where a large engine required a large radiator and duct, and that his freehand drawings may have helped persuade the BPC in order to order the aircraft that became the Mustang. Atwood is described as involved in marketing and credited with the successful sale to the British: 'Atwood spent three weeks in New York City in the converted hotel space utilized by the commission for its office. It was largely through his efforts that the agreement was reached to produce a new fighter in preference to the P-40.'[32] There is, however, firm evidence that the NAA presentation used much more than Atwood's freehand drawings, including three view drawings and Specs 1592 and 1593 by Schmued, Horkey and Ashkenas.

Atwood appears to have developed an obsession that his role in the conception of the Mustang was underappreciated and Schmued's was overdone. The 'Meredith effect' and his early recognition of it at the time when others were supposedly unaware of it appears to have been his vehicle for projecting his role – possibly even subconsciously.

Summary

To conclude Atwood's overarching claim that 'the "Meredith effect" of drag reduction was the basis of the Mustang design' is not valid in the way that he meant it when asserting that his 'concept was to take advantage of the [hot] cooling air to add momentum to it, which in those days was known as the 'Meredith effect'.[33] Thus, in Atwood's account from the outset the aircraft that became the Mustang was designed to incorporate this effect. In fact, it was quite possible for Schmued to have laid out the initial design of the Mustang, with its ventral aft radiator, without his having had any knowledge of Meredith or the 'Meredith effect'. Indeed, Schmued claimed the beneficial thermal impact of the radiator was only discovered later. What arguably did happen was that – as the design of the aircraft that was to be named the Mustang in December 1940 was developed – the cooling duct was refined by NAA aerodynamicists, Horkey and Ashkenas, and probably others, who both used NACA translated German work and NACA's own research that was based and built explicitly on Meredith's work. Also, arguably the NAA design was modified to incorporate features of the Curtiss XP-46 duct which the BPC knew to have been designed to exploit its ability to generate the 'Meredith effect' the designs of which the BPC wanted NAA to see. Thus, the 'Meredith effect' was the basis of the Mustang design, not because it was initially designed to exploit it, but because, as the design was developed, the 'Meredith effect' was enhanced. Eventually, this had the result that the 'Meredith effect' became so fundamental to the success of the design, evinced by its low cooling drag and consequent high speed, that it could indeed be called, with considerable justice, the Mustang's design's basis.

It might be noted that the 'Meredith effect' itself had two parts – as seen in Meredith's core equation: aerodynamic, where a well contoured duct with adjustable exit limits drag and keeps it constant (but cannot eliminate it); and thermodynamic, as added radiator heat can eliminate drag above certain speeds. Schmued emphasised the former and Atwood the latter. Both the aerodynamic and thermodynamic elements are inherent in a ducted radiator. Breevort and Leifer's NACA report 112, *Radiator design and installation*,[34] which broadly examined radiators and their installation, made an interesting observation. That is, 'a good radiator design without consideration of the thrust [from converting heat into kinetic energy] will also be the best design when the thrust effect is taken into consideration'.[35] Therefore, a radiator did not need to be designed specifically for the 'Meredith effect' for it to be effective at recycling waste heat – as long as aerodynamically, it efficiently used ducts and an adjustable exit to reduce cooling drag.

The next two chapters explore other aspects of Meredith's contribution to the design of the Mustang which strengthen the case that his ideas made a huge contribution to the overall success of the design.

Chapter 23

(2) Mustang and Meredith – duct entry

The most distinctive feature of the Mustang was perhaps its deep aft ventral radiator duct projecting below the fuselage with a pronounced gap between the aircraft and the duct. How did this distinctive 'lip' arise and what might it have owed to Meredith? Also, it will be seen that Schmued attributed the solution to 'British data'. What might this data have been?

In May 1935 Meredith wrote on the problems of duct entry, *Note on the problem of conducting a fluid into a duct with the minimum of losses.* This highlighted the problems created by the boundary layer. It regarded the ventral position as problematical due to the long build-up of the boundary layer. 'Ventral entries. Such a system is bound to lead to separation as the boundary layer is thick and the depression at the surface is accentuated by the curvature of the boundary, serious losses associated are therefore common.' This work was not externally published but, through internal circulation, must have alerted other RAE personnel who worked on the boundary layer and duct entry problems. These other RAE personnel addressed the problem in wind tunnel tests. Hartshorn, writing in a *Note on the installation of a ducted radiator in the ventral position* (November 1935), was pessimistic about: 'Entry losses [where] the conversion from kinetic energy to pressure energy cannot be accomplished without loss for a ventral radiator.'

Meredith's solution was first placed in the public domain in 1936 in his patent – which would have been noted by interested parties, that is aircraft manufacturers – *Improvements in or relating to aircraft and other craft or vehicles* (Stewart and Meredith, GB 454,266, complete specification March 1936). This recognised the problems but did see solutions:

> It is required that the entrance to the duct be designed to avoid the excessive entry loss associated with stream separation. In general this is difficult to achieve without special precautions to remove the boundary layer and the condition can most be easily met by avoiding surface in front of the entrance, or by arranging that the boundary layer over such surface, if it cannot be avoided, does not enter the duct.

The RAE was certainly well aware of the problem of ventral duct entry. In *A review of wind tunnel experiments on ducted radiators* (Hartshorn, July 1936) said of the 'ventral and aft position', these 'have an appreciable residual internal drag due, in the main, to the effect of the aeroplane surface in front of the duct entrance'. But 'the external drag should be slightly less than for a nose radiator since the external drag is less'.[1] *A review of the RAE cooling research*, (Perring, September 1936) stated on entry loss:

> When the entry of the radiator is near the nose of the fuselage, or is located in the leading edge of the wing, the entry loss is very small, but with the ventral and aft radiators there is an entry loss equivalent to a drag of 1.0 to 2.0lb which is due to a separation of the boundary layer from the surface immediately ahead of the radiator entrance.

After the Mustang's first flight on 26 October 1940, wind tunnel and flight tests showed the duct entrances for both the radiator and carburettor duct were unsatisfactory. In early 1941 subtle but significant changes were made to the Mustang's cooling and carburettor ducts. On both, a 'lip' was introduced to bypass the boundary layer from the duct entry.

The background was that on 18 January 'Britain's Air Ministry was contacted for support to assist in the redesign of the scoop'.[2] A week later Beverley Shenstone arrived. When employed at Supermarine he had designed the Spitfire's elliptical wing. Subsequently, he had been appointed to the British Air Commission (BAC) in the US which oversaw the improvement of airplanes built there destined for Britain using British experience. He was well qualified in boundary layer issues having worked in Germany under Prandtl, who had developed the boundary layer concept. Also, through his work at Supermarine, he would have been aware of RAE research on the layer. He can hardly fail to have remarked on the 'lip' introduced on the Hawker Hurricane which was wind-tunnel tested by the RAE in August 1936. 'After reviewing flight and wind tunnel data, Shenstone suggested that the upper lip of the scoop be dropped approximately 1½ in. from the bottom of the wing. The results derived from the GALCIT wind tunnel testing indicated significant improvements to the radiator face pressure distribution.'[3] Boundary layer problems were not confined to the ventral duct. A lip was also introduced for the carburettor scoop, above the engine, as the Alison engine had cut out during high-speed dives. The scoop was raised so the entry had a lip below it and the entrance moved forward to the spinner separation line.

Schmued commented twice on the introduction of the lip giving different explanations. In 1971 he said: 'A clever young fellow, an internal aerodynamicist named Joe Beerer. With the help of some British data, he fixed up that radiator.'[4]

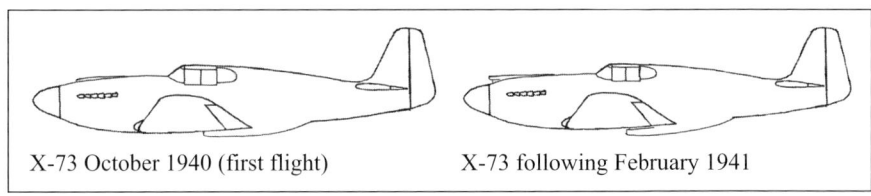

| X-73 October 1940 (first flight) | X-73 following February 1941 |

Figure 24.1 – Changes to cooling and air intake duct entries.

(2) MUSTANG AND MEREDITH – DUCT ENTRY

Beerer had been hired by NAA in 1940 as Chief Thermodynamicist to work on coolant problems on the Mustang. Also, in 1985, Schmued recorded material that was included in Wagner's 1990 book which gave a different story of indirect British involvement:

> The British Air Ministry was extremely helpful. Among others, they sent us Dr B.S. Shenstone to assist us. Dr Shenstone advised us to provide an upper lip on the radiator housing, which was about 1.5 inches below the fuselage contour. By doing this, we got a much better pressure distribution in the air scoop.[5]

This would seem to confirm Shenstone's central role. It might, however, be noted that Horkey gave a different account:

> Ed [Schmued] certainly looks at it from a different viewpoint than we in aerodynamics did at that time. Actually, with the one-quarter scale model at Cal Tech, Irving Ashkenas, who had been working with me [Horkey], came up with the idea of why not put a boundary bleed in. In other words, take that top line of the radiator duct and bring it down from the bottom line of the fuselage and let the turbulent boundary layer that built up under the fuselage go by the entrance and therefore you would get more efficient air into the duct. He went ahead one night and did this on the model and the results were great.[6]

The question of Ashkenas's role will be reviewed later.

Reverting to Schmued, he made it clear that there was British involvement either indirectly through Beerer or directly through Shenstone. Two solutions to redirect the boundary layer away from the entrance had been proposed in the UK: the boundary layer bypass and the 'lip'. The following drawings show the development of British ideas for dealing with the problem of the boundary layer and duct entry. The first drawing shows the solution given by Meredith in his 1935 paper.

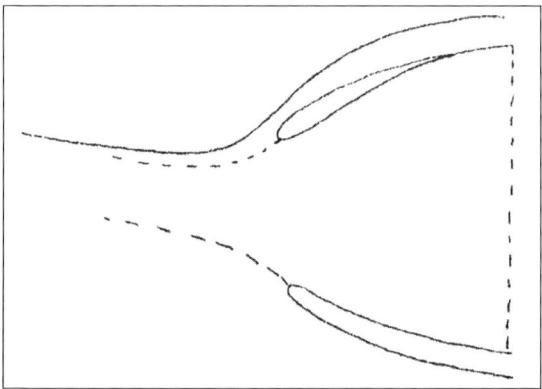

Figure 24.2 – Meredith's drawing of 'an auxiliary duct by-passing the cooling system for the purpose of removing the harmful boundary layer' applied to a 'ducted underslung radiator' from *Note on the problem of conducting a fluid into a duct with the minimum of losses* (Meredith, May 1935).

The second drawing shows Meredith's ideas for improving the Spitfire design in September 1935.

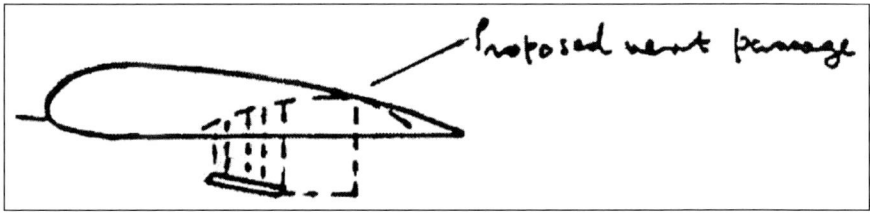

Figure 24.3 – Meredith's sketch made 11 September 1935 during visit to Supermarine showing proposed changes – addition of 'vent passage' and 'guide vanes' – to the F37/34 cooling system.[7]

The next image shows the first illustration found, dating from July 1936, of a 'lip' – here in the chin position.

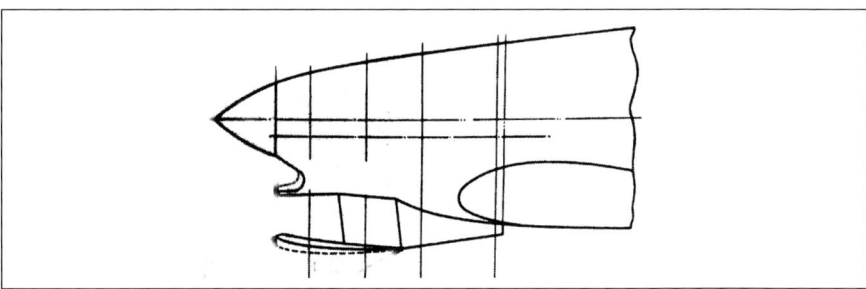

Figure 24.4 – Hawker Hart Model A with 'entrance lip' in *A review of wind tunnel experiments on ducted radiators* (Hartshorn, July 1936).

In the following month a 'lip' was wind-tunnel tested on the Hawker interceptor by the RAE.

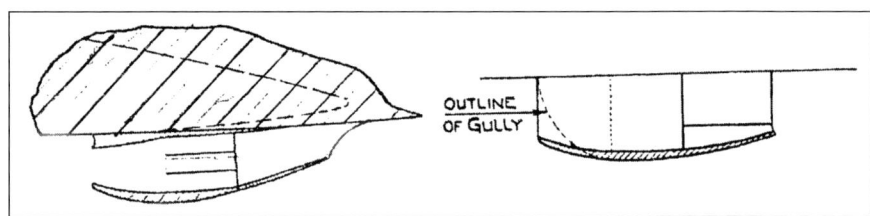

Figure 24.5 – Hawker Interceptor cowl with 'lip added' in *Addendum to Note on the installation of a ducted radiator in a ventral position* (Hartshorn, August 1936).

The RAE also tested a 'lip' on Hawker's planned successor to the Hurricane in 1938. (A bypass was also tested but is not shown here.) A 'lip' was also tested on the Spitfire Mk III as shown in the next two images. (As with the previous Hawker

(2) MUSTANG AND MEREDITH – DUCT ENTRY

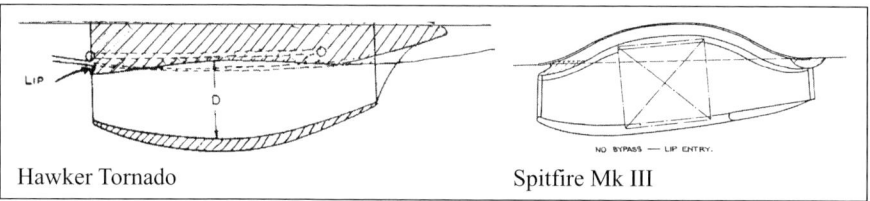

| Hawker Tornado | Spitfire Mk III |

Figure 24.6 – Hawker Tornado 'lip' in *A Preliminary note on an improvement in the design of ventral radiators*, (Patterson, August 1938) Spitfire Mk III 'lip' in *Tests on Spitfire radiators in the 24ft wind tunnel* (Reeman, July 1941).

aircraft a bypass was also tested.) The research paper was dated July 1941. It does, however, demonstrate that the RAE was testing 'lips' and 'bypasses' in the year Shenstone advised NAA.

These images show that there was no lack of British work for Beerer to have drawn on or Shenstone to have used in solving the Mustang's duct entry problems. Also, Meredith had originated this work in 1935.

Ironically, it might be noted that Meredith did not prescribe the aft ventral position as the optimum place to bury a ducted radiator. Indeed, he was implicitly critical of it due to the long build-up of the boundary layer. It was possibly Atwood's insight that the 'Meredith effect', that is the conception of a ducted radiator as a heat engine, could only be realised on a [small] single-engined aircraft in the ventral position. It was Meredith, however, who provided the solution to the boundary layer problem in his 1935 paper with a bypass, thus solving the problem of the ventral location.

It was noted above that Horkey gave credit to Ashkenas for the lip. 'Other people [an allusion to Beerer and Shenstone?] may have come up with that later on. I want to give full credit to Irving Ashkenas as really being the developer of the boundary-layer bleed.'[8] Given, however, that Schmued gave credit to British work both via Beerer and to a specific British individual, Shenstone, his account cannot be excluded. Therefore, if Ashkenas did play a role then this might again be seen as an example of parallel development, as was suggested with the duct location, as a way partially to reconcile Atwood and Schmued's accounts.

Chapter 24

(3) Mustang and Meredith – exhaust gas momentum

Meredith had a third conclusion in his 1935 paper on *Cooling of Aircraft Engines*: 'Finally, attention is drawn to the importance of the moment of the exhaust gases for a high-speed aeroplane, although no attempt is made to deal with this point quantitatively.' Under the heading, 'Effect of the momentum of the exhaust gases on the drag of an engine installation,' he continued, 'design to date has apparently been little affected by consideration of the momentum of the issuing gases'. He added:

> The thrust derivable from the rearward direction of the exhaust gases is given by the product of the mass flow and the velocity of the exit and the latter quantity depends upon the internal design of the exhaust system. The thrust power is, however, also proportional to the speed of flight. Thus, it becomes increasingly important to utilise this thrust as the speed of flight increases.

By correct design much of the energy of the exhaust gases could be retained and significantly add to thrust horsepower in high-speed flight. However, 'no attempt is here made to assess the power which may be available from this source. It is suggested, however, that if an appreciable proportion of the original energy of the exhaust gases can be preserved, this will provide an appreciable increment to the thrust horsepower of a high-speed aeroplane.[1]

Meredith's third conclusion had important consequences, first for the Spitfire and Hurricane, as their exhaust stacks were carefully redesigned by Rolls-Royce to exploit exhaust gas momentum. After this all high-speed inline powered aircraft had exhaust stacks redesigned or initially designed to exploit exhaust momentum. Therefore, the Mustang was not alone in having exhaust stacks designed to exploit exhaust gas momentum as recommended by Meredith. Given the Mustang's high speed it was clearly done in an efficient manner. Therefore, can any direct line be traced to Meredith?

As seen, T.P. de Paravicini had recently worked with Meredith at the RAE before joining Rolls-Royce in late 1935. Rolls-Royce was the first company to investigate systematically exploiting exhaust gas momentum on liquid-cooled

(3) MUSTANG AND MEREDITH – EXHAUST GAS MOMENTUM

Figure 25.1 – *Aircraft exhaust systems* (Paravicini (Rolls-Royce), GB 471,177, November 1935).

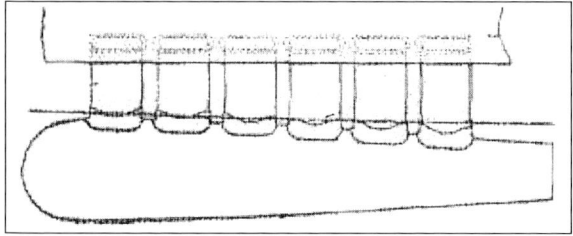

inline engines. On 30 November 1935, Paravicini applied for a patent, for *Aircraft exhaust systems* (Paravicini (Rolls-Royce), GB 471,177, November 1935).[2] 'In an exhaust discharge system for an aircraft capable of a speed of 250 miles an hour the exhaust is discharged into a rearwardly projecting manifold or manifolds.'[3]

Meredith's role was explicitly recognised in experiments made by Rolls-Royce on the Heinkel He 70 delivered in 1936 to Rolls-Royce's aerial test site at Hucknall where a Rolls-Royce Kestrel engine was installed. 'It was on this airplane [Heinkel] that Rolls-Royce, for the first time, developed jet exhaust stacks, of which the first suggestion in Britain had been made by Meredith in the same paper in which he had pointed out the possibility of recovering the energy in radiator heat.'[4]

Both the Spitfire and Hurricane were powered by the Rolls-Royce Merlin engine and quickly adopted the improved design by Rolls-Royce. 'Rolls-Royce believed that for the attainment of maximum speed in a fighter it was effective to make use of the energy in the exhaust by means of the jet exhaust stacks which it had developed, and which were used on all Spitfires and Hurricanes.'[5] The tests led to modifications of the Spitfire's design.

> A distinct improvement emerged from work by Rolls-Royce which indicated that directing the engine's exhaust gases directly rearwards would augment thrust. This thrust augmentation could amount to 70lb, equivalent to a 70hp increase at 300mph. In September 1937 ejector exhausts producing this effect were fitted to K5054 and its maximum speed rose to around 360mph.[6]

After the Spitfire and the Hurricane, all inline fighters exploited exhaust gas momentum.

E.W. Hives, and F.L. Smith of Rolls-Royce, in *High Output Aircraft Engines*, (Hives and Smith (Rolls-Royce), SAE, July 1939) said: 'Rolls-Royce Ltd have now developed and patented what is termed an ejector-type exhaust system in which the exhaust gases are discharged rearwards at high velocity through restricted outlets and their kinetic energy utilized to give propulsive effect which actually adds to the machine speed.'[7] (Rolls-Royce's work followed Paravicini's patent and experimentation on the Heinkel He 112).

In the US radial engines were tested before inlines. The US Navy asked NACA in July 1938 to establish how the exhaust system of a radial engine should be designed to obtain the maximum jet reaction from its waste gases. In the spring of

1939 NACA's Langley's Power Plants Division tested a Pratt and Whitney 1340 engine to determine the amount of thrust that could be obtained by projecting the waste gas rearwards through short exhaust stacks.[8] The report by Hives and Smith of Rolls-Royce was cited in *Experimental Determination of Exhaust Gas Thrust* (Pinkel and Voss, NACA, 1940) which described the experiments on radial engines. This stated: 'At full open throttle at sea level a gain in thrust horsepower of 18% using separate stacks.' The NACA report was then cited in NAA's Spec 1593, *The High Speed of the Allison Powered Pursuit,* by Horkey and Ashkenas, which was sent to the BPC on 18 March 1940.

The Mustang's exhaust system was not initially efficient and its refinement drew on work by NACA which used that by Rolls-Royce. The P-509 drawings and mock-up started after mid-March shows three doubled up exhaust stacks per cylinder bank. 'The engine exhaust stacks required further investigation to achieve optimum effect with minimum performance loss.'[9] These would be replaced by six single stacks. In late-March: 'The engine exhaust stacks required further investigation to achieve optimum effect with minimum performance loss.'[10]

The exploitation of exhaust gas momentum by the Mustang might appear to be part of Meredith's general legacy for inline liquid-cooled engines, as all such powered aircraft used this – unlike the 'lip' which was specifically employed by the Hurricane and the Mustang. (The boundary layer bypass was incorporated in the Messerschmitt Bf 109F and the Lockheed P-38J.) Notwithstanding, this was an idea advanced by Meredith and developed by Rolls-Royce that contributed to the high performance of the Mustang.

Considering this and previous chapters, as a general point, the Mustang embodied three aspects of Meredith's ideas, contained in two of his 1935 papers, in a combination that was probably more effective than any other Second World War fighter.

• *Cooling of Aircraft Engines With special reference to Ethylene Glycol Radiators enclosed in Ducts*	• 'Meredith effect' duct capable of jet propulsion • Stacks to exploit exhaust gas momentum
• *Note on the problem of conducting a fluid into a duct with the minimum of losses*	• Diverting the boundary layer away from the duct entrance – here with a 'lip'

Chapter 25

Mustang story completed

This chapter looks briefly at the further development of the Mustang. Questions are raised as to the explanation for the Mustang's higher speed. Was it the 'Meredith effect' radiator or the laminar flow airfoil? Also, the redesign of the duct for the P-51B is considered. Finally, the questions are asked: did the 'Meredith effect' work on the Mustang; and can any more light be thrown on Atwood's claims that the 'Meredith effect' was the basis of the Mustang's design?

Initial lack of US interest – improbable survival as a divebomber

The Mustang was of no interest to the US Materiél Division, now renamed Materiél Command, which had charge of USAAF procurement. Two aircraft, paid for by the British, delivered in 1941 and designated the XP-51, languished on Wright Field ignored in what can only seem like pique at NAA's temerity to refuse to be restricted to producing trainers and medium bombers. Therefore, when the British order was completed, how close would the Mustang become a footnote in aviation history?

On 8 October 1942, assistant air attaché at the US embassy in London, Major Thomas Hitchcock, wrote in a memorandum: 'It [the Mustang] arrived in England at a time when great emphasis was placed on high altitude performance, and because it was equipped with a low altitude engine, was of no particular interest to English Fighter Command.'[1] Therefore, it was used, almost by default, for low level intrusion and photo reconnaissance.

Hitchcock's memo had continued: 'Sired by the English out of an American mother, the Mustang has had no parent in the Army Air Corps or at Wright Field to appreciate and push its good points.'[2]

By the end of 1940 the British had ordered 620 Mustangs, the first of which came off the production lines in April 1941. In July a further 150 were ordered, ninety-three of which went to the British and fifty-five were retained by the US as the British ran out of funds. In February 1942, No 26 Squadron was the first of twenty-six to operate Mustangs. In May the Mustang attacked airfields in France and two months later demonstrated its legs by reaching the Ruhr in Germany. In August, over Dieppe, came the first confirmed kill.

Events forced the USAAF to take notice. On 7 December 1941, the Japanese had bombed Pearl Harbor, forcing a less partisan appraisal of aircraft capabilities, and in March 1942 flight testing of the XP-51 commenced. Following the tests the Mustang first entered service with the US when it received the fifty-five P-51 NAs from the July 1941 British order, and, after installation of oblique cockpit cameras, assigned them to photographic reconnaissance units in US as F-6A. In April 1943 came the first US Mustang missions by 154th Observation Squadron based in Tunisia.

The fate of Allison engined aircraft took a bizarre turn to secure survival. The A-36 fighter/bomber was an improvisation meant to keep production lines going. While there were no funds to employ the Mustang in a fighter role, which the turbocharged P-38 and P-47 were expected to fulfil in Europe, there was money for a dive bomber, the need for which was anticipated in North Africa. A contract for 500 A-36A aircraft was agreed on 16 April 1942. The main change was that the wing was redesigned to carry bombs and airbrakes. Of particular note to the cooling system, British experience had demonstrated no advantage from the variable cooling duct entry scoop and this was fixed.

The first A-36A Apache was delivered, in September 1942, with the first flight in October. In June 1943 the Apache flew its first combat mission in Morocco. A total of 500 A-36 dive bombers served in North Africa, the Mediterranean, Italy, and the China-Burma-India theatre. Also, it was used as a long-range escort fighter for B-25 Mitchell and B-26 Marauder missions in Italy. A-36As recorded eighty-four aerial victories and 177 fell to enemy action. The large ventral cooling system was a liability in a ground attack plane, leading to many of the losses being very vulnerable to ground fire. By June 1944, A-36As in Europe were replaced by Curtiss P-40s and Republic P-47s.

The simple truth was that a brilliant airframe was hobbled by an engine inadequate for war in Western Europe. This was not the fault of the Allison, which was a good engine, the same size as and with far fewer parts than the Merlin. It lacked, however, a versatile supercharger with excellent high altitude capability. (In the Soviet Union the otherwise little rated Allison-powered P-39 Airacobras were very successful as most fighting took place at low levels.)

Mustang high speed – 'Meredith effect' and laminar flow

The RAF routinely knocked off large numbers from the top speeds of US airplanes bought from the US. Having been told the Mustang could achieve 390mph the RAF cut it to 315mph and was stunned it reached 382mph. The Mustang was also considerably faster than the Spitfire Mk V at all except high altitude. A post-war US newspaper article recorded: 'Flight tests disclosed top speeds that the British disbelieved and put down to Yankee boasting. Hence, they gave P-51's meek reconnaissance jobs – until Spitfire fighter pilots complained that Mustangs were whizzing past them over the Channel.'[3] Hitchcock continued: 'Our P-51 was

35 miles an hour faster than the Spitfire V at around 15,000 feet. At 25,000 feet it went a few miles an hour faster and was pulling 290 less hp. That indicated there must be something aerodynamically good about the Mustang.'[4] Hitchcock added, 'The English became very enthusiastic about it'.[5]

The disparity of speed between the Allison-powered Mustangs and the single stage supercharger Merlin-engined Spitfire Mk Vs required explanation. Hitchcock, in a Memorandum dated 8 October 1942 wrote: 'The reasons for the remarkably low drag of the Mustang are not fully understood on this side of the ocean. The English think it [low drag] is only partly due to the laminar flow wing.'[6] And, 'The Farnborough [RAE] technicians were only willing to ascribe a small amount of the added speed to the laminar flow wing'.[7] US aerodynamicist Edward Warner went to England to investigate. He wrote to NACA on 25 August 1942 reporting the RAE comments:

> 'Well, it really hadn't much of a laminar-flow section'; that was subsequently modified to a suggestion that the wing design was such that laminar flow could only exist near the tips; and finally, that a skin joint running parallel to the span was sufficient to destroy any laminar flow beyond the first 25% of the chord. [8]

Hitchcock wrote on 8 October 1942: 'The reasons for the remarkably low drag of the Mustang are not fully understood on this side of the Atlantic. The English think it is only partly due to laminar flow.'[9]

The RAE anticipated 'compressibility' was probably the main advantage in practice of the laminar flow profile. Warner wrote: 'That they felt relatively little interest in the laminar-flow section as such, but a great deal in compressibility; and that it fortunately happened that the airfoil form favourable to laminar flow was also one favourable to keeping compressibility to a minimum.'[10] (Compressibility was meant here in the aerodynamic sense of variations in Mach numbers over different parts of the airframe and gave the Mustang its high diving speed.) Warner mentioned a 'Mr Squire' as having: 'Computed the effect of laminar flow on the P-51 performance as being 5 or 6mph at most. The remainder of the good performance was attributed to a variety of other small points, including an exceptionally good surface finish and the position of the radiator.'[11] Thus, the cooling duct attracted attention eventually, bringing into question Meredith's role with respect to the positioning of the radiator.

Herbert Brian Squire (1909-61) was the RAE's leading theoretical aerodynamicist after Herman Glauert, who had died in an unfortunate accident in 1934. He went to Göttingen where Prandtl did pioneering work on the boundary layer and wing theory post-First World War and on return to the RAE became the head of Aerodynamics. Squire had worked at Göttingen in 1932-33 (following Shenstone and Glauert). In 1933 he produced Squire's *Theorem on Hydrodynamic Instability,* which established when flow would be laminar or turbulent under certain conditions. In 1937, he and A.D. Young wrote, *The calculation of the Profile Drag of Aerofoils*, which enabled the boundary layer drag of aerofoils to be measured.[12] Squire worked, 'on the design of aerofoils to give prescribed pressure distributions, with the aim of delaying the onset of transition from laminar flow to turbulent flow, and also of avoiding shock wave formation at high speeds, which led to aerofoils, which should have reduced drag'.[13] In other words the man, 'Mr Squire', who Warner described as seeming to specialise in the matter of the effectiveness of the Mustang's laminar flow was possibly the man most qualified to do so in Britain. Putting the best man on the job showed the British took the question of the Mustang's low drag most seriously. (Squire was possibly yet another communist according to the Security Services. On 13 September 1937, they noted: 'If they suspend all of those on the list of communists it will include Meredith, Lockspeiser, Carter, Constance, Squire, Calvert, Hollingdale and Lord knows who. If they suspend all Socialists, they will have to close the Factory [RAE].'[14])

There is no evidence that the 'Meredith effect' was the subject of any attention when analysing the reason for the speed of the Mustang during the war years. The interest was in the location of the radiator not its internal structure or even its 'Meredith effect' possibilities. Attention focused on the radiator placing in order to reduce interference drag, that is drag caused by the intersection of airflows over different parts of the airframe, and not the 'Meredith effect' which involved thrust. On 20 August 1942 *Flight* wrote:

> Near the [wing] root there is a fairly sudden increase both in thickness and chord, the former being on the under surface and the latter on the leading-edge. In this way it has been possible to avoid large fillets on the upper surface. What probably helps to make this possible is the placing of the radiator under the fuselage, the cowling beginning under the wing and ending some way behind it.[15]

P-51B/C/D/H – major redesigns of the cooling duct

The story here of the Mustang and the impact of Meredith's ideas is now largely over with respect to the original design. There were, however, two major redesigns of the cooling duct for the P-51B and H which followed respectively from the merger with British Rolls-Royce engines with vastly improved high altitude performance and from British inspired efforts to lighten the airframe.

The Mustang was an airframe in search of an engine to fully exploit its potential. In 1940, developments began to the Merlin engine which would mean the full 'Meredith effect', that is negative drag or thrust, might realistically become possible, if mated to a highly efficient airframe like that of the Mustang. It was not the Merlin engine that transformed the Mustang. Its installation with a single stage supercharger had improved the performance of the Curtiss P-40 but not massively so. What made the difference was Rolls-Royce engineer Sir Stanley Hooker's two stage supercharger. Hooker predicted that maintaining power at high altitude could be achieved by using two superchargers in series, driven by the same engine gears.[16] In March 1940, detailed design began for the Merlin Mk 60 intended to power the high altitude version of the Vickers Wellington. This incorporated a supercharger, designed by Hooker for the failed Rolls-Royce twenty-four-cylinder Vulture to provide the second stage. Bench testing of the Merlin Mk 60 began in April 1941 and the first flight in a Wellington was in July. (The requirement for the Spitfire to be powered by the new engine was manifest when the Spitfire Mk V was thoroughly outclassed by the Focke Wulf Fw 190 which appeared in late 1941.) This resulted in the Spitfire Mk IX. The British now tried to unleash the potential of the Mustang airframe by marrying it with the most advanced version of the Merlin. Like many marriages the path to union faced challenges and had its advocates and detractors. It would require a complete redesign of the cooling system to match a much more powerful engine, resurrecting problems with the Mustang's ventral duct entry first highlighted by Meredith in 1935.

It was the British who recognised that the Mustang represented a new generation of fighter airframe. On 28 June 1942, Rolls-Royces Ernest Hives lamented to Air Chief Marshall Sir W.R. Freeman: 'We feel very depressed about the fighter position, both in this country and the U.S.A. and this has not improved since one of our pilots examined the Fw 190. The Spitfire 8 and 9 will make a big improvement.' Hives added: 'We are sold completely on the Mustang. The Merlin 61 goes into it with no alteration to the engine cowling or to the radiator cowling.'[17] Fortuitously, as has been seen, the Allison and the Merlin were the same size at 27 litres, while the inline powered, introduced to power French, German and Russian aircraft, were significantly larger at 36 litres.

That a US airplane could be married to the British designed Merlin was proved with the Curtiss P-40F Kittyhawk, first flight May 1941. This combined the P-40 with a Packard Merlin 28. Performance was improved on Allison-powered P-40s but not greatly so. The possibility of marrying the Mustang with the Merlin single-stage supercharger was first considered in 1941. On 11 March Kindleberger, frustrated in his dealings with Allison, asked the BPC to provide information on Rolls-Royce engines.[18] In April, 'Rolls-Royce, via US Senior Representative J.E. Ellor, sent an 18-page package of technical details for installing a Merlin XX engine'.[19] Also in April 1941, the British Air Commission considered the merger. Planning and Production Head C.R. Fairey wrote to Technical Department Head Air Vice-Marshal G.B.A. Baker asking, 'Will the NA 73 take the Rolls-Royce Merlin and has an installation been prepared. Am I right in assuming that such an installation has already been designed for the Kittyhawk?'[20]

On 30 April 1942, Ronnie Harker, Rolls-Royce's service liaison pilot flew the Mustang. The next day he submitted a very favourable report: 'The point which strikes me is that with a powerful and good engine like the Merlin 61, its performance should be outstanding, as it is 35mph faster than a Spitfire V at roughly the same power.'[21] The first flight of a Rolls-Royce Merlin powered Mustang was on 13 October 1942. That of the first flight of the Merlin Mustang, the XP-51B, in the US was 30 November 1942.

The more powerful engine necessitated a complete redesign of the radiator duct to accommodate a larger glycol and oil radiator. 'The new belly scoop which appeared on the P-51B, was a great achievement. Although Dr Beverly Shenstone suggested separating the scoop intake from the lower fuselage skin, it was Irving Ashkenas at NAA who designed the now-familiar scoop of the XP-51B.'[22] NAA took the advantage of the situation to make wholesale changes: the round radiator with the oil cooler in the centre was replaced by a square radiator combining the intercooler and the glycol radiator. The oil cooler radiator was removed from the centre of the annular radiator and placed in front of the engine radiator with its own mini-Meredith duct system with adjustable exit flap; and the upper lip was extended ahead of the lower lip.

A memo of 2 March 1943 from Ellor, Rolls-Royce's US representative at Packard, recorded there had been about thirty flights in the US, but they were short due to cooling problems. 'These [speeds of 426mph], however, are not regarded as representing the performance of the airplane since buffeting occurred in the regions of the radiator exit caused by a breakdown in air flow at the front of the duct.'[23] The problem of duct entry anticipated by Meredith in 1935 re-emerged with the redesigned duct. The situation was described by Ed Horkey:

> We got the boundary-layer bleed a little too small. What would happen was that it caused a duct rumble. [Test pilot] Chilton described it to us as somebody pounding on a locker. The boundary layer would build up, and airflow would go around the duct inlet, and then it would all of a sudden go inside again, and this would create a large impact load. [24]

Hair-raising full-scale wind tunnel tests were conducted:

> We also took an actual P-51B up to Ames Aeronautical Lab and cut the wingspan down a little and mounted it in the 16-foot high-speed wind tunnel. I took the first ride, and when we got up to 500mph in the tunnel, we got the rumble. It was quite a thrill. We lowered the top inlet of the radiator duct a small amount and also went to the cutback, or slanted, inlet shape and solved the problem on the P-51B. [25]

Another account is given in a history of the NACA Research Centre from the perspective of Ames's staff, again emphasising the boundary layer problem:

> North American engineers had considered the boundary layer in the design of the scoop and had lowered the scoop below the surface of the wing a little way to allow the boundary layer to pass harmlessly by. But for reasons of maintaining cleanness of line, they did not want the scoop to project downward any farther than necessary. In fact,

they had made it wide and shallow, thus, unfortunately, providing every opportunity for the ingestion of boundary layer. [26]

Credit for finding the solution was given to Smitty DeFrance of Ames:

> A number of minor modifications of the scoop were tried with little effect. The ever-present Smitty DeFrance, who seldom failed to advance his own recommendations, spoke forth on this occasion in no uncertain terms: 'Lower the damn thing!' This measure was pretty obvious, of course, but Manley [Hood] and his boys were searching for a somewhat more refined method of accomplishing the same end. Nevertheless, the lowering idea was tried and it, together with certain other modifications, was found to be a nearly perfect cure. North American people were delighted. [27]

The NACA Ames history concludes: 'Both NACA and North American had learned a valuable lesson. It concerned the importance of keeping boundary layer out of air scoops.'[28] Meredith and the RAE might have been almost disappointed that such a lesson had to be learnt again. Meredith had written his paper on duct entry eight years earlier in 1935.

The Mustang story marched on, but with the final design of the P-51B's ventral ducted radiator, the 'Meredith effect' story is largely complete. The British input, however, remained important. In passing there was the 'Malcolm' clear bubble cockpit canopy on the P-51B/C and later tear drop hoods on the P-51D and the *papier maché* drop tanks. The Mustang was made a fair more effective fighter with a much improved K-14 analogue gunsight based on a British Ferranti design gyroscopic gun sight that was fitted to the P-51D. (This was originally inspired by RAE work on applying gyroscopes to gunsights.)

There was one further major revision of the Mustang's design. British fighters were significantly lighter than those of the US, a point made by the British to the Americans. The empty weights of the Spitfire Mk V and the Mustang Mk I were 5,090lb and 6,500lb respectively. Gross weights were 6,770lb in 8,933lb. In January 1943, the Lightweight Mustang programme was begun and in February, Schmued visited England to investigate the issue and went to the Supermarine and Rolls-Royce factories. (Incidentally, the warm reception Schmued received as the designer of the Mustang appeared to have infuriated Lee Atwood.) Schmued had NAA's Field Service Department go to Spitfire repair depots and weigh parts to provide a previously unavailable Spitfire weight statement. In July 1943 the USAAF approved a contract with NAA to design and build a lightweight P-51. The result was the first complete redesign, which produced the P-51H powered by the Packard Merlin V-1650-9 producing 1,900 hp at 20,000 feet with water injection.

The cooling duct was totally redesigned. The radiator was increased in depth and size. The oil cooler was moved from the ventral cooling duct to in front of the oil tank ahead of the firewall removing the oil lines from the engine to the ventral duct. The oil was now cooled by a heat exchanger. (A heat exchanger is an oil radiator which uses the coolant fluid as a cooling medium instead of air.) The cooling duct inlet profile was not angled but square like the first P-51As. The carburettor chin duct inlet was reduced in size. The top speed was significantly increased to nearly 490mph at 25,000 feet.

Did the 'Meredith effect' actually work on the Mustang

Finally, the question might be asked to what extent the Mustang produced the full 'Meredith effect', that is, did it produce 'net drag' or thrust?

> There is still unresolved debate as to whether the 'Meredith effect', in practice, achieved 'negative drag'. This author [S.J. Miley in 1986] has no evidence to support this [Mustang produced net thrust]. The available literature [Meredith and Winter are among those cited] on the subject is entirely theoretical and is divided between the British position (pro) and the American and German positions (con). The weight of opinion at present is against realizing a net thrust from the cooling installation.[29]

There are no definitive texts. Therefore, the comments are somewhat subjective. There is no question that the Mustang duct itself produced thrust. The issue was whether this was sufficient to exceed the cooling system's drag. Gruenhagen wrote in 1969: 'Schmued and Horkey calculated that an aerodynamic duct formed at the entry and exit of the radiator could provide up to 300 pounds of thrust by utilizing ram air to eject the warmed airflow and thus overcome the drag offered to the fuselage by the duct itself.'[30] This implies cooling drag was at least neutralised. Ethell, in 1981, commented: 'Contrary to what some accounts have stated, the initial Mustang radiators on the P-51A and Mustang 1 did not produce thrust by virtue of the so-called "Meredith effect".'[31] By this is meant thrust sufficient to exceed cooling drag.

Schmued wrote:

> We also found out, later on [in wind tunnel tests], that the heat from the engine actually produced thrust in the radiator by increasing the velocity of the air flowing through.[32] That horsepower gained by the radiator was only discovered by wind-tunnel investigation. We were contractually required to wind-tunnel test the P-51, and long after the first airplane flew, we got around to test a model which had an electric motor to drive a three-bladed propeller. We found from wind-tunnel data that the P-51 should not be as fast as it was actually clocked. Our chief thermodynamicist, Joe Beerer, studied the problem and noticed the favorable effect of the radiator.[33]

194

Schmued said: 'Now, I would like to tell you that this radiator was so darned good aerodynamically that on the latest model we had in production, the D, that radiator duct produced 300hp thrust. That's a ramjet!'[34] (This radiator was the same as on the P-51B and C.) Clearly, Schmued saw the radiator thrust as significant, but he did not say that it exceeded cooling drag.

It has been claimed that the P-51H did actually produce the full 'Meredith effect', that is the cooling system unambiguously produced net thrust. Aviation writer Bill Gunston wrote: 'Drag of this installation type [ducted radiators] was always extremely low, and in some conditions the later installations, such as that of the P-51H, could give forward thrust.'[35] A decade earlier, in 1935, Meredith had produced an equation for calculating the net power lost and gained in the duct at a time when aircraft were designed to fly at around 300mph and the altitude he used was 14,000 feet. At 490mph, the P-51H's top speed, and 25,000 feet, Meredith's equation produces a much more positive result.

The key point is, however, not so much the extent that the Mustang duct produced thrust in excess of drag, but that it negated drag more than any other Second World War fighter.

Overall assessment of role of Meredith in the conception of the Mustang

As seen, in a published letter in *Air & Space*, October/November 1996, Atwood said: 'The simple fact is that it [the 'Meredith effect'] was the basis of the Mustang design, and its most efficient application required a buried radiator.'[36] It is not possible fully to support Atwood's claim that the 'Meredith effect' was the basis of the Mustang design on the evidence available for early 1940. It is arguable that the P-509 – with which British officials were familiar in 1939 and which was presented to the BPC in March 1940 – could have been developed without Meredith's work, on the basis that a buried 'oversquare' radiator was the most efficient form and this could only be located in the aft ventral position. Schmued, who is generally seen as the designer of the Mustang, claimed that he only found out later that the duct generated the 'Meredith effect' and the duct was a ramjet. (Schmued also swiped at Atwood, saying the latter only knew about the 'Meredith effect' after Shenstone told him about it – most likely in early 1941.) It is probable, however, that Atwood knew what the concept was, if not the name, earlier, as in Luttman's account, Atwood had discussed with him 'the ramjet character of radiator cooling'. Horkey and Ashkenas knew of Meredith's work through reading of NACA's translation of German papers (and probably NACA's own work) on the impact of heat in ducted radiators that was issued in 1938 and 1939. The radiator duct, in its early 1940 form, would have produced the 'Meredith effect' rather ineffectively. After the major revisions in February/March and May/June 1940, however, the duct would have produced this effect much more efficiently making Atwood's claim that the 'Meredith effect' was the basis of the Mustang design rather more valid. Also, the fact is that the Mustang was the most complete embodiment, in combination, of Meredith's ideas on ducts capable of creating thrust, duct entry to divert the boundary layer, and exhaust gas momentum. The last was common to all inline aircraft, but the efficacy of the Mustang's design of the first two was stimulated by the impact of Meredith's work through a number of routes analysed here.

(It might be added that Atwood also wanted the RAE, whose work has featured so prominently in this book so far, to be given its due credit. 'My second objective is to give proper credit to the Royal Aircraft Establishment at Farnborough, which sponsored the research that Meredith and R.S. Capon published in 1935 and 1936.'[37] On this basis could have been added the K-14 gunsight used on the P-51D, which was developed by the RAE and Ferranti and greatly enhanced allied aerial gunnery.)

Chapter 26

Meredith and US ramjets

Earlier three areas of Meredith's possible influence in the US were outlined that involved the evolution of the Mustang. A surprising fourth is the US ramjet as an independent form of propulsion. Atwood said the 'Meredith effect', 'involved discharging the heated air under as much pressure as was possible in a rear facing jet as in the yet-to-be-developed ramjet engine'. [1] The question of how the term 'Meredith effect' came into existence appears to be linked rather surprisingly with ramjet development in the US.

The earliest ramjet design was created by a French mechanical engineer, René Lorin, who in 1909 proposed using a jet engine to power a guided 'aerial torpedo' to defend against German airplanes. He published his theoretical ramjet design in 1913. René Leduc, however, applied for a patent in 1934 for a manned ramjet. NACA researchers who built the first US ramjet in 1941 exploiting the 'Meredith effect' were, 'unaware that there were several discussions of propulsive ducts in the literature starting with Lorin in 1913 and including later treatments by Carter, V. Leduc, Roy and others'. [2] The question then is whether in the US the ramjet concept was developed building on Meredith's insight that a ducted radiator was a heat engine.

There are two areas of investigation. The first is the overlap of personnel from NACA and NAA in 1940 who were working on the Mustang's laminar flow wing. These were coincidentally also involved in work on aspects of jet propulsion involving the Mustang's cooling duct and NACA's investigation of the motorjet, where a piston engine drives a compressor in a duct which channels into a combustion chamber where fuel is ignited. The second, possibly related, is NACA's investigation of the inlet and outlet drag at both ends of a tube which led to experimental work in 1941 where heat was added within the tube. The 1943 report of the 1941 material included the terms 'Meredith effect' and 'ramjet'. [3]

NAA and NACA overlap on the 'Meredith effect'

Looking at the first area of investigation, the overlap of NAA and NACA personnel working on jet propulsion, Eastman Jacobs (1902-1987) worked for NACA Langley from the 1920s to the 1940s focusing on wind tunnels, laminar flow, and the motorjet, that is jet propulsion using a ducted piston engine. US prospects for developing a jet engine had been hamstrung by the Buckingham report of 1923 which concluded: 'Propulsion by the reaction of a simple jet cannot compete, in any respect, with air screw propulsion at such flying speeds as are now in prospect.'[4] Therefore, alternative forms of jet propulsion were examined. In 1938 Jacobs started work on axial-flow compressors. He also sought the re-evaluation of Buckingham's 1923 report. In 1939 a NACA history of 1987 related Eastman Jacobs and Albert Sherman, 'proposed studying a ducted-fan system that used only dynamic pressure (that is, the pressure was not boosted by a fan) for compression and the Meredith cycle for thrust'.[5] Clearly what the 'Meredith cycle' stood for was understood at the time but the terms the 'Meredith cycle' (and the 'Meredith effect') were probably not yet used in the 1930s. The 1987 history explains:

> In 1936 [date of publication] Frank [Frederick] W. Meredith had pointed out in England that not all of the waste heat of a piston engine had to be lost when transferred to the cooling airflow of a radiator. If the pressure at the exhaust of the radiator tubes was higher than the free static pressure of flight, some of the dissipated heat could produce a small thrust.[6]

Clearly, this insight had been picked up by NACA personnel who realised that the heat source did not only need to be a radiator but could be the result of burning fuel. In 1940, Jacobs and NACA staff developed a jet propulsion test bed called Jake's 'Jeep'. 'This was a ducted-fan system, using a piston engine power plant to combine the engine's heat and exhaust with added fuel injection for brief periods of added thrust, much like an afterburner.'[7] In early 1940, NACA researcher, Russ Robinson, working from NACA's West Coast Liaison Office, visited NAA and was immediately coopted to work on airfoil pressure coordinates. NAA's own aerodynamicist Horkey related: 'Russ Robinson was a NACA aerodynamicist. He came by with [NACA's] Ed Hartman. They said that NACA had tested, in a wind tunnel, what was called a laminar-flow low-drag airfoil.'[8] Later, Robinson was joined by Jacobs who had been developing a motorjet at NACA. Jacobs and Robinson worked assisting NAA aerodynamicists Ed Horkey and Irving Ashkenas on the design of the Mustang's laminar flow wing in 1940. It might seem surprising if Jacobs' and NACA's work on his 'Jeep' motorjet were not discussed. Also, NAA personnel, including Lee Atwood, were familiar with 'the ramjet quality of radiator ducting'. A test rig for Jake's 'Jeep' was in operation during the spring of 1942 and there were plans to build an actual aircraft powered solely by such an engine.[9] As the US became aware of and more involved in gas turbine engines, Jacobs' ducted fan engine was cancelled in February 1943. (Jacobs was so frustrated he retired from NACA and later opened a successful beach restaurant in California.)

After NACA personnel had worked at NAA, NACA began to develop a ramjet seemingly quite independently of European ramjet work. Also, Meredith's name and the term, the 'Meredith effect' was later explicitly associated with this work.

NACA's 'Meredith effect' ramjet

Looking at the second area of investigation John Becker of NACA produced three interesting reports, starting in 1940, developing the idea of airflow entry and exit into ducts. The first two analysed the challenge of airflow through a body with a duct opening at the front and rear.

- J.V. Becker, *Wind-Tunnel Test of Air Inlet and Outlet Openings on a streamline Body*. NACA ACR, November 1940.[10]
- J.V. Becker, and D.D. Baals, *High-speed Tests of a Ducted Body with Various Air-Outlet Openings*. NACA ACR, May 1942.[11]

The third considered adding heat within the duct.

- J.V. Becker, and D.D. Baals, *Analysis of Heat and Compressibility Effects in Internal Flow Systems and High-Speed Tests of a Ramjet System*. NACA, January 1943.[12]

The 1943 report referred to experiments in 1941 by a team at NACA led by Becker, who started work on the possibilities of developing a ramjet engine, which was quite different to Jacob's design which had incorporated a piston engine in the duct. A later NACA history reported:

> In 1936, F.W. Meredith pointed out that the waste heat of a piston engine which is transferred to the cooling-air flow in a radiator is not all lost; it produces a small thrust provided the pressure at the exhaust of the radiator tubes is higher than the free static pressure of flight. This phenomenon became known as the 'Meredith effect'.[13]

Figure 27.1 – 'Heat model' used in NACA's investigation of a propulsive-duct (ramjet) system in early 1941, incorporating a 160-kw heater.[14]

Testing of the 'heat model' started in February 1941, the first NACA wind tunnel investigation of a propulsive duct producing thrust. At a Mach number of about 0.5, the propulsive effect had become equal to the internal drag, and beyond this speed substantial net thrust was developed by the internal flow. At the highest test speed, Mach 0.75, the heated duct developed the respectable thermal efficiency of some 9.5%, close to the expected theoretical value.[15]

The NACA researchers, 'achieved thrust equal to drag at about Mach 0.5, and net positive thrust at Mach 0.75, proving that the 'Meredith effect' was real, and also demonstrating the basic principles of operation of the ramjet engine'.[16] Also, 'clearly, the insignificant "Meredith effect" had the potential to become a primary jet-propulsion system'.[17]

As NACA researchers were, as above, 'unaware of the work of Lorin and later work by Carter, Leduc and Schmidt', where in the US did the idea of the ramjet using heat alone as opposed to a ducted piston engine come from? The answer might be sought in the first three references in the 1943 report:

- F.W. Meredith, *Note on the Cooling of Aircraft Engines with Special Reference to Ethylene Glycol Radiator Enclosed in Duct*, R & M No 1683, British ARC, 1936.[18]
- H. Winter, *Contribution to the Theory of the Heated Duct Radiator*, NACA TM No. 893, 1939.[19]
- A. Weise, *The Conversion of Energy in a Radiator*. NACA TM No, 869, 1938.[20]

Meredith, Winter and Weise analysed the impact of adding heat within a duct. Winter gave as his first reference Meredith and said it was Meredith who 'first pointed out the possible gain in power' that could so be obtained.[21] Thus, it may have been Meredith, followed by Winter and Weise, who inspired Becker to add heat to the ducts he was analysing in his first two reports. NACA personnel, Silverstein, Breevort and Leifer, had cited Meredith's work in 1939 when experimenting with cooling ducts as heat engines. It might be recalled also that Eastman Jacobs of 'Jakes Jeep' and Rus Robinson of NACA worked at NAA's California plant assisting aerodynamicists Ed Horkey and Irving Ashkenas in the design of the Mustang's laminar flow wing in 1940 at the same time.

In 1943, a NACA report included the first use found of the term the 'Meredith effect' here in the context of the impact of heat on cooling air within a radial engine: 'The power recoverable from the cylinder-cooling flow ("Meredith effect") in a typical air-cooled engine is shown in figure 20,' and, 'the power recoverable from the heat added to the cooling air ("Meredith effect") was found to be about 3 per cent of the brake horsepower for an existing air-cooled engine at a flight Mach number of 0.60 at sea level.'

In 1946, co-author Irving Ashkenas of NAA and others, discussing the possibility of functioning motorjets at very high speeds over Mach 1, questioned whether cooling was possible at exceptionally high speeds. They wrote: 'Without an inordinate expenditure of power is doubtful and depends on how much of the heat rejected to the cooling air can be utilized in jet propulsion (the so-called "Meredith effect").[22] This is the second use of the term the 'Meredith effect' found.

The 1980 NACA history says 'the term "ramjet" was not then in general use' at the time of the 1941 experiments.[23] The report *Analysis of Heat and Compressibility Effects in Internal Flow Systems and High-Speed Tests of a Ramjet System* (Becker and Baals, NACA, 1943) includes the term 'ramjet' which it would appear, became more familiar between 1941 and 1943.

How then did Becker's work on the 'Meredith effect' develop into an operational US ramjet? As the Second World War progressed the US Navy sought systems to defend against German guided anti-ship bombs and Japanese kamikazes. This resulted in *Operation Bumblebee* to develop surface to air missiles (SAMs). In turn the missiles required a propulsion system. Earlier NACA experiments by Becker in 1941 on 'Meredith effect' ramjets were reconsidered having initially failed to attract interest as jet propulsion had not been expected to produce thrust comparable to propellers. The US Navy Bureau of Aerodynamics produced, in December 1943, a report *Performance of Open Duct Propulsion Systems (Ramjets) at Subsonic Speeds* (Bollay and Redding, US Navy, 1943), which led to further research by Johns Hopkins Applied Physics Laboratory.[24] This resulted in the supersonic Talos ramjet missile which entered service in 1955.[25]

NACA histories claim that the US ramjet did not develop as the result of familiarity with the work of the Frenchman Leduc. This chapter has raised the possibility that the development of the ramjet in the US lay at least partly in the coincidence that NACA personnel who were already working on the motorjet ducted propulsion system were seconded to NAA to help it develop the Mustang's laminar flow wing profile. This was at the time that the same NAA personnel who were working on the wing were also refining the 'Meredith effect' cooling duct. Also, NACA personnel familiar with Meredith's work both directly in NACA's own report, and indirectly through German reports translated by NACA, experimented with adding heat within ducts whose inlet and exit drag was under investigation. There are a remarkable number of coincidences and overlaps. Thus, it seems at least possible that Meredith was an unsung father of the US ramjet which was explicitly recognised to incorporate the 'Meredith effect' from the first NACA investigations in 1941.

Chapter 27

Post-1941 national cooling systems

The Mustang went into British and US service in 1942 and set a new high standard for the application of the 'Meredith effect' cooling system, certainly for single-engined aircraft. (The in-wing system used by the twin-engined Mosquito, used as both a fighter and a bomber, was also very efficient.) In late 1943 the P-51B showed the potential of the Meredith system as, powered by the Merlin 61 it had greater power, particularly at altitude. This chapter looks at the possible impact of the Mustang design on other aircraft of different nations.

British design went in several directions. The Spitfire retained its aft wing located radiators and unlike the German Bf 109F no real effort was made to make them more efficient. It was followed in using this location by the Napier Sabre powered Martin Baker MB-3, first flight August 1942. The Merlin-powered Fairey Firefly had a chin located cooling system.

Tests on the ventral bath cooling system of the Hawker Tornado, first flight October 1939, showed that compressibility effects began to manifest themselves as speeds increased and it was decided that the ventral radiator bath was unsuitable for the speeds approaching 400mph that were being achieved for the first time. The radiator was therefore moved forward to the nose, a position already selected for that of the Type 'N', or Typhoon.

The adoption of the inefficient chin radiator on the Tempest seems particularly surprising as it wasted the potential of the wing which was much thinner than that on the Typhoon. Also, there were Tempest prototypes which showed what could be achieved with a superior cooling system. The Tempest 1 had a Sabre 4 engine with wing leading edge radiators. It proved capable of well over 460mph, but the wing leading edge radiator was considered vulnerable. The Tempest V was flown with a Sabre 2 engine with a chin radiator and a Sabre 6 with an annular radiator. The latter was faster but the Tempest V, with the proven Sabre 2 engine with an inefficient chin radiator, was adopted.

Later in the war some efforts were made to adopt more efficient systems. The Griffon-powered Firefly used in-wing radiators mounted ahead of the main spar like the Mosquito. This was very efficient and was used for the radial powered Hawker Sea Fury oil cooler radiator. The Martin-Baker MB-5 explicitly followed the P-51B demonstrating recognition of the superiority of this system for single-engined fighter aircraft. This design showed great promise but was not developed as other aircraft were available and jets soon supplanted piston engines anyway.

The US Curtiss P-40 was not developed further. Curtiss tried to recover sales with the cleaned up XP-40Q. This had a more powerful Allison engine and the radiators were moved from the chin to the wing leading edge position. The maximum speed increased to 422mph, which was less than the latest P-51 Mustangs and P-47 Thunderbolts, and no orders ensued. Interestingly, the Lockheed P-38J adopted a boundary layer bypass, a concept first proposed by Meredith in 1935. (As did the first operational US jet fighter, the P-80 Shooting Star, first flight 8 January 1944, at the jet engine duct entry.) The radial-engined Chance Vought F4U Corsair (first flight May 1940) had very efficient in-wing leading edge oil radiators with leading edge entrances.

In Germany the rear fuselage engine of the Dornier Do 335 which followed a line from UK patent 472,555 April 1936, through the Napier-Heston Racer and the Arsenal VG-60.

The Soviet Yak series was the most successful inline powered Russian aircraft. In 1943 the Yak 1-M and the Yak 3 first flew with engine radiators in a more buried and aft position that earlier Yaks. The Yak 9-P of 1945 followed this pattern. The

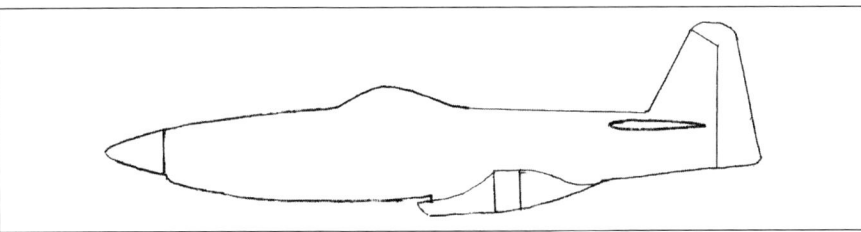

Figure 28.1 – Martin-Baker MB-5.

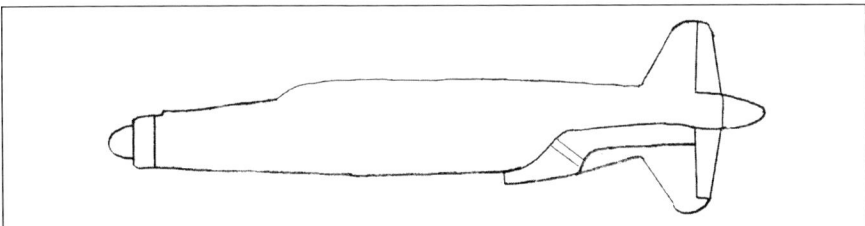

Figure 28.2 – Dornier Do 335.

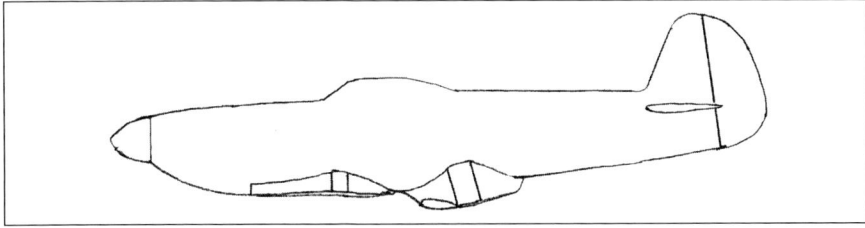

Figure 28.3 – Yak-3.

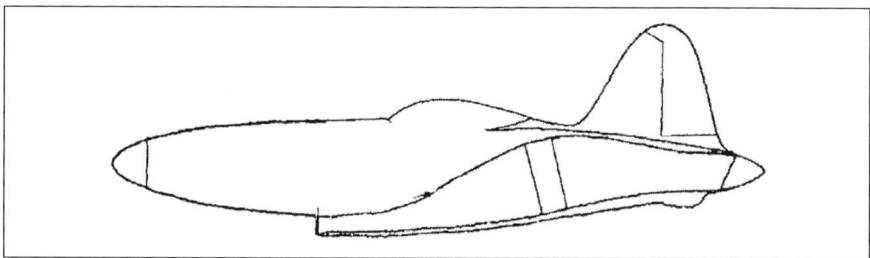

Figure 28.4 – VG-60.

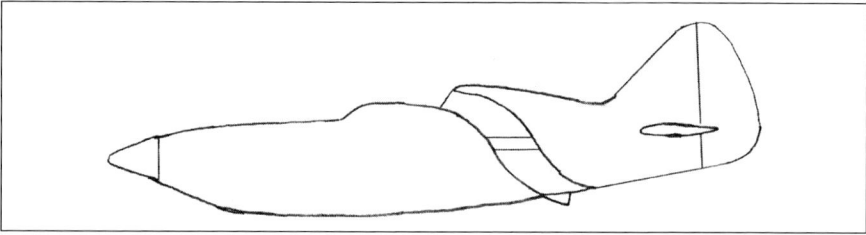

Figure 28.5 – SNCASE SE-580.

oil cooler radiators had entrances placed in the wing roots like the Bell Airacobra which proved successful in Soviet use. LaGG-3s of batch n°66 (the last one) were the fastest of the type, reaching 431mph, with eight exhaust pipes, redesigned nose radiator and ventral tunnel.

Italy continued with quite simple ventral radiators on the Reggianne Re-2005 and the Macchi C-205. The Kawasaki Hien Ki-61 also had a comparatively short central ventral radiator. Both the Re-2005 and the Ki-61 used vanes to equalise the pressure distribution over the radiator. (Meredith had suggested the use of vanes in 1935.)

In France, post-defeat by Germany in 1940, some design work continued in secret, including two interesting concepts. The VG-60 followed the Napier-Heston racer and anticipated the Dornier Do 335 in its use of a very long duct exiting at the tail.

Dewoitine became Sud-Est (SE) continuing to design developments of the Dewoitine 500 series. The SNCASE SE 580 had a large hump behind the cockpit which housed the duct inlet that directed air through a radiator positioned horizontally in the aircraft's rear fuselage and exited the fuselage via a ventral flap. The intake also incorporated a boundary layer bypass.

Overall, by the mid-Second World War certain cooling designs were becoming standardised for various nations, Russia, Italy, and Japan largely settled on the central ventral position with comparatively short semi-buried radiators. Germany used the aft-wing location for the Bf 109 but considerable effort was used to reduce the drag on operational aircraft with the F version. Only the British MB-5 unambiguously followed the Mustang, while the Yak series became more like the Mustang. France produced some very advanced designs, but occupation limited their development. Jets replaced piston engines before ending the opportunity for further development of fighter inline ducted cooling systems.

Epilogue

Meredith Reconsidered

Frederick William Meredith has the unusual distinction of having his services sought by both the Communist Soviet Union and the American military industrial complex America. Post-war, Dorothy Woodman told her interrogator that in 1935: 'One of her callers, fronting for the Russian, was particularly asked to see an expert in Meredith's subject, namely the remote control of aircraft.'[1] As Meredith had designed the Queen Bee he was clearly their man. In 1953, Meredith told his interrogators that a party of four Americans, engaged in parallel projects [guided missiles], would arrive in the country who had specifically asked to see him to discuss guided missile developments.[2]

In 1938, when Meredith left the RAE to join Smiths Instruments, the Security Services hoped Meredith would not be employed on military government work. On 16 May that year a Security Services letter from Colonel Jasper Harker of MI5 concluded:

> I think it is most fortunate that Meredith has left the RAE and [I] do not consider that any opportunity should be offered to him of re-entering Government service. In view of his valuable technical knowledge, I can quite understand that the position is a difficult one but hope that your technical branch will bear in mind in any future dealings with Meredith that he cannot be regarded as a loyal British subject.[3]

A vain hope. A letter to Harker of the Security Services of 10 May 1938 showed Meredith was still much valued after he had left the RAE. Smiths became the recognised place of expertise in stabilisation and guidance due to Meredith. 'I gather from our technical people that they still hope to take advantage of Meredith's knowledge, and it is probable that S. Smith & Son may become of increasing importance to the Department now that they have taken Meredith into their employ.'[4] Almost at once new work was directed to the RAE by Ivor Bowen of the Ministry of Air Production, who said that, 'Smiths was the best firm to approach' to develop the Navy's Automatic Dive Bomb Sight, 'because the Chief Research Engineer of this firm, Mr Meredith, is probably more acquainted with the design problems than any other person in the country outside the department,' and 'the only person the Air Ministry could trust with this difficult design task was Meredith'.[5] In order to develop the SEP1 autopilot introduced in 1945, 'to meet the British Air Staff requirements both for civil and military aircraft, the Research Organization of Smiths Aircraft Instruments Ltd was entrusted with the development of an all-electric automatic pilot system under the leadership of Mr F.W. Meredith'.[6]

Meredith's expertise in stability and remote guidance meant that Smiths was seen as the company best skilled to take on such missile work. In 1949 the GWD wished to place a secret contract with Bristol to sub-contract autopilot work to Smiths, meaning Meredith would be heavily involved. Two years later the Red Hawk air guided weapon project was given to Folland Aircraft, which was expected to sub-contract to Smiths for work on electrical guidance unit.[7] In 1952[8] Meredith said he would see Vickers to discuss a new contract for Smiths which was only coming to Smiths because of his position within it.[9]

So why were Meredith's scientific services so sought? Many reasons might be suggested and some examples of each provided; he was unique and irreplaceable; combined abilities in both aerodynamics and instruments; produced elegant counter intuitive solutions incorporating novel ideas; and was authoritative and compelling in a scientific situation.

Meredith has four large files compiled by the Security Services. These are veritable treasure troves of appraisal and praise of Meredith's abilities. Regardless of who is commenting the theme is remarkably consistent. Meredith was brilliant and unique. On 7 March 1949 it was stated baldly: 'Mr Meredith is in a high place in the category of indispensable people. This outweighs the security risk.'[10] On 25 October 1949 it was recorded Meredith, 'is so highly qualified I [Michael Serpell MI5 Counter Intelligence Officer] do not think we can suggest that his employment should be in any way limited'.[11] On 31 December 1952 and 6 January 1953 there were reports by Sir Stewart Mitchell, Controller Guided Weapons and Electrics (CGWL) and George Gardner, [Directorate of Guided Weapons (Research and Development, DGW (R&D)] on Meredith. The report by Mitchell on Meredith surmised: 'It would be well to reiterate the immense value of Meredith from the technological aspect of our guided weapon work. He is quite unique in this country and his value to us is extremely high. I would not say he is indispensable – nobody is – but it is fair to say that he is the leading expert in this country on matters such as automatic pilots for aircraft and guided missiles, etc.'[12]

Thus, on 6 April 1952, it was concluded that Meredith could continue on guided weapon work, subject to conditions on access to US material.[13] The author lamented: 'It is a great pity that this brilliant man should have this failing. He is unique and if he has to be removed from our scene I do not know how we would replace him'.

So why was Meredith so unique and irreplaceable? He combined remarkable expertise in both aerodynamics and avionics (or instruments). Earlier bizarre deaths in mid-1930s of RAE department heads were described, which put Meredith in charge of two major RAE units, Aerodynamics and Instruments, in quick succession, where he made major advances in both. Before 1935 Meredith worked in Instruments. *Flight International Magazine* reported on 26 July 1934: 'The instrumental problems and the aerodynamic requirements are not easily satisfied, and the credit for the practical development of the automatic pilot in this country belongs very largely to Mr F.W. Meredith, Mr P.A. Cooke and Mr P.S. Kerr.'[14] The Air Ministry, in January 1949, made clear both his versatility and indispensability. 'Mr Meredith is of such outstanding ability in the field of aerodynamics and auto-control [Instruments] that from technical considerations alone there is no one in the country whom the Department would be more anxious to employ.'[15] When asked about Meredith's qualities a Security Services briefing in 6 April 1951, discussing possible cooperation with the US on guided missiles, recorded: 'There is literally nobody in the country who can replace him. I am told that on account of his intimate knowledge of aerodynamics and instruments, he is unique.' [16]

Meredith not only combined knowledge and experience across aerodynamics and instruments he also, throughout his career, contributed elegant, counterintuitive solutions and novel solutions. At Aerodynamics in 1923 he pioneered automatic landing using only a trailing wire and the phugoid principle. In 1926 at Instruments he pointed out that the bombsight need not be stabilised if the aircraft were. At Aerodynamics in 1935 Meredith completely redefined the problem of ducted radiator cooling drag by presenting it as an opportunity rather than a cost. His counter-intuitive insight was that a cooling system, in the form of a ducted radiator, was a heat engine utilising the thermal energy released by the radiator to create thrust that above a certain speed could negate the drag of the cooling system.

Looking at Instruments in 1938 when Meredith was working for Smiths, he was allowed a fortnight over Christmas to analyse the problems, devising an Automatic Dive Bomb Sight (ADBS). In that period on 6 January 1939, he submitted a patent application for a pneumatic air-jet and chopper-block servomechanism incorporated in Second World War bombsights. In 1949, in a paper *The Modern Autopilot,* he 'reviewed the development of the hysteresis servomotor, an achievement made in the face of established authoritative theories as to the impracticality of such work'.[17] These were incorporated in the post-war SEP1 autopilot. During the war Meredith also addressed the problems of any gyroscope involving a spinning wheel, particularly bearing wear. His solution was a vibrating solid-state structure. This was the first known conception of a tuning fork gyroscope.

The record shows Meredith as authoritative in a scientific situation and ensuring his views were taken seriously. A report to the Security Services on 14 November 1938 recorded that Meredith addressed a scientist's group at the Cheddar Roast, 101 Great Russell Street. 'The meeting took the form of a lecture by F.W. Meredith, late Principal Scientific Officer in the Air Ministry, a very able speaker who held the attention of the thirty or so people in the room.'[18] When Meredith gave the Annual Lecture of the Measurement and Control Section on 7 May 1957, he 'took his audience on a fascinating excursion into the world of living things. ... the lecture was obviously very warmly appreciated'.[19]

Nor did Meredith mince words, as seen when he inspected the Spitfire design in September 1935. Meredith was not impressed by the aft wing positioning of the radiator. He 'expressed the opinion that the glycol radiator as proposed would cost us about 15% of engine HP, i.e., about 15mph in drag at top speed'.[20] He explained why 'the radiator position was not good'. Meredith was clearly a man whose views commanded attention and were to be considered carefully. As the result of the meeting, 'the Meredith radiator scheme was adopted for the F37/34'.[21] Meredith had specifically recommended wind tunnel testing. The Spitfire ducted radiator was the first designed for a particular aircraft to be tested in a wind tunnel. The tests were carried out in November 1935, although the final report was not dated until May 1936.[22]

The Automatic Dive Bomb Site (ADBS) had not passed the trial stage by mid-1941 and the results were deemed disappointing. Meredith rejected the critical RAE analysis. In the light of factual errors, Ivor Bowen of the Ministry of Air Production reported: 'We have had a fairly protracted argument with Mr Meredith of Smiths and as a result we are all agreed (RAE included) that the mechanism deserves further trial in an aircraft which is more suitable to diving attack than are the Skua and Swordfish.'[23]

In 1949 Meredith gave a paper to the Royal Aeronautical Society on the modern autopilot where he was withering about the inability of British manufacturers of valves to produce reliable valves.

> It is unfortunate that our manufacturers of valves cannot see their way to producing special valves for electronic equipment requiring a high degree of reliability. The American valve manufacturers have seen this and are producing special valves for the purpose. Unless something is done about it, either the job will be done without valves, or the art of electronic control will be in danger of becoming an American monopoly.[24]

In a scientific situation Meredith clearly presented his views in a compelling manner.

Summary of important contributions and their phases

Pre-Second World War

Meredith spent nearly all the interwar period at the RAE from 1919 to 1938. During this period he made huge contributions to both civil and military aviation, playing a leading part in ensuring that Britain and the Empire had British designed stabilising and autopilot designs. He also largely designed the stabilisation and control systems for the unmanned Larynx and Queen Bee. In 1935 he moved for nine months to head the Aerodynamics unit. This brief period resulted in what might be seen as his *annus mirabilis* with critical insights on radiator duct as heat engines and on duct entry. After the period at Aerodynamics Meredith returned to Instruments where he did important work on autopilot and bombsights (at a time when he was passing information to the Soviets).

Aerodynamics		
Automatic landing		
1924	*Automatic control of aeroplanes* (TNA, AVIA 6/1513)	Report following automatic landing tests in 1923 using the phugoid principle and incorporating a trailing wire landing aid.
Jet propulsion		
1935	*Invention relating to jet propulsion of aircraft* (TNA, AVIA 8/407)	Paper showing basic subsonic ramjet design.
Duct entry		
1935	*Note on the problem of conducting a fluid into a duct with the minimum of losses* (RAE paper Wind Tunnel Note No 267)	Proposed boundary layer bypass and vanes.
'Meredith effect'		
1935	*Cooling of Aircraft Engines With special reference to Ethylene Glycol Radiators enclosed in Ducts* (ARC, R&M No 1683, August 1935 (published 1936))	First (aerodynamic) conclusion 'The employment of low velocity cooling [placing the radiator behind a diffuser duct which slowed the cooling air] avoids the necessity of an increasing expenditure of power with increasing speed provided the exit conditions are adjusted to suit the speed [by a converging duct with a variable exit].' Second (thermodynamic) conclusion 'The combined effect of compressibility [here changes in temperature and density with that of pressure] and heat transfer from the radiator may reduce the power consumption to nothing if the size of the radiator is adequate.'
1935	*Improvements in or relating to aircraft and other craft or vehicles* (GB 454,266 patent)	With Stewart and Meredith treated ducted radiators as a heat engine.
1935	Meredith visits Supermarine in September	Comments (critically) on Spitfire cooling duct and other aerodynamic issues. Suggests wind tunnel tests.

'Meredith effect' (*Cont.*)		
1935/6	*Model tests of the Supermarine F.37/74 radiator cowl* (Shaw and Kirkby, TNA AVIA 6/2087, tests in November 1935)	Wind tunnel testing of Spitfire duct done following Meredith's recommendation.
Exhaust gas momentum		
1935	*Cooling of Aircraft Engines With special reference to Ethylene Glycol Radiators enclosed in Ducts* (ARC, R&M No 1683, August 1935 (published 1936))	Third (exhaust gas momentum) conclusion in: 'Finally, attention is drawn to the importance of the moment of the exhaust gases for a high-speed aeroplane, although no attempt is made to deal with this point quantitatively.'
Boundary layer suction		
1936	*The Possible Improvement in Aircraft Performance due to the use of Boundary-layer Suction* (With Griffith, TNA, E 3501, DSIR 23/5566, E/1976)	Griffith and Meredith produce the first equations for the boundary layer, moving along a similar surface but with regularly placed suction holes, with the result that the boundary layer has a constant thickness.
Instruments		
Automatic control		
Bombsight		
1926	*Problem of Lateral Stabilisation of a Bombsight* (TNA, AVIA 6/3131, RAE Report H.1138)	Pointed out that if the aircraft itself were stabilised then the bombsight need not be.
1936	*Memorandum on High Altitude Bombsights* (TNA, AVIA 53/233)	Asserted that in wartime a reflector stabilised vector sight would be in practice superior to a tachometric sight.
1939	*Improvements in or relating to apparatus for repeating the movements of a member such as the movable member of an instrument* (GB526,101A)	Pneumatic air-jet and chopper-block servomechanism.
Autopilot		
1930	Pilot assister (RAE)	The initial gyroscopic design used a pneumatically spun gyroscope to move the flight controls introduced by the RAE.

1931	Mk I (RAE/Smiths)	Production started of the RAE [two gyro, three axis] Mk 1 Automatic Control and was sold commercially as the Smith Automatic Control for civilian aircraft use.
1935	Mk IV (RAE/Smiths)	Standard Second World War British pneumatic two gyroscope three-axis autopilot developed under Meredith in the mid-1930s.
1937	*Aeroplane Stability and the Automatic Pilot* (With Cooke, Royal Aeronautical Society, Vol. XI, No. 318, June 1937)	Account of the results of the early efforts was presented by Meredith and Cook of the RAE.
Blind flying		
1930	*Air Transport in Fog* (*Journal of the Royal Aeronautical Society,* February 1931)	Stated: 'air transport in fog is immediately practicable: but it involves an element of risk.'
1930	*Improvements in or relating to electrical indicating systems* (With Smith, GB 357,968)	An invention that 'applied to wireless direction-finding apparatus for giving a continuous and instantaneous indication of the bearing of a transmitting station, for example for use on aircraft'. In 1935 Marconi announced it had acquired the rights for Meredith's Radio Azimuth patent.
Unmanned stabilised aircraft		
1925	Larynx (RAE)	Flying bomb controls.
1933	Queen Bee (RAE/de Havilland)	Air Ministry Specification F 18/33 for a wireless-controlled pilotless target aircraft to provide gunnery practice incorporating Meredith's ideas on automated landing and autopilot with auto-controls based on the Smiths Mk la automatic pilot.
Gunsight		
1937	*Note on the problem of aiming fixed guns in aeroplanes* (RAE, Departmental Note No. H 242)	Proposed simplifying the task of the pilot by designing the aeroplane and training the pilot for control in two axes control to aid obtaining the required angle of bank.

1938	*Improvements in or relating to controlling aircraft* (With Gardner, GB 576,359)	Dealt with the problem of stabilisation (using gyroscopes) of a plane of sight during a banked turn.
Award		
1937	RAeS Silver Medal for outstanding achievement award (The Royal Aeronautical Society)	Honoured outstanding achievers in the global aerospace.

The Second World War

It has been argued here that few men made a broader contribution to the war in the air over Western Europe. After Meredith's and Capon's 1935/36 papers virtually all inline engined powered fighters were designed with ducted radiators of very varying efficiency. The Spitfire was the first aircraft to have a cooling duct system specifically intended to produce the 'Meredith effect'. All powerful inline engines had exhaust stubs designed to exploit exhaust gas momentum as Meredith specified. The Hurricane incorporated a 'lip' on the cooling duct to divert the boundary layer in 1936. The Mustang embodied with rare efficiency all aspects of Meredith's aerodynamic drag reduction and thrust addition ideas: ducts as heat engines, boundary layer lips, and exhaust gas momentum.

Remarkably, Meredith's contributions extended into the field of instruments. All larger British aircraft incorporated his designs in the form of Mk IV and Mk VII autopilots. Meredith advocated the use of vector in preference to tachometric bombsights. He also suggested employing a reflector mechanism to reduce its length. Both of these features were part of the successful stabilised Mk XIV sight. Meredith's air-jet and chopper servo mechanism was also an important feature of the design.

Solid state gyroscope		
1942	*Improvements in or relating to devices for detecting or measuring rate of turn* (GB 611,005)	Tuning fork (solid state) gyroscope.
Autopilot		
1942	Mk VIII (Smiths)	Simpler MK VIII was developed with a single gyroscope using Meredith's patents.
Bombsight		
1942	Mk XIV (RAE/various manufacturers)	Reflector vector type incorporating Meredith's air-jet and chopper servomechanism.
Autopilot		
1943	*Improvements in electric motors* (GB 576,248)	Hysteresis electronic servo motor.

Post-Second World War

In the post-war period the SEP1 civil and Mark IX military autopilot, the first successful rate/rate system, designed by Smiths under Meredith, was used in all larger British aircraft. Meredith had designed the autopilot so it could be linked to radios for automatic landings, a particular problem for frequently fogbound Heathrow. The Mark XIV bombsight continued in use until the 1960s. By the 1950s the days of the manned aircraft were seen (wrongly) as numbered. Meredith was regarded as essential to the development of the guidance systems of British missiles.

In 1941 NACA researchers had tested the 'Meredith effect' in a high-speed wind tunnel, using electrical heaters in a propulsive duct. Generally, however, aviation experts considered that jet engines could not produce as much thrust as a propeller, so this work was ignored until 1943, until US Navy researchers were looking for ways to power missiles to shoot down glided bombs and kamikazes. This produced the supersonic Talos ramjet missile which entered service in 1955.

Autopilot		
1945	SEP1, Mark 9 (Smiths)	First rate/rate autopilot incorporating hysteresis motors.
1949	*The Modern Autopilot: A Dissertation on the Fundamentals of Modern Autopilot Design* (*Flight*)	Article following Royal Aeronautical Society presentation.
Solid state gyroscope		
1949	*Control of Equilibrium in the Flying Insect* (*Nature*)	Pointed out *halteres*, small oscillating structures on some insects, enabled them to stabilise themselves in flight.
1957	*Invention and Nature* (Annual Lecture of the Measurement and Control Section)	Highlighted the *halteres* in flies, rod like vibrators behind the wings, which act like alternating gyroscope stabilisers. 'A detailed account of the efforts of various inventors, including himself, to make use of this same principle (that of Foucault's pendulum) to stabilize aircraft. Man has here been less successful than nature.'
Award		
1953	Wakefield Gold Medal (Royal Aeronautical Society)	Award for outstanding contributions to air safety (not given every year).

On 13 December 1953, C.G.W.L. Mitchell gave it as his opinion that the Ministry of Supply should make plans gradually to fade Meredith out of defence work. Gardner, on the other hand, thought that his value to us was so great that he should be retained on the present basis.

> He [Gardner] said we were well ahead of all other countries in Meredith's field and that this was solely due to Meredith. We might be able to retain our leading position for a year or two without Meredith while we were still exploiting his ideas, but if we did not have his continuing services we should undoubtedly fall behind in the future.[25]

After that nothing is heard of Meredith's scientific activities. An internet message board for ex-flight staff recently bemoaned: 'Whatever happened to British avionics? We were the cutting edge in the fifties yet lost the plot entirely in less than ten years.'

Meredith's legacy lives on to the present. He put special importance on managing the boundary flow at duct entry when he proposed isolating the boundary layer from the duct. The engines of the Northrop Grumman B-2 Spirit Stealth bomber (first flight 1989, in service 1997) are buried within its wing to conceal the engines' fans and minimize the exhaust signature. The gap below the air intake keeps the boundary layer out of the jet engine. Many jet fighters have a boundary layer splitter plate, for the example, the McDonnell F4 Phantom, and is perhaps fitting that its efficiency should be enhanced by another aspect of Meredith's work, boundary layer suction: that is perforation on the plate and remove the fresh boundary layer which builds up on the plate. Many splitter plates have a series of holes drilled into the surface closer to the engine side of the intake. Suction is applied to these holes, further reducing the boundary layer. A splitter plate with suction holes can be seen on the BAE Typhoon.

Remarkably, during the war Meredith patented a solid state 'tuning fork' gyroscope. This was a concept that would be extraordinarily important in the modern era. Solid state gyroscopes are incorporated in smart phones and gaming devices, multimotor drones, robot controls, photographic stabilisers, and transportation devices like segways.

Meredith – the national dilemma

Meredith presented a huge problem to any authority. His work was seen as indispensable to the national interest and he was regarded as uniquely capable of doing it. But he also presented an unquantifiable national security threat, particularly after he was identified as having actually passed secret material to the Soviets. As an official wrote in the later 1940s: 'This [Meredith's] case presents the problem of "Communism in industry" in as acute a form as I have seen it.'[26] The question was, could the problem be managed?

Pre-war, on 15 March 1934, however, when considering suspending communists:

> It was suggested that it was preferable to have the benefit of
> Meredith's brains at the RAE and run the risk of a possible leakage.
> It was pointed out that if Meredith were dismissed, he might quite
> possibly go to Russia where the Air Ministry would be completely
> deprived of his services and brain, which they value very highly.[27]

Post-war, on 6 April 1952, it was concluded that Meredith could continue on
guided weapon work, subject to conditions on access to US material. The author,
as seen, lamented: 'It is a great pity that this brilliant man should have this failing.
He is unique.'[28]

In the interwar period it was decided Meredith was best left alone. Despite
repeated informant reports for years, it was considered that little could be done
about the Meredith problem at RAE. 'As far as Meredith's open communist
sympathies were concerned, the Air Ministry did not consider – in view of the lack
of a definite policy at the time [pre-Second World War] – that any action could be
taken.'[29] The Security Services decided not to warn Smiths when Meredith was
about to join them:

> We are inclined to agree that no warning about the Official Secrets
> Act should be given. Actually, he will have less opportunity now to
> acquire really secret information than he has had in the past: perhaps
> 'acquire' is not the correct word, for much of the secret information
> in his possession emanates from his own brain.[30]

After the war, when it was known Meredith had passed material to the Soviets,
on 18 January [1949] the decision was made that the government could not afford
not to employ Meredith, who had a wife and family to maintain and enjoyed his
work. On 7 March it was concluded Meredith was not currently associated with the
Communist party and unlikely to divulge classified information to Russians. 'Mr
Meredith is in a high place in the category of indispensable people. This outweighs
the security risk.'[31]

Analysis of the Security Services records reveals that to a remarkable extent
Britain was not a police state and the very circumscribed powers of those services.
There were quite extreme views on the left and right. As seen: 'The local police
are inclined to think that the majority of employees in the RAE are out-and-out
Bolsheviks.'[32] The head of Instruments, Leonard Bygrave, was killed in a riding
accident during a Legion of Frontiersmen exercise. Post-war 'Tubby' Vielle, who
was employed by the RAE pre-war, wrote a paper: 'Suggesting that, for the benefit
of future world peace, and before Russia developed their own atomic bomb, the
US and Britain should threaten Moscow immediately with an atomic bomb attack
unless Moscow disarmed completely and opened up their country to us.'[33]

The Security Services failed completely in efforts to restrict large numbers of
RAE personnel visiting the Soviet Union, where on his third trip in 1937, Meredith

provided secret information. In 1932 it was recorded that: 'The Authorities were aware that Meredith and the others were sympathetic to the Soviet regime, but considered that, as long as the former was allowed to express his opinions openly, no harm would result.'[34] When considering the risk of Meredith's defection on 12 April [1952], the Security Service record states: 'No power exists whereby a British subject can be prevented from leaving the country if he wishes to do so, unless evidence exists which will justify his detention under warrant.'[35] Also: 'The plain fact is that a British subject with a head full of knowledge and ideas can leave the country at his own sweet will, and I do not think that any department ought to be allowed to entertain the notion that there is anything which the Security Service can do about it.'[36]

In October 1953, 'Meredith said he was continuously heckled by his colleagues and admitted that in self-defence he had from time to time spoken rather wildly'.[37] This particular Meredith problem was resolved not by shooting or incarceration in the Gulags. Rather, 'a special dining room has now been arranged for the four senior men in the factory, which includes Meredith'.[38] On 29 May 1952, the Guided Weapons [Directorate] said it was becoming difficult to keep American information from Meredith and sought advice. There was the 'impression that Meredith in fact had knowledge of a considerable amount of the latest developments, both British and American, in this special field and that it was therefore possible that the Ministry of Supply restrictions were so ineffective that Meredith was not aware of them'.[39]

The last entry in Security Service file KV2/2202 was on 8 June 1953, reporting a meeting that discussed whether Meredith should be included on a list for internment in the event of war or emergency. It was decided not, but that the question would be addressed again in six months when a Home Office Committee had discussed how best to deal with, 'communists or communist sympathisers who have access at their place of employment to classified government work'.[40] The file noted: 'We are, however, really in the position that if we trust M, it is in our belief in bourgeois honesty and in the face of his past record and his proclaimed Marxist view.'[41]

On a personal level there was a certain amount of old-fashioned British tolerance, even black humour. Gardner commented: 'In discussing political theory, he had not the same control over his emotions, and his colleagues tended to discount a great deal of what he said on that account.'[42] An informer revealed that: 'In the old days at Farnborough [name redacted] had often told him if ever his revolutionary friends came to power, Meredith would be the first person they would shoot.'[43] The point was that this was a joke. While Soviet communists might well have shot him, the British Security Services did not.

Meredith appears to have led a charmed life in his brushes and collisions with authority. He disappeared for some months, as far as the army was concerned, during the First World War with no repercussions. He openly espoused revolution in the inter-war period. After the Second World War he was identified as having been a pre-war Soviet spy and he refused to renounce his pro-Soviet, anti-American views. He enjoyed a long and secure retirement in Cheltenham which included much croquet.

Meredith was a man of exceptional intelligence. Therefore, what drove him to a position seen as perverse, even immature, by those who recognised his scientific brilliance? The sympathetic Gardner stated: 'I found that he had an extremely generous disposition, and possibly this, more than anything else, led him to champion the underdog and to become interested in Socialist and Communist theories.'[44]

Gardner added an insight into the apparent contradiction between the rationality of his scientific method and the ferocity (or naïvety) of his political views. 'About 1930 or 1931, when there was a great growth of political consciousness in the country, Meredith spent a lot of his time studying current political problems.'[45] In December 1952, Mitchell was harsher:[46]

> My general impression is that Meredith politically is extremely juvenile and adolescent. He appears to be still in the stage usually passed by long haired types of students by the time they reach the age of about 22 [Meredith was in his mid-fifties]. Meredith certainly has not passed through that stage, and I doubt very much whether he will ever now get through it. My own view is that to some extent Meredith has a split personality and that that portion which shows itself in his political views is probably quite unaffected by the other half of his personality which deals with his business and domestic affairs.[47]

It might be recalled that Meredith was an Irishman. He was born in Ireland and went to prep-school there. After public school in England he studied for his BA at Trinity Dublin. He visited Ireland frequently. That he was an Irishman was recognised early in his Security Services file in 1927. A redacted source in 1927 reported that Meredith was 'responsible on the Aerodynamics side for serial target (W/T [wireless telegraphy] controlled aeroplanes [possibly the Queen Bee or an antecedent]): that he was a very reserved Irishman, believed to hold extreme Sinn Fein views'.[48] An informant reported before his marriage in 1935: 'The trouble with Meredith is that he has had a very unhappy private life and bears a grudge against the world. He could best be described as an embittered Irish rebel.'[49] (It might be added that Security Services sources all recorded that Meredith's marriage seemed very happy.) On 22 March 1952, the Security Services concluded that Meredith was still a Marxist but, 'he is not now a very serious one and may well maintain his views more from Irish perversity than from conviction'.[50]

Is it, however, possible to construct a counterfactual argument that Meredith was actually accurate in his political analysis and justified in his behaviour? As Gardner stated: 'About 1930 or 1931, Meredith spent a lot of his time studying current political problems.'[51] Political developments made Meredith increasingly susceptible to Soviet approaches. His post-war interrogator in the late 1940s reported:

> In 1935 he [Meredith] was quite satisfied that the British Government was pursuing the wrong foreign policy. It was showing a blind hatred of Russia and watched with equanimity the rearmament of Germany.

> At an early stage he, Meredith, realised that if Germany succeeded in beating Russia, it would turn on the West. He thought that his country was being dishonoured by its foreign policy, a view which was confirmed by the rape of Spain.[52]

Also,

> He felt that war between Hitler and Russia was inevitable, and that it was owed to the future of humanity that Russia should not lose this war. He realised that he had to pay a very high price in grave personal risk in taking some positive action, but that in the circumstances this risk was well warranted.[53]

Arguably, Meredith's political analysis was right. Nazi Germany was indeed a profound threat. Also, Meredith believed his motives for recruitment as a Soviet spy were based on the most principled motives. 'He therefore had to communicate to the Russians anything that might be of military advantage to them in the war with Germany which he felt completely convinced was inevitable.'[54] Meredith saw himself as an honourable spy: '[He] decided to exercise certain moral scruples and to pass on nothing which was not a child of his brain. He felt no wrong was done by sharing his own ideas, inventions and the like with his Russian friends.'[55] It might be noted now that: 'He resolutely refused to become an active spy, confining his disclosures always to matters arising from his own inventive mind.'[56] The range of areas embraced by that 'inventive mind' was, however, vast indeed.

Before the discovery that Meredith had been a practising spy in the later 1940s, his behaviour as a known communist sympathiser in the 1930s was perforce tolerated given his irreplaceability. Indeed, to have excluded from public life and office all those who had been Soviet sympathisers in the 1930s and 1940s would have involved an impossible loss to the intellectual and political life of the nation. On 13 September 1934, the Security Services recorded: 'If they suspend all of those on the list of communists it will include Meredith, Lockspeiser, Carter, Constance, Squire, Calvert, Hollingdale and Lord knows who. If they suspend all Socialists they will have to close the Factory [RAE].'[57] Most had honourable motives – distress at the welfare crisis caused by the Depression, itself perceived as a consequence (not then entirely unreasonably) of the failure of capitalism, and horror at the rearmament of the appeased fascist Germany. But these Soviet sympathisers largely rejected Soviet communism when the reality – the purges, the Molotov-Ribbentrop pact, of the gulags, and the suppression of independence movements in adjacent countries – became clear. But not so, apparently, Meredith.

Yet Meredith was not a spy like Philby, Burgess, Maclean, or Beurton (Agent Sonya), who worked to spread Soviet hegemony and whose activities resulted in many deaths. He provided only information stemming from his fertile mind that might help strengthen the Soviet Union against attack, inevitably from Germany, possibly from the US and/or the UK. (Vielle's paper, proposing a pre-emptive western nuclear strike on the Soviet Union, might be recalled.) The Security Services and the Government had an impossible challenge whether to risk allowing Meredith to continue work in areas where his skills were deemed unique, or remove him, close down the security risk, but lose the opportunity for him to do work at which he was deemed the best in the country. For nearly three decades it was decided to take the risk – a decision conditioned by a remarkable respect for established legal systems and constitutional structures, leavened by bourgeois tolerance and good British humour. In this case the decision does look right as Britain, and the US, got the benefit of his expertise for most of the span of a working life and he retired into deep, but it seems, not at all unpleasant obscurity. This was almost certainly a risk worth taking, particularly for the 'Meredith effect', pioneered on the Spitfire and perfected on the Mustang, the two most important allied fighters in Second World War Western Europe.

APPENDICES

Appendix 1

Cooling issues

It might be useful to set out certain technical themes and challenges this book tackles. As seen, F.W. Meredith examined many of these areas and made novel proposals for solutions.

Piston engine as 'heat engines' – focus on exhaust stage

A piston engine is a form of 'heat engine', that is a system which converts heat energy into mechanical energy. There are four stages: intake, compression, power and exhaust. Much attention has been paid to the first three stages involving superchargers and engines and relatively little to the exploitable energy in the fourth. The focus of this book is on this last stage. A piston engine is not efficient, as roughly only about 25% of the energy in the fuel results in horsepower that drives the propeller; roughly another 25% needs to be removed as heat by the engine's cooling systems; and there is a further loss of about half of the energy as hot exhaust gas. The energy, however, from the last two need not be entirely lost.

There are two types of cooling, depending on whether heat is transferred directly to the air or through a liquid medium: an air-cooled engine functions by guiding the cooling air directly over the engine itself and particularly the cylinder heads; a liquid-cooled engine uses that liquid to take the heat away from the engine to a radiator where it is transferred to the air. (A radial engine cannot entirely avoid having a radiator, as the oil required to lubricate the engine, which also provides a cooling medium, must itself be cooled. Hence, both radial and inline engines have an oil cooling radiator which is about a third of the size of the radiator required to cool the liquid jackets of an inline engine.)

The heat energy – that either goes directly to the air that passes through the radial's fins, or indirectly, resulting from passing through an inline engine's radiator – can be converted into kinetic energy in a duct. Thus, there is a second heat engine where intake results from the forward motion of the aircraft, compression from impact on the engine cooling fins or radiator face, power from the addition of heat from the fins or in the radiator, followed by exhaust behind the engine or radiator. Also, the engine exhaust gas momentum can either be directed rearwards or used to power a turbocharger; or it can be added to the air heated through the cooling process to increase greatly the kinetic energy in a duct behind the radiator.

'Cold' and 'hot' cooling systems

Axiomatically, a cooling system might be considered as 'cold'. It was Meredith's particular insight to perceive it as 'hot' and that a ducted or cowled cooling system could be, as seen, a second heat engine. The purpose of a system regarded as 'cold' was solely to cool the liquid going through the radiator. Thus, temperature changes in the air, not only while it went through the radiator, but also before and after, were ignored. Thus, the focus is on drag and its reduction. In practice, however, a cooling system is 'hot' as it involves the transfer of heat and is a heat engine in its own right.

Drag and power

Airflow drag results from forcing the aeroplane through the medium of air. The change in the amount of power needed to overcome the drag of an object through a fluid (here air) varies as a cube of the ratio of velocities. Thus, the power required when doubling the airspeed in level flight from 150mph to 300mph is 125 horsepower times (300/150) cubed (125 times 2^3 equals 1,000 horsepower). Reducing cooling drag to a minimum cuts wasted power and that becomes increasingly important as speeds increase. External drag can be largely eliminated by burying the cooling system and exhausting the cooling air in a way that avoids disrupting the exterior airflow.

Four types of cooling drag

The cooling system was a source of additional drag. The Royal Aircraft Establishment (RAE) outlined four types of liquid systems cooling drag:

Internal

- The minimum internal drag is caused by the radiator itself when receiving sufficient air for cooling.
- Residual internal drag is that total measured through the duct less the minimum drag.

The problems tended to be largely at the duct entry created by ingestion of the boundary layer – that is slower moving air adjacent to the airframe surface.

External

- The minimum external drag is that caused by the additional external surface area of the duct.
- The residual drag is that resulting from other drag resulting from the relationship of the duct with the airframe and airstream.

Laminar and turbulent airflow

Airflow may be smooth (laminar) or turbulent, resulting in much higher drag. Maintaining laminar flow by controlling the pressure distribution on an airfoil is called natural laminar flow (NLF). (Active laminar flow control (ALFC) includes suction through perforations, a method analysed by RAE scientists, A.A. Griffith and Meredith.)

Boundary layer and duct entry

The boundary layer is air in contact with the airframe that moves more slowly than the surrounding airstream. If the cooling duct entrance is at the front of the fuselage or wing there is no boundary layer problem, but if it is, as in practice for ducted cooling systems, in the fuselage ventral or the underwing aft position, then the layer has had time to build up. The ingestion of both slower moving boundary layer air and faster moving air outside that layer into the duct causes turbulence and thus drag. (The challenge is to divert the boundary layer from entering the duct. Meredith was particularly aware of the problem of duct entry and proposed important solutions.)

Pressure drop across the radiator

As air passes through the radiator its pressure drops. The reduction in the momentum at the front and rear of the radiator creates thrust in the reverse 'wrong' direction, following Newton's second law of motion which requires engine power in order to overcome that negative thrust or drag. Therefore, the amount of power, and hence of cooling air going through the radiator, should be restricted to no more than necessary for cooling. As the volume of air needed to cool the engine is much more in a climb than in the cruise condition the challenge is to find the means to adjust the pressure drop to no more than necessary for cooling in a given flight condition, by either increasing or reducing the duct entrance or exit area.

Different requirements for power at various speeds in level and climbing flight

The most severe conditions for engine cooling are found when climbing rapidly near the ground in hot weather, when the engine is developing maximum power and the temperature difference between the air and the fluid in the radiator is low. (The higher the temperature difference the more heat can be transferred.) Accordingly, the radiator must be designed to meet this condition if it is not to overheat in these conditions. Therefore, some means of reducing the cooling air flow in less demanding conditions, must be found or power will be wasted in unnecessary cooling. This could be: shutters before the radiator; making the radiator retractable;

or variable flaps behind the radiator controlling the volume of air flowing out of and hence into the duct. The first two required the radiator to be exposed directly in the airstream resulting in higher drag – while the last, in practice, required placing the radiator in a duct.

Key cooling duct dimension ratios

Placing a radiator between a diverging and a converging duct greatly reduces drag by slowing the air before it reaches the radiator and then after the radiator accelerating it to close to the external air velocity. Therefore, decisions are required as to the length of the diverging or converging ducts and the ratio of the areas of the duct entrance or exit and the radiator area. On these decisions will depend the extent that cooling air is decelerated and accelerated. The location of the duct will impose constraints on the lengths and ratios which are a function of frontal area.

In practice the important ratios are:

- Firstly, the ratio of duct entrance and radiator frontal area. This determines the extent that the air is slowed before hitting the radiator according to Bernoulli's theorem (a decrease in the speed of a liquid flow results in a drop in its pressure – and vice-versa). Therefore, a large radiator frontal area would seem preferable, but this could create very high external drag if the duct cannot be buried due to its location. The ratio can be varied by making the duct entrance area variable with an adjustable flap.
- Secondly, there is the ratio of radiator frontal diameter and the radiator length. The radiator has to dissipate heat. This is done most efficiently when the cooling air temperature is raised by 85% of the difference between the temperature of the air entering the radiator and coolant liquid temperature. This requires radiator tubes of a sufficient length relative to their calibre.

There is an inherent dichotomy between the two ratios. A larger radiator frontal diameter, implying shorter tubes means less power is needed to overcome drag. Longer tubes, and thus a smaller radiator frontal diameter, results in more efficient heat dissipation. There is thus a choice between radiators that are: 'oversquare' or with larger frontal width than tube length; or 'undersquare', the converse. As seen, R.S. Capon's work at the RAE could be interpreted as favouring an 'undersquare' radiator. In August 1935, he had written: 'It is advantageous to use a radiator of small frontal area having long tubes: the optimum conditions indicate a tube length which will cause the rise of temperature of the air to be about 85% of the radiator-air temperature difference.'[1] This presupposed two factors: the radiator was substantially unburied so the frontal area needed to be relatively small to avoid inordinate drag; and the absolute optimum was required – when in practice a satisfactory result could be achieved at a significantly lower percentage. In practice a figure far less than 85% is practicable, making 'oversquare' radiators preferable as the air is slowed more below the radiator provided this can be carried.

Summary of key cooling issues

This book repeatedly comes back to certain issues. These are: restricting the airflow through the radiator to no more than needed for cooling for a given flight condition; managing the airflow into the duct entry so the boundary layer does not create turbulence; optimising the balance of the ratio of radiator frontal width to tube length; and the conception of a cooling system as 'cold' or 'hot'. In the former the focus is on reducing drag by efficient use of diverging and converging ducts. In the latter it is to create thrust from the heat engine cycle.

Interceptors and escort fighters

In the period between 1935 to 1945, fighters were largely conceived of as being two types. Interceptors were defensive fighters tasked to destroy bombers or reconnaissance aircraft relatively close to base. They needed to be able to climb fast to attack incoming aircraft. They required only sufficient fuel to climb, attack and return soon to base when ammunition was expended. They were generally characterised by small size, and short range. (Long range capability was a disadvantage here as a large weight of fuel would detract from rapid climb, and ammunition carrying.)

The concept of the escort fighter developed during the war as it became brutally clear, contrary to pre-war doctrine, that bombers could not defend themselves in the daytime against interceptors. Such fighters would protect the strategic bombers on their long-range missions. The high fuel load and the perceived requirement for a navigator was initially seen as necessitating twin engines. The top speed was similar to the interceptor, but size and weight made them less manoeuvrable. Thus, they were vulnerable to the interceptors unless, like them, they were single engined. These two types had different cooling requirements: the interceptor needed cooling maximised for rapid climbing and high-speed combat; and the escort's cooling had to be efficient for both long range cruising and high-speed combat.

In practice the Second World War showed that the heavy twin engined escort fighter was largely a flawed concept as it was not able to defend itself against the interceptors. (Twin engine escort fighters, however, proved adequate bomber interceptors, provided air superiority could be established over any single-engined escorts defending the bombers.) Eventually, it was realised that escort fighters could be single-engined as the navigator proved unnecessary, at least during the day, providing they could be built with large enough fuel capacity and sufficiently aerodynamically efficiency to provide the range necessary to accompany bombers. Such efficiency meant reducing drag from cooling to a minimum.

Appendix 2

Development of cooling systems before the Spitfire

The earlier development of the aircraft cooling systems, prior to F.W. Meredith and the Supermarine Spitfire, might be briefly revised.

Radials I – From rotaries to radials

During the First World War air-cooled aero engines were largely rotaries where the crankshaft was stationary and cylinders revolved, combining minimalist design with good cooling. These had surprisingly advanced looking cowls – unlike early radials which were generally not covered. The cowls, however, were not there to improve drag reduction and cooling but to guide away the copious spray from total loss oil lubrication systems. The bottom part of the cowling was cut away to allow the expelled oil to escape without drenching the pilot. The limitation created by gyroscopic forces, as power increased, meant the rotary was supplanted in the immediate post-war years by the radial where the crankcase and cylinders were fixed and the revolving crankshaft turned the propeller. As these did not expel oil from the exhaust manifolds, like those of the oil total loss rotaries, there was no perceived need for a cowling and the cylinders were initially fully exposed as this was thought to enhance cooling.

Inlines I – Junkers' pioneering work

In the First World War, British, French and American large water cooled inlines increasingly had radiators placed between the propeller and the engine with variable front shutters to adjust airflow according to the flight condition. Shutters of the Venetian window-blind type, however, added greatly to the drag of the radiator when closed, while their drag when open was not negligible. During the First World War inline design developed so that, by its end, water cooled V-12s like the Rolls-Royce Eagle and the US Liberty engines were becoming common for larger allied inline powered aircraft aeroplanes.

Figure A2.1 – Junkers J2, 1916, showing *Düsenkühler*.

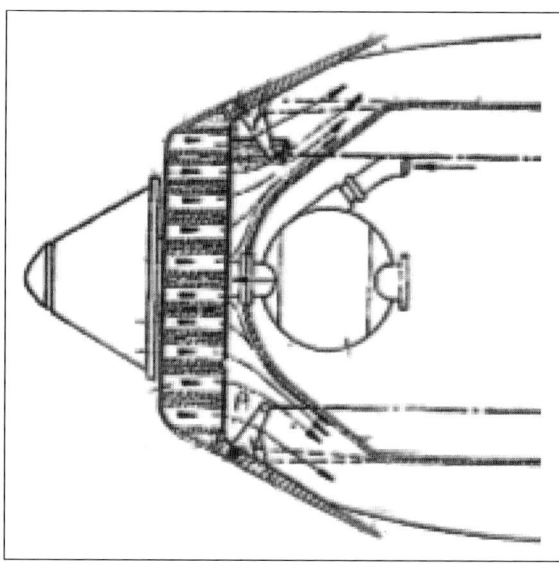

Figure A2.2 – Junkers patent US 1,464,765A (1920) originally German in 1918, showing adjustable flaps behind the radiator.

A precocious early ducted radiator system was designed by Hugo Junkers, 1859 to 1935, who had been Professor of Thermodynamics at the Technische-Hochenschule in Aachen. In 1915, Junkers patented a *Düsenkühler* or jet cooler.[1] This was actually incorporated in the remarkably advanced Junkers J2 of 1916. Not only was this an all-metal monoplane, unique for the period, but it had a ventral radiator duct.

Junkers also proposed the control of the volume of air exiting the cooling system so cooling drag was minimised. He applied for a German patent in February 1918. The US patent of 1920 said: 'I [Junkers] further attach to the side walls of the radiator adjustable flaps extending rearwardly. By varying the position of these flaps the cross-sectional area of the passage for the air leaving the radiator can be altered.'[2] Thus, Junkers had designed and patented both the key aspects of a ducted radiator system, albeit separately, the diffusing and converging ducts and the adjustable exit.

Willy Messerschmitt, in the late 1930s, praised the Junkers *Düsenkühler* as the most important single contribution to high-speed flight as it cut down the otherwise prohibitive cooling drag.

> The introduction of the *Düsenkühler* by Junkers makes it possible to significantly reduce the resistance of the cooling system. The advantage of the cooler was that the cooling capacity became independent of speed and that the air speed in the cooler and thus the power required for the cooler, could be kept constant.[3]

Radials II – cowls and cowl flaps

By 1927 the radial drag problem was so serious that in the US the National Advisory Committee for Aeronautics, or NACA, was requested to investigate. Underlying, there were two issues: the air passing through and around the cylinder fins became excessively turbulent; also, more air than necessary went through the cylinder fins creating excessive cooling drag that unnecessarily wasted power in other than rapid climb.

Townend Ring

The issue of turbulence was first tackled by the Townend Ring, developed by Dr Hubert Townend of the British National Physical Laboratory in 1929. This was a narrow chord, aerofoil section, cowling ring fitted around the cylinders. The ring ducted the air onto the cylinder heads and directed a streamlined flow rearwards. This ring was widely used between 1930 to 1935.

NACA cowling 1 – without flaps

In the US NACA developed a wide chord cowling which restricted flow into the cowl and reduced turbulence. At the front the cowling extended in front of the cylinder heads. At the rear was a fixed gap between the cowling and the fuselage. The NACA cowling directed cool air to flow through the engine across its hottest parts. Turbulence after the air passed the cylinders was greatly reduced. Drag was lowered by nearly two thirds. Nearly every radial-engined aircraft was equipped with this cowling after the mid-1930s.

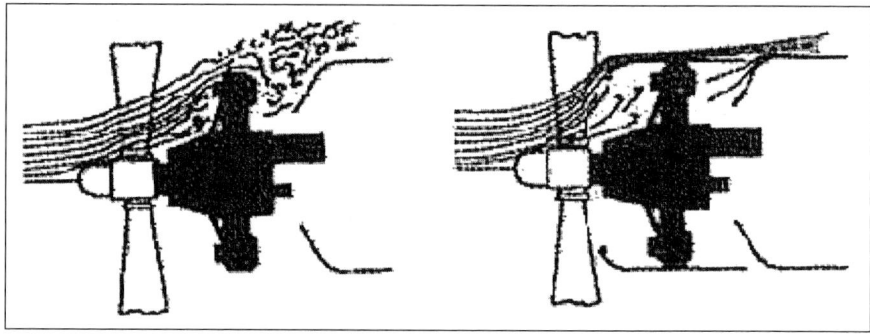

Figure A2.3 – Radial engine showing airflow without and with a NACA cowling.

NACA cowling 2 – with Beisel's flaps

In 1934 The US Vought group under aeronautical engineer R.B. Beisel, aided by radial manufacturer Pratt and Whitney, made cooling more efficient by directing the airflow to the cylinder rear with baffles.[4] Also, 'they invented rear cowl flaps to vary the size of the exit opening and so to regulate efficiently the airflows to the minimum value required for cooling in each condition of flight'. The efficiency of the combination of the fully cowled engine with adjustable flaps exceeded expectation. In April 1936, D.H. Wood, senior NACA investigator, wrote: 'Recent experiments on the cooling of air-cooled engines have shown that the mechanism of cooling is more complicated than was previously imagined; yet the efficiency with which cooling is accomplished is better than anticipated, in fact, better than some theoretical maximum estimates.'[5] Radial engines now incorporated the key aspects of a ducted cooling system: a cowling creating a duct and cowl flaps.

Inlines II – introducing Rolls-Royce

The role of Rolls-Royce in developing inline cooling systems is often overlooked. The Kestrel engine, first run 1926, used supercharging at all altitudes and there were two important innovations in the cooling system during its life, pressurisation and the addition of ethylene glycol.

1) Pressurisation
As the engine size increases a greater amount of cooling fluid has to be used, along with an increasingly large radiator to cool it. The Kestrel used a pressurised cooling system to maintain pressure sufficient to keep the boiling point at about 150 °C. Water boils at 100 °C, at ground level, but this temperature decreases with altitude. Since the amount of heat carried out of the engine is a function of the temperature difference between the incoming air and the coolant, the greater the difference, the better.

2) Ethylene Glycol

The second key development was the addition of ethylene glycol, which had a boiling point considerably higher than that of water. Therefore, the radiator could be run much hotter, increasing the temperature difference between the incoming air and the radiator, so the necessary heat dissipation could be accomplished with a smaller and lighter radiator holding less coolant.

Shutters and retractable radiators

The airflow volume could also be adjusted by the use of shutters in the cowl which covered the full frontal area of the engine. Front shutters were shown to be one of the least efficient drag reducing techniques. In June 1935, RAE mathematician and scientist R.S. Capon wrote: 'the radiator is inevitably converted into a bluff body when the shutters are closed, [so] no very large diminution of drag would be expected.'[6]

Pressurising the system and using ethylene glycol could make radiators smaller and more efficient but did not deal with the problem that a radiator configured for a full power climb wasted power in the level flight condition. With radials this was managed with Beisel's adjustable cowl flaps. The problem, where radiators were used, could be solved by either restricting the airflow through a radiator of constant area by adjusting the entry area with front shutters or the area of the radiator exposed to the airstream by making it semi-retractable.

Front shuttering produced a high drag bluff surface directly facing the airflow, which was very inefficient. Retracting the radiator during the cruise condition while leaving exposed an area sufficient for cooling, still resulted in high frontal drag on the exposed radiator area. Also, there was turbulence, as much cooling air simply went around the radiator exterior. (Another system in which there was the great, but ultimately, futile hope, was evaporative cooling, where the gaseous cooling agent was condensed within the airframe. This was fine for fast level flight, but it was incompatible with the violent manoeuvres required of combat aircraft.)

By the mid-1930s the challenge of cooling the radial engine – cowling the air flow round the cooling surface and controlling the volume of flow by shuttering – had been largely resolved. The same concepts could be applied to the liquid cool engine but had yet to be done systematically to a modern fighter plane. NACA's Wood, quoted earlier, said in April 1936 that following the huge advances in radial cooling: 'The radiator problem should be approached with an open mind and without preconceived notions. It will not be surprising if the radiator drag can be reduced to less than half of its present value. The liquid-cooled engine will then become a most serious competitor of the air-cooled engine in the high powers that are now ahead.' [7] In Britain these developments were already well underway at Rolls-Royce and the RAE by early 1935.

Appendix 3

'Meredith effect' formula derivation

Meredith's 1935 paper *Cooling of Aircraft Engines With special reference to Ethylene Glycol Radiators enclosed in Ducts* was outlined earlier in the main text. The derivation of its main conclusions are analysed here in more depth.

Breakdown of Meredith's coefficients

The boxed sections below show how Meredith established the coefficients 0.177 and 1.725 in his equation.

$$\text{Percentage of engine power} = 0.177 \ (V/100)^2 - 1.725 \ (V_0/100)^2$$

	gained	lost
	from radiator	in duct
	heat	

Power gained from radiator heat

The value of 0.177, the first term is derived as follows:

				0.345	$(V/100)^2$	percentage of thermal energy converted into kinetic energy at pressure behind radiator
0.345	x	0.46	=	0.158	$(V/100)^2$	proportion of engine heat transferred to glycol coolant
0.158	x	1.10	=	0.177	$(V/100)^2$	power gained due to lower temperature at altitude of 14,000 feet

There is an adjustment $(1-(4/3)(V/V_0)^2$ for adding heat at pressure behind the radiator expressed in terms of V_0. (This adjustment is negative in overall effect if V_0, the velocity through the radiator, is greater than 100mph and the converse if less.)

$0.177(V/100)^2$	x	$(1-(4/3)(V_o/V)^2)$	=	$0.177(V/100)^2$	-	$\dfrac{0.175(V/100)^2}{(4/3)(V_o/V)^2}$	
$0.177(V/100)^2$	-	$\dfrac{0.175(V/100)^2}{(4/3)(V_o/V)^2}$	=	$0.177(V/100)^2$	-	$0.233(V_o/100)^2$	

Power lost in duct

The power lost, the value of 1.725, is derived as follows:

				4.0	$(V_o/90)^2$	power required to overcome drag at 90mph of a cold radiator is 4% of the power it will dissipate at this speed for a temperature difference of 67°C
4.0	x	0.46	=	1.84	$(V_o/90)^2$	power expressed as percentage of BHP, instead of heat, dissipated (0.46 of BHP)
1.84	x	(67/125-23)	=	1.21	$(V_o/90)^2$	correction for temperature difference of 102°C for ethylene glycol
1.21	x	$(100/90)^2$	=	1.5	$(V_o/100)^2$	velocity adjusted to 100mph from 90mph
1.5	x	0.6	=	0.9	$(V_o/100)^2$	reduced power expended in drag for a ducted radiator is about 0.6 for an exposed radiator
0.9	x	1.15	=	1.035	$(V_o/100)^2$	increased power required due to adiabatic temperature increase through compression before the radiator reducing the available temperature difference through the radiator
1.035	x	1.14	=	1.2	$(V_o/100)^2$	increased power required due to the radiator being hot
1.2	x	1.231	=	1.48	$(V_o/100)^2$	increased power required due to lower density at altitude

There are thus three terms:

$0.177(V/100)^2$	-	$0.233(V_o/100)^2$	-	$1.48(V_o/100)^2$

These can in turn be simplified by adding the last two V_0 terms to give Meredith's formula:

$$0.177(V/100)^2 \quad - \quad 1.725(V_0/100)^2$$

The full 'Meredith effect' occurs when, 'the power expended on cooling does not increase with the speed of flight, but it should diminish to vanishing point at a practicable speed beyond which the cooling system contributes to propulsion'.

Gains and losses in formula

Gains

- The major gain is derived from putting the radiator in a duct. (This is given by Meredith as reducing the power lost by 0.6.)
- There is also a gain from the lower temperature at altitude. This increases the temperature difference between the coolant liquid and the cooling air. In the formula the altitude assumed is 14,000 feet.

Losses

- Compression – the adiabatic temperature increase, due to compression before the radiator, reduces the available temperature difference across it.
- Radiator – power is lost due to the increase in temperature and the fall in pressure and density across the radiator.
- Pressure – the heat is added behind the radiator at a lower pressure (provided V_0 is equal or greater than 100mph) which is likely to be the case as otherwise the radiator would be too large.

There is a further loss not related to heat addition:

- Density – loss due to the lower density at higher altitude.

Maximising the 'Meredith effect'

Treated as a mathematical exercise the 'Meredith effect' is maximised by:

- making the ratio of V to V_0 as large as possible. That is flying as fast as possible (V) while reducing the air speed through the radiator (V_0) as much as possible. Clearly there are limits on both. A higher airplane speed is determined by increasing power and reducing drag overall. Speed through the radiator depends on how large and therefore heavy the radiator is and there are clearly limits in practice. (Meredith thought a radiator large enough for V_o less than 100mph would be impractical.)

- flying as high as possible where the temperature difference between the coolant and the air is greater. This depends on an adequate supercharger.

Breakdown of coefficients – formula where exhaust heat is added

Meredith also gave a formula where waste heat was added. This required the following initial adjustment:

			0.16	$(V/100)^2$	from above
0.16	x	7/3	= 0.373	$(V/100)^2$	ratio of waste heat to indicated power
0.373	x	1/0.46	= 0.811	$(V/100)^2$	assuming all heat transferred

Adjusting for the temperature gain gave the first value.

0.8	x	1.10	= 0.88	$(V/100)^2$	power gained due to lower temperature at altitude

The second value was calculated as above.

$0.88(V/100)^2$	x	$(1-(4/3)(V/V_o)^2$	= $0.88(V/100)^2$	-	$\dfrac{0.88(V/100)^2\,(4/3)}{(V/V_o)^2}$
$0.88(V/100)^2$	-	$\dfrac{0.88(V/100)^2}{(4/3)(V/V_o)^2}$	= $0.88(V/100)^2$	-	$1.172(V_o/100)^2$

The third value $(1.48(V_o/100)^2)$ is unchanged.

There are thus three terms.

$0.88(V/100)^2$	-	$1.172(V_o/100)^2$	-	$1.48(V_o/100)^2$

These can in turn be simplified to give Meredith's formula.

$0.88(V/100)^2$	-	$2.67(V_o/100)^2$

Appendix 4

RAE Wind tunnel Test Programme

In the main text some key wind tunnel tests have been analysed. The RAE conducted a remarkable systematic programme of wind tunnel research. Other key reports are outlined here. The ventral, aft wing and chin locations were tested.

Ventral location

Note on the installation of a ducted radiator in the ventral position (Hartshorn, November 1935). – The RAE completed a study of a partly buried ventral radiator duct. This was an obvious candidate for investigation as the Hawker Hurricane

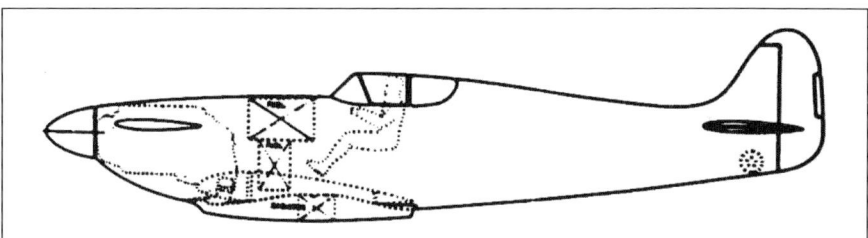

Figure A4.1 – Supermarine 312 – design study for specification F.37/35 for a four-cannon aircraft.

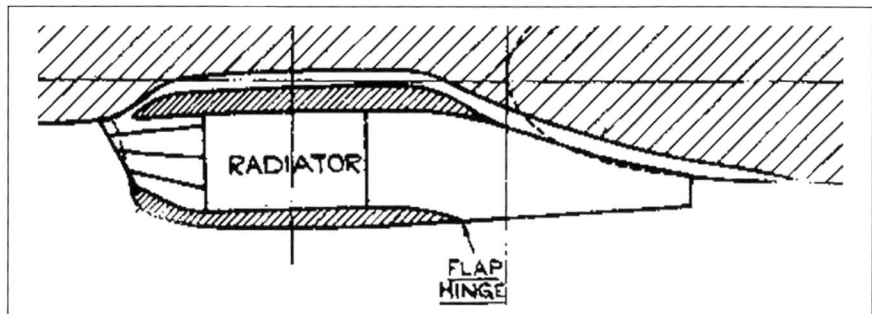

Figure A4.2 – Ventral radiator Model 2 with by-pass in *Note on the installation of a ducted radiator in the ventral position* (Hartshorn, November 1935).

and the proposed Supermarine 312 had ducted ventral radiators. Air Ministry specification F37/35 was issued in 1935 for a four-cannon aircraft. The Type 312 prototype was ordered from Supermarine but later cancelled to allow the company to focus on the Spitfire.

The wind tunnel test was of a ventral position with some similarities to but not the same as the 312.

The radiator was semi-recessed into the fuselage in front of the leading edge of the wing and the cowl was continued backward over the front of the wing. The cooling flow was controlled by a flap which altered the exit area of the duct.

The tests showed the following internal and external losses, the exit adjusted for a flight speed of 300mph.

Internal losses.
(1) Radiator loss	0.5lb. at 100 fps	
(2) Entry loss	1.25	
(3) Wake loss	0.25	
		2.00

External losses
(1) Skin friction on extra surface	0.25	
(2) Extra drag of a fairly well-designed cowl	1.5	
		1.75

(3) Avoidable losses		
(a) Absence of fillets	1.0	
(b) Re-entrant flap	1.0	
(c) Sharp entry	3.0	

The report identified the particular problem of the boundary layer with the ventral location. This had been discussed by Meredith in his Wind Tunnel Note No 267, *On the problem of conducting a fluid into a duct*. On entry loss the report stated, 'the conversion from kinetic energy to pressure energy cannot be accomplished without loss for a ventral radiator'. The extent of entry loss was clearly serious, 'at top speed this entry loss is two to three times the loss through the radiator'. The boundary layer was identified as the cause of loss. 'This entry loss is probably linked up with the combination of a well established boundary layer on the undersurface of the fuselage.'

The methods tried to reduce this loss were:

a. Dividing the entry into separate compartments.
b. Placing deflector vanes near the entry.
c. By-passing the boundary layer near the duct entrance through a separate slot.

These methods, which had been proposed by Meredith in his paper on entry ducts, were only partly successful. Of note for future practice the perceived serious boundary layer problem of the ventral position might be resolved by moving the radiator forward. 'Further tests are to be made with radiator moved forward so that the duct entry in the plane of the nose of the fuselage. It is hoped that the entry loss will be reduced considerably.' That this was so would be demonstrated with tests by Rolls-Royce using its Heinkel He 70, see below. This was done with the Curtiss XP-40 and the Hawker Tornado, the predecessor of the Typhoon.

This paper is of considerable interest for the insight it gives into the very real problems of ventral radiators, even those semi-recessed and with a boundary layer bypass. The wind tunnel tests revealed the problem of boundary build-up with the ventral position which were regarded in Britain as nearly intractable. This unsatisfactory early experience may have tended to predispose British designs against the ventral position. (The Hawker Hurricane had already been designed with a ventral radiator following Hawker's biplane practice.)

Aft wing location

Model tests of the Supermarine F.37/34 radiator cowl (Shaw and Kirkby, May 1936). – The partially buried aft wing location was used by the Supermarine Spitfire and was discussed above. Notes taken in September 1935 record Meredith, when inspecting the Supermarine F37/34 mock-up on a site visit, had recommended that the cooling system, which he made clear was sub-optimal, 'might be improved considerably by tunnel testing a model'.[1] These tests were carried out in November 1935 before the F37/34 was flown and the radiator ducts were revised in the light of the texts. The tests showed that radiator design was not as efficient as Meredith predicted. The inefficiency was attributed to duct entry loss – an issue that had particularly concerned Meredith. The report was not finalised until May 1936 and is dealt with above in conjunction with texts on the Hawker Hurricane cooling system.

Chin location

Note on tests of a ducted radiator fitted to the nose of a ¼ scale Hart (Patterson, April 1936). – In April 1936, the RAE investigated the chin location using a quarter scale Hawker Hart model. (In the November 1935 investigation of the ventral position it was proposed that drag, caused by boundary layer build-up might be reduced by moving the radiator to the chin position.) The design was modified by revising the profile of the duct upper surface to make it straighter.

	Original design	Modified design
(lbs at 100ft/sec at 300mph)		
External skin friction drag	0.40lb	0.40lb
Minimum internal drag	0.70	0.70
Residual internal drag	0.05	0.05
Residual external drag	1.20	0.70
Total cooling drag	2.35	1.85

Figure A4.3 – Chin location in *Proposed radiator installation for K. 2969 Hart in 24ft tunnel* (Patterson, April 1936).

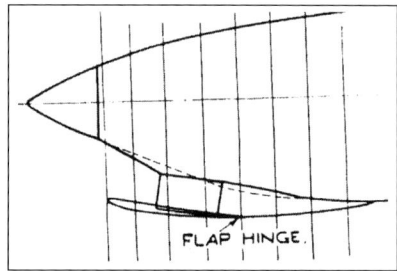

The chin location was superior to the aft-wing and ventral positions, but inferior to the in-wing, largely as there was no boundary layer build-up. Thus, moving the cooling system from the ventral to the chin location was seen as a rational decision. (The later *A review of wind tunnel experiments on ducted radiators* (Hartshorn, July 1936) revealed that a 'lip' was also applied to the Hart chin radiator.)

Further wind tunnel tests

A review of the RAE cooling research (Perring, September 1936). – This paper covered both air-cooled radials and inlines and provided a table giving a detailed breakdown of the different types of drag for the latter. This report developed previous papers by tabulating their results. The following table summarises the key results in a larger table in the report.

Position	Type	Reference	Internal		External		
			Minimum	Residual	Friction	Residual	Total
Leading edge	enclosed	1 Engine and radiator in wing	1.6	0.1	0	-0.5	1.2
Nose	exposed	2 Hart	0.6	0.2	0.5	0.7	3.0
Aft wing	semi-recessed	3 Supermarine Spitfire	1.3	1.5	0.35	0.55	3.7
Ventral	exposed	4 Hawker Interceptor with 'lip'	1.2	1.2	0.5	1.3	4.2
Ventral	semi-recessed	5 Hawker Interceptor with rounded profile entrance	1.6	2.2	0.4	0.7	4.9
Ventral	exposed	6 Hawker Interceptor without 'lip'	1.2	2.0	0.4	1.7	5.3

1	A scheme for a radiator in a wing (1227)	(R.A. Shaw	October	1935)
2	Note on tests of a ducted radiator fitted to the nose of a ¼ scale Hart (1291)	(G.N. Patterson.	April	1936)
3	Model tests of the Supermarine F37/34 (1297)	(R.A. Shaw, F.W. Kirkby	May	1936)
4	Model tests on the Hawker Interceptor radiator cowl (1298(a))	(R.A. Shaw, D. Cameron	August	1936)
5	Note on the installation of a ducted radiator in the ventral position (1254)	(A.S. Hartshorn	November	1935)
6	Model tests on the Hawker Interceptor radiator cowl (1298)	(R.A. Shaw, D. Cameron	May	1936)

The identified entry loss in ventral positions very precisely anticipated the problems of the Mustang and the solution.

> When the entry of the radiator is near the nose of the fuselage, or is located in the leading edge of the wing the entry loss is very small, but with the ventral and aft radiators, there is an entry loss equivalent to a drag of 1.0 to 2.0lb which is due to a separation of the boundary layer from the surface immediately ahead of the radiator entrance.
>
> The effect can be partly overcome by lowering the entry relative to the main surface, so that the retarded boundary layer instead of entering the duct is deflected around the outside of the cowl in the gully formed above the 'lip'. With this type of cowl entry the entry loss is about 1.0lb.

Meredith's ideas for recycling otherwise waste energy were noted. On exhaust gas momentum: 'The possibility of recovering some of the heat energy of the exhaust gases, or of making best use of the momentum of these discharging gases is receiving consideration.' Also, on recycling heat, 'The recovery of some part of the heat energy from the heated cooling air in the case of an air-cooled engine or ducted radiator is also receiving attention'.

Note on present position of cooling drag of aero engines (Douglas, April 1937). – This report largely reiterated earlier summaries. On the benefits of divesting the boundary layer from the dual entry, it said: 'The entry loss with ventral and aft radiators can be partly overcome by causing the retarded boundary flow ahead of the cowl to avoid the entry and pass around the outside of the cowl.' The RAE was working with engine and airframe manufacturers. 'Tests on practical nacelle-wing installations are being arranged for the 24ft tunnel in collaboration with Messrs Rolls-Royce and Messrs Westland Aircraft Ltd. Meredith's ideas for recycling waste heat had been taken aboard. Also, now that the focus was moving on from aircraft capable of exceeding 300mph to 400mph this now became a much more practicable proposition.

> The possibilities of regenerative cooling are now well understood, and a correction can be made to estimates of cooling drag based on cold tests. Such an estimate made for the proposed 750 horsepower Bristol flat engine suggests a 0.9lb. at a 100 fps. for a flight speed of 400mph at 15,000ft, which would neutralise the cooling drag.

The RAE was investigating another of Meredith's ideas. 'Work is, however, proceeding to reduce the drag of exhaust systems and to make best use of the exhaust momentum.'

Replacements for the Hurricane and Spitfire Mks I and II

By the late 1930s the design of replacements and developments of the Hurricane, already obsolescent, and the Spitfire were underway. The Hawker Tornado was powered by a new engine, the 24-cylinder Rolls-Royce Vulture, the Spitfire Mk III, which incorporated significant design changes, by the Rolls-Royce Merlin XX. Wind tunnel testing of the cooling duct of both were carried out in the late 1930s and early 1940s. (In these two tests external drag was no longer split between minimum and residual drag, presumably because the determination of minimum drag was seen as arbitrary.)

Hawker Tornado

Preliminary note on an improvement in the design of ventral radiators (Patterson, August 1938). – Hawker intended to replace the Hurricane with an all metal fighter designed around the Rolls-Royce Vulture engine. This was basically four Peregrine (based on the Kestrel) 6-cylinder blocks in an X shape around a common crankshaft. It was never developed sufficiently to overcome crankshaft lubrication problems. (The Napier Sabre was H shaped with two crankshafts and was made reliable once

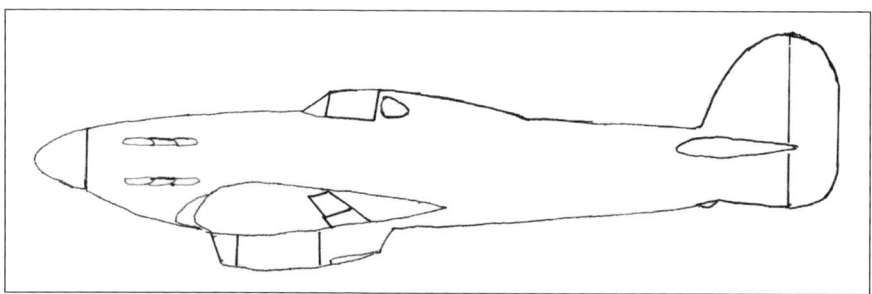

Figure A4.4 – Hawker Tornado first prototype showing original ventral radiator.

Bristol resolved the sleeve valve problems.) The first Tornado prototype (P5219), first flight on 6 October 1939, had a large ventral duct.

RAE wind tunnel research had already highlighted in many reports the problems of ventral cooling systems. The introduction to the 1938 report outlined the problems of the ventral position as perceived in Britain. (Ventral here meant in practice at the point of greatest fuselage depth below the wing.)

> When the entry is in a rear position e.g., under the fuselage or wing, the boundary layer on the surface extending ahead of the entry is subjected to a large reversed pressure gradient and a separation of the flow occurs at the entrance to the duct. There is therefore a large increase in the cooling drag and a reduction in the maximum flow through the duct.

(This problem was anticipated in Meredith's 1935 *Wind Tunnel Note No. 267* on duct entry which stated separation was inevitable, 'as the boundary layer is thick

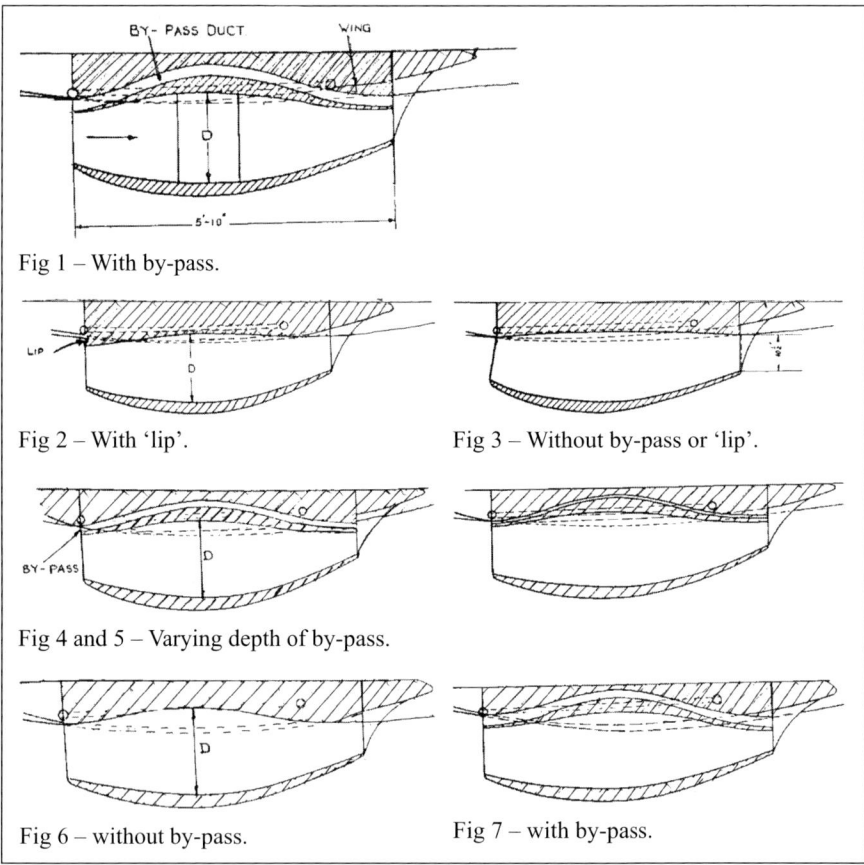

Fig 1 – With by-pass.

Fig 2 – With 'lip'.

Fig 3 – Without by-pass or 'lip'.

Fig 4 and 5 – Varying depth of by-pass.

Fig 6 – without by-pass.

Fig 7 – with by-pass.

Figure A4.5 – Ventral ducts in *Preliminary note on an improvement in the design of ventral radiators* (Patterson, August 1938).

and the depression at the surface is accentuated by the curvature of the boundary'.) Burying the ventral radiator did not reduced drag. 'This effect is still more pronounced when the radiator is recessed.' Thus, 'the reduction of cooling drag, which should be obtained by recessing the radiator, has not therefore been realised in practice'. This RAE report is of note because it is the first to conduct detailed tests on a boundary layer bypass to reduce drag. 'In order to prevent the separation of the flow at the duct entrance a by-pass was developed which consisted of a duct of uniform depth joining a forward-opening slot at the entrance of the cooling duct to a backward-opening slot at the entrance.' There followed a thorough investigation of many duct configurations.

The tests were divided into three parts:

	Figures	By-pass depth (ins full-scale)	Recess depth (proportion above fuselage line)	Minimum internal drag (full-scale at 100 fps)	Residual internal drag (full-scale at 100 fps)	External and by-pass drag (full-scale at 100 fps)	Total cooling drag (full-scale at 100 fps)
(a) Three types compared the normal type of entry 'lip' by-pass duct	Fig. 3	0	0.13	3	3.8	1.7	8.5
	Fig. 2	2.5 in	0.13	3	1.9	3.4	8.3
	Fig. 1	2.5 in	0.13	3	0	3.3	6.3
(b) the radiator was recessed in stages deepest recess medium recess shallowest recess	Fig. 6	0	0.25	3	3.9	0.9	7.8
	Fig. 5	0.83 in	0.21	3	2.9	1.5	7.4
	Fig. 4	1.67 in	0.17	3	0	2.8	5.8
(c) a well recessed radiator with a by-pass duct was tested	Fig. 7	2.5 in	0.25	3	0	2.2	5.2

- First, three types of entry were compared: a normal entry (Fig 3); a 'lipped' entry (Fig 2) and a 2.5 inch deep bypass (Fig 1). In all three cases 13% of the duct depth was recessed in the fuselage. The 'lipped' entry (8.3lbs at 100 fps drag) was a slight improvement on the normal entry (8.5lbs at 100 fps). The bypass eliminated residual internal drag and produced a better result of 6.3lbs at 100 fps.
- Second, having established that the bypass gave the best result different depths of bypass and amounts of recess (1.67 inches and 17% recessed (Fig 4), 0.83 inches and 21% recessed (Fig 5), and no bypass and 25% buried (Fig 6)) were tested. (The smaller the bypass the greater the recess.) The 1.67 inch bypass with 17% recess produced the best result.
- Thirdly, a bypass depth of 2.5 inches and 25% recess (Fig 7) was tested and this produced the best result as there was no residual internal drag and low external drag. 'The results for the design shown in Fig 7 indicate that it is possible to recess a radiator when using a by-pass. The result is a ventral radiator which is equally as good as a nose radiator.'

Overall, the results might seem obvious:

- A larger recess produces less external drag.
- A larger bypass produces less internal residual drag but there is no gain from having a bypass with a greater depth than 1.67 inches. (A bigger bypass depth does produce somewhat greater residual drag.)

Thus, a combination of recessing and bypassing produces the best result.

When the prototype actually flew, compressibility effects (where air density changes differentially at higher speeds) began to manifest themselves and it was decided that the ventral radiator bath was unsuitable for the speeds approaching 400mph that were being achieved for the first time. The radiator was therefore moved forward to the nose, a position already selected for the Type 'N', or Typhoon. Rolls-Royce's tests with the Heinkel He 70 had showed moving the cooling duct from the ventral to the chin position could produce good results. 'Moving the radiator forward into the fuselage frontal area and greatly increasing the duct length produced a great improvement.'[2] On radiator location: 'The experiments included tests of a radiator entirely within the frontal area of the Heinkel, although not actually inside the airplane, and showed this was the most desirable location.'[3]

Spitfire Mk III

Improved radiator tests on Spitfire radiators in the 24ft wind tunnel (Reeman, July 1941). – The Spitfire Mk III was the first major redesign of the Spitfire. The new aircraft was based around the Merlin XX, a 1240hp engine with a two speed supercharger designed by Stanley Hooker. The cooling system incorporated a boundary layer bypass. (This concept had first been proposed by Meredith in

1935.) The Spitfire Mk III first flew on 16 March 1940. Testing of the aircraft continued despite the Battle of Britain. The RAF placed a production order for over 1,000 aircraft with deliveries in1941.

In 1941 the RAE tested the cooling systems of the Mk I, II, and III Spitfires. The exercise highlighted some perhaps unexpected problems with the Mk III design, underlining the problems of reducing drag with aft underwing radiators. Tests were conducted on the following radiator installations:

- Spitfire I cowl with 320 x 7 mm honeycomb radiator.
- Spitfire II cowl with a Morris fin and tube radiator. (This complied to the 5 to 1 rule whereby a radiator was most efficient when the area of metal exposed to the air was five times that to the cooling liquid.)
- Spitfire III cowl having a 2 inch bypass duct. Modifications with a reduced bypass duct, 1 inch, and with no bypass duct were also tried.

The tables which follow consolidate the results for the Spitfire Mk I and Mk II. The radiator was tested both 'cold' and 'hot'. Thus, the full 'Meredith effect' was examined.

Spitfire	Mk I		Mk II	
	honeycomb radiator	hot radiator	Morris fin and tube radiator	hot radiator
Drag lb at 100 fps				
Minimum internal	1.6		1.6	
Residual internal	1.9		2.1	
Total internal	3.5	3.4	3.7	4.1
External	1.3	1.0	0.8	0.6
Total cooling	4.8	4.4	4.5	4.7

With the radiator 'cold' overall, the fin and tube radiator was superior as higher internal drag was offset by lower external drag, possibly because of the smaller frontal area. The 'hot' results appear contradictory. The honeycomb radiator on the Mk I showed an improvement. The Morris fin and tube radiator saw a deterioration. (Presumably the characteristics of the fin and tube radiator meant the increase in the resistance of the 'hot' radiator offset the thrust obtained from heat regeneration.)

A full range of entries were tested for the Mk III including a 2 inch and a 1 inch bypass (suggested by Meredith in 1935 when inspecting the Spitfire design), a 'lip', and a 'normal' entry. The Mk III had higher drag than the earlier Mks despite the addition of a bypass vent. In part this was because the more powerful engine created more unavoidable minimum internal drag.

> The elimination of entry losses with this type of cowl can usually
> be achieved if the boundary layer is diverted round the outside of

the cowl by a suitable lip at entry or is bypassed by an auxiliary duct over the top of the radiator. [The ventral radiator test discussed above showed a well-designed bypass duct, a saving to total cooling drag of about 2lb.] For this reason the radiator duct of the Spitfire III (which has a more powerful engine than the Spitfire I and II) has been designed to have a bypass.

The bypass vent did reduce other 'residual' internal drag. But external drag increased because the bypass vent added depth to the partially buried radiator making it project further into the airstream. 'On the Spitfire III the arrangement with a 1 inch bypass had the least total cooling drag and showed a saving of 1.5lb over modified forms of the cowl without bypass duct and the same radiator recess.'

Spitfire III	Normal entry	'Lip' entry	2 inch bypass	1 inch bypass
Drag lb at 100 fps				
Minimum internal	2.1	2.1	2.1	2.1
Residual internal	2.3	1.7	1.4	0.9
External	2.3	2.6	2.0	2.1
Total cooling	6.7	6.4	5.5	5.1

The comments on the 'lip' entry are worth noting as this was the solution adopted for both the Hawker Hurricane and the North American Mustang. The bypassed entries showed a considerable improvement over the normal entry – albeit drag was still high. The 'lipped' entry was marginal, but the radiator dimensions made a 'lip' difficult to be made fully efficient.

These results show that the cowl with a reduced bypass area at entry and exit gives a saving of 1.6lb in total cooling drag over a duct with a normal type entry. Owing to the amount of radiator recess it was difficult to obtain a satisfactory lip entry without unduly restricting the duct entry area. Thus, the lip type cowl showed little improvement over the cowl with normal entry.

The fitting of the bypass still had a cost in terms of increasing external drag because the bypass reduced the space available for recessing. 'From these results it will be seen that the reduction in residual internal drag obtained by fitting the bypass is largely offset by the internal drag of the bypass and the greater external drag of the internal cowl.'

The Spitfire Mk III 'hot radiator' was tested with both a 2 inch and a 1 inch bypass. 'The increase in the resistance of the hot radiator largely offset the thrust obtained from the heat regeneration effect.'

	Spitfire III		Spitfire III	
	2 in. bypass	hot radiator	1 in. bypass	hot radiator
Drag lb. at 100ft/sec				
Minimum internal	2.1		2.1	
Residual internal	1.4		0.9	
	3.5	3.8	3.0	3.2
External + bypass	2.0	1.8	2.1	1.6
Total cooling	5.5	5.6	5.1	4.8

In both cases the hot radiator produced greater internal drag, presumably because of the increased radiator resistance when hot. The external drag, however, fell again, presumably because of the thrust effect. The report concluded: 'A one inch bypass should be adequate and gives a saving of 1.6lb in total cooling drag over a cowl with the normal entry and the same depth of radiator recess.'

The aft-wing location of the Spitfire's radiator continued to hamstring the overall design. Firstly: 'With a lip entry little improvement can be expected over a normal type cowl owing to the difficulty in obtaining a satisfactory lip entry without undue restriction of the duct entry area.' Secondly: 'With the limited length of cowl the fitting of a bypass duct restricts the radiator duct entry area, thus the full advantages of the bypass are not realised. Owing to this the Spitfire III cowl shows little improvement on the standard cowl which allows the use of a more deeply recessed radiator.' It remained that, overall, the Spitfire radiator location made it very difficult to improve its performance.

An order was placed for mass production of the Mk III, but it was soon cancelled. The Merlin XX was used in the Hawker Hurricane Mk II project which had a higher priority as the Hurricane needed the powerful engine more than the Spitfire to remain reasonably competitive in combat with the Bf 109. Rolls-Royce had anyway developed the Merlin 45, which could be used in a Mk I or Mk II fuselage, becoming the Mk V.

The problems created by the Spitfire's cooling system's aft location meant that it was difficult to reduce the overall cooling drag for the Mk III compared to the Mks I and II, but at least, given the greater engine power and thus potential higher drag, the redesign did well to restrict drag. Other factors, the greater engine power, the retractable tail wheel, the revised cockpit canopy and the reduced wingspan meant that the Mk III was capable of 400mph. The exigencies of war meant that it was easier to re-engine the Mk II with an engine (Merlin 45) more powerful than that proposed for the Mk III (Merlin XX) to create the Mk V which, despite the more powerful engine, was slower than the Mk III. A price, however, would be paid with arrival of the Focke Wulf Fw 190 which comprehensively outclassed the Mk V. The top speed of the Mk V was 375mph on 1515 HP. The Mk III was capable of 385 to 400mph, depending on sources, on 1240 HP. Thus, the Mk III was faster than the Mk V on lower power and was capable of matching the Allison-powered Mustang I.

Twin engined airplanes

British twin engined airplanes included the Westland Whirlwind and the de Havilland Mosquito. Both had wing leading edge duct entries between the fuselage and the engine nacelle and radiators buried in the wing. The placement of the undercarriage system within the nacelle restricted the radiator duct to the inefficient chin position if this were placed in the nacelle. This was acceptable in larger bombers but undesirable in aircraft designed for speed. In the Whirlwind and the Mosquito, the location of the radiator and the duct were quite different. In the first design type the ducts passed through the wing spars. In the second, much simpler design, the wing chord was extended ahead of the front spar and the whole duct placed before that spar with the exit below the wing. The Whirlwind's radiators were behind the main spar and the wing flap also varied the air flow through the cooling duct which exited at the rear. There was also a slat which opened to allow increased airflow when the flaps were down. The Mosquito's radiators were ahead of the main spar where the wing chord was increased to contain the radiators and the ducts. The exit was ahead of the main spar and pointed downwards. Both airplanes' solutions were tested by the RAE.

Through in-wing design – Westland Whirlwind

The Whirlwind was built to the same specification as the Supermarine 312, which called for a fighter with four cannons that could have either one or two engines. Westland's design had two Rolls-Royce Peregrine engines, a development of the successful 21 litre Kestrel.

Wind tunnel tests on a radiator in a wing (Kerr, December 1936). – The report, *A Scheme for a radiator in a wing* (Shaw and Curtis, October 1935), showed buried radiators with leading wing entry had very low drag. Therefore, a full-size test was carried out to confirm this result. In the December 1936 test the radiator only and not the engine was buried in the wing. The radiator was situated between two spars.

These tests showed in-wing location resulted in low drag of, '1.2lb, representing approximately 2 per cent of the BHP [650 hp Kestrel]. The internal drag is 0.8lb, leaving an external drag of only 0.4lb at 100 fps.'

Note on present position of cooling drag of aero engines (Douglas, April 1937). – This recorded tests on practical nacelle-wing installations that were being arranged for the 24ft tunnel in collaboration with Messr Rolls-Royce and *Messrs Westland Aircraft Ltd*. These will show the drag cost of the practical details of a nacelle installation, and the possibilities of an underslung radiator on a nacelle which must also provide accommodation for a retractable undercarriage.

Thus, in the design process the Whirlwind's ducted radiator was changed from the nacelle to the wing.

Further tests in the 24ft tunnel tests on a radiator in a wing (Kerr, Shaw, Tye, Pretorius, July 1937). – In 1937 further tests were carried out in order to, 'provide

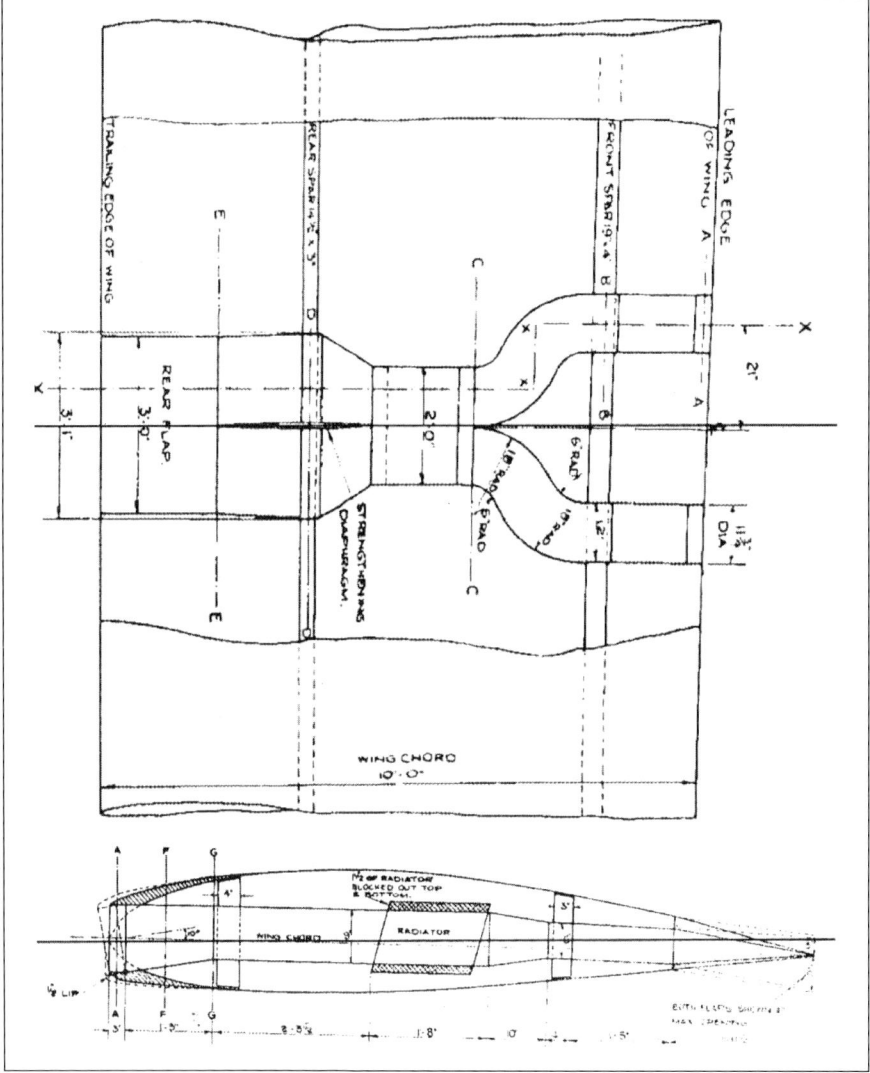

Figure A4.6 – In-wing cooling duct in *24ft wind tunnel tests on a radiator in a wing* (Kerr, December 1936).

further date on duct and entry designs'. This was based on a larger 1,000hp engine. 'The most successful system yet tested was a slit entry with an internal expanding duct [which] would increase the drag of the bare wing by 1.6lb at 100 fps. [1.5lb internal, 0.1lb external].'

1st Addendum to Further tests in the 24ft tunnel tests on a radiator in a wing (Tye, Pankhurst, November 1937). – There was particular concern that the duct entry in the leading edge could interfere with lift and impair flow throw the duct, particularly at higher angles of incidence. A new entry was tested which improved flow at the cost of increase in drag. Modifications to the upper lip resulted in 1.9lbs at 100 fps but, 'the maximum flow through the duct at climbing incidence was slightly improved by the new entry'.

2nd Addendum to Further tests in the 24ft tunnel tests on a radiator in a wing report (McInerney, Kerr, November 1938). – The in-wing design created problems due to the need to constrict the duct as the wing thickness contracts behind the rear duct and immediately ahead of the adjustable exit flap hinges. This resulted in a small increase in internal drag that, 'will have a negligible effect on the top speed performance'.

Tests of a Peregrine nacelle wing unit in the 24ft tunnel (Shaw, McInerney, May 1938). – This tested an alternative location for a nacelled Peregrine engine. This was placed in a chin duct below the power plant 'cowled nose radiator'. This produced the following cooling drag in pounds at 100 feet per second.

	300mph	400mph
Internal cooling drag	5.0lbs	1.6lbs
External cooling drag	2.3lbs	2.9lbs
	7.3lbs	4.5lbs
Faired shape drag	5.8lbs	5.8lbs
	13.1lbs	10.3lbs

(The sharp fall in internal cooling drag from 5lb to 1.6lb between 300 and 400mph is not commented on.) Clearly this set-up was much less efficient than the in-wing design which was fixed upon by Westland. The company produced a highly original configuration. Both the entry and exit were adjustable. Leading edge slats opened when the rear trailing edge split flap passed a quarter of its travel. The fowler trailing edge flap was also the radiator flap. The Whirlwind's ducted radiator had a number of unique and unusual features. It was the only aircraft in general use where the duct went through the full wing chord. The duct entrance was adjustable. Also, it anticipated aspects of the Bf 109 aft wing radiators: the use of the flaps to control duct exit (Bf 109E) and the adjustable entrance (Bf 109F).

In wing ahead of front spar – de Havilland Mosquito

The 'wooden-wonder' Mosquito started as a private venture that would not utilise strategic materials or in-demand metal working skills. A full-scale mock-up was inspected on 29 December 1939 after which the project received official backing. On 25 November 1940, the prototype made its first flight. The de Havilland design. like the Westland Whirlwind. had in-wing radiators. The entire cooling duct, however, placed ahead of the main spar. required the chord to be extended forward. Rather surprisingly, the Mosquito's configuration was anticipated in early German research in 1937 by Willy Messerschmitt.

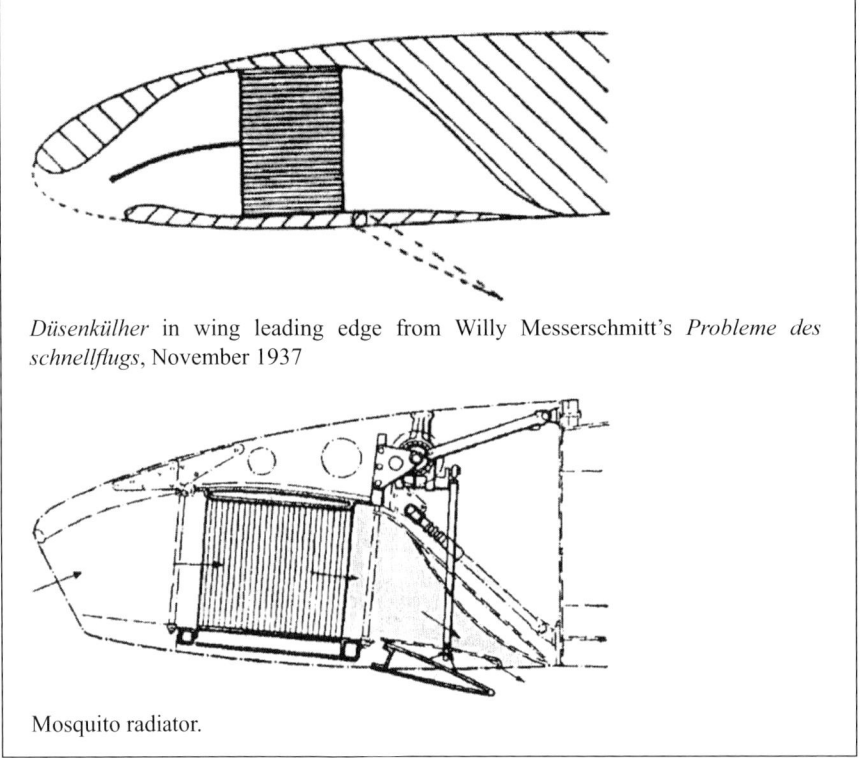

Düsenkülher in wing leading edge from Willy Messerschmitt's *Probleme des schnellflugs*, November 1937

Mosquito radiator.

Figure A4.7 – Willy Messerschmitt's 1937 design for a *Düsenkülher* in wing leading edge' and the de Havilland Mosquito's ducted radiator ahead of the main spar.

In this position the ducts had to be quite short. This limited the extent that the radiator frontal area could exceed the duct entrance if sufficient cooling air was to be admitted. When the rear flap was open it makes a 'lip' that generates low pressure behind it – effectively sucking the air out. The design was tested by the RAE before the first flight.

Note on an in-wing radiator installed ahead of the front spar (Smelt, Smith, Stott, June 1940). – The Introduction noted the advantages and problems of the in-wing position:

> The in-wing radiator, with leading-edge entry and trailing-edge exit for the cooling duct, is known to be the most efficient form of radiator installation yet designed. In spite of this, it is only rarely used because of the difficulty of leading ducts through the wing spars. The scheme considered here avoids this difficulty by installing the whole of the radiator and duct ahead of the main spar and exit on the undersurface of the wing just forward of the spar.

The early RAE tests were for 300mph at 15,000ft with a 1,000hp engine. For the Mosquito the results were scaled up so the results are for 400mph. A range of duct entries were examined with subtle changes in the relationship between actual entrance and airfoil profiles.

Drag of cold radiator – lb at 100 fps ground level	Minimum internal	Residual internal	External	Total
Entry 1	1.2	0.0	0.3	1.5
Entry 2	1.2	0.0	0.0	1.2
Entry 3	1.2	0.6	0.0	1.8

These losses indicate that the losses of the system are extremely small. In fact, zero external and internal loss is quite possible, as in entry 2. In this respect the system is as efficient as the in-wing radiator with trailing-edge exit.

Nacelle position – Blackburn B-20

The Blackburn B-20, first flight March 1940, was a remarkable flying boat design which had a retractable lower hull to reduce fuselage depth. This also allowed for propeller clearance when on the water and a far smaller frontal area when in the air. The very efficient looking nacelle – which did not have to contain the undercarriage – may have contributed to the high speed. The B-20 prototype was lost after breaking up due to severe vibration on 7 April 1940 during a high-speed run. It reached 345mph – a point that might be worth remarking given that this was a twin engined flying boat. The absence of landing gear in the engine nacelle meant the radiator could be optimally placed below and behind the engine with a lipped duct entrance and an exit straight out of the rear of the nacelle. The duct was also comparatively long. The efficient design might have contributed to the high speed.

Appendix 5

'Meredith effect' meaning and first use

Meredith did not coin the term, the 'Meredith effect'. This Appendix looks at what Meredith described and when the term the 'Meredith effect' originated and developed.

Meredith account as in Meredith's work and describing his work on the Spitfire

The following shows in the first three columns Meredith's own words describing his key insights about ducted radiators in 1935 and 1936, taken from a variety of his documents. The first column gives his description of jet propulsion in the form of a subsonic ramjet. The second and third column provided his descriptions as in his seminal paper and his patent. The fourth column gives a description of his ideas from 2006 in the context of the Spitfire, where they were first applied.

Meredith *Invention relating to jet propulsion of aircraft*, RAE, February 1935[1]	Meredith June 1935 RAE report, *Cooling of Aircraft Engines With special reference to Ethylene Glycol Radiators enclosed in Ducts*, August 1935[2]	Stewart and Meredith *Improvements in or relating to Aircraft and other Craft or Vehicles*, GB 454,266 March 1936 submitted September 1936[3]	Akroyd *The Aerodynamics of the Spitfire*, Journal of Aeronautical History, 2016[4]
Aerodynamic element			
It has been proposed to propel aircraft or the screws of aircraft by the principle of the internal combustion reaction motor.	The employment of low velocity cooling avoids the necessity for an increasing expenditure of power with increasing speed provided the exit	It is known to enclose the cooling surfaces of an aircraft engine in a duct and it is also known to decrease the drag on the aircraft caused by frictional losses in the duct by shaping the duct	As to the radiator, 'cometh the hour, cometh the man', in this case F.W. Meredith of the RAE with his proposal in 1935 for a ducted radiator system

253

Meredith *Invention relating to jet propulsion of aircraft*, RAE, February 1935[1]	Meredith June 1935 RAE report, *Cooling of Aircraft Engines With special reference to Ethylene Glycol Radiators enclosed in Ducts*, August 1935[2]	Stewart and Meredith *Improvements in or relating to Aircraft and other Craft or Vehicles*, GB 454,266 March 1936 submitted September 1936[3]	Akroyd *The Aerodynamics of the Spitfire*, Journal of Aeronautical History, 2016[4]
For this purpose an internal duct is provided in which the air is compressed, by passing through an expanding passage,	conditions are adjusted to suit the speed.	so that the kinetic energy of the stream flowing through it is converted to pressure before the cooling surfaces are reached and is reconverted to kinetic energy before being discharged from the duct. These conversions are achieved by shaping the forward part of the duct so that the streamlines of the stream entering the same are expanded either in front of or inside the duct and by contracting the walls of the duct after the cooling surfaces have been passed. Adjustment of the throat area of the nozzle is required to limit the stream through the duct to that required for cooling the engine.	which would greatly reduce radiator drag. Meredith's proposal rested on two interlinked ideas. The first reduces the drag of the radiator matrix itself, this varying as the square of the local air speed, by reducing the latter at the radiator. This is accomplished by capturing the cooling air in a duct which increases in area up to the radiator, the flow speed dropping progressively according to the continuity principle as the duct area increases.

Meredith *Invention relating to jet propulsion of aircraft*, RAE, February 1935[1]	Meredith June 1935 RAE report, *Cooling of Aircraft Engines With special reference to Ethylene Glycol Radiators enclosed in Ducts*, August 1935[2]	Stewart and Meredith *Improvements in or relating to Aircraft and other Craft or Vehicles*, GB 454,266 March 1936 submitted September 1936[3]	Akroyd *The Aerodynamics of the Spitfire*, Journal of Aeronautical History, 2016[4]
Thermodynamic element			
… after which heat is added before the air expands in a contracting passage from the end of which the jet of augmented momentum issues.	The combined effect of compressibility and heat transfer from the radiator may reduce the power consumption to nothing if the size of the radiator is adequate.	According to this invention the kinetic energy of the stream at its discharge from the duct is raised by transferring to the stream part waste heat from the engine. By means of this invention it is possible with an internal combustion engine of an aircraft given a substantial head of pressure at the front of the duct such as is available with an aircraft travelling at about 300 miles per hour, to reduce the drag in a properly designed duct, to a figure which we believe has not hitherto been achieved and it may even be found possible to reduce such drag below nothing as that the duct produces a thrust on the aircraft.	The second idea is to utilise the heat energy released by the radiator. The combination of the continuity principle and the energy equation of a thrust-producing high-speed jet by passing the radiator efflux through the convergent duct. This would counteract the residual drag of the enclosed radiator. The scheme was introduced to the Spitfire's design.

The table shows clearly how the 'Meredith effect' concept broadly split into two parts corresponding to the thermodynamic and aerodynamic elements of his equation.

'Meredith effect' as used by NACA and NAA personnel

The actual term the 'Meredith effect' appears to have been first used by people at NAA and NACA, some of whom were associated with the design of the Mustang. NACA's Becker experimented on ramjets in 1941 and produced a report in 1943. Irving Ashkenas joined NAA in 1939 and worked with Ed Horkey, who was NAA's aerodynamicist on the Mustang's cooling duct. Eastman Jacobs was seconded to NAA from NACA in early 1940 to work on the laminar flow wing after he was working on a motorjet at NACA in 1940. After NACA personnel were at NAA, work then initiated at NACA in 1941 on a ramjet as well as a motorjet.

J. Becker, and D.D. Baals, *Analysis of Heat and Compressibility Effects in Internal Flow Systems and High-Speed Tests of a Ramjet System.* 1943[5]	I. Ashkenas [NAA] et al. *Aerodynamics and Aircraft Design,* Matériel Command, 1946[6]	J.V. Becker, *The High-speed Frontier: Case Histories of Four NACA Programs, 1920-1950,* 1980[7]	J.R. Hansen, *Engineer in Charge: A History of the Langley Aeronautical Laboratory,* 1987[8]
The power recoverable from the cylinder-cooling flow ('*Meredith effect*') in a typical air-cooled engine is shown in figure 20. [p. 35] The power recoverable from the heat added to the cooling air ('Meredith effect') was found to be about 3 per cent of the brake	Whether this [adequate cooling of conventional engines in very high-speed flight] can be accomplished without an inordinate expenditure of power is doubtful and depends on how much of the heat rejected to the cooling air can be utilized in jet propulsion (the so-called '*Meredith effect*').	In 1941 a team at NACA led by John Becker started work on the possibilities of developing a ramjet engine, which was quite different to Jacob's design, which had incorporated a piston engine. In 1936, F.W. Meredith pointed out that the waste heat of a piston engine which is transferred to the cooling-air flow in a radiator is not all lost; it produces a small thrust provided	A NACA history relates how Eastman Jacobs and Albert Sherman proposed studying a ducted-fan system that used only dynamic pressure (that is, the pressure was not boosted by a fan) for compression and the *Meredith cycle* for thrust. In 1936 Frank [Frederick] W. Meredith had pointed out in England that not all of the waste heat of a piston engine had to be lost when transferred to the cooling airflow of a radiator. If the pressure at the exhaust

J. Becker, and D.D. Baals, *Analysis of Heat and Compressibility Effects in Internal Flow Systems and High-Speed Tests of a Ramjet System.* 1943[5]	I. Ashkenas [NAA] et al. *Aerodynamics and Aircraft Design,* Materiél Command, 1946[6]	J.V. Becker, *The High-speed Frontier: Case Histories of Four NACA Programs, 1920-1950,* 1980[7]	J.R. Hansen, *Engineer in Charge: A History of the Langley Aeronautical Laboratory,* 1987[8]
horsepower for an existing air-cooled engine at a flight Mach number of 0.60 at sea level. [p. 36]		the pressure at the exhaust of the radiator tubes is higher than the free static pressure of flight. This phenomenon became known as the '*Meredith effect*'.	of the radiator tubes was higher than the free static pressure of flight, some of the dissipated heat could produce a small thrust.

The first known use of the term the 'Meredith effect' is found in a NACA paper of 1943 which built on experiments done in 1941. Ashkenas's co-authorship of a book published in 1946 might indicate that the term the 'Meredith effect' was in use at NAA during the war years.

Description of radiator duct prior to Atwood's 'Origin the Mustang fighter plane' without the term 'Meredith effect'

The first major book on the Mustang, Robert W. Gruenhagen's *Mustang: The Story of the P-51 Fighter*, was published in 1969. This does not mention either Meredith or the 'Meredith effect'. This might indicate that the terminology remained something familiar only to the NAA and NACA personnel who had worked on the Mustang's cooling duct, motorjets and ramjets. Ed Schmued, who has generally been regarded as the designer of the Mustang, claimed he was unaware of the 'Meredith effect' at the time and learned of its impact only later. Ed Horkey was familiar with Meredith's work, at least indirectly, as will be seen, through German research, if not in 1940 the specific term, the 'Meredith effect'.

R.W. Gruenhagen, *Mustang The Story of the P-51 fighter,* 1969[9]	Ed Schmued, *Conception and Development of the P-51 Mustang,* 1971, in NAAR 2015[10]	Ed Schmued (1985 manuscript in), *Mustang Designer Edgar Schmued and the P-51,* 1990[11]	Ed Horkey (interview 1988), *Mustang Designer Edgar Schmued and the P-51,* 1990[12]
Schmued and Horkey calculated that an aerodynamic duct formed at the entry and exit of the radiator could provide up to 300 pounds of thrust by utilizing ram air to eject the warmed airflow and thus overcome the drag offered to the fuselage by the duct itself.	Now, I would like to tell you that this radiator was so darned good aerodynamically that on the latest model we had in production, the D, that radiator duct produced 300 hp thrust. That's a ramjet.	We also found out, later on, that the heat from the engine actually produced thrust in the radiator by increasing the velocity of the air flowing through. That horsepower gained by the radiator was only discovered by wind-tunnel investigation. We were contractually required to wind-tunnel test the P-51, and long after the first airplane flew, we got around to test a model which had an electric motor to drive a three-bladed propeller. We found from wind-tunnel data that the P-51 should not have be as fast as it was actually clocked. Our chief aerodynamicist, Joe Beerer, studied the problem and noticed the favourable effect of the radiator. (The author Wagner then comments: 'This added thrust is called the "*Meredith effect*", after the British engineer F.W. Meredith, who described it in a paper published in 1935.')	Meredith had brought forth the theory or proposal to take in air at a high velocity and slow it down, which, of course, builds up pressure. As it goes through the radiator core, the pressure helps some, but primarily you have more dwell time. Then with the increased pressure and temperature, you squeeze the air down again as it goes out the back and you actually get some thrust from this, or what can be called negative radiator drag.

Texts drawing on Atwood's unpublished 1970s memo '*The Origins of the Mustang Fighter Plane*'

The term, the 'Meredith effect' may have entered the general public domain as the result of drawing on material in Atwood's unpublished memo, *The Origins of the Mustang Fighter Plane*, dated 1973, as a response to Gruenhagen's 1969 book which gave Atwood a vital marketing but not design role. The principle may indeed have been developed at NACA, NAA and the RAE, but the term the 'Meredith effect' does not seem to have disseminated in generally available literature before books drawing on Atwood's unpublished memo was published.

L. Carson, *Persue and Destroy*, 1978[13]	R. Murray, *Lee Atwood … Dean of Aerospace*, 1980[14]	B. Yenne, *Rockwell the Heritage of North American*, 1989[15]
In January 1940, Atwood produced a *concept* which put the radiators [glycol and oil] aft of the wing, housed in a well-contoured inlet that would recover some of the energy lost in the cooling process ('*Meredith effect*'). The principle involved is one of 'radiator propulsion' where the radiator heat is added to the cool airstream in a properly contoured duct, which causes the air to slow down for a short distance and then to expand with heat from the radiator and eject out the rear with increased speed and momentum. The reaction to the increased momentum is a propulsive force in the direction of flight which opposes the effect of the drag of the whole radiator system.	My *concept* was to take advantage of the cooling air to add momentum to it, which in those days was known as the '*Meredith effect*'. It wasn't anything new aerodynamically.	I [Atwood] evolved a design *concept* which involved placing the cooling radiators back of the wing and designed a ducting system to recover some of the cooling energy in an efficient manner. The principle had been developed to some extent in literature, both in the [US at] NACA and in England as the '*Meredith effect*'. It involved discharging the heated air under as much pressure as was possible in a rear facing jet as in the yet-to-be-developed ramjet engine. Thus, the cooling drag could be reduced to very little or even nothing at all in theory.

At the beginning of this part of the book Lee Atwood's claim that the 'Meredith effect' was the basis of the Mustang's design was outlined. No evidence has been found that the term existed when the Mustang was designed. By the early 1980s other authors to those drawing on Atwood's unpublished memo were using the 'Meredith effect' term. Jeffrey Ethell in, *Mustang, A Documentary History*, 1981, did not refer to Atwood's memo but wrote: 'Contrary to what some accounts have stated, the initial Mustang radiators did not produce thrust by virtue of the so-called "Meredith effect".'[16]

Abbreviations

AIAA	American Institute of Aeronautics and Astronautics
ARC	Aeronautical Research Committee
articles-nasa-langley	https://authorzilla.com/zNWjO/articles-nasa-langley-gis-team-home-page.html (Mustang articles)
Atwood IWM 21441	Papers of J.L. Atwood, Imperial War Museum, Document 21441
JRAeH	Journal of the Royal Aeronautical History
Hansen 2009	J.R. Hansen (Editor), *The Wind and Beyond: A Documentary Journey into the History of Aerodynamics in America*, NASA SP-2007-4409, NASA History Division, 2009
NACA	National Advisory Committee for Aeronautics
Marsh 2019	S.H. Marsh, *The Air Ministry and the Bomb Dropping Problem: Bombsights, Scientists and Techno-Military Invention, 1918-45,* King's College London, 1 June 2019
RAE	Royal Aircraft Establishment
RAeS	Royal Aeronautical Society
SAE	Society of Aeronautical Engineers
TNA	The National Archive

Bibliography

Meredith

TNA papers

Meredith F.W., *Automatic Control of Aircraft*, TNA, AVIA 6/1513, RAE Report B A 520, December 1924.

Meredith F.W., Memorandum on High Altitude Level Bombsights, in *Automatic self-setting bombsight: user claim*, TNA, AVIA 53/233, RAE Report H 255, February 1938 (in Marsh 2019).

Meredith, F.W., *Problem of Lateral Stabilisation of a Bombsight,* TNA, AVIA 6/3131, RAE Report H1138, November 1926.

Meredith F.W., *Invention relating to jet propulsion of aircraft,* TNA, AVIA 8/407, 28 February 1935.

Meredith F.W., *Cooling of Aircraft Engines with special reference to Ethylene Glycol Radiators enclosed in Ducts,* TNA, AVIA 6/2020, BA 1213, June 1935.

Also:

Griffith A.A., F.W. Meredith, *The possible improvement in aircraft performance due to the use of boundary layer suction,* TNA, E 3501, DSIR 23/5566, E/1976, March 1936.

Griffith A.A., F.W. Meredith, *Improvements in or relating to aircraft,* TNA, AVIA 8/416, May 1936.

RAE papers

Meredith F.W., *Note on the problem of conducting a fluid into a duct with the minimum of loss,* RAE, Wind Tunnel Note No 267, May 1935.

Meredith F.W., *Note on the problem of aiming fixed guns in aeroplanes,* RAE, Departmental Note No H 242, October 1937.

ARC papers

Meredith F.W., *Cooling of Aircraft Engines with special reference to Ethylene Glycol Radiators enclosed in Ducts,* ARC, R&M No 1683, August 1935 (published 1936).

BIBLIOGRAPHY

Patents

Meredith F.W., C.H. Holt, *Improvements in or relating to electrical indicating systems,* GB 357,968, applied 1930, published 1931.

Stewart C.J., F.W. Meredith, *Improvements in or relating to Aircraft and other Craft or Vehicles,* GB 454,266, applied 1935, accepted 1936.

Meredith F.W., G.W. Gardiner, *Improvements in or relating to Controlling Aircraft,* GB 576,359 applied 1938, accepted 1940, published 1946.

Meredith F.W., *Improvements in electric motors,* GB 576,248, applied 1943, published 1946.

Meredith F.W., *Improvements in or relating to devices for detecting or measuring rate of turn,* GB 611,005, applied 1942, publication 1948.

Articles

Meredith F.W., Air Transport in Fog, *JRAeS,* February 1931.

Meredith F.W., Ducted Radiators: The Theory of Low-Velocity Cooling, with a basis for Calculating the Drag, *Aircraft Engineering,* August 1936.

Meredith F.W., P.A. Cooke, Aeroplane Stability and the Automatic Pilot, *JRAeS,* June 1937.

Meredith F.W., On the Social Impact of Air War, *The Modern Quarterly,* 1938.

Meredith F.W., The Modern Autopilot: A Dissertation on the Fundamentals of Modern Autopilot Design, *Flight,* 13 January 1949.

Meredith F.W., Control of Equilibrium in the Flying Insect, *Nature,* 1949.

Meredith F.W., Bats, Bees and Brains, *London Report,* August 1957.

Letter

Meredith F.W., British Autopilot Claims More Reliability, *Aviation Week,*
[https://archiveorg/stream/Aviation_Week_1947-1208/Aviation_Week_1947-12-08_djvutxt], 8 December 1947.

TNA—biographical

Meredith F.W., Mrs M.G. Meredith, *Frederick William Meredith, Margaret Gwendoline Meredith, Soviet Intelligence Agents and Suspected Agents,* TNA, KV 2/2199, 1927-1937.

Meredith F.W., Mrs M.G. Meredith, *Frederick William Meredith, Margaret Gwendoline Meredith, Soviet Intelligence Agents and Suspected Agents,* TNA, KV 2/2200, 1937-1949.

Meredith F.W., Mrs M.G. Meredith, *Frederick William Meredith, Margaret Gwendoline Meredith, Soviet Intelligence Agents and Suspected Agents,* TNA, KV 2/2201, 1949-1952.

Meredith F.W., Mrs M.G. Meredith, *Frederick William Meredith, Margaret Gwendoline Meredith, Soviet Intelligence Agents and Suspected Agents,* TNA, KV 2/2202, 1952-1953.

2/lieutenant Frederick William Meredith, Royal Garrison Artillery, 1915-1918, 1930, TNA WO 339/44412.

Also in:
Benjamin Lockspeiser, alias Benny Lockspicer, KV 2/3059, 1918-1937.

J. Leland Atwood

Meredith, the 'Meredith effect', Mustang articles and papers
Atwood J.L., *The Origin of the Mustang fighter plane*, (unpublished paper), 8 August 1973.

Atwood J.L., Origin and Evolution of the Mustang, *Air Power History Journal* (Journal of Air Force History Foundation), Vol 40, No 3, Fall 1993.

Atwood J.L., *The Spitfire and the Mustang (The Meredith Mystery)*, 15 August 1994 (revised 14 July 1995).

Atwood J.L., *The Spitfire and the Mustang (The Meredith Mystery)*, *Friends Journal*, Vol 18, No 4, Winter 1995.

Atwood J.L., *A Lo-Tech Analysis of the Meredith Effect on the P-51 Mustang Aeroplane*, 1 June 1996.

Atwood J.L., Mustang Margin: a reappraisal, *Air Power History: The Journal of Air and Space History*, Vol 43, No 3, Fall 1996.

Atwood J.L., *The Mustang's Margin, Aviation History: A Clarification*, 1996.

Atwood J.L., The P-51 The Real Story – Rebuttal, *American Aviation Historical Society*, Summer 1997.

Atwood J.L., Mustang Design Retrospective, *FlyPast Special*, Atwood IWM 21441, 1997.

Atwood J.L., An Engineer's Perspective on the Mustang, *Flight Journal*, June 1999.

Atwood J.L., 'We can build you a better airplane than the P-40', *Aeroplane*, May 1999.

Atwood J.L., A View of the Mustang, *484th Bomb Group Association*, Spring – Summer 2001.

Atwood – letters
Atwood J.L., letter to George C. Larson, (Air & Space/Smithsonian), 20 August 1996.

Atwood J.L., letter to Mrs Kathy Stonich of the North American Trainer Association, Atwood IWM 21441, 9 June 1997.

Atwood J.L., letter to Sir W. Self, in North American Aviation 1940-1941, AVIA 38/733, TNA.

Atwood – letters – published
Atwood J.L., 'Mustang Memories', published letter to *Air & Space*, October/November 1996.

Books

Spitfire
Cole L., *Secrets of the Spitfire: The Story of Beverley Shenstone, The Man Who Perfected the Elliptical Wing,* Pen & Sword, 2012.
Morgan E.B., E. Shackladay, *Spitfire: The History,* Guild Publishing, 1986.
Price A., *Spitfire: A Documentary History,* Macdonald and Jane's, 1977.
Quill J., *Spitfire: The amazing personal story of a Spitfire test pilot and RAF fighter,* Arrow Books, 1983.

Also presentation
Davis E.J., *The Basic Design of the Prototype Spitfire* The 30th R.J. Mitchell Memorial Lecture [Delivered at the Southampton Branch of the Royal Aeronautical Society] Royal Aircraft Museum Hendon, File AC 93/14/25, 4 March 1986.

Mustang
Birch D., *Rolls-Royce and the Mustang,* Rolls-Royce Heritage Trust, 1987.
Carson L.K., *Pursue and Destroy: 8th Air Force's Fighter Group in World War II,* Sentry Books, 1978.
Chorlton M., *Allison-Engined P-51 Mustang,* Osprey, 2012.
Christgau J., *Sierra Sue II: The Story of a P-51 Mustang,* Great Planes Press, 2000.
Ethell J., *Mustang: A Documentary History,* Jane's, 1981.
Marshall J.W., L.F. Ford, *P-51B North American's Bastard Stepchild that saved the Eighth Air Force,* Osprey, 2020.
Francillon R.J., *High-Spirited Mustang Volume I: The saga of the North American Aviation P-51 Mustang - Part 1: Development and Production,* Eirl Aerosphere Research, 2017.
Graff C., *P-51 Mustang: Seventy-Five Years of America's Most Famous Warbird,* Zenith Press, 2015.
Gruenhagen R.W., *Mustang: The Story of the P-51 Fighter,* Arco Publishing, 1969.
Kinzey B., *P-51 Mustang Part 1,* Squadron/Signal Publications, 1996.
Ludwig P.A., *P-51 Mustang: Development of the Long-Range Escort Fighter,* Classic Publications, Sussex, 2003.
Meekoms K.J., *The British Air Commission and Lend-Lease,* Air-Britain (Historians) Ltd, 2000.
Murray R., *Lee Atwood ... Dean of Aerospace,* Rockwell International Corporation, 1980.
O'Leary M., *Building the P-51 Mustang,* Speciality Press, 2010.
Pace S., *Mustang: Thoroughbred Stallion of the Air,* Fonthill Media, 2012.
Wagner R., *Mustang Designer Edgar Schmued and the P51,* Orion, 1990.
Yenne B., *Rockwell: The Heritage of North American,* Bison Books, 1989.

Also:

anon, Aeroplane and Armament Experimental Establishment, Boscombe Down, Mustang, AG 351 and AG383, [wwwwwiiaircraftperformanceorg/mustang/ ag351handlinghtml], 13 August 1942.

Other

Anderson J.D., *The Grand Designers: The Evolution of the Airplane in the 20th Century,* Cambridge University Press, 2018.

Baughen G., *The Rise and Fall of the French Airforce,* Fonthill Media, 2018.

Buttler T., *British Secret Projects: Fighters and Bombers 1935-1950,* Midland Publishing, 2004.

Cousins F.W., J.L. Hollington, *The Anatomy of the Gyroscope, Part III,* Advisory Group For Aerospace Research And Development Neuilly-Sur-Seine (France) 1990.

Glauert H., *Elements of of Aerofoil and Airscrew Theory,* Cambridge University Press 1926.

Gunston B., *Development of Piston Aero Engines,* J.H. Haynes & Co, 2007.

Hooker Sir S., *Not Much of an Engineer,* Airlife, 1984.

McRuer D.T., D. Graham, I. Ashkenas, *Aircraft Dynamics and Automatic Control,* Princeton University Press, 1973.

Redman J., *The British Stalinists and the Moscow Trials*, March 1958.

Schlaifer R., *Development of Aircraft Engines (The Rolls-Royce Liquid-Cooled Engines),* Boston, Harvard University, 1950.

Smith P.C., *Skua: The Royal Navy's Dive Bomber,* Pen & Sword Aviation, 2006.

Tsien H.A., W.R. Sears, I. Ashkenas, C.N. Hasert, N.M. Newmark, *Aerodynamics and Aircraft Design* , Headquarters Air Matériel Command 1946.

Vielle E.E., *Almost a Boffin: Why he invented the Cruise Missile,* Dolman Scott, 2013.

West N., *Historical Dictionary of British Intelligence,* Scarecrow Press, 2005.

West N., *Mask: MI5's Penetration of the Communist Party of Great Britain,* Routledge, 2006.

Non-English

Breuget L., R. Devillers, *La technique des radiateurs d'aviation et de leur carénage,* Dunod – Paris, 1939.

Eckert E.R.G., *Einführung in den Wärme – und Stoffaustausch,* Springer, 1966.

Messerschmitt W., *Probleme des Schnellflugs: (Problem of high-speed airplanes),* Schriften Der Deutschen Akademie der Luftfahrtforschung (Publications of the German Academy of Aviation Research), Heft 31 November 1937, 1937/38.

Nußelt W., *Die Theorie der Wärmekraftmaschinen,* De Gruyter, 1951.

von Gersdorf K., et al, *Deutsche Flugmotoren und Strahltriebwerke,* [DRP 299799, 7 July 1915], Bernard & Graefe, 2004.

anon, *Schriften der Deutschen Akademie der Luftfahrtforschung,* Schriften Der Deutschen Akademie der Luftfahrtforschung (Publications of the German Academy of Aviation Research) Heft 10 1939.

Journal/Paper

British

Ackroyd J.A.D., The Aerodynamics of the Spitfire, *JAeH,* Paper No 2016/03 2016.

Ackroyd J.A.D., Aerodynamics as the Basis of Aviation: How Well Did It Do? *JAeH,* Paper No 2018/01 2018.

Hall A., M. Morgan Bennet Melville Jones, 28 January 1887-31 October 1975, *The Royal Society Publishing,* Vol 23 (November 1977).

Howard R.W., Automatic Flight Controls in Fixed Wing Aircraft, *Aeronautical Journal,* (Royal Aeronautical Society) 1973.

Lednicer D.A., Technical Note: A CFD Evaluation of Three Prominent World War II Fighter Aircraft *Aeronautical Journal,* (Royal Aeronautical Society) June/July 1995.

Melville-Jones B., The Streamline Airplane, *Aeronautical Journal,* Vol, 33, 1929.

Shenstone B.S., Sucking Off the Boundary Layer *Aeroplane* Vol 52, 27 January 1937.

Warren H., The Royal Aircraft Establishment during World War II some personal reminiscences, *Journal of Aeronautical History,* Paper No 2012/04 2012.

US

Beisel R.B., Why Use Cowl Flaps, *Journal of Aeronautical Sciences,* March 1937.

Lednicer D.A. and I.J. Gilchrist, A Retrospective: Computational Aerodynamic Analysis Methods Applied to the P-51 Mustang, *AIAA,* paper 91-3288, September 1991.

Lednicer D.A., World War II Fighter Aerodynamics, *EAA Sport Aviation,* January 1999.

Miley S.J., Review of Liquid-Cooled Aircraft Engine Installation Aerodynamics, AIAA paper 86-2587 29 September, 1 October 1986.

Miley S.J., Review of Liquid-Cooled Aircraft Engine Installation Aerodynamics, *Journal of Aircraft,* Vol 25, No 3 March 1988.

Pellegrini M., L. Piancastelli, The bonus of aircraft piston engines, an update of the Meredith effect *International Journal of Heat and Technology* 25(2):51-56 December 2007.

Piancastelli L., L. Frizzeiro, G. Donnici, The Meredith Ramjet: An Efficient Way to Recover the Heat Wasted in Piston Engine Cooling, *Journal of Engineering and Applied Sciences,* Vol 10, No 12, July 2015.

Piancastelli L., S. Pica, G. Donnici, High Altitude Operations with Piston Engines Powerplant Design Optimisation Part III: The Diffuser critical design, *Journal of Engineering and Applied Sciences,* Vol 11, No 7, April 2016.

Rauscher M. [MIT], W.H. Phillips [NACA], Propulsive Effects of Radiator and Exhaust Ducting, *AIAA*, 27 November [received] 1942.

Spinardi G., R. Slayton. Greener Aviation Take-of (Delayed): Analysing Environmental Transitions with the Multi-Level Perspective, *Science & Technology Studies,* 1/2015.

Non-English

Breguet L., R. Devillers, La Technique des Radiateurs Carénés, *La Science aérienne,* Paris, 1 v no 6, Nov-Dec 1938.

ARC—Reports & Memoranda

Bottle D.W., T.V. Somerville, *Tests on the Hurricane L 1696 in the 24-ft Wind Tunnel,* ARC R&M No 2562, August 1941.

Capon R.S., *The cowling of cooling systems,* ARC R & M No 1702, March 1936.

Hartshorn A.S., L.F. Nicholson, *The Aerodynamics of the Cooling of Aircraft Reciprocating Engines,* ARC R&M No 2498, May 1947.

Hartshorn A.S., M.A. Nicholson, *The Aerodynamics of the Cooling Aircraft Reciprocating Engines,* ARC R&M No 2498, May 1947.

Mair [ed] W.A., *Research on High Speed: Aerodynamics at the RAE From 1942 to 1945,* ARC R&M No 2222, 1950.

Somerville T.V., R.R. Duddy, G.H.L. Buxton, *Tests on a Whirlwind Aircraft in the Royal Aircraft Establishment 24-ft Wind Tunnel,* ARC R&M No 2603, June 1940.

Squire H.B., A.D. Young, *The calculation of the Profile Drag of Aerofoils,* ARC R & M No 1838.

RAE reports

Anderton Brown C., F.G. Barlow, *Heat Dissipation of ethylene glycol radiators and comparison with water radiators,* TNA AVIA 6/5367 E 3462, May 1935.

Capon R.S., *The cowling of cooling systems,* TNA AVIA 6/2017, BA 1208 June 1935.

Capon R.S., *The cowling of cooling systems (2nd report),* TNA AVIA 6/2017, BA 1208 A, August 1935.

Carpenter L., High Altitude Level Bombsights, in Automatic self-setting bombsight: user claim, TNA, AVIA 53/233, RAE Report H255, February 1938. In S.H. Marsh, *The Air Ministry and the Bomb Dropping Problem: Bombsights, Scientists and Techno-Military Invention,* 1918-45, King's College London, 1 Jun 2019.

Davies H., *Wind tunnel note no 354Note of scale effects on entry and duct losses in cooling systems,* TNA AVIA 6/9434, May 1938.

Douglas G.P., *Note on present position of cooling drag of aero engines,* TNA BA 1399, April 1937.

Griffith A.A., *An Aerodynamic Theory of Turbine Design,* RAE Report H1111, 7 July 1926.

BIBLIOGRAPHY

Hall A.A., H. Constant, *Note on the development of additional power for aircraft by jet reaction*, TNA, AVIA 6/2357, 1940.

Hartshorn A.S., *A review of wind tunnel experiments on ducted radiators,* TNA AVIA 6/2111, BA 1322, July 1936.

Hartshorn A.S., *Note on performance data for honeycomb radiators in a duct,* TNA AVIA 2043 BA 1245, November 1935.

Hartshorn A.S., *Note on the installation of a ducted radiator in the ventral position,* TNA AVIA 6/2050, BA 1254 November 1935.

Hartshorn A.S., K.V. Diprose, G.N. Patterson, *On the thrust obtainable from exhaust momentum,* RAE BA 1578 BA 1578, March 1940.

Kerr C.E., *24ft Wind tunnel tests on a radiator in a wing,* TNA AVIA 2140, BA 1356, December 1936.

Kerr C.E., R.A. Shaw, W. Tye, W.J. Pretorius, *24ft Tunnel: further tests on a radiator in a wing,* TNA DSIR 23/6411, BA 1413, July 1937.

Patterson G.N., *Note on tests of a ducted radiator fitted to the nose of a ¼ scale Hart,* TNA AVIA 6/2081, BA 1291, April 1936.

Patterson G.N., *Some wind tunnel tests on internal expansion in duct entries,* TNA AVIA 6/2172, BA 1402, May 1937.

Patterson G.N., *Preliminary note on an improvement in the design of ventral radiators,* TNA AVIA 6/2254 BA 1498, August 1938.

Patterson G.N., F. Smith, B.M. Rimmer, *Note on model tests of ventral ducted radiators underslung from a Vulture nacelle installation,* TNA AVIA 6/2291, April 1939.

Perring W.G.A., *A review of the Royal Aircraft Establishment cooling research,* TNA AVIA 6/2127, September 1936.

Perring W.G.A., *A review of RAE cooling research,* TNA BA 1342, September 1936.

Reeman J., *Tests on Spitfire radiators in the 24ft wind tunnel,* TNA AVIA 6/2447, BA 1694, DSIR 23/11196, July 1941.

Seddon J., E.A. Harrison, *A Collection of Wind Tunnel Test Data on the Exit Static Pressures of Engine Cooling Ducts,* TNA AVIA 6/9952, AERO 2127, March 1946.

Seddon Dr J., *Aerodynamics of Radiator Cooling,* RAE Report No 2290, May 1947.

Shaw R.A., W.H. Curtiss, *A Scheme for a radiator in a wing,* TNA AVIA 6/2028 BA 1227, October 1935.

Shaw R.A., F.W. Kirkby, *Model tests of the Supermarine F37/34,* TNA AVIA 6/2087 BA 1936, May 1936.

Shaw R.A., D. Cameron, *Model tests of the Hawker Interceptor radiator cowl,* RAE BA 1298, May 1936.

Shaw R.A., *Addendum to Report No, BA 1298 – Model tests of the Hawker interceptor radiator cowl,* RAE BA 1298, August 1936.

Shaw R.A., M.J. McInerney, *Tests of a Peregrine nacelle wing unit in the 24ft tunnel,* TNA AVIA 6/2221, BA 1460, May 1938.

Shaw R.A., *The use of a trailing edge flap to reduce the induced drag of a nacelle,* TNA AVIA 6/2222, 1938.

Smelt R., H. Davies, C. Callon, *Recovery of energy from a ducted cooling system,* TNA AVIA 2134, BA 1348, November 1936.

Smelt R., F. Smith, P. Abbott, *Data on an in-wing radiator installed ahead of the front wing spar,* TNA AVIA 6/2369, June 1940.

Also:

anon, *North American Aviation file 1940 – 1941,* TNA AVIA 38/733, 1940-1941.

anon, TNA Aircraft: Equipment (Code B, 5/21): Automatic dive bombsight for Fleet Air Arm: development and trials, TNA AIR 2/3524.

British – other

Rolls-Royce, Estimation of the increase in performance obtainable by fitting a continuously variable radiator flap, *Experimental Department Report,* 10 August 1942.

NACA/NASA

Book

Becker J.V., *The High Speed Frontier, Case History of Four NACA Programs, 1920-50,* NASA Scientific and Technical Information Branch, https://historynasagov/ SP-445/ch5-3htm, SP-445 NASA 1980.

Bilstein R.E., *Orders of Magnitude, a History of NASA, 1915-1990,* SP-4406 NASA 1989.

Hansen J.R., *Engineer in charge: a history of the Langley Aeronautical Laboratory 1917-1958,* NASA History Series, SP-4305 NASA 1987.

Hartman E.P., *Adventures in Research: A History of the Ames Research Center 1940-1965,* NASA History Series, SP-4302 NASA 1970.

Report

Becker J.V., Baals D.D., *Analysis of Heat and Compressibility Effects in Internal Flow Systems and High-Speed Tests of a Ramjet System* NACA, National Advisory Committee for Aeronautics, NACA ACR, Report No 773, January 1943.

Becker John V., *Wind-Tunnel Test of Air Inlet and Outlet Openings on a streamline Body,* NACA ACR, National Advisory Committee for Aeronautics, NACA ACR, Report No 1038, November 1940.

Becker J.V., Baals D.D., *High-speed Tests of a Ducted Body with Various Air-Outlet Openings NACA ACR,* National Advisory Committee for Aeronautics, NACA ACR, May 1942.

Bollay W., E.M. Redding, *Performance of Open-Duct Propulsion Systems (Ramjets) at Subsonic Speeds,* Power Plant Memorandum No 5, Bureau of Aeronautics, US Navy, December 1943.

BIBLIOGRAPHY

Brevoort M.J., M. Leifer, *Radiator Design and Installation,* National Advisory Committee for Aeronautics, Special Report No 112, May 1939.

Buckingham E., *Jet propulsion for Airplanes,* NACA Report No 159, in Ninth Annual Report of NACA-1923 Washington, 1924.

Bushnell D.M., M.H. Tuttle, *Survey and bibliography on attainment of laminar flow control in air using pressure gradient and suction,* NASA, Scientific and Technical Information Branch, 1979.

Dearborn C.H., A. Silverstein, *Drag Analysis of Single Engine Military Airplanes Tested in the NACA Full-Scale Wind Tunnel,* NACA Wartime Report L-89 – Langley Memorial Aeronautical Laboratory 1940.

Matthews H.F., F. Howard, *Elimination of Rumble from the Cooling Ducts of a Single-Engine Pursuit Airplane,* NACA Wartime Reports A-70 – Ames Aeronautical Laboratory, August 1943.

Nickle F.R., W.J. Nelson, *Tests of the XP-46 Airplane in the NACA Full-Scale Wind Tunnel 1940 (20140000028),* Langley Research Center, January 1940.

Pinkel B., F. Voss, *Experimental Determination of Exhaust Gas Thrust,* Special Report No 139, February 1940.

Silverstein A., *Experiments on the recovery of waste heat in cooling drag,* NACA Special Report No 111, May 1939.

Tifford A.N., *Radiator Design and Installation – II,* National Advisory Committee for Aeronautics, January 1942.

Ulbrich N., *A High-Speed Full-Scale Wind Tunnel Test of the XP-51B in the Ames 16t Wind Tunnel,* American Institute of Aeronautics and Astronautics, 5-8 January 2009.

Reports – translated from German

Göthert B., *The Drag of Airplane Radiators with Special Reference to Air Heating (comparison of theory and experiment),* NACA Technical Memorandum 896 (first published in Germany in 1938), 1939.

Weise A., *The Conversion of Energy in a Radiator,* NACA Technical Memorandum 869, (first published in Germany in 1937), 1938.

Winter H., *Contribution to the Theory of the Heated Duct Radiator,* NACA Technical Memorandum 893 (first published in Germany in 1938), 1939.

SAE

Beisel R., B.A. MacClain, F. Thomas, The Cowling and Cooling of Radial Air-Cooled Aircraft Engines, *SAE Technical Paper Series 340089,* 1934.

Hives E.W., Smith F.L., High Output Aircraft Engines, *SAE Journal (Transactions),* Vol 46, No 3, 1940.

Miley S.J., Aerodynamics of Liquid-Cooled Aircraft Engine Installations *SAE Technical Paper Series 850896,* April 1985.

Wood D.H., Engine Nacelles and Propellers and Airplane Performance, *SAE Journal (Transactions),* Vol 31, April 1936.

Wood H., Engine Nacelles and Propellers and Airplane Performance, *SAE Journal (Transactions),* Vol 31, April 1936.

Wood H., Liquid-Cooled Aero Engines, *SAE Journal (Transactions),* Vol 39, No 1, July 1936.

Wood H., Author's Conclusion to Discussion of 'Liquid-Cooled Aero Engines', *SAE Journal (Transactions),* Vol 39, No 4, 1936.

Worth W., Radiator Proportions Discussed, *SAE Journal (Transactions),* Vol 39, No 1, July 1936.

Other NACA/NASA

Driggs I.H., Aviation Design Research Branch, Bureau of Aeronautics, Navy Department, Washington, DC, to Experiments and Developments Branch, Document 4-28(g), in J.R. Hansen (Editor), *The Wind and Beyond: A Documentary Journey into the History of Aerodynamics in America*, NASA SP-2007-4409, NASA History Division, 2009.

Warner E., London, to Dr George W. Lewis, NACA, Washington, DC, Document 4-28(e), 25 August 1942, in J.R. Hansen (Editor), *The Wind and Beyond: A Documentary Journey into the History of Aerodynamics in America*, NASA SP-2007-4409, NASA History Division, 2009.

Magazine/Newspaper

British

Douglas G.P., Cooling Problems with Particular Reference to the Work of the RAE Tunnel, *The Aircraft Engineer*
Supplement to Flight, 28 February 1937.

Dunnell B., Power House [Rolls-Royce Experimental], *Aeroplane,* February 2017.

British *Flight* (all anon)

Two New Marconi Devices, *Flight*, January 1935.

Liquid Cooling Today, *Flight,* 30 September 1937.

Auxiliary Propulsion, *Flight,* 22 April 1937.

'Ideas of Mr Meredith …', *Flight*, 2 December 1937.

Air-cooled v Liquid-cooled Aircraft, *Flight,* 13 March 1941.

Unobtrusive Cleverness, *Flight,* 20 August 1942.

Mustang Squadron, *Flight,* 30 July 1942.

A New Autopilot General Survey of Smith's Electric Pilot: Entirely New Basis of Control: Maintenance Eliminated, *Flight,* 15 September 1947.

A New Autopilot, *Flight,* 25 September 1947.

Flight, The Modern Autopilot, A Dissertation on the Fundamentals of Modern Automatic Pilot Design, *Flight,* 13 January 1949.

Tuning Fork and Laser, *Flight International,* 27 June 1967.

US (all Mustang)

Buckingham D., The Effect of the North American P-51 Mustang on the Air War in Europe, *IBH 20th Century History,* 1995.

Churchill E., Mighty Midget, *Flying Magazine,* January 1944.

Cox J., *The Restoration of the XP-51 Sport Aviation,* December 1975.

Ethell J., [Title not given in NAAR source], *Air Force Magazine,* 1981.

Ford L., M. 'Mac' Blair, A Ghost from the Distant Past, *NAAR Bulletin,* Fall 2003.

Ford L., Mustang – The True Birthright, *NAAR Bulletin*, Summer 2009.

Ford L., The Extended Range Mustang, *NAAR Bulletin,* Winter 2007.

Fredrickson J., The P-51's Turbulent Development, *Air Force Magazine,* 2016.

Galen D., P-51 Mustang in action, *Aircraft No 45,* squadron/signal publications, 1981?

Garrison P., Who made the Mustang? *Air & Space,* August/September 1996.

Garrison P., In the Mustang's Wake, *Aviation History Magazine,* 7 February 2015.

Horkey E., The P-51: The Real Story, *AAHS Journal,* (American Aviation Historical Society) pp 178-190, 1996.

Rees E., A Tribute To Dutch Kindleberger: The Mustang – A Great War Horse, *The Air Power Historian* (Air Force Historical Foundation) Vol 9, No 4, October 1962.

Rees E., How the North American P-51 Mustang emerged from the shadows and helped assure Allied air superiority over Europe, *Air Force Magazine*, 1 March 1964.

Schmued E., Conception and Development of the P-51 Mustang, *NAAR,* Fall 2015.

Other

anon, Merchant of Speed, *Saturday Evening Post,* 19 February 1949.

Patent

British

Ellor (1), *Improvements in Cowling for Liquid Cooled Internal Combustion Engines for Aircraft,* GB 447,283 Rolls-Royce applied 1934, accepted 1936.

Ellor (2), *Improvements in Radiator Cowling for Aircraft,* GB 456,335, Rolls-Royce applied 1935, accepted 1936.

Ellor J.E., T.P. de Paravicini, *Improvements in aircraft [Heston-Napier racer],* GB 472,555 Rolls-Royce applied 1936, accepted 1937.

de Paravicini T.P., (Rolls-Royce), *Improvements in exhaust discharge arrangements for internal combustion engines,* GB 471,177, applied 1935, accepted 1937.

de Paravicini T.P., (Rolls-Royce), *Oil coolers for aircraft,* GB 463,303, applied 1935, accepted 1937.

Non-British
Junkers H., Radiator, US 1,464,765A, [see Espacenet], 28 June 1920 filed.

Various

PhD
Boylan B.L., *The Development of the Long-Range Escort Fighter,* USAF Historical Studies, no 136, I June 1955.
Linett J.A., *A vibratory system for measuring rates of turn,* Thesis submitted for the degree of Doctor of Philosophy, University of Edinburgh, March 1968.
Marsh S.H., *The Air Ministry and the Bomb Dropping Problem: Bombsights, Scientists and Techno-Military Invention, 1918-45,* King's College London, 1 June 2019.

Letter, email
Ethell J., Letter (private) to Jack Reeder, https://authorzillacom/zNWjO/articles-nasa-langley-gis-team-home-pagehtml, 2 April 1979.
Oram J,A., Letter, 'Sir Your report on the vibrating gyro reminds me that just after the war F.W. Meredith …', *New Scientist,* 14 March 1963.

Website
Anon, *Jets45, List of Engines/Engines USA,* https://tanks45tripod/Jets45/List of Engines/EnginesUSAhtm
Hays P.R., *History of the Talos Ramjet Engine,* https://wwwokieboatcom/Ramjet%20historyhtml,
Wjaworski W., *Blog Virtual Aircraft 3D modeling as a hobby,* http://wjaworskipl/blog/p-40/0101-06jpg
anon, *Blasius boundary layer,* https://enwikipediaorg/wiki/Blasius_boundary_layer
anon, *Meredith Effect and the P-51*, WW2AIRCRAFTNET, https://ww2aircraftnet/forum/threads/meredith-effect-and-the-p-5116845/page-8

Endnotes

Introduction

1. J. Quill, *Spitfire: The Amazing personal story of a Spitfire test pilot and RAF fighter,* Arrow Books, 1983, p 79.
2. J.L. Atwood, 'Mustang Memories', letter, *Air & Space,* October/November 1996.
3. *KV 2/2201*, TNA, p 62.
4. R.W. Howard, Automatic Flight Controls in Fixed Wing Aircraft – The First 100 Years, *Aeronautical Journal,* November 1973.
5. R. Farnham, *The Meredith Effect – Fact or Fiction? Can a properly ducted radiator offset all internal cooling drag and produce thrust?,* 2015. https://www.kitplanes.com/the-meredith-effect-fact-or-fiction/
6. D. Lednicer, World War II Fighter Aerodynamics, *Sport Aviation*, January 1999.
7. R. Schlaifer, *Development of Aircraft Engines (The Rolls-Royce Liquid-Cooled Engines),* Boston, Harvard University, 1950, p 237, fn 46.
8. *ibid,* p 237, fn 46.
9. G. Spinardi, R. Slayton, Analysing Environmental Transitions with the Multi-Level Perspective, *Science & Technology Studies,* 1/2015.
10. anon, *Blasius boundary layer.* [https://en.wikipedia.org/wiki/Blasius_boundary_layer]
11. anon, The Modern Autopilot, A Dissertation on the Fundamentals of Modern Automatic Pilot Design, *Flight*, 13 January 1949.
12. F.W. Meredith, P.A. Cooke, Aeroplane Stability and the Automatic Pilot, *Journal Royal Aeronautical Society,* June 1937.
13. F.W. Meredith, British Autopilot Claims More Reliability, *Aviation Week*, 8 December 1947.
14. anon, A New Autopilot. General Survey of Smith's Electric Pilot: Entirely New Basis of Control: Maintenance Eliminated, *Flight,* 15 September 1947.
15. J.A. Linett, *A vibratory system for measuring rates of turn,* Thesis submitted for the degree of Doctor of Philosophy University of Edinburgh, March 1968.
16. *KV 2/2200*, TNA, p 23.
17. *KV 2/2201*, TNA, p 63.

275

PART 1: MEREDITH AND THE SPITFIRE

1935 – *annus mirabilis* sees two critical developments

1. F.W. Meredith, *Cooling of Aircraft Engines with special reference to Ethylene Glycol Radiators enclosed in Ducts*, ARC, R&M No 1683, August 1935 (published 1936).
2. *Programme of Aeronautical Research at RAE 1935,* Aerodynamics Sub-committee, Aeronautical Research Committee, 1935.

Chapter 1: Supermarine, Rolls-Royce and RAE – and the cooling challenge

1. D. Birch, *Rolls-Royce and the Mustang,* Rolls-Royce Heritage Trust, 1987, p 20.
2. E.B. Morgan, E. Shackladay, *Spitfire: The History,* Guild Publishing, 1986, p 22.
3. R.S. Capon, *The cowling of cooling systems*, ARC R&M 1702, March 1936.
4. E.B. Morgan, E. Shackladay, *Spitfire: The History,* Guild Publishing, 1986, p 21.
5. *ibid,* p 22.
6. E.J. Davis, *The Basic Design of the Prototype Spitfire,* The 30th R.J. Mitchell Memorial Lecture, 4 March 1986.

Chapter 2: Royal Aircraft Establishment and Frederick William Meredith – Bolshevism rampant

1. J.L. Atwood, 'Mustang Memories'.
2. *KV 2/3059*, TNA, p 122.
3. E. Warner, London, letter to Dr George W. Lewis, NACA, Washington, D.C., Document 4-28(e), 25 August 1942, (in Hansen 2009)   .
4. E.E. Vielle, *Almost a Boffin, Why he invented the Cruise Missile,* Dolman Scott 2013, p 163.
5. *ibid,* p 314.
6. *KV 2/2200*, TNA, p 101.
7. *ibid*, p 23.
8. *ibid*, p 101.
9. *KV 2/2201*, TNA, p 62.
10. *KV 2/2199*, TNA, p 32.
11. *2/lieutenant Frederick William Meredith, Royal Garrison Artillery*, 1915-1918, 1930, TNA, WO 339/44412.
12. *ibid.*

13. *KV 2/2200*, TNA, p 41.

14. *ibid*, p 31.

15. *KV 2/2202*, TNA, p 26.

16. *KV 2/2200*, TNA, p.41.

17. S.H. Marsh, *The Air Ministry and the Bomb Dropping Problem: Bombsights, Scientists and Techno-Military Invention, 1918-45*, King's College London, 1 June 2019.

18. R.W. Howard, Automatic Flight Controls in Fixed Wing Aircraft – The First 100 Years, *Aeronautical Journal,* November 1973.

19. *ibid.*

20. *KV 2/2200*, TNA, p 154.

21. F.W. Meredith, *Automatic Control of Aircraft*, TNA, AVIA 6/1513, RAE Report B. A 520, December 1924, (in Marsh 2019).

22. D.T. McRuer, D. Graham, I. Ashkenas, *Aircraft Dynamics and Automatic Control,* Princeton University Press, 1973, p 31.

23. F.W. Meredith, *Automatic Control of Aircraft*, TNA, AVIA 6/1513, RAE Report B. A 520, TNA, December 1924, (in Marsh 2019).

24. RAeS Membership Records, *KV 2/2200*, TNA, p 101-3.

25. *KV 2/2200*, TNA, p 154.

26. F.W. Meredith, Air Transport in Fog, *Journal of the Royal Aeronautical Society,* February 1931.

27. D.T. McRuer, D. Graham, I. Ashkenas, *Aircraft Dynamics and Automatic Control,* Princeton University Press, 1973, p 31.

28. *ibid,* p 31.

29. F.W. Meredith, C.H. Holt, *Improvements in or relating to electrical indicating systems,* GB 357,968, applied 1930, published 1931.

30. anon, Two New Marconi Devices, *Flight,* 31 January 1935.

31. F.W. Meredith, *Problem of Lateral Stabilisation of a Bombsight,* November 1926.

32. *KV 2/2199*, TNA, p 12.

33. *ibid*, p 12.

34. *KV 2/2200*, TNA, p 154.

35. E.E. Vielle, *Almost a Boffin, Why he invented the Cruise Missile,* Dolman Scott 2013, p 170.

36. *KV 2/2199*, TNA, p 43.

37. *ibid*, p12.

38. *ibid*, TNA, p 32.

39. *KV 2/2202*, TNA, p 13.

40. *ibid*, p 14.

41. *KV 2/3059*, TNA, p 97.

42. *ibid*, TNA, p 95.
43. *KV 2/2199*, TNA, p 36.
44. *ibid*, p 35.
45. *ibid*, p 45.
46. *ibid*, p 36.
47. *KV 2/3059*, TNA, p 72.
48. *KV 2/2199*, TNA, p 35.
49. *ibid,* p 38.
50. *ibid*, p 44.
51. *KV 2/2200*, TNA, p 38.
52. *KV 2/2199*, TNA, p 187.
53. *KV 2/2200*, TNA, p 187.
54. *KV 2/2202*, TNA, p 43.
55. *ibid*, p 43.
56. *KV 2/2199*, TNA, p 42.
57. *ibid*, p 56.
58. *ibid*, p 57.
59. *ibid*, p 55.
60. *ibid,* p 38.
61. *ibid,* p 40.
62. *ibid*, p 47.
63. *ibid*, p 40.
64. *ibid*, p 19.
65. *ibid,* p 12.
66. *ibid*, p 64.
67. *ibid*, p 37.
68. *ibid*, p 14.
69. *KV 2/3059*, TNA, p 11.
70. H. Glauert, *Elements of Aerofoil and Airscrew Theory*, Cambridge University Press, 1926.

Chapter 3: Meredith's papers on jet propulsion and duct entry

1. *KV 2/2200*, TNA, p 154.
2. F.W. Meredith, *Invention relating to jet propulsion of aircraft,* TNA, AVIA 8/407, 28 February 1935.
3. *ibid.*
4. *ibid.*

5. A.A. Hall, H. Constant, *Note on the development of additional power for aircraft by jet reaction*, TNA, AVIA 6/2357, 1940.
6. E.B. Morgan, E. Shackladay, *Spitfire: The History,* Guild Publishing, 1986, p 26.

Chapter 4: Rolls-Royce and RAE Patents for ducted radiator systems

1. Schlaifer, *Development of Aircraft Engines,* p 237, fn 46.
2. anon, Auxiliary Propulsion, *Flight*, 22 April 1937.

Chapter 5: Meredith and Capon ARC research papers on inline engine cooling

1. Davis, *The Basic Design of the Prototype Spitfire.*
2. F.W. Meredith, *Cooling of Aircraft Engines with special reference to Ethylene Glycol Radiators enclosed in Ducts*, ARC, R&M No 1683, August 1935 (published 1936)..
3. Davis, *The Basic Design of the Prototype Spitfire.*
4. G.P. Douglas, Cooling Problems with Particular Reference to the work of the RAE Tunnel, *The Aircraft Engineer*, 28 November 1935.
5. G.P. Douglas, Cooling Problems with Particular Reference to the work of the RAE Tunnel, *The Aircraft Engineer*, 28 November 1935.
6. *ibid.*

Chapter 7: First aircraft with ducted radiators – Meredith critical of the Spitfire's

1. WW2AIRCRAFT.NET, Meredith Effect and the P-51, https://ww2aircraft.net/forum/threads/meredith-effect-and-the-p-51.16845/page-8
2. E.B. Morgan, E. Shackladay, *Spitfire: The History,* Guild Publishing, 1986, p 25.
3. *ibid,* p 25-26.
4. F.W. Meredith, *Note on the problem of conducting a fluid into a duct with the minimum of loss,* RAE Wind Tunnel Note No 267, May 1935.
5. E.B. Morgan, E. Shackladay, *Spitfire: The History,* Guild Publishing, 1986, p 25.
6. Davis, *The Basic Design of the Prototype Spitfire.*
7. *ibid,* p 25.
8. *ibid,* p 25.

9. Davis, *The Basic Design of the Prototype Spitfire.*
10. E.B. Morgan, E. Shackladay, *Spitfire: The History,* Guild Publishing, 1986, p 26.
11. *ibid,* p 26.
12. E.B. Morgan, E. Shackladay, *Spitfire: The History,* Guild Publishing, 1986, p 26.
13. Davis, *The Basic Design of the Prototype Spitfire.*
14. Quill, *Spitfire,* p 79.

Chapter 8: Spitfire and Hurricane wind tunnel tests

1. E.B. Morgan, E. Shackladay, *Spitfire: The History,* Guild Publishing, 1986, pp 25-26.

Chapter 9: Spitfire a pionneering but flawed design

1. Davis, *The Basic Design of the Prototype Spitfire.*
2. *ibid.*
3. Quill, *Spitfire,* p 79.
4. A. Price, *Spitfire: A Documentary History,* Macdonald and Jane's, 1977, p 23-24.
5. *ibid.*
6. Lednicer, World War II Fighter Aerodynamics.
7. E.B. Morgan, E. Shackladay, *Spitfire: The History,* Guild Publishing, 1986, p 26.
8. *ibid.*
9. A.S. Hartshorn, M.A. Nicholson, *The Aerodynamics of the Cooling Aircraft Reciprocating Engines,* ARC R&M 2498, May 1947.
10. D. Lednicer, World War II Fighter Aerodynamics, *Sport Aviation,* January 1999.
11. J.A.D. Akroyd, The Aerodynamics of the Spitfire, *Journal of Aeronautical History,* 2016.
12. *ibid.*
13. Rolls-Royce, Estimation of the increase in performance obtainable by fitting a continuously variable radiator flap, *Experimental Department Report,* 10 August 1942.

Chapter 10: Rolls-Royce buys Heinkel He 70 for flight testing including radiators and exhaust stubs

1. Schlaifer, *Development of Aircraft Engines,* p 237.
2. E.B. Morgan, E. Shackladay, *Spitfire: The History,* Guild Publishing, 1986, p 37.

3. *ibid,* p 37.
4. Schlaifer, *Development of Aircraft Engines,* p 237-8.
5. Sir S. Hooker, *Not much of an engineer,* Airlife, 1984.
6. Schlaifer, *Development of Aircraft Engines,* p 237.
7. *ibid,* p 229.
8. T.P. de Paravicini, (Rolls-Royce), *Improvements in exhaust discharge arrangements for internal combustion engines,* GB 471,177, applied 1935, accepted 1937.
9. *ibid.*
10. Akroyd, Aerodynamics.
11. Hooker, *Not much of an engineer,* Airlife, 1984.
12. Schlaifer, *Development of Aircraft Engines,* p 229.
13. *ibid,* p 237, fn 46.

Chapter 11: Wind tunnel analysis in 1935 and 1936

1. *KV 2/2199*, TNA, p 38.
2. Meredith, *Note on the problem of conducting a fluid.*

Chapter 12: Ducted radiators on aircraft generally

1. W. Messerschmitt, Probleme des Schnellflugs: (Problem of high speed airplanes),*Schriften Der Deutschen Akademie der Luftfahrtforschung (Publications of the German Academy of Aviation Research),* Heft 31 November 1937, 1937/38.
2. Lednicer, World War II Fighter Aerodynamics.
3. G. Baughen, *The Rise and Fall of the French Airforce,* Fonthill Media, 2018, np online.
4. L. Breguet, R. Devillers, La Technique des Radiateurs Carénés, *La Science aérienne,* Paris, 1 v. no. 6, Nov-Dec 1938.

Chapter 13: Meredith scientific contribution post 1935

1. A.A. Griffith, *An Aerodynamic Theory of Turbine Design,* RAE, Report H1111, 7 July 1926.
2. *KV 2/3059*, TNA, p 125.
3. B. Melville-Jones, The Streamline Airplane, *Aeronautical Journal,* Vol, 33, 1929.

4. F.W. Meredith, A.A. Griffith, *Improvements in or relating to aircraft,* AVIA 8/416, TNA, May 1936.

5. F.W. Meredith, A.A. Griffith, *The possible improvement in Aircraft Performance due to the used of boundary layer suction,* DSIR 23/5566, 1936.

6. D.M. Bushnell, M.H. Tuttle, *Survey and bibliography on attainment of laminar flow control in air using pressure gradient and suction,* NASA, 1979.

7. J.L. Atwood, An Engineer's Perspective on the Mustang, *Flight Journal,* June 1999.

8. P.C. Smith, Skua! *The Royal Navy's Dive-Bomber, Pen & Sword Aviation,* 2006 (Dive Bomb-Sight Sub-Committee: papers, 20/4155, TNA), p 23-24.

9. *ibid,* p 22.

10. *ibid,* p 30.

11. F.W. Meredith, *Memorandum on High Altitude Bombsights,* AVIA 53/233, TNA, 21 April 1937, (in Marsh 2019).

12. *ibid.*

13. Marsh, *The Air Ministry and the Bomb Dropping Problem.*

14. *Aircraft: Equipment (Code B, 5/21): Automatic dive bombsight for Fleet Air Arm: development and trials,* Minute 3, 19/01/1939, AIR 2/3524, TNA, (in Marsh 2019), p 118, fn 114.

15. *ibid,* p 116 fn, 104 (in Marsh 2019).

16. Minute 11, 02/03/1939, AIR 2/3524, TNA, (in Marsh 2019), p 117, fn 107.

17. F.W. Meredith, *Note on the problem of aiming fixed guns in aeroplanes,* RAE, Departmental Note No. H 242, October 1937.

18. F.W. Meredith, G.W. Gardner, *Improvements in or relating to controlling aircraft,* GB 576,359, October 1938.

19. F.W. Cousins, *The Anatomy of the Gyroscope, Part III,* Advisory Group for Aerospace Research And Development, 1998.

20. *KV 2/2200,* TNA, p 158.

Chapter 14: Meredith – From Spitfire to Spy

1. *KV 2/2200,* TNA, p 64.

2. *ibid,* p 64.

3. *ibid,* p 64.

4. *ibid,* p 46.

5. *ibid,* p 46.

6. *KV 2/2199,* TNA, p. 37.

7. *KV 2/2201,* TNA, p. 87.

8. *ibid,* p 87.

9. *KV 2/2200*, TNA, p 152.
10. *KV 2/2202*, TNA, p 13.
11. *KV 2/2200*, TNA, p 46.
12. *ibid*, p 46.
13. *KV 2/2201*, TNA, p 87.
14. *KV 2/2200*, TNA, p 95.
15. *ibid*, p 85.
16. *ibid*, p 64-5.
17. *ibid*, p 47.
18. *ibid*, p 102.
19. *ibid,* p 102.
20. *ibid*, p 47.
21. *ibid*, p 102.
22. *ibid*, p 135.
23. *ibid*, p 14.
24. *ibid*, p 102.
25. *ibid*, p 47.
26. *ibid,* p 137.
27. *ibid*, p 137.
28. J. Redman, *The British Stalinists and the Moscow Trials,* March 1958. https://www.marxists.org/archive/pearce/1958/03/trials.html,
29. *KV 2/2200*, TNA, p 189.
30. *ibid,* p 167.
31. *ibid*, p 102.
32. *ibid*, p 164.
33. *ibid*, p 163.
34. *ibid,* p 98.
35. *ibid*, p 47.
36. *Ibid,* p 47.
37. *ibid*, p 71.
38. *ibid*, p 185.
39. *ibid*, p 51.
40. *ibid,* p 86.
41. *KV 2/2201*, TNA, p 87.
42. *KV 2/2200*, TNA, p 47.
43. *ibid*, p 47.
44. *ibid,* p 98.
45. *ibid*, p 137.
46. *KV 2/2201*, TNA, p 119.

Chapter 15: Meredith's War years

1. F.W. Meredith, British Autopilot Claims More Reliability.
2. F.W. Meredith, Memorandum on High Altitude Level Bombsights, in *Automatic self-setting bombsight: user claim*, TNA, AVIA 53/233, RAE Report H.255, February 1938, (in Marsh 2019).
3. Smith, *Skua!* p 93.
4. Bowen to DTD, 13/02/1942, AIR 2/3524, TNA, (in Marsh 2019), p 118, fn 114.
5. Marsh 2019, p. 118.
6. Marsh 2019, p. 119.
7. Cousins, *The Anatomy of the Gyroscope.*
8. A. Hall, M. Morgan, Bennet Melville Jones 28 January 1887 – 31 October 1975, *The Royal Society Publishing*, November 1977.
9. F.W. Meredith, *Improvements in electric motors,* GB 576,248, applied 1943, published 1946.
10. F.W. Meredith, The Modern Autopilot: A Dissertation on the Fundamentals of Modern Autopilot Design, *Flight,* 13 January 1949.
11. F.W. Meredith, *Improvements in or relating to devices for detecting or measuring rate of turn,* GB 611,005, applied 1942, published 1948.
12. J.A. Oram, letter, 'Sir. Your report on the vibrating gyro reminds me that just after the war…', F.W. Meredith …, *New Scientist,* 14 March 1963.
13. anon, Tuning Fork and Laser, *Flight International,* 27 June 1967.
14. *KV 2/2200*, TNA, p 23.
15. *ibid*, pp 136-7.
16. *ibid*, p 23.
17. *ibid,* p 8.
18. *ibid,* p 9.

Chapter 16: Meredith post-1945

1. anon, A New Autopilot, *Flight,* 25, September 1947.
2. Meredith, British Autopilot Claims More Reliability.
3. anon, 'A New Autopilot. General Survey of Smith's Electric Pilot: Entirely New Basis of Control: Maintenance Eliminated', *Flight,* 15 September 1947.
4. Meredith, British Autopilot Claims More Reliability.
5. Meredith, *Improvements in electric motors.*
6. F.W. Meredith, The Modern Autopilot: A Dissertation on the Fundamentals of Modern Autopilot Design, *Flight,* 13 January 1949.
7. *ibid.*

8. Meredith, *Improvements in or relating to devices for detecting or measuring rate of turn*.
9. F.W. Meredith, Control of Equilibrium in the Flying Insect, *Nature*, 1949.
10. F.W. Meredith, Bats, Bees and Brains, *London Report,* August 1957.
11. *KV 2/2202*, TNA, p 24.
12. *KV 2/2201*, TNA, p 6.
13. *KV 2/2202*, TNA, p 30.
14. *KV 2/2200*, TNA, p 94.
15. *ibid*, p 23.
16. *ibid*, p 14.
17. *ibid*, p 41.
18. *ibid*, p 41.
19. *ibid*, p 20.
20. *ibid*, p 23.
21. *ibid*, p 62-65.
22. *ibid*, p 63.
23. *ibid*, p 31.
24. *KV 2/2200*, TNA, p 29.
25. *KV 2/2201*, TNA, p 9.
26. *ibid*, p 71.
27. *ibid*, p 71.
28. *ibid*, p 76.
29. *ibid*, p 8.
30. *ibid*, p 9.
31. *ibid*, p 10.
32. *ibid*, p 62.
33. *ibid*, p 63.
34. *ibid*, p 63.
35. *ibid*, p 13.
36. *ibid*, p 14.
37. *ibid*, p 15.
38. *ibid*, p 58.
39. *ibid*, p 19.
40. *ibid*, p 37.
41. *ibid*, p 40.
42. *ibid*, p 35.
43. *ibid*, p 26.
44. *KV 2/2202*, TNA, p 3.
45. *ibid*, p 32.
46. *ibid*, p 32.

47. *ibid,* p 30-31.
48. *ibid*, p 24.
49. *ibid*, p 26.
50. *ibid*, p 18.
51. *ibid*, p 17.
52. *ibid*, p 16.
53. *ibid*, p 11.
54. *ibid*, p 9.
55. *ibid*, p 8.

PART 2: THE 'MEREDITH EFFECT' AND THE MUSTANG

1939 – North American Aviation's Lee Atwood discovers Meredith

1. Atwood, 'Mustang Memories'.
2. *ibid.*
3. anon, Vista Morning Press, 6 June 1984, p 11 (in Wagner, fn 20, p. 230).
4. Atwood, 'Mustang Memories'.
5. J.L. Atwood, Origin and Evolution of the Mustang, *Air Power History Journal,* 1993.
6. Marshall, Ford, *P-51B North American's Bastard Stepchild,* p. 27.
7. *ibid,* p 27.
8. L.K. Carson, *Pursue and Destroy: 8th Air Force's Fighter Group in World War II,* Sentry Books, p 32.
9. *ibid.*

Chapter 17: (1) The Mustang and Meredith – the 'Meredith effect'

1. Atwood, 'Mustang Memories'.
2. F.W. Meredith, *Cooling of Aircraft Engines with special reference to Ethylene Glycol Radiators enclosed in Ducts*, ARC, R&M No 1683, August 1935 (published 1936).
3. J.V. Becker, *The High Speed Frontier, Case History of Four NACA Programs, 1920-50,* NASA, 1980, p 161.
4. J.V. Becker, D.D. Baals, *Analysis of Heat and Compressibility Effects in Internal Flow Systems and High-Speed Tests of a Ramjet System*, NACA, Report No. 773, January 1943.
5. E. Rees, Mustang! How the North American P-51 Mustang emerged from the shadows and helped assure Allied air victory, *Air Force Magazine*, 1 March 1964.

6. L.F. Ford, M. 'Mac' Blair, A Ghost from the Distant Past, *NAAR Bulletin,* Fall 2003.

7. *ibid.*

8. L.F. Ford, Mustang – The True Birthright, *NAAR Bulletin,* Summer 2009.

9. *ibid.*

10. R.S. Capon, The *Cowling of cooling systems (2nd report),* AVIA 6/2017, August 1935.

11. D.H. Wood, Engine Nacelles and Propellers and Airplane Performance, *SAE Journal (Transactions),* Vol. 31, April 1936.

12. *ibid.*

13. H. Wood, Liquid-Cooled Aero Engines, *SAE Journal (Transactions),* vol 39, No 1, July 1936.

14. *ibid.*

15. *ibid.*

16. *ibid.*

17. *ibid.*

18. W. Worth, Radiator Proportions Discussed, *SAE Journal (Transactions),* vol 39, No 1, July 1936.

19. M.J. Breevort, M. Leifer, *Radiator design and installation,* NACA, Special Report No 112, May 1939.

20. L.F. Ford, Mustang – The True Birthright, *NAAR Bulletin,* Summer 2009.

21. *ibid.*

22. *ibid.*

23. *ibid.*

24. *ibid.*

25. *ibid.*

26. *ibid.*

27. E. Horkey, The P-51: The Real Story, *AAHS Journal,* 1996.

28. R. Wagner, *Mustang Designer Edgar Schmued and the P51,* Orion, 1990, p 46.

29. J. Fredrickson, The P-51's Turbulent Development, *Air Force Magazine,* 2016.

30. L.F. Ford, Mustang – The True Birthright, *NAAR Bulletin,* Summer 2009.

31. K.J. Meekcoms, *The British Air Commission and Lend-Lease,* Air-Britain (Historians) Ltd, 2000, p 23.

32. *ibid,* p 16.

33. *ibid,* p 17.

34. *ibid,* p 22-23.

35. *ibid,* p 23.

36. L.F. Ford, Mustang – The True Birthright, *NAAR Bulletin,* Summer 2009.

Chapter 18: The availability and impact of Meredith's work in the US

1. A. Weise, *The Conversion of Energy in a Radiator*, NACA Technical Memorandum 869, (first published in Germany in 1937) 1938.
2. Winter, *Contribution to the Theory*.
3. B. Göthert, *The Drag of Airplane Radiators with Special Reference to Air Heating (comparison of theory and experiment)*, NACA n°896, May 19 Is this date correct?
4. Marshall, Ford, *P-51B North American's Bastard Stepchild*, p 68.
5. *ibid*, p 68.
6. P.A. Ludwig, *P-51 Mustang: Development of the Long-Range Escort Fighter*, Classic Publications Sussex, 2003, p 221, fn 18 (ch 6).
7. Winter, *Contribution to the Theory*.
8. Horkey, The P-51: The Real Story.
9. A. Silverstein, *Experiments on the recovery of waste heat in cooling drag*, NACA Special Report No. 111, May 1939.
10. Becker, Baals, *Analysis of Heat and Compressibility Effects*.
11. A. Silverstein, *Experiments on the recovery of waste heat in cooling drag*, NACA Special Report No. 111, May 1939.
12. Breevort, Leifer, *Radiator design and installation*.
13. C.H. Dearborn, A Silverstein, *Drag Analysis of Single Engine Military Airplanes Tested in the NACA Full-Scale Wind Tunnel*, NACA Wartime Report L-89 –, 1940.
14. *ibid*.
15. J.L. Atwood, The Spitfire and the Mustang (The Meredith Mystery), *Friends Journal*, 1995.

Chapter 19: The 'Meredith effect' and some US and non-US aircraft

1. W. Wjaworski, *Blog Virtual Aircraft 3D modeling as a hobby.* http://wjaworski.pl/blog/p-40/0101-06.jpg
2. R.W. Gruenhagen, *Mustang: The Story of the P-51 Fighter*, Arco Publishing 1969, p 13.
3. J. Ethell, *Mustang: A Documentary History*, Jane's, 1981 p 10.
4. A.S. Hartshorn, *Note on the installation of a ducted radiator in the ventral position*, TNA, AVIA 6/2050, November 1935.
5. E.B. Morgan, E. Shackladay, *Spitfire: The History*, Guild Publishing, 1986, p 37.

6. Marshall, Ford, *P-51B North American's Bastard Stepchild,* p 57.
7. *ibid,* p 71.

Chapter 20: Stages in the evolution of the Mustang

1. L.F. Ford, Mustang – The True Birthright, *NAAR Bulletin,* Summer 2009.
2. *ibid.*
3. *ibid.*
4. L. Piancastelli, S. Pica, G. Donnici, High Altitude Operations with Piston Engines Powerplant Design Optimisation Part III: The Diffuser critical design, *Journal of Engineering and Applied Sciences,* Vol. 11, No. 7, April 2016.
5. L.F. Ford, Mustang – The True Birthright, *NAAR Bulletin,* Summer 2009.
6. Wagner, *Mustang Designer Edgar Schmued,* p 51.
7. L.F. Ford, Mustang – The True Birthright, *NAAR Bulletin,* Summer 2009.
8. Ford, Blair, A Ghost.
9. P.A. Ludwig, *P-51 Mustang: Development of the Long-Range Escort Fighter,* Classic Publications, Sussex, 2003, p 220, fn 17.
10. *ibid,* p 220, fn 17.
11. J.W. Marshall, L.F. Ford, *P-51B North American's Bastard Stepchild that saved the Eighth Air Force,* Osprey 2020, p. 49-50.
12. J.L. Atwood, Origin and Evolution of the Mustang, *Air Power History Journal,* 1993.
13. Gruenhagen, *Mustang: The Story,* p 35.
14. L.F. Ford, Mustang – The True Birthright, *NAAR Bulletin,* Summer 2009..
15. Marshall, Ford, *P-51B North American's Bastard Stepchild,* p. 86.
16. L.F. Ford, Mustang – The True Birthright, *NAAR Bulletin,* Summer 2009.
17. J.L. Atwood, Origin and Evolution of the Mustang, *Air Power History Journal,* 1993.
18. B. Yenne, *Rockwell: The History of North American,* Bison Books, 1989, p 49.
19. Ethell, *Mustang,* p 14.
20. Wagner, *Mustang Designer Edgar Schmued*, p 57.
21. J. Marshall, Ford, *P-51B North American's Bastard Stepchild,* p 80.
22. J.L. Atwood, letter to Sir W. Self, 1 May 1940, in *North American Aviation 1940-1941*, AVIA 38/733, TNA.
23. Marshall, Ford, *P-51B North American's Bastard Stepchild,* p 57.
24. *ibid,* p 71.
25. J.L. Atwood, letter to Sir W. Self, 1 May 1940, in *North American Aviation 1940-1941*, AVIA 38/733, TNA.
26. Ford, Blair, A Ghost.

27. F.R. Nickle, W.J. Nelson, *Tests of the XP-46 Airplane in the NACA Full-Scale Wind Tunnel 1940*, Langley Research Center, 11 January 1940.
28. J.L. Atwood, Origin and Evolution of the Mustang, *Air Power History Journal,* 1993.
29. R. Wagner, *Mustang Designer Edgar Schmued and the P51*, Orion, 1990.
30. *ibid,* p 54.
31. anon, Vista Morning Press.
32. S. Pace, *Mustang: Thoroughbred Stallion of the Air*, Fonthill Media, 2012, np (online).
33. Ethell, *Mustang,* p 14.
34. Nickle, Wilson, *Tests of the XP-46.*

Chapter 21: Atwood's subsidiary claims re-examined

1. J.L. Atwood, Origin and Evolution of the Mustang, *Air Power History Journal,* 1993.
2. J.L. Atwood, Mustang design retrospective, *FlyPast Special*, November 1997.
3. *ibid*, p 51.
4. Meekcoms, *The British Air Commission*, p 25.
5. J.L. Atwood, Origin and Evolution of the Mustang, *Air Power History Journal,* 1993.
6. J.L. Atwood, The Mustang Margin A Reappraisal, *Air Power History: The Journal of Air and Space History*, Autumn 1996.
7. J.L. Atwood, An address to the Yorkshire Air Museum in June 1998 by Lee Atwood (in Atwood IWM 21441).
8. J.L. Atwood, Mustang design retrospective, *FlyPast Special*, November 1997.
9. Atwood, The Spitfire and the Mustang.
10. *ibid.*
11. G.P. Douglas, Cooling Problems with Particular Reference to the work of the RAE Tunnel, *The Aircraft Engineer*, 28 November 1935..
12. anon, Auxiliary Propulsion, *Flight,* 22 April 1937.
13. Breguet, Devillers, La Technique des Radiateurs Carénés.
14. Baughen, *The Rise and Fall.*
15. Davis, *The Basic Design of the Prototype Spitfire.*
16. J.L. Atwood, *The P-51 The Real Story-Rebuttal, 1996-1997* (in Atwood IWM 21441).
17. Atwood, Mustang design.
18. Yenne, *Rockwell,* p 49.
19. *ibid,* p 48.

20. J.L. Atwood, Origin and Evolution of the Mustang, *Air Power History Journal,* 1993.
21. Gruenhagen, *Mustang: The Story,* p 35.
22. Horkey, The P-51: The Real Story.
23. Atwood, *The P-51: The Real Story.* Two different names, same book title???
24. J.L. Atwood, Origin and Evolution of the Mustang, *Air Power History Journal,* 1993.
25. Yenne, *Rockwell,* p 49.
26. Ethell, *Mustang,* p 14.
27. Yenne, *Rockwell,* p 49.
28. M. O'Leary, *Building the P-51 Mustang,* Speciality Press, 2010, p 24.
29. Meekcoms, *The British Air Commission*, p 25.
30. Becker, Baals, *Analysis of Heat and Compressibility Effects.*
31. Carson, *Pursue and Destroy.*
32. R. Murray, *Lee Atwood ... Dean of Aerospace,* Rockwell International Corporation, 1980, p 29.
33. Yenne, *Rockwell,* p 48.
34. Atwood, Mustang's Margin.
35. Atwood, Yorkshire Air Museum.

Chapter 22: Atwood's overarching 'Meredith effect' claim re-examined

1. Atwood, 'Mustang Memories'.
2. Marshall, Ford, *P-51B North American's Bastard Stepchild,* p 57.
3. E. Rees, A Tribute To Dutch Kindleberger: The Mustang – A Great War Horse, *The Air Power Historian (Air Force Historical Foundation),* Vol. 9, No. 4, October 1962.
4. *ibid.*
5. E. Churchill, Mighty Midget, *Flying Magazine,* January 1944.
6. E. Rees, A Tribute To Dutch Kindleberger: The Mustang – A Great War Horse, *The Air Power Historian (Air Force Historical Foundation),* Vol. 9, No. 4, October 1962.
7. Rees, Mustang!
8. Carson, *Pursue and Destroy*, p 34.
9. *ibid,* p 50.
10. R. Murray, *Lee Atwood ... Dean of Aerospace,* Rockwell International Corporation, 1980, p 29.
11. Yenne, *Rockwell,* p 48.

12. *ibid,* p 48.
13. Wagner, *Mustang Designer Edgar Schmued.*
14. J. Cox, The Restoration of the XP-51, *Sport Aviation*, December 1975.
15. L.F. Ford, Mustang – The True Birthright, *NAAR Bulletin,* Summer 2009.
16. *ibid.*
17. E. Schmued, The Conception and Development of the Mustang, 1971 symposium, *NAAR Bulletin*, Fall 2015.
18. Wagner, *Mustang Designer Edgar Schmued*, p 61.
19. *ibid,* p 61.
20. *ibid*, p 51.
21. *ibid,* p 35.
22. Horkey, *The P-51: The Real Story.*
23. Winter, *Contribution to the Theory.*
24. Horkey, *The P-51: The Real Story.*
25. *ibid.*
26. E. Churchill, Mighty Midget, *Flying Magazine*, January 1944.
27. J. Ethell, letter to J. Reeder, 2 April 1979 (in articles-nasa-langley).
28. Wagner, *Mustang Designer Edgar Schmued*, p 55.
29. Atwood, Engineer.
30. Birch, *Rolls-Royce and the Mustang*, p 87.
31. J.L. Atwood, letter to G.C. Larson, in *Air & Space/Smithsonian,* 20 August 1996 (in articles-nasa-langley).
32. Gruenhagen, *Mustang: The Story,* p 35.
33. R. Murray, *Lee Atwood ... Dean of Aerospace,* Rockwell International Corporation, 1980, p 29.
34. Breevort, Leifer, *Radiator design and installation.*
35. *ibid.*

Chapter 23: (2) Mustang and Meredith – duct entry

1. A.S. Hartshorn, *A review of wind tunnel experiments on ducted radiators,* TNA AVIA 6/2111, July 1936.
2. Marshall, Ford, *P-51B North American's Bastard Stepchild,* p 105.
3. *ibid,* p 106.
4. Schmued, The Conception and Development of the Mustang.
5. Wagner, *Mustang Designer Edgar Schmued*, p 61.
6. Ludwig, *P-51 Mustang: Development,* p 35.
7. E.B. Morgan, E. Shackladay, *Spitfire: The History,* Guild Publishing, 1986, p 22.
8. Ludwig, *P-51 Mustang: Development,* p 35.

Chapter 24: (3) Mustang and Meredith – exhaust gas momentum

1. F.W. Meredith, *Cooling of Aircraft Engines with special reference to Ethylene Glycol Radiators enclosed in Ducts*, ARC, R&M No 1683, August 1935 (published 1936)..

2. T.P. de Paravicini, (Rolls-Royce), *Improvements in exhaust discharge arrangements for internal combustion engines,* GB 471,177, applied 1935, accepted 1937.

3. *ibid.*

4. Schlaifer, *Development of Aircraft Engines,* p 237, fn 46.

5. *ibid,* p 229.

6. Akroyd, Aerodynamics.

7. E.W. Hives, F.L. Smith, High Output Aircraft Engines, *SAE Journal (Transactions),* vol 46, 1940.

8. J.R. Hansen, *Engineer in charge: A history of the Langley Aeronautical Laboratory 1917-1958,* NASA, SP-4305, 1987.

9. Marshall, Ford, *P-51B North American's Bastard Stepchild,* p 68.

10. *ibid,* p 68.

Chapter 25: Mustang story completed

1. Birch, *Rolls-Royce and the Mustang*, p 38.

2. *ibid,* p 38.

3. anon, Merchant of Speed, *Saturday Evening Post,* 19 February 1949.

4. Birch, *Rolls-Royce and the Mustang*, p 147.

5. *ibid,* p 147.

6. *ibid,* p 37.

7. *ibid*, p 38.

8. Warner, London, letter to Lewis, p 914.

9. Birch, *Rolls-Royce and the Mustang*, p 37.

10. *ibid.*

11. *ibid.*

12. H.B. Squire, A.D. Young, *The calculation of the Profile Drag of Aerofoils*, 1937. ARC, R & M No. 1838, 193.

13. H. Warren, The Royal Aircraft Establishment during World War II: some personal reminiscences, *Journal of Aeronautical History,* Paper No. April 2012.

14. *KV 2/3059*, TNA, p 11.

15. anon, Unobtrusive Cleverness, Flight, 20 August 1942
16. Hooker, *Not much of an engineer*, p 53-6.
17. Birch, *Rolls-Royce and the Mustang*, p 20.
18. Marshall, Ford, *P-51B North American's Bastard Stepchild,* p 108.
19. *ibid,* p 109.
20. C.R. Fairey, letter to Air Vice-Marshal Baker, in *North American Aviation 1940-1941,* 17 April 1941, AVIA 38/733, TNA .
21. Birch, *Rolls-Royce and the Mustang*, p 10.
22. Ludwig, *P-51 Mustang: Development,* p 87.
23. J.W. Birch, Rolls-Royce and the Mustang, p. 65.
24. Wagner, *Mustang Designer Edgar Schmued*, p 62.
25. *ibid,* p 63.
26. E.P. Hartman, *Adventures in Research: A History of the Ames Research Center 1940-1965,* NASA SP-4302 1970.
27. *ibid.*
28. E.P. Hartman, *Adventures in Research: A History of the Ames Research Center 1940-1965,* NASA SP-4302 1970.
29. S.J. Miley, Review of Liquid-Cooled Aircraft Engine Installation Aerodynamics, *American Institute of Aerodynamics and Astronautics,* AIAA paper 86-2587, 29 September, 1 October 1986.
30. Gruenhagen, *Mustang: The Story,* p 39.
31. Ethell, *Mustang,* p 11.
32. Wagner, *Mustang Designer Edgar Schmued*, p 61.
33. *ibid.*
34. Schmued, The Conception and Development of the Mustang.
35. B. Gunston, *Development of piston aero engines*, PSL, Haynes Publishing, Sparkford, 1999.
36. Atwood, 'Mustang Memories'.
37. *ibid.*

Chapter 26: Meredith and US ramjets

1. Yenne, *Rockwell,* p 48.
2. J.V. Becker, *The High Speed Frontier*, p 162.
3. J.V. Becker, D.D. Baals, *Analysis of Heat and Compressibility Effects.*
4. E. Buckingham, *Jet propulsion for Airplanes,* NACA Report No. 159, Washington, 1924.
5. Hansen, *Engineer in charge.*
6. *ibid.*

7. R.E. Bilstein, *Orders of Magnitude, a History of NASA, 1915-1990,* SP-4406, NASA 1989.

8. Wagner, *Mustang Designer Edgar Schmued*, p 190.

9. Bilstein, *Orders of Magnitude.*

10. J.V. Becker, *Wind-Tunnel Test of Air Inlet and Outlet Openings on a streamline Body*, NACA Report No. 1038, Nov 1940.

11. J.V. Becker, D.D. Baals, *High-speed Tests of a Ducted Body with Various Air-Outlet Openings,* NACA, May 1942.

12. J.V. Becker, D.D. Baals, *Analysis of Heat and Compressibility Effects.*

13. J.V. Becker, *The High Speed Frontier*, p 161.

14. *ibid*, p 163.

15. *ibid*, p 164.

16. P.R. Hays, *History of the Talos Ramjet Engine.* https://www.okieboat.com/Ramjet%20history.html

17. J.V. Becker, *The High Speed Frontier*, p 162.

18. F.W. Meredith, *Cooling of Aircraft Engines with special reference to Ethylene Glycol Radiators enclosed in Ducts*, ARC, R&M No 1683, August 1935 (published 1936).

19. Winter, *Contribution to the Theory.*

20. Weise, *The Conversion of Energy.*

21. Winter, *Contribution to the Theory.*

22. H.A. Tsien, W.R. Sears, I. Ashkenas, C.N. Hasert, N.M. Newmark, *Aerodynamics and Aircraft Design*, Headquarters Air Matériel Command, 1946, pp 41-42.

23. J.V. Becker, *The High Speed Frontier*, p 162.

24. W. Bollay, E.M. Redding, *Performance of Open-Duct Propulsion Systems (Ramjets) at Subsonic Speeds*, Power Plant Memorandum No 5, Bureau of Aerodynamics, US Navy, December 1943.

25. Hays, *History of the Talos Ramjet.*

Epilogue: Meredith Reconsidered

1. *KV 2/2201*, TNA, p 87.

2. *ibid*, p 37.

3. *KV 2/2200*, TNA, p 163.

4. *ibid*, p 164.

5. Minute 3, 19/01/1939, AIR 2/3524, TNA, (in Marsh 2019), p 116, fn 104.

6. anon, A New Autopilot, *Flight,* 25 September 1947.

7. *KV 2/2201*, TNA, p 6.

8. *ibid*, p 71.
9. *ibid*, p 76.
10. *KV 2/2200*, TNA, p 31.
11. *ibid*, p 9.
12. *KV 2/2202*, TNA, p 24.
13. *ibid,* p 63.
14. anon, *Flight International Magazine,* 26 July 1934.
15. *KV 2/2200*, TNA, p 41.
16. *KV 2/2201*, TNA, p 62.
17. F.W. Meredith, The Modern Autopilot: A Dissertation on the Fundamentals of Modern Autopilot Design, *Flight,* 13 January 1949.
18. *KV 2/2200*, TNA, p 158.
19. F.W. Meredith, Bats, Bees and Brains, *London Report,* August 1957.
20. E.B. Morgan, E. Shackladay, *Spitfire: The History,* Guild Publishing, 1986, p 37.
21. *ibid.*
22. Davis, *The Basic Design of the Prototype Spitfire.*
23. *Aircraft: Equipment (Code B, 5/21): Automatic dive bombsight,* p 116-7, fn 106.
24. anon, The Modern Autopilot: A Dissertation on the Fundamentals of Modern Automatic Pilot Design, *Flight,* January 13, 1949.
25. *KV 2/2202*, TNA, p 32.
26. *ibid,* p 23.
27. *KV 2/3059*, TNA, p 95.
28. *KV 2/2201*, TNA, p 63.
29. *KV 2/2200*, TNA, p 101.
30. *ibid*, p 31.
31. *KV 2/2200*, TNA, p 31.
32. *KV 2/3059*, TNA, p 122.
33. E.E. Vielle, *Almost a Boffin, Why he invented the Cruise Missile,* Dolman Scott 2013, p 314.
34. *KV 2/2199*, TNA, p 32.
35. *KV 2/2201*, TNA, p 13.
36. *ibid*, p 14.
37. *ibid*, p 35.
38. *ibid*, p 35.
39. *KV 2/2201*, TNA, p 26.
40. *KV 2/2202*, TNA, p 8.
41. *KV 2/2201*, TNA, p 9.
42. *KV 2/2202*, TNA, p 26.

43. *ibid*, p 43.
44. *ibid*, p 26.
45. *ibid*, p 26.
46. *ibid*, p 24.
47. *ibid*, p 24.
48. *KV 2/2199*, TNA, p 12.
49. *KV 2/2202*, TNA, p 43.
50. *KV 2/220*, TNA, p 9.
51. *KV 2/2202*, TNA, p. 26.
52. *KV 2/2200*, TNA, p 64.
53. *ibid*, p 64.
54. *ibid*, p 64.
55. *ibid*, p 66-7.
56. *ibid*, p 47.
57. *KV 2/3059*, TNA, p 11.

APPENDICES

Appendix 1: Cooling Issues

1. Capon, The *Cowling of cooling systems (2nd report)*, AVIA 6/2017, August 1935.

Appendix 2: Development of cooling systems before the Spitfire

1. K. Von Gersdorf, et al., *Deutsche Flugmotoren und Strahltriebwerke*, DRP 299799, 7 July 1915, Bernard & Graefe, 2004, p. 196.
2. H. Junkers, Radiator, *Invention relates to the arrangement of the radiator in motor-driven vehicles and quite especially in flying machines*, US1464765A, 28 June 1920.
3. W. Messerschmitt, Probleme des Schnellflugs.
4. R.B. Beisel, A. MacClain, F. Thomas, The Cowling and Cooling of Radial Air-Cooled Aircraft Engines, *SAE Technical Paper 340089*, 1934, also, R.B. Beisel, Why Use Cowl Flaps, *Journal of Aeronautical Sciences*, March 1937.
5. D.H. Wood, Engine Nacelles and Propellers and Airplane Performance, *SAE Journal (Transactions)*, Vol. 31, April 1936.
6. R.S. Capon, *The Cowling of cooling systems (1st report)*, AVIA 6/2017, June 1935.
7. Wood, Engine Nacelles and Propellers.

Appendix 4: RAE Wind tunnel Test Programme

1. E.B. Morgan, E. Shackladay, *Spitfire: The History,* Guild Publishing, 1986, p 22.
2. *ibid*, p 32.
3. Schlaifer, *Development of Aircraft Engines*, p 237, fn 46.

Appendix 5: 'Meredith effect' meaning and first use

1. F.W. Meredith, *Invention relating to jet propulsion of aircraft*, AVIA 8/407, TNA, 28 February 1935.
2. F.W. Meredith, *Cooling of Aircraft Engines with special reference to Ethylene Glycol Radiators enclosed in Ducts*, ARC, R&M No 1683, August 1935 (published 1936)..
3. F.W. Meredith, C.J. Stewart, *Improvements in or relating to Aircraft and other Craft or Vehicles,* GB 454,266, applied 1935, accepted 1936.
4. Akroyd, Aerodynamics.
5. J.V. Becker, D.D. Baals, *Analysis of Heat and Compressibility Effects.*
6. Tsien, Sears, Ashkenas, Hasert, Newmark, *Aerodynamics and Aircraft Design*, pp 41-42.
7. J.V. Becker, *The High Speed Frontier*, p 161.
8. Hansen, *Engineer in charge*
9. Gruenhagen, *Mustang: The Story,* p 39.
10. Schmued, The Conception and Development of the Mustang.
11. Wagner, *Mustang Designer Edgar Schmued*, p 61.
12. *ibid,* p 61.
13. Carson, *Pursue and Destroy,* p 34.
14. R. Murray, *Lee Atwood ... Dean of Aerospace,* Rockwell International Corporation, 1980, p 29.
15. Yenne, *Rockwell,* p 48.
16. Ethell, *Mustang*, p 11.

Index